D1457352

WISE AS SERPENTS,
INNOCENT AS DOVES

WISE AS SERPENTS, INNOCENT AS DOVES

American Mennonites Engage Washington

Keith Graber Miller

THE UNIVERSITY OF TENNESSEE PRESS

KNOXVILLE

Earlier versions of portions of this work, which are reprinted here by permission,
appeared in the following articles: "Bumping into the State: Developing a Washington
Presence," *Mennonite Quarterly Review* 70 (1) (Jan. 1996): 81-106;
"Mennonite Lobbyists in Washington: Wise as Serpents, Innocent as Doves?"
The Annual of the Society of Christian Ethics (Nov. 1995): 177–99;
"Whirling Toward Similitude? Mennonite Lobbyists in the U.S. Capital,"
Conrad Grebel Review 12 (3) (Fall 1994): 283–97.

The paper in this book meets the minimum requirements of the
American National Standard for Permanence of Paper for Printed
Library Materials. ∞ The binding materials have
been chosen for strength and durability.

Library of Congress Cataloging-in-Publication Data

Graber Miller, Keith, 1959–
    Wise as serpents, innocent as doves : American Mennonites engage Washington / Keith
Graber Miller. — 1st ed.
        p.   cm.
    Includes bibliographical references and index.
    ISBN 0-87049-936-X (cloth : alk. paper)
    1. Mennonites—United States—Political activity.   2. Mennonite Central
Commitee—History. I. Title.
BX8116.G73   1996
289.7'73—dc20   95-41822
                                                                            CIP

To Ann and Niles

CONTENTS

ILLUSTRATIONS

ACKNOWLEDGMENTS

This text has benefited immensely from the critical reviews of earlier drafts by persons representing a variety of fields. From the beginning, my mentor, adviser, and friend Nancy T. Ammerman has provided critical insight, assistance, and support far beyond the call of duty. Among other persons who read and critiqued all or part of the manuscript are John Richard Burkholder, Ted Koontz, Steve Tipton, Jon Gunnemann, Theodore Weber, C. Arnold Snyder, Mark Chaves, Leo Driedger, J. Robert Charles, Theron Schlabach, John D. Roth, J. Lawrence Burkholder, Harlan Beckley, Levi Miller, Pete Gathje, Richard Kauffman, Minnie Graber, and Russell D. Buhite. Thorough reviews by seasoned Mennonite historian Albert N. Keim and by Allen D. Hertzke, whose *Representing God in Washington* provided inspiration for my own research, have strengthened the text considerably. I also am grateful for the insightful and unself-serving feedback I received from the following Mennonite Central Committee administrators, some of whom are scholars as well as church persons: John A. Lapp, Linda and Titus Gehman Peachey, Harold Nussbaum, Bob and Judy Zimmerman Herr, and the late William T. Snyder.

Of course, this analysis would not have been possible were it not for MCC Washington's receptivity to my work. From the beginning, long-time director Delton Franz made himself available to me by submitting to multiple interviews and giving me complete freedom to rifle through his voluminous filing cabinets, a floor-to-ceiling closet full of records and clippings dating back to 1968, his personal phone logs, his minutes to meetings, and his correspondence. For twenty-six years, Franz served as the "public face" of Mennonites and Brethren in Christ on Capitol Hill, and most of his professional energies have been expended in developing the MCC Washington office—the office I probed, prodded, and picked apart for nearly two years.

I also am grateful to the other MCC Washington staffers who served as my confidants and friends over the course of my participation and observation in the capital. Staffers and service personnel who contributed much to this analysis were Keith Gingrich, Greg Goering, Jalane Schmidt, Ken Martens Friesen, and Karl Shelly, all of whom allowed me to follow them to coalition meetings, gave me access to their files, spoke openly on the record, and critiqued earlier versions of my chapters. These MCC Washington workers were among the nearly fifty persons interviewed for this project. Without their assistance, and the assistance of dozens of legislative aides, directors of other religious advocacy offices, theologians and ethicists, MCC administrators, church leaders, and others who willingly sat for interviews, this book never would have been completed.

In addition, I owe an immense debt of gratitude to the Schowalter Foundation and the Indiana University Center on Philanthropy, both of which provided grants for my research expenses during the 1992–93 year; and to the Louisville Institute for the Study of Protestantism and American Culture, whose 1993–94 fellowship allowed me to teach only part-time that year. Without the fellowship, and without Goshen College's release of teaching time, this manuscript undoubtedly still would be in process. Donald B. Kraybill's friendship, encouragement, and wise counsel through the stages of publishing likewise have been essential in bringing this work to print.

I also want to thank Hesston, Jean, and Jason Lauver, who frequently gave me a home away from home during the weeks I was in Washington; Dennis Stoesz and other staffers who facilitated my research at the Mennonite Archives in Goshen, Indiana; Mennonite Historical Library staff persons, who helped me find important texts and did not hound me about having books out months overdue; and my students at Goshen College, who put up with reading some sections of an earlier draft and forced me to more clearly articulate my views. In addition, University of Tennessee Press editors Meredith Morris-Babb and Scot Danforth provided astute critiques, careful editing, and collegial support throughout the process of publication. My multitalented teaching assistant Bethany Swope graciously assisted me with the tedious tasks of proofreading and index preparation.

Finally, I want to thank my family—and not simply because it is customary. For most of the years since we were married in 1987, Ann has provided our primary income while she has pursued her career as a professor, graphic designer, and fine artist. Her work allowed me to finish both my master's degree and doctoral studies. In large and smaller ways, she also has reminded me to see beauty in all things; to schedule time to rest; to use both sides of my brain; to not take myself or my work too seriously; to live with passion and intensity; to invest time in relationships; and to allow myself to experience grace. Her companionship and partnership have contributed immensely to the completion of this project.

And I am grateful to our son, Niles, who shares his birthdate with the inception of this text. During my early months of research, Niles often accompanied me to the library in a backpack. Sometimes he listened as I read aloud portions of obtuse theological and ethical texts in an effort both to continue my work and entertain him during the weeks and months we were home together. Niles and Ann have helped me realize that as much as I enjoy the rigors of academia, and as much as I live for teaching and writing, it is the roles of father and husband that I have found the most gratifying. It is to Ann and Niles that I dedicate this work.

1

ENGAGING THE QUIET

Mennonites demonstrated some experience and skill in Washington. . . .
[They] can be wise as serpents, and innocent as doves.

—*James F. S. Amstutz, "Dialogue with Washington:*
Mennonites and the Test of Faith"

"The preaching of the Gospel is the church's primary task," Mennonite
Church leader Guy F. Hershberger wrote at mid-century. "For it to become or to maintain a lobbyist organization, for the shaping of the nation's
foreign policy, would be a perversion of its purpose and function."[1] Ironically, less than two decades later Hershberger supported Mennonites' plans
to establish a Washington, D.C., outpost for monitoring legislative, judicial,
and administrative actions. In a February 1968 article for his denomination's
weekly publication, Hershberger said that Mennonites "ought to have an
office in Washington to keep in closer touch with the working of the federal government than is possible under present circumstances."[2] The office,
which had been under consideration for nearly fourteen years, was opened
in July 1968. Since then, the Mennonite Central Committee's Washington
branch has listened, observed, informed, and advocated in the nation's capital.

In the last half century, American Mennonites have moved dramatically
from being *die Stillen im Lande* ("the Quiet in the Land") to being politically engaged, a shift riddled with anxieties for Mennonites and perhaps for

U.S. political culture as well. Although formerly excluded or withdrawn from public discourse, U.S. Mennonites, partly through MCC's advocacy office on Capitol Hill, now participate daily in the sphere of national politics, seeking to bring critical, experiential insight to bear "in defining America's version of a good society."[3] This political engagement has placed Mennonites in settings that push at their boundaries, however; settings that elicit cautious responses from some within the Mennonite traditions.[4] The shift toward Mennonite political involvement—sometimes in the form of "prophetic" involvement—is one that perceptive religious historian Martin E. Marty lamented a dozen years after MCC Washington was founded. After attending a Mennonite conference on the Kansas prairies, Marty reported his discomfort with hearing repeated calls for the Anabaptists to be prophetic in America. Today, he said, prophecy generally means radical criticism of society—"and that is cheap." Marty suggested that Mennonites, who number fewer than three hundred thousand in the United States, should allow the critical and prophetic burden to pass to others, while they "keep doing what they do best." For Marty that "best" included "praising God in song and art and prose, simply. Loving the soil and helping bring forth its fruit." It involved "being among the first with almost the most to meet boat people or share know-how or grain. Sending a large percentage of their young into service occupations. Providing alternative service."[5] These things, said Marty, may speak more clearly than "being prophetic" and to do them would *be* "being prophetic."

What is striking about Marty's recommendation is that "doing what they do at their best" contributed to Mennonites' recent reentry into political life, prophetic and otherwise. Since the formation of Mennonite Central Committee in 1920, Mennonites have extended their service involvements in North America and around the world. Just as MCC has broadened its concerns and its work, so has the American state expanded with new programs and interests at home and all over the globe. When the U.S. government provides services for the public good, such as providing health care, social welfare, or education, the Mennonites—and other religious groups—have become allies with the state. At other times, the U.S. government's programs and policies have conflicted with the work of Mennonites and other church groups. As Mennonites have reached out in their relief and service work, they have repeatedly "bumped up against" the American state, whose involvements often do have a direct impact—whether for good or ill—on the persons with whom Mennonites work. MCC volunteers, often placed in "trouble spots" in Asia, the Middle East, Africa, and Latin America, repeatedly encounter the U.S. government, which sometimes sets up goals, practices, and institutions that make MCC's service and relief work more difficult.

The Washington office of MCC was created partly as a response to this historical reality, functioning as a bridge between desires for authentic service and the constraints of the state. Mennonite ethicist John Richard Burkholder says that in this century, Mennonites have been "catapulted" into the world. "A new internal dynamic in the life of the church—in particular its tremendously expanding global mission and service activity—has interacted with the cataclysmic events of external history—world wars, revolution, famine—to bring about significant change in the way Mennonites have come to think and act in the political realm," Burkholder writes. He notes that increasingly Mennonites have found themselves involved with the government at various levels, "needing to deal both with the positive welfare functions of the state and with the more problematic areas."[6] A recent MCC brochure states, more simply, that as MCC workers serve around the world, "they often find that the human needs they work to meet—such as poverty, hunger, poor health and education—are caused by governments' political decisions and actions." The brochure adds that, because of this, "MCC sometimes calls on governments to change policies that harm people."[7] Mennonite Central Committee's lobbying office is the institutionalized setting where Mennonites hope to speak out of their domestic and international experience with people affected by American policies.

NONRESISTANCE LEADS TO NONINVOLVEMENT

Historically, American Mennonites' commitment to pacifism, or "biblical nonresistance," exacerbated their noninvolvement in politics. Historian Richard K. MacMaster documents that in colonial Pennsylvania, Maryland, and Virginia, Mennonites voted, helped select candidates, and held certain local offices. Prior to the American Revolution, MacMaster contends, pacifism was considered compatible with good citizenship.[8] By the early stages of the revolution, however, the test of membership in the newly forming American state was willingness to participate in local "associations" and to pledge to bear arms to protect American liberties. Nonresistant Mennonites "failed the test." Although patriots sought to include Mennonites in the new democracy, Mennonites felt increasingly alienated. Eventually, observes MacMaster, "the revolution induced in Mennonites a mood and strategy of inwardness and withdrawal."[9] In subsequent years this pacifistic withdrawal was solidified with the public "outsider" status given to Mennonites in a nation frequently at war. Before long, nonresistant Mennonites were among the most politically marginalized religious groups in the country.

By the twentieth century, multiple theologians, sociologists, and philosophers perceived this apoliticism as normative for religious pacifists—

those unwilling to "dirty their hands" in a realm necessitating coercion and violence. The phrase, a reference to the dilemma of seeking to uphold an important moral principle while responding to avoid some looming disaster, is echoed in the statement made by Communist leader Hoerderer in Sartre's play of that name: "I have dirty hands. Right up to the elbows. I've plunged them in filth and blood. . . . Do you think you can govern innocently?"[10] The answer given by most post–World War I theologians and other observers is "No." The problem with principled pacifists, claim critics, is that they uphold the important moral principle of nonviolence without sufficient concern for potential disaster in a "fallen" universe.

Moreover, for some moderns, in the liberal political paradigm public policy discourse is based on principles and moral rules to which all rational individuals could assent.[11] Such philosophical liberals fear the active participation of religious groups, and in particular those committed to pacifism, because of their religiously bound versions of the good life. Although these critics' primary concerns are with office holding, they also have effectively contributed to the silencing of pacifist voices. In "Politics as a Vocation," sociologist Max Weber writes about two "irreconcilably opposed" ethical systems: an ethic of ultimate ends and an ethic of responsibility. The former he attributes to the radical pacifist sects, and the latter, argues Weber, is necessary for politicians:

> This is not to say that an ethic of ultimate ends is identical with irresponsibility, or that an ethic of responsibility is identical with unprincipled opportunism. Naturally nobody says that. . . . However, there is an abysmal contrast between conduct that follows the maxim of an ethic of ultimate ends—that is, in religious terms, "The Christian does rightly and leaves the results with the Lord"—and conduct that follows the maxim of an ethic of responsibility, in which case one has to give an account of the foreseeable results of one's actions.[12]

Weber adds that "he who seeks the salvation of the soul, of his own and of others, should not seek it along the avenue of politics, for the quite different tasks of politics can only be solved by violence." For Weber, "the genius or demon of politics lives in an inner tension with the god of love, as well as with the Christian God as expressed in church."[13]

Theologian and "political realist" Reinhold Niebuhr follows in the stream of Weberian thought, developing the sociologist's observations on theological grounds. Niebuhr nuances Weber, however, by distinguishing between the "heretical pacifism" of early-twentieth-century religious liberals, whose perspective was rooted in "unrealistic" hopes for humanity, and the Mennonites' nonresistant ethic, an ethic rooted in the biblical witness. Niebuhr considers the Mennonites' nonviolent ethic as consistent with the nonresistant love taught by Jesus, and he sees sacrificial love as the foundation for the Christian ethic.[14] However, he also contends that such an ethic is impossible to achieve in a world peopled by fallen human beings. Niebuhr suggests that if Mennonites are sufficiently humble, they can serve as a prod to the nation's conscience, reminding pragmatically oriented persons that love is the ideal toward which Christians strive. However, Niebuhr expects Mennonites to remain disengaged from the real world of politics, where compromise is essential to effecting change and violence is an inherent part of governing.

Mennonites, many of whom welcomed Niebuhr's mid-century backhanded compliment, already had sought out other ways to be good American citizens.[15] They recognized that there is a certain kind of institution in American society—usually implicit but now sometimes spoken by presidents or used against candidates in election campaigns—that insists that service to the country is something everyone must undertake. If persons are unwilling, for reasons of faith or conscience, to serve in the military forces, they must contribute to the country in some other way.[16] Drawing partly on their centuries-old traditions of discipleship and humble service, Mennonites had offered themselves for nonmilitary social needs. As early as the French and Indian War, they had given relief to war sufferers. In the revolutionary colonies, some Mennonites pleaded for exemption from militias on the grounds that they had done some prior meritorious public service.[17] In the Civil War, Mennonites responded with humanitarian assistance and, in some cases, "compromised" to the point of providing wagons and other military-related supplies.

When Niebuhr wrote his affirmations of Mennonite quietism, Mennonites already had institutionalized their tradition of service in the Mennonite Central Committee. While earlier various Mennonite groups had formed short-term relief organizations to meet specific needs, the institutionalization of Mennonite service did not occur until a crisis involving Russian Mennonites arose just after World War I. The Mennonite Central Committee, now internationally known for its development and conciliation efforts, was organized in 1920 to provide relief to these overseas cousins of American Mennonites. Gradually, MCC evolved into a stable, highly structured organization with involvements around the world. The formation of MCC coincided with the development of multiple Mennonite missions, publishing, and educational ventures, paralleling similar institutionalization in American Protestant denominations.[18]

James C. Juhnke, in one of the first analytical accounts of the development of the Mennonite Central Committee, suggests that World War I forced Mennonites to accommodate to the nature of twentieth-century nationalism. "Their felt need for some corresponding positive act through which they, like their fellow Americans, could stand up among people without shame was at the core of their postwar behavior."[19] P. C. Hiebert, the first chair of the Mennonite Central Committee, and MCC leader Orie O. Miller write that there was "little satisfaction in just maintaining a negative position toward war." Hiebert and Miller said that what was needed was "an opportunity to disprove the charges of cowardice and selfishness made against the conscientious objectors, and to express in a positive, concrete way the principles of peace and goodwill." When the call came for young men to do relief and reconstruction work in war-stricken Europe, it "proved to be just the opportunity sought."[20] Juhnke contends that the Mennonite tragedy was not that they became Americans so slowly, but that "they so desperately wanted to be good American citizens and could not fulfill the requirements without violating their consciences or abandoning the traditions of their forebears." Juhnke attributes to this tension "whatever was creative in the Mennonite experience"—relief programs, development of positive alternatives to military service, and scattered criticism of American nationalism from a pacifist perspective.[21]

COMPELLED TO SPEAK

Juhnke appears to be accurate in his observation that the tension between nonresistance and American citizenship, between the calls of God and country, prompted Mennonites to develop and institutionalize the service emphases embryonic in early Anabaptism. One ought not suppose, of course, that Mennonites' tradition of service is simply an effort to cover their pacifist flanks from patriotic attacks. Feeding the hungry and clothing the naked—both within and outside the fold—were part of Anabaptist-Mennonitism from the early years of the movement.[22] In 1553 a group of German Anabaptists had provided aid to Calvinists fleeing persecution in England. During the seventeenth century, Hutterites gave food and shelter to strangers who sought refuge in their colonies. Dutch Mennonites, who had lived through persecution but were now tolerated in their land, aided their sisters and brothers in Danzig, Poland, Moravia, Switzerland, and the Palatinate between 1660 and 1700. A decade later, in 1710, the Dutch Mennonites formed the Dutch Relief Fund for Foreign Needs, the first foreign Mennonite relief agency. Mennonite communities in colonial America responded to Indian raids in 1755 with relief assistance, including wagon loads of food and clothing for those who had fled their frontier farms. The following year they joined the Quakers in working at peace with Native Americans by seeking to right the wrongs done to them by whites.[23]

Even Juhnke, who makes the most of "wartime persecution sen[ding] Mennonites to seek a moral equivalent to war's sacrifices," also acknowledges the deeper roots of Mennonite benevolence. He notes that Mennonite leaders often cited two sources, the Bible and Anabaptist-Mennonite history, to challenge their people to give generously.[24] Biblical passages frequently referred to include Matthew 25:35-36 ("For I was hungry, and you gave me food") and Galatians 6:10 ("So then, as we have opportunity, let us do good to all people, and especially to those who are of the household of the faith"). Former MCC worker Peter Dyck once said that the Handbook of the Mennonite Central Committee reads, in part, "like a modern Midrash on the New Testament."[25] Juhnke suggests that by citing biblical passages, Mennonites were implying that their calling was to continue the work that God had done in Christ, carrying forth the message of incarnation. "Relief work of a church taking the way of Christ must do it from a heart of love that is ready for 'fellow suffering' in service," states one early MCC publication. "With such a spirit of suffering witness in service the entire personnel of our relief program will be welded into a fellowship of holy purpose that will be an honor to the Christ we serve."[26] The gospel's call for active, humble service is one significant motivating and authorizing source for Mennonites' humanitarian efforts.

Still, throughout American history, assisting with social needs did allow Mennonites to participate responsibly in local, state, and national culture without militarily defending their country or engaging in the potential violence of politics and political administration.[27] This study suggests further—without drawing direct lines of causation—that these experiences in domestic and international service contributed to the reentry of apolitical American Mennonites into the political realm. Observing firsthand at the local level how America's policies affected persons in the United States and elsewhere around the world elicited Mennonites' increased political engagement. Newly active in the world at home and overseas, Mennonites witnessed the results of government policies and felt compelled to speak. Persons who served in Mennonites' various outposts also saw the limits of traditional nonresistance and sought new ways to do active peacemaking, including international conciliation work and advocacy in the world's power centers. The Mennonite Central Committee's Washington office is one institutionalized expression of this recent movement from withdrawal to service to political engagement, a movement that has coincided with theological shifts away from a rigid two-kingdom view that posits a deep chasm between "the church" and "the world."

Mennonite Central Committee service worker Janine Kennel Rands, left, teaches sewing skills to refugees in Somalia. Often MCC Washington channels field workers through Capitol Hill offices, where they speak about their experience with people "on the ground." Photo by Frances Weaver Grill, courtesy of Mennonite Central Committee Photograph Collection, Archives of the Mennonite Church, Goshen, Indiana.

From the capital office, Mennonites have sought to speak out of their national and international experience with people "on the ground"—persons and communities whose lives have been affected by American institutions, policies, and practices. One of MCC Washington's primary responsibilities is to channel returning service workers through Washington's legislative and administrative corridors. Often, staffers' letters to members of Congress cite stories from MCC volunteers in the Philippines, Sudan, Brazil, or Nicaragua. The stories, whether told by service workers or MCC Washington staff persons, have implications for American policy. Such advocacy efforts usually are compatible with the work of the "mainline" denominations' religious lobbies,[28] with whom MCC Washington regularly joins forces. But, on occasion, Mennonites' lobbying runs against the grain of established norms and practices, and MCC Washington staffers find themselves justifying to their lobbying peers their reluctance to enter into some alliances or their unwillingness to agree with some coalitional statements.

At times, MCC's advocacy has influenced the office's peers in Washington's lobbying milieu, making a mark on others' discourse and practices. But MCC often finds itself under tremendous pressure to operate precisely like other religious advocacy offices, which have—no doubt—had a significant impact on the way Mennonites lobby in Washington. Mennonites also have been influenced by their interactions with legislators and government administrators, as well as other nongovernmental organizations (NGOs) in the capital. At times, the temptation has been to adapt too fully to what may be called the "instrumental rationality"—or the "Washingtonian specialist language"—of the state.

This analysis argues that Mennonite theological-ethical traditions, including pacifism, humility, and service—and the concrete, ground-level experiences such traditions have provided—should continue to inform not only the content but also the style of Mennonites' formal national-political involvement. Mennonites are far too few in number to be a politically significant force. In their dialogue at the walls of power in Washington, their only credibility and influence lies in an astute and accurate analysis of how the world really works and in the integrity of their witness and confession to the "truth" as they see it. Such congruence with Mennonites' history and traditions has been possible for MCC Washington because of its institutional ties back to its parent organization and its constituent denominations, which are placed well outside the highly charged context of the nation's capital. This book, then, offers an inside view of how a set of theological and ethical precepts—precepts bound within particular institutional contexts which both give them power and constrain them—are working themselves out in the pragmatic world of politics. It is intended to provide a thick description of what an attempt at faithful, Mennonite political praxis looks like in one key location.

Along the way, the text also addresses, from both theological and sociological perspectives, the questions of legitimacy. How does a lobbying organization that is deeply embedded in an international service and relief organization—which is in turn supported by diverse types of Anabaptist-Mennonites, some of whom are quite uncomfortable with any political engagement—find legitimation from its supporting bodies? Also, how does a lobbying agency with its own religious discourse, traditions, and practices legitimate itself in the context of a political lobbying culture with its own institutionalized practices and long-established discourse? Because MCC Washington is attempting to negotiate its way through the dense thickets of religious advocacy, the study sheds light on how such lobbying groups have evolved. Since the office also redefines what it means to be Mennonite, it illuminates transformations in this one small denominational grouping in the United States.

LOOKING THROUGH THE MCC WASHINGTON LENS

The lens through which we are looking—Mennonite Central Committee's advocacy office on Capitol Hill—is probably Mennonites' most "public" face. It is involved in multiple, complex institutional relationships. Most significantly, the lobbying office is a branch of Mennonite Central Committee, an international service and relief organization devoted to what, by initial appearances, is a vastly different agenda. The organization's mission statement holds that MCC "seeks to demonstrate God's love through committed women and men who work among people suffering from poverty, conflict, oppression, and natural disaster." MCC sees itself serving as "a channel for interchange between churches and community groups where we work around the world and the North American churches who send us, so that all may grow and be transformed." The mission statement adds that "MCC strives for peace, justice, and dignity of all people by sharing our experiences, resources, and faith in Jesus Christ."[29]

Concentrating on the American Mennonites' Washington lobbying office ought not suggest that this is the only setting where the denominations monitor government activity or do advocacy.[30] Nor, more importantly, should it imply that lobbying is the primary locus of Mennonites' justice, peacemaking, and mission activities. Mennonites—whether as individuals, or through their other denominational institutions, or through ecumenical organizations—are actively involved at the grassroots level in urban centers, in Appalachia, and around the world, teaching, assisting, listening, and living alongside persons placed outside their host society's mainstream. Nor should the focus of this analysis imply that the Washington office is *MCC's* principal avenue for working for peace and justice; in fact, only a fraction of MCC's resources are devoted to the Capitol Hill lobbying efforts. More than 99 percent of the organization's money and energies go toward relief, service, development, justice, and conciliation projects in North America and overseas.

Some observers also may notice that this focus on a lobbying office sidesteps actual political office holding or political administration, the more concrete concerns of pacifism's critics. Mennonite Central Committee, whether from its home base in Pennsylvania or from Washington, does not make governmental policy decisions. Certainly many Mennonites hold local political offices in the United States, and some have taken on statewide responsibilities. However, no Mennonite has held a national office in the United States since 1938, and prior to that only three Mennonites were elected to Congress.[31] For complex reasons, some of which will be sketched below, far more *Canadian* Mennonites run for and are elected to provincial and national political posts.[32] One criticism that American Mennonites will continue to hear is that while they generally are unwilling to "dirty their hands" with actual political involvement, they freely critique government policies and practices, both individually and through the MCC Washington office.[33]

The headquarters for Mennonite Central Committee are in Akron, Pennsylvania, located in rural Lancaster County, home to thousands of Mennonites and Amish. Although the trip between Washington and Akron takes only about two hours by car, the cities seem far more distant by social, theological, philosophical, or political transport. On the way to Akron one passes through miles of pastoral, rolling farmland, encountering horse-drawn black buggies and bike-riding, bonnet-wearing women along the way. MCC's headquarters, in the midst of a residential area, are housed in 1970s-style brick-and-wood buildings. Administrative offices in these buildings are located in a large, open spaces with short dividing walls marking individual cubicles. The chief executive officer of the organization manages MCC's 33.5-million-dollar-a-year operations from behind one of the room dividers, tucked into a corner.

In contrast to the simplicity of the office and its surroundings, however, are the activities and international resources of the Mennonite Central Committee. Historian Paul Toews observes that staff members, who are "coming and going to every corner of the earth," can "talk knowledgeably about virtually every global issue." MCC's small library houses the world's major newspapers. "The coffee conversation roams around the world," observes Toews. "The Akron telexes relay urgent messages to and from Nicaragua, Vietnam, Lesotho, India and many other places. The phone conversations are carried on in multiple languages."[34] In addition to keeping up with current events around the world, many of MCC's administrative staff members served overseas before settling in Akron, so they have firsthand experience in international settings.

Mennonite Central Committee draws its support from a number of theologically, socially, and politically diverse Anabaptist branches: the General Conference Mennonite Church and the Mennonite Church—which are in the process of merging as they move into the twenty-first century—are on one end of the spectrum, while the Old Order Mennonite and Beachy Amish Church are on the other.[35] Toews writes that persons seeing the quaintness of the Mennonite-Amish family in Lancaster County, or in similar rural settings around the country, do not recognize that other Mennonites—including some of those within the walls of MCC—are thoroughly modern:

While some travel with horses to a family farm to worship in time-honored ways, others gather in a meetinghouse to debate the latest fashions in Western theology. Some congregations sing the traditional melodies of the *Ausbund* (a sixteenth-century hymnal), while others do contemporary religious jazz and Bach cantatas with orchestral accompaniment. Some Lancaster Mennonite congregations are populated by bankers, lawyers, psychiatrists, professors and businessmen whose firms do an annual business worth hundreds of millions of dollars. These folks are integrated into the intellectual, economic and professional elite of Western culture. Although they inhabit differing intellectual, cultural and economic universes, none are any less the bearers of the Mennonite tradition than the others. English tweed, the broad-rimmed Amish hat and MCC volunteer fatigues are compatriots in this world.[36]

MCC represents or maintains contacts with most of the larger Mennonite and Brethren in Christ groupings, pulling together these motley bodies into a common mission. Beyond these denominational links, MCC's Washington office relates *directly* to congregations and individuals by maintaining a three-thousand-member mailing list.

Further complicating these inter-institutional relationships is the division of Mennonite Central Committee into three distinct organizations with their own governing boards: Mennonite Central Committee (sometimes referred to as MCC International); Mennonite Central Committee Canada;[37] and Mennonite Central Committee U.S. MCC International's thirty-eight board members meet each January to wade through more than two hundred single-spaced pages in the annual workbook. "To the casual observer," wrote one reporter, "[MCC] may be the ultimate church committee—in the best and worst sense. . . . [It has] an infrastructure so involved that the lines of accountability resemble Charlotte's web more than an organizational flow chart."[38] The agency's Washington office comes under the supervision of MCC U.S., even though many of its communications to the federal government involve international issues.

MCC Washington personnel spend about 70 percent of their time and energies facilitating and educating those within the larger Mennonite family who feel "called" to make their witness heard by government officials. For example, the office annually publishes a scorecard for representatives and senators related to their records on issues of concern to MCC and makes newsletter subscribers aware of important legislation under consideration. In addition, the office works extensively with ecumenical "peace and justice" lobbying groups,[39] sharing information and consolidating energies to form a more substantial bloc for lobbying on Capitol Hill. Many of these religious allies are located alongside MCC in the Methodist Building, directly across from the Capitol and the Supreme Court building, at the historic center of the American religious lobbying universe.[40] The MCC Washington office, with nearly three decades of history behind it, provides provocative fodder for sociological, theological, and ethical analysis. Here we will focus on the years 1968 to 1993, when the office was under the direction of Delton Franz.

THE MENNONITE MOSAIC

As is clear from the above description of MCC's diverse constituencies, Mennonites are far from monolithic. The "Mennonite" designation can be used for a score of religious bodies, some with only a few hundred members. All totaled, baptized Mennonite and Brethren in Christ adults in the world number almost 975,000, with around 288,000 in the United States and 118,000 in Canada. The largest Mennonite bodies in North America include the Mennonite Church (formerly "Old" Mennonites), with about 110,000 members; the Old Order Amish, with 63,000; and the General Conference Mennonite Church, with about 60,000.[41] Some Mennonites, in particular the Old Order Amish and some Hutterites, often are identifiable by their clothing, while the majority of Mennonites cannot be readily distinguished from other moderns. Some Mennonites send their children to their own private schools, but most Mennonite youths are fully integrated into public schools. Although the perception may be that most Mennonites are farmers or live in rural communities, the reality is that only 15 percent of Mennonites now farm, and nearly half of the Mennonites in North America live in urban centers, where they work in a variety of professional occupations.[42] During the twentieth century, Mennonites have undergone a radical transformation, by most standard measures, from being primarily a socially "separated" people to being largely "acculturated." The MCC Washington office is a public reflection of this recent "coming of age" of Mennonites—a "coming of age" prompted by multiple changes in wealth, education, professionalization, and other sociological factors.[43]

All Mennonites trace their historical origins to the sixteenth-century Anabaptists, who were part of what has become known as the "left wing" of the Protestant Reformation. The Anabaptists agreed with much of what the Reformers were seeking to do, but believed the Reformers were not going far enough on some issues. Of central importance to Conrad Grebel, Felix Manz, Michael Sattler, Menno Simons, and most other early Anabaptist leaders to whom contemporary Mennonites trace their ancestry was the autonomy of the church from the state in matters of worship and religious practice; the separation of Christians from the "worldly" realm of politics; the necessity for baptism into the church to be voluntary, based on an adult commitment to follow in the way of Christ; and rejection of "the sword." Not all early Anabaptists, or persons called Anabaptists, were pacifists, but the surviving groups of Mennonites' ancestors were.[44] Both because some Anabaptists were violent, and because the pacifist Anabaptists refused to obey civil authorities on some matters such as infant baptism, they were perceived as a threat to social order. Within months after their beginnings in 1525, their first martyrs were killed, first at the hands of Catholic authorities and later by Protestants. Over the course of the next century, thousands of Anabaptists were killed, and those in the movement fled to other lands and rural areas safe from the avenging arm of religious and civil authorities. Although the movement began in Switzerland and south Germany, soon many Anabaptists came to be called Menists and then Mennonites, after the Dutch Anabaptist leader Menno Simons, who managed to avoid early martyrdom.

Over the centuries, various factions and divisions resulted in a variety of Mennonite branches. The Hutterites, a communal group, emerged in the early decades of Anabaptism and continue their shared living in eastern and midwestern pockets of the United States and Canada. In the late seventeenth century, Jakob Ammann led a group of followers in forming what became the Amish—an attempt to counter Mennonites' perceived compromises with society. Earlier in that century, Mennonites began coming to the New World, lured by the hope for religious freedom. Gradually, multiple other splits occurred in North America, resulting in most of the contemporary groupings. Present Mennonite bodies include the Mennonite Church, General Conference Mennonite Church, Mennonite Brethren Church, and Brethren in Christ, all of which are part of the Mennonite Central Committee "family." The Mennonite Church (MC), the oldest and largest North American Mennonite grouping, includes persons mostly of south German and Swiss origin.[45] The General Conference Mennonite Church (GCMC) was formed about 1860 from a group of persons newly immigrated to the United States and an 1847 schism in the Franconia Conference of the Mennonite Church. More progressive than their MC sisters and brothers, GCMC leaders sought to follow the principle of "unity in essentials, liberty in nonessentials, and love in all things." The Mennonite Brethren Church (MB), now numbering about forty-three thousand in North America, became a separate church in Russia prior to their arrival on American shores. The Brethren in Christ, with about twenty thousand members in the United States and Canada, emerged in the 1770s in Pennsylvania as an attempt to synthesize Anabaptism and Pietism.

In the past decade, much internal ado has been made about the differences between Mennonites with a strong Swiss-German heritage and those more deeply rooted in the Dutch-Russian experience. James C. Juhnke has developed the thesis of a "bipolar mosaic" that has "foundationally conditioned" North American Mennonites' self-understandings. The two poles include the south German–Swiss stream, which was transplanted to Pennsylvania in the late seventeenth and eighteenth centuries and spread from the "Pennsylvania-German" heartland. The other stream is the Dutch–north German one, which first went to Prussia and South Russia before migrating to North America in waves in the 1870s, 1920s, and 1940s. "These two streams have definably different historical memories, cultural characteristics, and theological preferences," contends Juhnke.[46] The Swiss–south German Anabaptists were shaped by their origins on the radical wing of Ulrich Zwingli's reform, the two-kingdom separatism of their early self-definition in the 1527 Schleitheim Confession, their years of persecution and repression, and the major schism between Mennonites and Amish in 1693. "Subordination and subservience led them to special emphasis on certain themes present in Anabaptism from the beginning: a decisive dualism of church and world, reluctance or refusal to become involved in public life, and a rejection of worldly pride accompanied by a premium upon humility," writes Juhnke.[47]

The Dutch Mennonite tradition was considerably different, says the historian. In the Netherlands Mennonites were tolerated as early as 1570, and they experienced growth and cultural renaissance in the seventeenth century. Some early Dutch Mennonite refugees had fled eastward toward Prussia and then moved into the farmlands of the Ukraine. Until World War I and the Communist Revolution, they developed autonomous political and cultural communities in Russia, creating a modified "Christendom." "Russia's Mennonites learned to accept responsibility for public affairs and to wrestle with the contradictions of an Anabaptist remnant which had achieved a measure of worldly power," notes Juhnke. "Even while they saw the politics of nations and empires as alien and worldly, Dutch-Russian immigrants . . . assumed that they as Christians could be involved positively in local public institutions. They were active in the social, economic, religious, and to some extent the political tasks of building a Mennonite place in the world."[48]

The divergent experiences of the two Mennonite streams, while diluted over the past century of North American experience, still should be noted in an analysis of Mennonites and national politics. Most members of the Mennonite Church in the United States and Canada are of Swiss–south German origin, so their understandings of the church and state are shaped, in part, by a long heritage of governmental persecution and political alienation. The majority of those in the General Conference Mennonite Church, on the other hand, share the Dutch-Russian experience of self-government.[49] The same is true for the Mennonite Brethren Church, whose members are nearly all of Dutch-Russian background. Further stratification of the two streams can be made along geographic and national boundaries. Most Swiss–south German Mennonites can be found east of the Mississippi and in the United States rather than Canada. In contrast, Dutch-Russian Mennonites populate western states in the United States and are far more prevalent in Canada. The distinctions become relevant when examining Mennonites' relationships to the state in the United States versus similar church-state relationships in Canada.

CANADIAN MENNONITES AND POLITICS

Partly because of Canadian Mennonites' more pervasive Dutch-Russian heritage, and—more important—because of Canada's distinctive history and form of government, Mennonites in Canada generally respond differently to their state than do Mennonites in the United States.[50] Canadian Anabaptists view the state more positively, with less suspicion and distrust, seeing it as an agency established by God for the good of creation. They also have freely entered into joint ventures with state authorities, including everything from foreign aid to publication to victim-offender programs to other forms of humanitarian assistance.[51] In addition, Canadian Mennonites have moved more rapidly and more broadly into political participation, running for and being elected to high offices and civil service posts. One longtime observer of Mennonites and politics in Canada notes that usually one or more Anabaptists can be found in the legislatures of each of the five western provinces—with several holding cabinet rank—and hundreds have run for provincial offices. In several elections, all three or four candidates for a provincial seat were of Mennonite heritage.[52]

Mennonite Brethren scholar John H. Redekop suggests multiple reasons for the differences between U.S. and Canadian Mennonites' political activity. In addition to the Dutch-Russian experiment in self-government, and the heavier concentration of Dutch-Russian rather than Swiss–south German Mennonites in Canada, Redekop mentions a number of other sociological, historical, religious, and political factors.[53] One sociological factor is that Mennonites, while less numerous, are more significant numerically in Canada than in the United States. About one out of every 900 people in the United States is Mennonite or Mennonite-related, while the Canadian ratio is one out of 230. In some towns and rural areas Mennonites constitute a majority and determine electoral and policy matters, Redekop says. He also notes that immigrants to Canada did not come to a country that had revolted against political exploitation and oppression, nor is there a presumed "wall of separation" between church and state. Further,

Christianity in Canada has not become politicized as it has in the United States. "Canada has experienced nothing analogous to the development of Christian-Americanism," Redekop claims, nor is there a Canadian equivalent of American "Manifest Destiny." Canada has no Moral Majority or religious far right of any consequence, so Canadian Mennonites are able to express their conservative religious concerns without differentiating themselves from passionate Christian defenders of the political establishment or other religious extremists. Redekop also notes that Canada has not set itself up as a religious entity: Canada's founders are not revered as saints (there are no holidays devoted to them); national buildings are not shrines, and national political holidays have almost no religious content. He suggests that when a state makes no claim to being an object of worship, Anabaptists have less reason to react negatively to it.[54] Canada's place among the world powers may also contribute to Mennonites' response: it is a middle power with no major military role on the world stage. It has not developed a nuclear arsenal, and it has only a relatively small military budget of about 9 percent of total government expenditure. "Canada has a different profile in the world," contends one politically involved Mennonite. "The facts aren't always as good as the myth, but the myth looks pretty good."[55] In short, Mennonites have less to be threatened by and less to critique in Canada than in the United States.

All of these factors make political comparisons between Mennonite persons and institutions in the United States and Canada tremendously complex. One particular institution that must be mentioned in this context, however, is the Ottawa office of Mennonite Central Committee Canada, which has a mandate similar to that of MCC Washington. When MCC was debating where to place its first national "listening post," both Washington and Ottawa were considered. In many ways, because of Canadian Mennonites' more amicable relationship with the state, one might have expected the office to be placed in Ottawa, seat of the Canadian government. However, it was precisely the *antagonistic* relationship with the state that prompted MCC's selection of Washington over Ottawa. When the District of Columbia office was founded in 1968, U.S. Mennonites were embroiled in two related tensions with their government: conscription and the military involvement in Vietnam.[56]

After nearly seven years of board meeting discussions—and experimentation with having a part-time person monitor and report national government activity in Canada—MCC Canada decided in 1974 to establish its Ottawa office the following year.[57] The "Functions of an Ottawa Office," developed by J. M. Klassen and adopted by MCC Canada at its annual meeting, 11–12 January 1974, almost directly parallel the original guidelines for the MCC Washington office.[58] During the 1960s and early 1970s there had been a limited religious presence on Parliament Hill in Ottawa, but until 1975 no church organization had a full-time lobbyist assigned to working with government there. Ironically, MCC Canada was the first.[59] Hired as director for the Mennonites' office was William Janzen, who earlier had done MCC service in the Republic of the Congo (now Zaire) and who was completing a Ph.D. in political science at Carleton University.[60]

In his initial months, Janzen first tried to establish contact with Members of Parliament who also were members of churches represented by MCC Canada. Over the years he has researched and written numerous briefs, scheduled government appointments for other Mennonite delegations, met with MPs, and testified before committees. Each year MCC Canada, either independently or in coalition with other organizations, submits more than one hundred communications to Canadian departmental staff or elected officials.[61] Janzen suggests that having so many Mennonites in government sometimes makes his job more interesting. He reports that once when he went to speak to officials in the External Affairs Department, on the *other* side of the table was a member of his congregation. "Of course, he had to hold the government line," says Janzen, "but in church on Sunday morning he would come to me and say, 'Bill, don't give up. Keep doing it.'"[62] Such an encounter, which happened on other occasions as well, would be far more rare in Washington.

A thorough comparison and contrast of Mennonites' work in Canada and the United States would highlight the distinctive ways politically engaged Mennonites function in the two national settings. Because of the contextual differences and the immense complexity of the varying social, historical, religious, and political "locations" of Washington and Ottawa, however, the Ottawa office's work will not be examined here. The U.S. situation throws the issues analyzed in this study in higher relief, and therefore is a more appropriate context for this discussion. It is hoped that, at some point, the framework used here can be adapted for a more concentrated look at Mennonites and the Canadian government, and then can be fruitfully compared with the following findings regarding MCC Washington.

WISE AS SERPENTS, INNOCENT AS DOVES

According to the gospel accounts, when Jesus was speaking with his disciples about moving beyond the security of their close-knit group, he encouraged them to be "wise as serpents" as well as "innocent as doves." The biblical passage that makes reference to wisdom and innocence comes as a transition, in Matthew's account,[63] between Jesus' sending his followers out into the mission field (Matthew 10:1–16) and his explanation that they may suffer persecution for doing so (Matthew 10:17–25). According to the text, Jesus tells the disciples that they will be as "sheep among wolves," a metaphor used elsewhere both in Jewish and Greek literature. As one biblical commentator, Eduard Schweizer, argues, "The band of disciples is not a safe haven for sheep; they must venture out not only into insecurity but even into defenselessness." While the disciples are not to seek martyrdom, they should recognize that suffering will be a part of their faithful existence. "The caution of the disciples," observes Schweizer, "is to consist not in clever diplomatic moves but in the purity of a life that is genuine and wears no masks."[64]

One might ask what inferences are being made by the references to serpents and doves, since the biblical metaphors can be quite ambiguous and the language tremendously dense. Was this serpent the type that tempted and misled Adam and Eve in the story from Genesis 3? Or was it the serpent that Moses created from his rod, in the presence of Pharaoh, to prove that he was speaking for Yahweh? (Exodus 7:10) Or was it the brass serpent set on a pole in the wilderness, a serpent that brought a homeopathic kind of healing to all who looked at it? (Numbers 21:9)[65] Was the dove referring to the type Noah sent out, according to Genesis 8, to determine the safety of venturing from the ark? Were Matthew's readers expected to be reminded of God's spirit descending "like a dove" on Jesus at the time of his baptism? (Matthew 3:16) Or was Matthew thinking of the prophet Hosea's dove, "silly and without sense, calling to Egypt, going to Assyria" (Hosea 7:11)?

The precise interpretation of the Greek terms *phronimoi* and *akeraioi* have been variously translated. Schweizer renders the terms as "cautious" as snakes and "gentle" as doves.[66] W. F. Albright and C. S. Mann translate the phrases as "be as prudent as serpents, and as candid as doves."[67] Max Zerwick and Mary Grosvenor's respected New Testament grammatical analysis suggests that *phronimoi* means "sensible, wise in a practical way" and that *akeraioi* means "guile-less, simple, unsophisticated."[68] Regardless of the precise biblical meaning, a number of persons within Mennonite Central Committee have called attention to the biblical charge in reference to the Washington office. To one degree or another, they have taken on the charge, and have recognized the tensions between wisdom and innocence. At least four explicit allusions should be mentioned here.

First, in a 1977 description of "The Establishment of the Washington, D.C. and Ottawa Offices," MCC's William Keeney called attention to the "vortex of power which whirls around the centers of political influence" and "the pressure to try to establish the kingdom of God by selling out to the expedience of political and military power." "The offices need constant reminders," contends Keeney, "that the task is first of all to be faithful, to be wise as serpents and harmless as doves."[69]

Second, former staffer Greg Goering writes in his perceptive paper "Learning to Speak Second Languages" about a friend offering him a book titled *The Power Game: How Washington Works.*[70] He says he initially did not want to read the book, since it went against his previous assumptions about the role of an MCC office in Washington. "My reluctance stems primarily from seeing the church's role in Washington as a prophetic one," he writes, "a church standing at a distance from the center of worldly power rather than as an insider influencing decisions behind the scenes. A church wearing sackcloth and ashes delivering oracles from outside the temple rather than a special interest group donning three-piece suits and ties." Goering adds that the "lure of power" is great, and "its seduction infiltrates well-meaning humanitarians all too quickly. How can we become wise as serpents about the way Washington works yet remain innocent as doves?"[71]

A third reference to Jesus' words is found in a 1991 *Peace Office Newsletter.* Although Atlee Beechy's remarks in this location are not directed specifically at the work of MCC Washington, it is appropriate to mention them here. Beechy, a psychologist and MCC supporter for many years, writes that the "world has learned well her ways of making enemies, weapons and wars." He then asks whether MCC and its constituents can be "wise as serpents and harmless as doves? Can we live and teach Christ's reconciling way of making enemies into friends in our daily walk and across the world?" He holds that "these days" call for much fasting, prayer, and "inner cleansing and commitment to the biblical foundations of our Anabaptist peace and justice witness." He suggests that self-righteousness, hate, and fear impede that witness, while hope, trust, and love "release and enhance our witness." He concludes by saying, "Let us express our witness with confidence, humility and joy."[72]

A fourth reference can be found in an article by James F. S. Amstutz. In his 1992 discussion of MCC and MCC Washington's work in the capital on Selective Service System issues, Amstutz lists six learnings from the decade-long dialogue between Mennonite representatives and SSS administrators. Among those learnings is that "Mennonites can be wise as serpents and innocent as doves." Amstutz claims Mennonites made "systematic use of Capitol Hill" during the selective service discussions. While this was "not lobbying in the strict definition of the term," he contends, phone calls and letters from Mennonite voters did make a difference. "Persistence was needed to reach a satisfactory resolution," Amstutz writes. "As Mennonites witnessed to their historic, faith-based position of conscientious objection, they did so through available means. They neither stood by passively while SSS implemented unacceptable alternative service plans, nor refused to deal outright with SSS in the business of making plans for a smooth running conscription." Amstutz concludes by saying that "it was a compromise position that kept the best interests of the wider church and the personal integrity of those directly involved in some kind of balance."[73]

Based on these four references—and others in MCC documents over the years—it is clear that the agency is seeking to strike a balance between wise engagement in the political world in which it is located and the relative clean-handedness of Mennonites' humble, nonresistant, service-oriented faith traditions.

LOOKING AHEAD

In chapter 2, the expansion of both Mennonite Central Committee and the American state will be addressed, with the focus on the founding of MCC Washington as a bridging or mediating institution. The three central chapters—3, 4, and 5—will develop, respectively, the notions of pacifism, humility, and service in the work of MCC Washington. Chapter 3 will examine Mennonites' alliances and coalitions with "mainline" Protestant, Catholic, Jewish, and nonreligious lobbyists in Washington, showing the mutual influence of the various advocacy groups. The fourth chapter will look more closely at the lobbying practices of MCC Washington, comparing its work with that of its religious lobbying peers. Chapter 5, which stands at the heart of the text, will detail MCC Washington's international connectedness and illustrate how being embedded in a service and relief organization shapes its work and makes its advocacy distinctive in the Washington milieu. While most of this study's focus is on lobbying *practices*, the sixth chapter will look more specifically at MCC Washington's political and religious *discourse*. The final chapter will draw together a number of the observations made throughout the text.

By examining the struggles and involvements of MCC Washington, readers should gain a clearer vision of contemporary Mennonites, the once-peculiar people who make up the agency's constituent body. The analysis of the office's work will evidence tensions between various persons, groups, and branches within Mennonitism and should illuminate to what extent the office remains embedded in Anabaptist-Mennonite traditions. Not surprisingly, the political transformation of Mennonites is affected by many of the same modernizing influences that have so deeply affected the American religious scene— urbanization, specialization (professional occupations), rationalization (education), stratification (more middle-income members), and mobility. Mennonite ethicist J. Lawrence Burkholder wrote more than 30 years ago:

The Mennonite church is caught in a tug-of-war between opposing forces. It is a struggle between the traditional Mennonite "way of life" and social involvement. The logic of Mennonite theology, ethics and history points in the direction of radical rejection of social responsibility for the sake of a "new and separated" people. However, the logic of present day social, economic and educational tendencies among Mennonites points toward greater involvement and responsible participation in the affairs of the world. . . . The question is whether American Mennonites, who are now increasingly caught in the "whirl" of American life, will be able to avoid at least some of the adverse experiences of other sects by the knowledge of the problem gained through modern social sciences. Will it be possible for at least one dissenting group of the Reformation to maintain some of the peculiar doctrines and practices of the faith in the modern period in the face of the seemingly relentless forces of conformity to the general practices of society? What is, of course, more important than the question of holding on to traditional patterns is the question of how to make what is genuinely Christian in the Mennonite position relevant to the Christian church as a whole and relevant also to the world.[74]

This study hopes to show how living, breathing theological-ethical traditions may, at their best, prove relevant to the world. The MCC Washington office is one concrete example of where the dynamic of Mennonite traditions, infused in individuals as well as institutions, comes face-to-face with the previously rejected political world.

2

BUMPING INTO THE STATE

> The 1940s marked a watershed in expanded exposure to the larger world
> for Mennonites. As conscientious objectors, hundreds of our young men
> and many women were immersed in new realities. As volunteers in state
> mental hospitals and in overseas refugee relief assignments, Mennonites
> were exposed to new dimensions of pain and suffering. Then followed
> the revolutions in African and Asian colonies. Our missionaries, relief
> workers, and North American churches were increasingly exposed to
> larger global realities, and their Washington connections. When the civil
> rights movement, the war on poverty, the U.S. immersion in the Vietnam
> War and the revival of the draft all coincided in the '60s, the era of our
> innocence, like that of the larger Christian community, effectively ended.
> A new-found servant posture called forth a prophetic voice.
>
> —*Delton Franz, "How We Do Our Work: The Mennonite Voice to Government"*

For the first half of the twentieth century, U.S. Mennonites communicated
with official Washington infrequently and reluctantly. During those decades Mennonites' disengagement, deeply rooted in more than 350 years
of relative noninvolvement with the political world, increasingly came into
tension with broadening Mennonite experience.[1] Within a decade after the
sixteenth-century beginning of the Anabaptist movement in Europe, most
of those on the Reformation's left wing had found themselves espousing a
rather radical separation of the roles and responsibilities of the church and

the state. Shifts in American Mennonites' theological and ethical under-standings of the relation of the church to the state emerged gradually as they began their mission, service, and relief work around the globe and found themselves placed in contexts that pushed at their boundaries. While this outreach was initiated in the late nineteenth century, it expanded dra-matically in the early and mid-twentieth century, prompted by the experi-ences of the two world wars. American Mennonites' attempts to serve in a meaningful way during and after the wars brought them face-to-face with persons and situations that elicited new responses—sometimes political ones—to the more interconnected world in which they now lived.[2]

The founding of Mennonite Central Committee in 1920—and its sub-sequent growth and change—is an integral part in the story of what could be called the "institutional politicization" of Mennonites. MCC began with a humble agenda: to feed and clothe Mennonites' suffering sisters and broth-ers trapped in a volatile Russia. Soon the vision and the work of the relief organization grew beyond the narrow scope of persons in their own faith traditions, taking them to countries where Mennonites had no previous experience but where natural disasters or difficult living conditions called for a humanitarian response. Just as MCC deepened and extended its in-volvements around the world, so did the U.S. government, both at home and overseas. Motives for the U.S. development work abroad and also for MCC's service work were complex, and they ranged from self-legitimation as an organization or nation to authentic humanitarian concerns to—in the case of the U.S. government—imperialistic intentions. These motivations, however, are less important than the fact that Mennonites repeatedly found themselves bumping up against the American state.

HUMBLY APPROACHING THE STATE

American Mennonites' twentieth-century reticence to speak to the state is evident in their limited and narrowly focused formal communications to government officials from 1900 to 1950. Most of the letters and statements to government leaders related to Mennonites' exemptions from military service, although others witnessed more generally on issues of war and peace, commending or protesting the actions of the federal government. From 1915 up through at least the 1960s, observes one person who ana-lyzed official statements, letters, and public presentations, Mennonite Church communications to political leaders reflected a tenor of "nonresistance and willingness to suffer (the 'way of the cross'), rather than demanding rights or expressing harsh judgment."[3] Such a tone suggests an ongoing percep-tion of the relationship of Mennonites to the state as one of subjects to rulers rather than as citizens participating in a democracy.[4] In an effort to legitimate their concerns, Mennonites' statements to government leaders throughout this century also consistently have provided an overview of Mennonites' historic peace witness.[5] Because of their long history as "outsiders" in the political process, Mennonites apparently have believed that they need to justify their voice when speaking.

While they initially intended, by all accounts, to have been a movement within the Protestant Reformation, sixteenth-century Anabaptists soon found themselves at odds with other Reformers. The event precipitating the Swiss Anabaptists' break with Reformer Ulrich Zwingli was ostensibly the baptism of infants, but the larger issue was the linking of the church with the political authorities, who demanded that infants be baptized. Soon after a final confrontation between the Anabaptists and Zwingli in Zürich in early 1525, the Anabaptists defiantly rebaptized themselves and refused cooperation with political officials.[6] The rejection was mutual, and soon Anabaptists faced imprisonment and torture and, within a few months, martyrdom.

In the turmoil of the sixteenth century, religious and political officials were concerned with persons and groups threatening what minimal order existed. The Anabaptists were speaking radically about both the government and the economic system. They were outspoken about economic injustice, especially when the clergy were responsible for such injustice. Also, they generally agreed that in God's kingdom there should be no "mine" and "thine," and the Hutterite branch developed this into a complete community of goods. While the Anabaptists did not intend for their convictions to be normative for the whole society, their manner of living and their public pronouncements about oppression of the poor represented a threat to the stability of society.[7] The Anabaptist leaders, the magistrates believed, might undermine both the political and economic order through their "seditious" ramblings about the poor and through their refusal to cooperate with those wielding governmental power.[8]

Although some Mennonites and others have depicted the Anabaptists' withdrawal from political involvement as a unique attempt at social change, it is more likely that—at least once they established their radical religious boundaries—they were politically disengaged because noninvolvement was their only option. Sociologist Leo Driedger argues that the Anabaptists "refused to participate in the magistracy usually because they did not have a choice, so they withdrew to what they considered more pressing matters." The early Anabaptists, Driedger observes, "sought to change government neither from within nor from without—they simply withdrew. Because of their radical religious and discipleship views, the early Anabaptists had their hands more full trying to find a means of survival."[9] Ironically, this mutual rejection of the Anabaptists and their culture led to an anticipation of modernity. Among the characteristic modern features germinating in this rejection and subsequent structuring of Anabaptist life were voluntarism, secularization of the nation, pluralization of society, increasing differentiation, privatization of faith, and the separation of the church and state.[10] Historian George W. Forell writes that "the view of the Church held by most Christians in America owes more to this Anabaptist vision than to the teachings of the sixteenth-century Jesuits, Lutherans, or Calvinists."[11]

The earliest Anabaptists were primarily drawn from the craft and farming occupations. One study of Anabaptist occupational stratification estimated that 41 percent were craftspeople in cities, small towns, and villages, and just under 24 percent were farmers.[12] Within two generations, the percentages shifted dramatically as Anabaptists, under persecution, were driven to rural areas and into primarily land-based occupations. Those in towns and villages also refused to participate in guilds, which then became hostile to such innovators. A good number of the Anabaptist leaders were drawn from the clergy and were relatively well educated, although most of these leaders were killed within the first several years of the movement. Public executions of Anabaptists, who continued to be politically suspect, lasted from 1525 to 1614, and others died later in prison.

In spite of their own untimely deaths at the hands of the civil authorities, most of the early Anabaptists agreed with Martin Luther's theological perspective that governing institutions had a *preservative* function, curbing and controlling the power of sin.[13] This perspective, rooted in the biblical story of humanity's "fall," suggests that originally God did not intend for there to be political institutions, but humanity's actions necessitated establishing institutions of government as a "dike against sin." This view contrasts sharply with the theological understanding of the state found in Thomas Aquinas and the Roman Catholic natural law tradition, in which the state is part of the good that God created, a natural outgrowth of who we are as relating humans. Political institutions simply help us cooperate and reach our full potential.[14]

The Lutheran view suggests that if everyone were Christian, there would be no need for political authority: the state is ordained for the sake of order in a fallen world. Most early Anabaptists agreed with Luther on this point, adopting some version of a dualistic, two-kingdom understanding of the world, building on the writings of St. Augustine and of their contemporaries.[15] The surviving strains of Anabaptism, however, parted ways with Luther on the issue of the Christian's role in the two kingdoms. For Luther, Christians stood squarely in the midst of both kingdoms: in their private, personal lives, they were in the kingdom of God, and in their public lives they were in the earthly kingdom. Persons were essentially split down the middle in their loyalties: Christian love called them to act in both kingdoms, abiding by the ethic of each when working in that realm and not expecting to effect much change in the earthly kingdom. For most of the Anabaptists, it was the *world,* not individuals, who were split: faithful Christians lived in the kingdom of God and abided by its ethic, and others were in the earthly kingdom. God had instituted civil government, the Anabaptists said, and therefore it should be obeyed—up to the point where the state's demands clearly contradicted God's authority. Because of their understandings of the commandments of Christ, however, they believed the Christian could not kill—even when the state had legitimated killing in the cases of war or capital punishment. Therefore, although they believed the state was divinely instituted, most Anabaptists said the true Christian could not participate in the government's work, because the civil realm required the use of violence for maintaining order and was therefore "outside the perfection of Christ."[16] Even Anabaptist leader Pilgram Marpeck, who himself served as a civil engineer, said, in effect, that one can be a Christian magistrate, but not for long.[17]

Although few Anabaptists served in the civil government, on occasion they communicated their opposition or praise to the princes and rulers. Menno Simons frequently referred to the governing authorities in his works, and in 1552 he wrote "A Pathetic Supplication to All Magistrates," requesting kinder treatment of Anabaptists and urging the "noble sirs" to repent, serve God, do justice to widows, orphans, and strangers, and to follow after the way of Christ.[18] With extensive persecution during the first century of European Anabaptism, many of the statements Anabaptists made to government authorities came in the midst of intense confrontations—such as at trials—and therefore they involved some measure of self-defense.[19] Often, as was the case in Simons' "Supplication," the Anabaptists sought to remind civil servants of their Christian duty. In the century following Anabaptism's founding, followers of Menno and other Anabaptist leaders became more withdrawn and politically disengaged, prompted by persecutorial necessity and unwillingness to compromise.

Mennonites, as a group, first arrived in the "New World" in the mid-seventeenth century, lured by a vision for an experimental community which would share goods and have religious freedom.[20] In 1662 about twenty-five Dutch Mennonite families came to establish the communal colony along the Delaware River. However, two years later, when English troops were battling the Dutch for their new empire, the Mennonite settlement was captured and completely destroyed. Not until two decades later did Mennonites, wooed by their Quaker friends, come to the colonies to establish what became a permanent community. The wooing took some years, since some

European Mennonites in the 1670s and 1680s saw political reasons for remaining aloof from the Quakers. Quakers had attempted to make converts of Mennonites and had refused to pay some war-related taxes, bringing renewed persecution. "Many Mennonites by contrast cherished their hard-won toleration and preferred to be 'the quiet in the land,'" writes historian Richard K. MacMaster. "So the Mennonites paid all taxes and tithes to state churches [in Europe], and stayed clear of evangelism and political expression and whatever else might bring them trouble."[21] Once they did come to America, the Mennonites quickly settled into primarily agrarian occupations, building on the land management techniques they had developed in Europe. Their farming practices modernized slowly, partly because they lacked any theology that blessed money making and partly because the ban against suing in law courts—even for just cause—limited their involvement in the potential expansiveness of modern forms of economic enterprise.[22]

In colonial America Mennonites occasionally addressed government officials with their concerns. In 1688 some Germantown Mennonites or Mennonites-turned-Quakers joined with other Friends in publicly protesting slavery.[23] In May 1755, several Mennonite deacons and ministers in Lancaster County wrote to the Pennsylvania assembly asserting their loyalty to the king and expressing their willingness to pay taxes and comply with laws, but declaring that they would not defend the king with the sword.[24] It was only with the coming of the American Revolution—when being a member in the newly forming American state meant pledging to bear arms to protect its liberties—that Mennonites found themselves again alienated and, eventually, socially and politically withdrawn.[25] In the years following the revolution American Mennonites were only episodically politically active, and even then actions generally were taken by individuals and not congregations or larger bodies. The same was true, in general, during most of the nineteenth century. Historian Theron F. Schlabach reports that throughout the century some Mennonites voted and held local offices, but that others believed that office holding *as well as* voting were inappropriate for those within the Mennonite fold. At the end of the century, notes Schlabach, Mennonites "still put little faith in government to perform God's work," and while some voted, "they had done so more as persons woven into their local communities than as people caught up in modern nation-building." Following the Civil War, Schlabach says, American Mennonites took some steps toward political activism, prompted by Russian Mennonites' immigration to the United States and Canada, increasing progressivism in some Mennonite denominations and the call for Prohibition. "Yet on the whole Mennonites had not let themselves get caught up in politics and nationalism."[26] With the exception of late-nineteenth-century Prohibition—on which there also was ambivalence within the Anabaptist denominations—American Mennonites generally did not participate in public political protests or campaigns. Their involvements with the national government were limited to the contacts necessary to assist their Russian sisters and brothers in their immigration to the United States and Canada.

In comparison with their earlier centuries of virtual silence, American Mennonites' twentieth-century communications to and with their national government seem an explosion. However, for at least the first half of this century, Mennonites' telegrams and letters to national leaders, and the formal, "politically-oriented" position statements made by various Mennonite denominations, were modest and restricted to several issues surrounding peace and warfare. One collection of formal statements between 1900 and 1978 lists a total of nine statements to government from the General Conference Mennonite Church during that period; four statements from the Mennonite Church; four from the Mennonite Brethren Church; and two from the Brethren in Christ.[27] By far most of the Mennonite *denominational* communications to government during this period were devoted to or touched on issues of conscription and conscientious objection.[28] Evident in reviewing the formal statements to government is the broadening of peace concerns after a half century of almost exclusive attention to draft-related concerns. After 1950 one finds multiple Mennonite statements on industrial relations, refugees, race relations, birth control and abortion, persecution in Third World countries, civil disobedience, world hunger, amnesty, the death penalty, stewardship of energy resources, and other broadly defined peace issues. Mennonites' increasing interconnection with their world, brought about through the programs of organizations such as MCC, expanded their vision of peace and peacemaking.

CREATING THE MENNONITE CENTRAL COMMITTEE

When the Mennonite Central Committee was founded on 27 July 1920, few could have anticipated its institutional permanence or growth into an organization with more than nine hundred workers in some fifty countries around the world.[29] No one would have expected that someday it could include programs not only for disaster relief but for international mediation and reconciliation, prison ministries, mental health services, agricultural development, international visitor exchanges, Self Help Crafts, and—perhaps most remarkably—advocacy or lobbying in the nation's capital.[30] MCC was born out of a specific situation and a particular need: Mennonites who had migrated to Russia and lived comfortably under the Russian czarist state were now suffering as a result of the revolution and civil war. The internal war resulted not only in direct casualties, but also contributed to widespread famines and the spread of various epidemics. By the time of the crisis in Russia, American Mennonites were primed to serve in some way, motivated partly by their guilt of not suffering—even *prospering* economically—during World War I, while others in their country had lost their spouses, children, or livelihoods while in military service.[31] After the war, President Woodrow Wilson had written a brief memo that concluded with "[i]t will now be our fortunate duty to assist by example, by sober, friendly counsel, and by material aid in the establishment of just democracy throughout the world." Mennonites realized that by giving material aid, they could again be perceived as patriotic.[32] John A. Lapp, later the executive secretary of the Mennonite Central Committee, states in a 1970 article that "the nonresistant peace testimony rested right at the heart of the existence of MCC. . . . It was the search to find positive ways of helping [humanity] while refusing to serve in the military that motivated Mennonite and Brethren in Christ churches to organize service agencies," Lapp contends. "In a truly dialectic fashion relief service helped to authenticate the peace testimony."[33]

Information about the suffering of Mennonites and others in Russia came through several sources, including their various relief workers. Following a 1919 mission to deliver aid to destitute Mennonites in Siberia, three General Conference Emergency Relief volunteers reported on the debilitating conditions they had observed in Russia. Three Mennonite Church Relief Commission workers assigned to France cabled back to their Scottdale, Pennsylvania, headquarters the same year that there was an "appalling need for clothing, bedding, hospital supplies, fat and milk. Recommend unit for Russia and cooperation Central Europe."[34] The Russian Mennonites themselves sent a study commission to Europe, Canada, and the United States to tell of their plight. In mid-July the Russian study commission reported to an inter-Mennonite group from Kansas and Oklahoma. That group then called a meeting of representatives from the various Mennonite relief organizations for late July at the Prairie Street Mennonite Church in Elkhart, Indiana. Thirteen men from Pennsylvania, Minnesota, Iowa, Kansas, and Indiana attended the meeting. Recognizing that many in their denominations distrusted cooperative efforts, even with other Mennonites, the group arranged for the organization they birthed to be a temporary one, responsible only for relief aid to Russia. They explored a variety of options for unified relief work, and on 27 July they finally adopted a resolution that said the representatives present "deem it well and desirable to create a Mennonite Central Committee, whose duty shall be to function with and for the several relief committees of the Mennonites in taking charge of all gifts for South Russia, to make all purchases of suitable articles for relief work, and to provide for the transportation and equitable distribution of the same."[35] Seven Mennonite conferences and relief organizations sent representatives to MCC's first official meeting, which took place in Chicago 27 September 1920. Between December 1921 and 1925 MCC distributed 1.3-million-dollars' worth of resources in Russia, saving perhaps as many as 9,000 Mennonites—and many others—from starvation.[36]

While the relief effort was considered successful, MCC's work also was considered *finished*. While food and clothing still were being distributed in Russia, Mennonites in the states already were talking about disbanding the organization. The organization's administrative staff amounted to one part-time person, so eliminating the organization entirely and returning to the prior decentralized structure of multiple relief organizations was possible. However, since MCC was never formally disbanded, it became, partly by default, the primary cooperative Mennonite relief organization, and its directors finally incorporated the organization in 1937. In MCC's original statement of purpose, leaders wrote that it was to serve "in the relief of human suffering and distress and in aiding, rehabilitating, and re-establishing Mennonite and other refugees, and generally to support, conduct, maintain and administer relief and kindred charitable projects."[37]

During the 1930s most of MCC's limited energies were devoted to the Russian Mennonite resettlement projects in the Paraguayan Chaco. In the late 1930s and early 1940s, however, the organization's programs expanded exponentially, in response to the devastation of World War II.[38] "The war-peace conviction is integral to the genesis and growth of the MCC," claims MCC relief worker and administrator Robert Kreider. Kreider observes that, beginning in 1940, "house was added to house" in Akron, Pennsylvania, to accommodate the growing administrative headquarters, and scores of Civilian Public Service workers were sent to Akron to administer the burgeoning programs. "The MCC archives bear witness to a paper explosion in the files," he says. "As opportunities opened for sending workers and supplies abroad, bridgeheads of relief and refugee programs were established overseas."[39] While the war still raged, MCC gained permission from the United States and other national governments—including Germany, which allowed MCC to work in some of the countries it had overrun—to provide food, clothing, and medical supplies to war-torn Poland, France, and England. In a letter of instruction to another MCC worker, Orie O. Miller wrote that "our work, as you know, is entirely nonpartisan—relief to be extended without preference as to race, nationality, or otherwise, with particular attention to relief needs among war suffering women and children."[40] The letter, which also said the "Mennonite folks of Europe" should receive prior consideration, was representative of MCC's pattern during the war years.[41] The focus on the nonpartisan nature of MCC's work continues to this day. During and after the war years MCC also expanded its relief efforts into Puerto Rico, the Middle East, India, China, the Philippines, Japan, the Netherlands, Italy, Belgium, Hungary, Austria, Germany, Switzerland, and elsewhere. In addition to giving food and clothing to those devastated by the war, MCC service workers helped refugees find temporary shelter and more permanent homes, necessitating frequent contacts with government officials.

Back in the United States, thousands of Mennonites and other religious objectors to war had special assignments in Civilian Public Service, which was administered in part by Mennonite Central Committee. CPS was the mechanism Mennonites, Friends, and the Church of the Brethren worked out with the Selective Service System between 1940 and 1942 to avoid reliving the unfortunate experiences of World War I.[42] With CPS, conscientious objectors could provide humanitarian service in programs funded by and orchestrated by the churches rather than serve in noncombatant roles under the U.S. military, as was the case in the earlier war. CPS allowed Mennonites, Friends, and Brethren to serve in constructive ways in work "of national importance" without militarily defending their country. MCC administered 73 base camps, units, and special projects, nearly half of the 152 total units supervised by agencies of the various denominations. MCC's special projects included 26 mental hospital units, which contributed to the revolutionizing of mental health care in the United States following the war.[43] MCC also carried responsibility for units that worked in dairying, soil conservation, forestry, public health, national parks, and agriculture and with the Bureau of Reclamation. About half of the total 12,000 CPS workers served under MCC during the nearly six-year life span of CPS.[44]

In the process of developing Civilian Public Service, Mennonites birthed another branch of MCC: the MCC Peace Section, which in the early 1990s was reabsorbed into the parent organization. The Peace Section sought "to keep the lines clear and distinct in the matter of Christian witness to the nonresistant way of life," "to keep the peace concerns of the churches before the proper persons at the proper time," and "to interpret the attitude of government officials and the general public toward the peace position of the churches."[45] In conjunction with the earlier formed National Service Board for Religious Objectors (NSBRO), a cooperative project of the Friends, Church of the Brethren, and Mennonites, the Peace Section was responsible for monitoring changes in selective service.[46] In addition, it was charged with conducting peace education for MCC's multidenominational constituency, parts of which had lost sight of the pacifism or nonresistance of their heritage. Peace Section's initial mandate also included serving as the government contact agency for Mennonites and Brethren in Christ on matters of war and the draft. Another focus of the Peace Section's involvements that evolved over the years was "the expansion of peacemaking or reconciliation into conflict situations or the promotion of peace concerns among Christians who are not of this persuasion."[47]

As was true for the overall organization, the Peace Section's agenda and staff grew considerably in the several decades following its formation in 1942. Over the years, the Peace Section—where eventually the lobbying office was lodged—served as a kind of lightning rod for Mennonite Central Committee, receiving the brunt of the constituency's criticism about MCC's cooperative peace efforts and political involvements. Although the lines were not clearly drawn, the division of tasks between the larger MCC and the Peace Section allowed some of MCC's supporting bodies to affirm the service, relief, and development work of the organization while separating these involvements from the more controversial "peace" or "political" work that the organization sponsors.

During the 1950s and 1960s, while MCC's relief and development projects continued to increase dramatically, the Peace Section sponsored several significant conferences to reflect on issues that had emerged in the context of the Brethren in Christ and Mennonites' broadening experiences.[48] Robert Kreider suggests that MCC has allowed Mennonites to confront afresh issues that Christians have wrestled with for centuries: "Persons of relatively sheltered experience have been thrust into situations in MCC work where there is no escape from responding to these issues." Among the many questions MCC volunteers and administrators encounter, notes Kreider, are the following:

> Service in the inner city in America presents a whole new set of issues. Workers in the inner city who are committed to nonresistance may feel increasingly that the plight of the poor can only be relieved with the threat of force. . . . Shall we use government surpluses and government funding of ocean freight for relief shipments? If we choose to maximize our resources by using government funds do we minimize our witness? If one chooses to make use of government funds in MCC programs, another question arises. Does one have a right, a responsibility to speak out in criticism against actions of one's benefactor—the government? When you know so much more than you once did about the inner city of Cincinnati or the refugees of Jordan or the corruption in Saigon or the brutality in Hue—dare you keep silence? Dare the peaceable Mennonites become the outspoken Mennonites? . . . One senses in MCC work a progressive unfolding of awareness of the deep-rooted causative factors in social evils— evils which cannot be touched with temporary first aid.[49]

The study conferences that MCC and MCC Peace Section planned or supported sought to respond to these and other questions. Of primary import during the Peace Section's early years was a 9–12 November 1950 meeting at Winona Lake, Indiana. Representatives from most of MCC's constituent bodies attended the meeting, seeking to come to consensus on a unified statement of the essence of Mennonite and Brethren in Christ faith, especially as it related to issues of peace. Out of the conference came an inter-Mennonite statement, "Declaration of Christian Faith and Commitment," which provided a theological backdrop for MCC's work for the next four decades.[50]

MCC Peace Section also sponsored Mennonite participation in a series of theological discussions known as the Puidoux conferences, which took place in Europe over more than a decade beginning in 1955. The conferences grew out of cooperative efforts between Mennonites and other denominations and organizations to present a unified peace position in ecumenical settings. Some persons with prior experience with MCC, or persons who went on to become visionary leaders of MCC, participated in the Puidoux conferences.[51] In addition to the Puidoux meetings, multiple other inter-Mennonite or more ecumenical peace-related conferences—some sponsored by MCC and some not—took place during the 1950s and 1960s.[52] What's important in this context is to recognize that these theological and ethical discussions generally were *responses* to the situations encountered in Mennonites' broadening mission and service experiences. Mennonites working with organizations such as MCC, as Robert Kreider says, faced "the inescapable necessity of responding to issues which are not posed in the home community."[53] In most cases, the theological sorting that Mennonites were doing was epiphenomenal, an attempt to understand and articulate the tensions and dilemmas they had encountered in the field.[54] The limits of traditional, withdrawn nonresistance were clear: the task was to find new ways of making peace.

While Mennonite graduate students, theologians, and ethicists—many of whom were also MCC personnel—wrestled with issues of peace and war on paper in the decades after the Second World War, Mennonite Central Committee kept plugging away in the United States, Canada, and in units scattered around the world—now also including parts of Asia, Africa, and Latin America.[55] The organization also gradually shifted its primary emphasis away from providing emergency relief in crisis situations. Delton Franz, longtime director of MCC Washington's lobbying office, sometimes characterizes this shift as the "passages" of MCC from emergency relief in the 1920s. These passages included a switch to service projects, including refugee resettlement and house reconstruction, in the 1940s in Europe; to

Third World development projects in the 1950s; to justice issues in the 1970s and following years. Franz and others at MCC often cite the well-worn adage "If you *give* a family a fish, the family will eat for a day. If you *teach* a family to fish, they'll know how to fish for a lifetime. If you *provide access* to the fish pond, they'll truly be able to feed themselves forever." MCC does still distribute fish and teaches persons to fish, but its present emphases are on job creation, the environment, and peacemaking. The transitions MCC has made are largely related to its cumulative experience, which has evidenced the complexity of causal factors related to hunger, violence, and other forms of oppression. One of those factors, and the most relevant one in this discussion, is the role of various governments—in particular, the United States.

A number of persons have called attention to the growth and expansion of the activities and programs of twentieth-century nations, including the U.S. government. John Boli-Bennett, who studied the ideological extension of nation-state authority over the course of a century, claims—a bit too hyper-critically—that we have witnessed the rise of the "universal, omnivorous state."[56] Much of the literature on the growth of political institutions calls attention to the effects such expansion has on religious organizations and other entities in the "voluntary sector," which once carried primary responsibility for health, education, and social welfare needs.[57] The United States is simply one among many nations where government interests and programs have expanded in response to social, economic, and technological changes.[58]

Sociologist Robert Bellah and his associates argue that the expansion of government responsibilities is part of the modern expansion of the public sphere—the arena in which problems are defined as public and political rather than private. "For better or worse, we have developed an activist state, which in its own confused, fragmented way not only provides for the welfare of individual citizens but manages the local economy—setting interest rates, guaranteeing bank deposits, bailing our failing corporations, regulating the stock market." The *Good Society* authors note that now the U.S. government subsidizes college education, guarantees home loans, underwrites much of the scientific research that fuels the national economy, provides unemployment insurance, guarantees or provides medical coverage and income in old age, and protects persons from job discrimination. Still concentrating on domestic concerns, they claim, "More and more we think of problems that government cannot or will not solve—infant mortality in poor communities, the AIDS epidemic, rising drug use—as public problems for which government is responsible."[59] In many cases in this century, national politicians have responded to these social needs with increased programs, funding, and services.

State expansion can be measured in a variety of ways, including budgetary and personnel changes. Researcher David Harrington Watt notes that total U.S. government expenditures (federal, state, and local) increased dramatically in this century. Total combined expenditures were 20 billion dollars in 1940, 70 billion dollars in 1950, 151 billion dollars in 1960, 333 billion dollars in 1970, 959 billion dollars in 1980, and 1,696 billion dollars in 1986. Harrington Watt observes that, at the turn of the century, the federal government employed under 240,000 civilians. In 1940 the figure was 1,000,000, and by 1988, 3,100,000 civilians received paychecks from the federal government. Active-duty military personnel went from 140,000 in 1900 to about 460,000 in 1940 to 2,200,000 in 1988. Harrington Watt says that allowing for inflation does not make the trend disappear: expressed in constant dollars (based on fiscal year 1982), federal budget outlays increased from 83 billion dollars in 1940 to 699 billion dollars in 1980 and an estimated 870 billion in 1988.[60]

During these developmental years, states Harrington Watt, expenditures were concentrated in two areas: social welfare, which by 1984 had risen to 671 billion dollars (52 percent of total government outlays and 18 percent of the Gross National Product), and military spending. At times during the postwar era, he claims, military outlays accounted for as much as 62 percent of total federal expenditures. The United States spent more of its GNP on the military than did France, Japan, West Germany, or the United Kingdom, allowing the country to develop "a military arsenal that far outstripped those of its allies and rivals and that was without precedent in world history."[61] David H. Kamens and Tormod K. Lunde develop the notion that nation-states have become the only imaginable way of organizing and rationalizing international order. "States are no longer seen as 'nightwatchmen'—even in the United States. Current world culture defines them as important problemsolvers," they observe. "As a consequence, states have acquired a new range of activities that they are expected to carry out."[62] These activities include national planning and international development, as well as problem solving in conflicts between and within other countries. Often, in the case of conflicts, the United States has responded both diplomatically and with military intervention.

As major nations, including the United States, have intervened politically, militarily, or economically into developing countries, the result has not always been constructive.[63] In recent decades some church organizations have recognized the debilitating effects major outside interventions may have on the economic growth and stability of indigenous state structures—especially as they have witnessed the results in the local communities in which they serve. As they have worked at the grassroots level, seeking to meet humanitarian needs through education and support of local development efforts, they have often encountered governmental organizations working to resolve some of the same problems or have felt the effects of governmental programs and policies.

BUMPING INTO EACH OTHER "ON THE GROUND"

As the American government has extended its interests and involvements, both domestically and overseas, it sometimes has found itself working alongside mission, relief, and development volunteers of nongovernmental organizations, including Mennonite Central Committee. At times government policies and programs, especially during the nineteenth and early twentieth centuries, furthered Protestant and Catholic churches' mission work, making their activities possible. MCC's John A. Lapp notes that churches' missions developed at the same time as the colonial empires expanded. "Missions and missionaries are very much a part of the historical situations in which we find ourselves," says Lapp in a 1976 speech. "There is a macro political situation that we cannot escape. . . . ." While the cultural and political alliances that fueled the engine of both imperialism and missions are now widely discredited, says Lapp, mission agencies must acknowledge their past interconnection with the cultural forms and empires of the West.[64]

Much of the church-state experience in this century, and especially in recent decades, has contrasted sharply with that of earlier eras, when nations were building their empires. Rather than riding the wave of their nation's efforts, U.S. church organizations now sometimes find themselves in opposition to the domestic and overseas initiatives of their government. On occasion NGO volunteers find themselves supporting the revolutionary claims of disempowered nationals who clamor for peace and justice, while their government provides funding for the regimes that oppress those with whom they work. In such cases and in many other settings, the U.S. government's programs and policies contradict and constrain those of NGOs, adding to the suffering the service agencies seek to relieve. "During the Korean War in the '50s, the expanded exposure of our people to suffering from Appalachia to Africa became the bridges that allowed us to move back and forth from the tranquillity of rural America to the revolution in the Congo," wrote MCC Washington workers years later. "The *governmental* connections to warmaking and peacemaking were taking on new reality."[65]

Mennonite Central Committee began its relief and development work devoid of political aspirations and likely unaware of the political ramifications of its service. Only gradually did MCC workers, administrators, and constituents recognize that "our service cannot escape the realities of power in the world system."[66] Partly through its attention to world hunger, one of MCC's foci since its founding in 1920, the organization has come to realize that all service is woven into social and political structures. In a 1993 presentation on world hunger, MCC's food and disaster coordinator listed seven causes of hunger, four of which were directly related to government practices. The first four causes, holds Hershey Leaman, are poverty, war, misguided economic policies, and destruction of the environment. Among the specific points Leaman mentions are the lack of access to resources, the destruction of productive farmland and transportation routes through warfare, destructive trade policies, embargoes, and boycotts, and Third World debt to Western banks. MCC now realizes, suggests Leaman, that "helping people grow more food, teaching them to read, promoting good nutritional practices, [and] helping provide better health care" will not reduce hunger unless other social, political, and economic restructuring occurs.[67]

Over the years, MCC workers in the field, who daily have contact with those whose lives are affected by United States government policies, have made the organization aware of the need for change beyond the "ground level." In the 1960s MCC volunteers in Appalachia and urban settings in the United States asked, "Is there no money available to make our cities human? Can't the welfare system be changed so that it won't break up the family and destroy a person's dignity? If we remain quiet are we in a sense giving our nod of approval to the status quo?"[68] In 1950 MCC's J. N. Byler reported on his exploratory trip to the new nation of Israel and his visit with some of the nearly one million displaced Arab-Palestinian refugees. Byler noted that the United States, United Nations, and Great Britain had recognized the State of Israel, while the Arab states did not recognize the country. While the displaced people wanted to return to their homes, the political situation, complicated by the support of the world powers, made this impossible. Byler asked, "How long [the refugees] can sit in their fast-deteriorating tents, mud huts, make shift shelters, and over-crowded housing is a real sixty-four dollar question."[69] Years later MCC's country director in Jordan said that when he and other workers distributed Christmas bundles from Mennonite children in North America one year, one recipient rejected the gift. The woman, who was living in a Palestinian refugee camp, looked at the bundle, threw it back at the MCC worker, and remarked, "We get Christmas bundles and the Israelis get Phantom jets. You keep your Christmas bundles and you have your country keep its Phantom jets."[70]

MCC began assisting with medical, nutritional, and other human needs in South Vietnam in 1954, years before U.S. troops were sent to the country. In time MCC workers questioned their efforts to mop up after their government's destruction. It was in Vietnam, however, where American

MCC workers most frequently found their government at cross-purposes with their relief aid.[71] At a 1966 meeting of relief workers in South Vietnam, one Vietnamese national said, "If any of you are not ashamed for what your country is doing here, you might as well go home right now. You will never do my people any good."[72] For many years MCC workers in Vietnam wrote back to Akron headquarters that as soon as they bound up wounds, there would be more American bombs, more deaths, and more destruction.[73] In May 1965, fifty representatives of religious groups, including five Mennonites, visited Washington to discuss Vietnam with administration officials and members of Congress. The Washington visitation coincided with President Lyndon Johnson's request for a special appropriation of seven hundred million dollars for continuing the Vietnam conflict through June 1965.[74] The following year, members of the Vietnam Mennonite Mission Council wrote to their supporting constituent bodies that they were "troubled by the great suffering the Vietnamese people have had to endure due to acts of terrorism, fighting, bombings, and shellings." The council noted that thousands were being killed or maimed, "social fabric is being torn and the morality of the people adversely affected. . . . . We are concerned because the justification for our country's heavy military involvement here is open to question. The issue is not so clear-cut as those who defend United States military actions would have us believe."[75]

Later that summer MCC Board Chair C. N. Hostetter Jr. and Executive Secretary William T. Snyder wrote to President Johnson, calling attention to the organization's twelve years of service work in South Vietnam. After specifying their disagreements with U.S. policy, they wrote that out of the context of Vietnam "we have felt increasingly . . . a contradiction and a paradox in our efforts, trying to help the people on the one hand while at the same time our government was engaged in an escalating war that was devastating the countryside and creating enormous tragic suffering for the civilian population." Snyder and Hostetter contended that "the time has come when we can no longer maintain faith with the homeless, the hungry, the orphaned and the wounded to whom we minister unless we speak out as clearly as we can against the savage war in which our country is engaged."[76] Hostetter and Snyder added that MCC workers are willing to suffer with their Vietnamese brothers and sisters, "but we do not want our efforts to be a palliative on the conscience of a nation seeking to do good on one hand while spreading destruction on the other." In clear terms, they expressed their opposition to the escalating military efforts that "increase the dimensions of human suffering."

In 1967 Hostetter, Snyder, and three others went to the White House to present another letter to President Johnson. The letter echoed many of the concerns expressed in the 1966 correspondence. Hostetter and other MCC representatives said Mennonites were not abandoning their tradition of responding to conflict by serving the victims rather than participating in the conflict. However, the letter said, "Our consciences protest against providing clothing and food and medical care for refugees while remaining silent about a policy which generates new refugees each day."[77] The correspondence to the president, both in 1966 and 1967, was based on the firsthand observations of Mennonite workers living through the devastation of the war.

Perhaps more than any other single event or experience, this involvement in Vietnam led Mennonites—via Mennonite Central Committee—toward recognizing the political impact of their service work. John K. Stoner, then executive secretary of MCC U.S. Peace Section, states in 1977 that although none of MCC's actions—such as providing relief to war sufferers in Vietnam, aiding the families of political prisoners, or visiting Christians in pre-*perestroika* Russia—are political in the popular sense of the word, they all have their political impact. "MCC and its constituency will have grown in our understanding when we recognize this fact and outgrow the ignorance or naiveté which seeks to ignore it," claims Stoner.[78] Vietnam also made MCC keenly aware of the impossibility of serving authentically

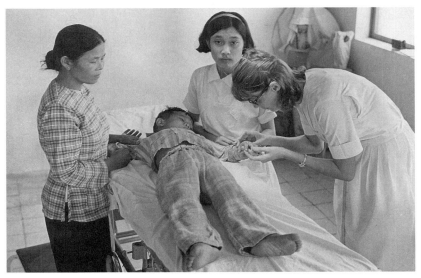

MCC service worker Mary Sue Helstern, right, works with a young Vietnamese boy in 1966 while his mother and an assistant observe. Photo by Lance Woodruff, courtesy of Mennonite Central Committee Photograph Collection, Archives of the Mennonite Church, Goshen, Indiana.

without speaking to the governments contributing to human suffering. In the years following the Vietnam War and after the founding of MCC Washington, MCC workers in the nation's capital frequently mentioned sociologist Peter Berger's observation that, in the twentieth century, for the first time in human history, the tide has turned whereby more human suffering is caused by the policies and actions of governments than by natural disasters. "The only political commitments worth making are those that seek to reduce the amount of human suffering in the world," holds Berger.[79] Berger's words have become part of the mantra MCC Washington workers recite as they justify their lobbying efforts on Capitol Hill.

MOVING INTO WASHINGTON

In his mid-century book *The Mennonite Church in the Second World War,* Mennonite Church historian and peace leader Guy F. Hershberger noted the contacts his denomination's Peace Problems Committee had made with government officials. He referred to the committee's 1927 letter to national politicians that encouraged them to pursue a policy of friendship and good will in international relations and expressed concern for the increase in military training in colleges and universities and the breakdown of relationships between the United States and some other countries. While affirming that such letters or visits to government officials may be appropriate, Hershberger suggested that the amount of energy the church devotes to these activities is a question. As already noted, he believed that for the church to maintain or become a lobbyist organization "would be a perversion of its purpose and function."[80] But in his 1968 article in *Gospel Herald,* Hershberger listed a number of reasons why Mennonites *ought* to have an office in the nation's capital. Among the reasons he listed was the fact that Mennonites' domestic and foreign relief and service programs, educational institutions, and hospitals "are daily affected, for good or ill, by a host of government agencies . . ."[81]

In the seventeen years between publication of Hershberger's 1951 text and the 1968 article, Mennonites' relationship to American politics had changed dramatically. American Mennonites had experienced two more wars, and the latter directly affected their service work. A few had participated actively in the Civil Rights movement, marching alongside Martin Luther King Jr. and inviting him to speak on their college campuses. Mennonite young people were becoming increasingly vocal about their opposition to the U.S. military presence in Vietnam. Congress had nearly accepted a proposal that would have continued to recognize conscientious objectors to military service, but only after inducting them into the service and then assigning them to civilian units supervised by the military. Denominational and academic leaders were hosting study conferences to re-examine the relationship of the church and state. Mennonites also were changing demographically: more persons in the churches were getting advanced degrees and settling into professional occupations. Slowly but surely, they were moving from their rural enclaves into the suburbs and the city. All of these transformations—but especially the experience in Vietnam and the trauma of the Selective Service System's 1967 revisions—made the notion of a permanent Mennonite "presence" in Washington more palatable to MCC's still reluctant constituency.

For many years before MCC Washington opened in 1968, Mennonites had the semblance of an office in the capital. MCC Peace Section's mandate included keeping abreast of legislative and policy action on Capitol Hill, especially on conscription issues, so Akron employees often traveled to Washington for legislative visits or congressional testimony.[82] During the development of Civilian Public Service in 1940, they had joined with other peace churches to form the National Service Board for Religious Objectors. From at least 1945 until the early 1960s, Mennonites had one person on staff at NSBRO, often serving as director of the organization, who regularly reported to the Peace Section.[83] NSBRO's work, like that of Peace Section's own occasional Washington work in the 1940s and 1950s, generally was confined to issues of draft legislation, although at times staffers tracked legislation on immigration laws and U.S. policies on world hunger.

While the NSBRO connections gave Mennonite Central Committee a toehold in Washington, some within the organization and its constituent denominations continued to push for a more sustained presence in the capital. By the mid-1960s many religious bodies already had Washington offices. Among them were various Baptist denominations, Catholics, Church of the Brethren, Methodists, Seventh-Day Adventists, Lutherans, African Methodist Episcopal Zion Church, Christian Church (Disciples of Christ), Presbyterians, Jewish groups, Unitarian-Universalists, the United Church of Christ, the National Council of Churches, and the National Association of Evangelicals. The Quakers have had a continuing Washington presence since 1940, first under the Friends War Problems Committee, then the National Service Board for Religious Objectors, and finally under the Friends Committee for National Legislation.[84] The Friends Committee was the first—and for several decades the *only*—religious organization to openly register as a lobby.[85]

In 1955 MCC Peace Section commissioned Irvin B. Horst to study the "Washington and New York scenes," making note of Mennonites' present involvements there and determining whether there would be additional areas "where our witness may be given consistently with what we believe to be the Biblical standards for Christian life and work in this world."[86] Horst visited with representatives from the Friends Committee on National Legislation, the National Association of Evangelicals, and the National Council of Churches, seeking their counsel on witnessing to government and UN leaders.[87] Horst's uncompleted study was concluded in 1956.[88]

The following year Peace Section's executive committee reviewed Horst's brief report and agreed to plan a two-day conference on "Christian Responsibility to the State," a conference that took place that November.[89] Then Peace Section, at the prompting of the General Conference Mennonite Church's Board of Christian Service, agreed to consider sponsoring an inter-Mennonite Washington study seminar in 1961.[90] In the meantime the Institute of Mennonite Studies, located at Associated Mennonite Biblical Seminaries in Elkhart, Indiana, commissioned John H. Yoder to undertake a "Study Program on the Mennonite Witness to the Social Order." Yoder's study resulted in the publication of his significant *The Christian Witness to the State*.[91]

In 1962 MCC Peace Section's new executive secretary, Edgar Metzler, reopened the discussion about an increased voice in Washington, hoping to keep alive the idea of a permanent office. In a 1963 projection of Peace Section's future, Metzler and other administrators suggested that within five years a full-time staff person would be located in Washington to help Mennonites "move beyond the limited witness of the past."[92] "The exact program for the future, the message, and its method of communication, is unclear," the projection said. "The great challenge here is to work at contemporary problems within a biblical understanding of the state. The temptation will be merely to follow the familiar patterns of ecclesiastical social action."[93]

At the time Peace Section made its five-year projection, graduate student John D. Unruh was serving in a one-month "Washington Witness to Government" assignment under the Peace Section's direction. The assignment was geared to the civil rights crisis and the limited nuclear test-ban treaty, partly in response to "the feelings of guilt among some Mennonites that we have only witnessed to government on matters pertaining to our own immediate interests and needs—such as the conscientious objector provisions on draft legislation."[94] In his report, Unruh argued that, although "the place of the idealist in Washington will always be difficult," the idealistic witness should be given in such settings and that "all too frequently when Mennonites speak with legislators we approach them too gingerly and accord them excessive reverence." Unruh said Mennonites should be more courageous in presenting their testimony to busy members of Congress, spending less time engaging in "delightful banter," story telling, and discussing mutual acquaintances. Unruh recommended that similar summer programs be implemented in New York and again in Washington and that an Akron-based person be more responsible for monitoring legislation. He stopped short, however, of recommending establishing a permanent Washington office, "for I think we need to be clearer than we now are about what we would be seeking to accomplish in Washington, and why." But Unruh concluded with a pointed question: "In the legislative arena some of the questions starkly facing modern [people] are being debated— must not the church be there to give its witness and its testimony?"[95]

In 1964–65 MCC Peace Section sponsored an extensive church-state study, surveying 150 churches across the United States and Canada. The study prompted another major conference on church-state issues in October 1965. According to participant Keeney, the conference helped some to accept a new understanding for church-state relations, knocking some blocks out of the theoretical wall separating church and state. He contends that the modern state does not function only as an enforcer of the law: it also provides many services for the public good, just as the church does. In areas such as providing health care, social welfare, education, and other similar services, the church and state are frequently allies: "[t]o erect a wall of separation would be a disservice to the persons needing help." Overall, Keeney observes, the church–state study conference "led many participants to conclude that the traditional Mennonite stance of isolation from the government was not always the wisest."[96]

At its 8 June 1966 meeting, Peace Section's executive committee dealt with the issue of a Washington witness once again. In the committee's minutes, members state: "Our traditional willingness to testify when our own interests were involved in relation to conscientious objection have led to suggestions that we should also be willing to testify when the rights of others are involved. Various study conferences of Peace Section constituent groups have expressed a growing concern that witness to the state should be a dimension of our service of Christian compassion." The executive committee's remarks were prompted by actions taken 6 November 1965 by the Peace and Social Concerns Committees of the Mennonite Church and General Conference Mennonite Church. It was these *denominational* peace committees, especially the General Conference committee, that put pressure on Mennonite Central Committee to establish an office.[97]

Feeling encouraged by their two largest constituent denominations, Peace Section commissioned yet another study of witness possibilities in Washington. This time Dwight Y. King, a Harvard Divinity School student, was asked to speak with Mennonites and others in Washington, especially representatives of other religious organizations, and to make specific recommendations for action. King's resulting thirty-two-page, heavily footnoted, theologically sensitive document is a gold mine for those interested in the history of religious lobbying.[98] King quotes some of the fifteen denominational and ecumenical leaders he interviewed in Washington, as well as Mennonites who lived and worked in the capital. The researcher argues in favor of a distinctively Mennonite peace witness in Washington: "most moralists speaking to public issues are operating under models identical to those which political scientists and policy makers are using," such as just war theory. "A Washington office would provide us a platform for articulating other models to government officials and to the various denominational groups."[99] King cautions, however, that the office should function *primarily* as a "listening post." Helpful concepts to guide MCC Peace Section's thinking, he suggests, might include the following: to see it as an *enabling agency* for constituents seeking to be more effective servants; to view it as *preventive maintenance*—anticipating change and proposing solutions to problems; and to understand interest in public affairs and social action "as a legitimate spiritual gift in the church."

King, ever attuned to the concerns of MCC's constituent denominations, argues that the office would need to be careful in selecting the issues "we might be more prophetic about." He also readily admits that, whatever the issues, "the decision to open an office in Washington will have effects on the *future* and identity of the Mennonite denomination." King mentions that the Washington agencies that most clearly understand "what they are about in Washington, both in terms of government and in terms of their denomination, are the ones operating most effectively, and with least frustration." He says denominations have found that establishing Washington offices has "definite repercussion" on the sponsoring groups, noting that understandings of "mission to the 'state' will be closely related to a group's understandings of its mission to the world and its concept of the church."[100] Although it was two years before the MCC Washington office opened, King's report was taken seriously. His astute observations provided much of the material for the documents that would guide MCC Washington's work.

At the 19 January 1967 annual meeting of MCC Peace Section, the board adopted a motion "that we favor in principle increased representation in Washington and that the Peace Section Executive Committee be instructed to work out a recommendation for implementation."[101] Then, in May 1967, the U.S. Congress provided the final impetus Mennonites needed to actually establish the office they had been planning for more than a decade. Unaware of draft legislation making its way through Congress, Mennonites almost "missed the boat," as one leader described it.[102] That spring, Congress had considered a variety of alterations to selective service guidelines, since the Selective Service Act was scheduled to expire 30 June. During the congressional proceedings in April and early May, MCC leaders William Keeney and John E. Lapp testified before the Senate and House Armed Services Committees. The Senate passed a bill that left the conscientious-objector provision relatively unchanged. But the Mennonites were unprepared for the House Armed Services Committee's bill, which was proposed 18 May. While the bill still provided exemptions for conscientious objectors, the provision took religious objectors back to the days of World War I: it required conscientious objectors, like other young men of age, to be inducted into the military service, and then furloughed them out into alternative service. The alternative service, however, still would be under military supervision, an arrangement that the peace churches had rejected in their 1940 discussions with Selective Service System. Mennonites learned of the bill from the National Service Board for Religious Objectors, which became aware of it only after it had passed the House and gone through the Senate Armed Services Committee. A week later, after a burst of Capitol Hill activity from peace church leaders, a second bill maintaining the earlier provisions was passed by the House and then the Senate.[103] The incident made Mennonite leaders realize the difficulty of monitoring legislation from outside Washington. They also discovered that many members of Congress did not know them as well as they had hoped. In his justification for opening a Mennonite office in the capital, Guy F. Hershberger wrote: "If they didn't know our views on induction, how can they know what we think on scores of other questions? And if we didn't know what was going on in Washington affecting us on the conscription issue, what do we know about what is going on in scores of other areas affecting our concerns and interests?"[104]

In June the committee instructed the executive secretary, Ivan J. Kauffman, to explore the possibility of opening a Washington office, and to seek out possible office space in the capital.[105] Finally, at the 18 January 1968 Peace Section Executive Committee meeting, a "Report and Recommendation Concerning a Washington Office" was approved.[106] The approval was the final formal step necessary for opening MCC Washington, the Mennonite and Brethren in Christ "bridge" between their service commitments and the American state. In the following months, the Peace Section was busy making plans for its Washington "listening post," interviewing candidates for the director's position, raising funding for the venture, and talking with constituents.[107] That July the office's opening marked a significant turning point in Anabaptist-Mennonite history. After more than a quarter century of painstaking gestation, MCC Washington was birthed in an eight-by-ten foot third-floor cubicle at the headquarters of the Friends Committee on National Legislation.

DELTON FRANZ, LONGTIME MCC WASHINGTON DIRECTOR

Chosen to direct the activities of MCC's new Capitol Hill office was Delton Franz, a General Conference Mennonite Church pastor. Franz learned of the Washington opening while on a year-long sabbatical in 1967–68 at Union Theological Seminary in New York, where he was taking courses in social and political science and practical theology. "I have felt increasingly the need for the church to be in communication with our federal government," he wrote to MCC that spring. "Such an assignment would receive my greatest efforts."[108] In April 1968 MCC Peace Section's chair, William Keeney, invited Franz to become director of the office. Three months later thirty-six-year-old Franz and his spouse, Marian, moved with their two children to the capital. When they arrived in Washington, some city blocks were still smoldering from the riots following Martin Luther King Jr.'s assassination, the tents of Resurrection City were just beginning to come down, the Vietnam War dominated American consciousness, and capital activists were planning civil rights marches. Franz and his family settled in northwest Washington, where they remained throughout Franz's nearly twenty-six years of leadership at MCC Washington. Franz retired from the director's position in December 1993 and continued as a consultant through the following December. Staffer Ken Martens Friesen served as interim director from January to August 1994. J. Daryl Byler, a former pastor and attorney, became the office's second director in August 1994.

Over the years, Franz became intimately identified with MCC's work on Capitol Hill, serving as the primary spokesperson and image bearer for Mennonites and Brethren in Christ in the city. For most of MCC Washington's years, Franz's personality and style—soft-spoken and yet passionate—has embodied the tenor of the office itself. Franz's personal passage from the rural, sheltering wheat fields of Kansas to one of the world's power centers parallels, on a personal level, the transformations within MCC and the denominations he represented. He was born in 1932, during the early years of the Depression, to parents of Russian-Mennonite heritage. During his elementary years he moved with his family from his birthplace, Hutchinson, Kansas—a Mennonite and Republican stronghold—to nearby Buhler.[109] Later Franz was educated in Mennonite institutions, first at Bethel College in North Newton, Kansas, and then, following two brief interim pastorates in Kansas, at Mennonite Biblical Seminary in Chicago. The move to Chicago was a "baptism by fire" for the twenty-three-year-old. Seminary students lived on the city's south side, an African-American community with nearly eighteen hundred persons per square block, triple the population before the neighborhood's racial transition—and twice the number in the entire town where Franz grew up. Families in multistory tenement buildings were squeezed into cramped apartments drastically downsized by slum landlords. Infant mortality and crime rates were high, and 40 percent of Franz's neighbors were on welfare. The Franz children were among only six whites out of the twenty-six hundred students at the neighborhood school, Shakespeare Elementary.

A year after moving to Chicago, Franz was asked to be student pastor at Woodlawn Mennonite Church, and after finishing seminary in 1958 he became a full-time minister there. Under his leadership and that of pastor Elmer Neufeld and associate pastor Vincent Harding, an African-American Seventh-Day Adventist-turned Mennonite, the formerly white church became interracial and intercultural. Among the members were white Mennonite Ph.D. students at the University of Chicago, former sharecroppers from the south, African-American case workers employed by the Department of Social Welfare, and welfare recipients. As a pastor and community worker, Franz participated in nonviolence workshops, boycotts, pickets, and sit-ins with Jesse Jackson. He became active in Jackson's Operation

Longtime MCC Washington Director Delton Franz experienced an awakening into political awareness while attending seminary and living in an urban African-American community on Chicago's south side during the late 1950s and 1960s. Franz, third from right in the front row, helped organize a seminar on "Christ, the Mennonite Churches, and Race Relations" in April 1959, when he was a co-pastor at Woodlawn Mennonite Church. Photo by Paul King, courtesy of Mennonite Central Committee Photograph Collection, Archives of the Mennonite Church, Goshen, Indiana.

Breadbasket (later Operation Push), which sought to upgrade the job status of African-American employees. He marched with Martin Luther King Jr. in the segregated Chicago neighborhood of Gage Park and later visited King's home, where King was recovering from a stabbing wound. Franz also provided leadership in the Hyde Park-Kenwood Council of Churches and Synagogues, meeting with state and city politicians about employment, education, housing, and public welfare needs of the poor. His work with the council and with Kenwood-Oakdale Community Organization, he contends, helped him learn firsthand what it means to address structures and systems—to question the economic underpinnings of the whole welfare system—instead of only providing humanitarian assistance. Working for social justice while studying theology and preaching in an urban congregation left an indelible impact on Franz and his understandings of active faith, a faith rooted both in the biblical texts and in concrete experience.

Franz suggests that his move from Chicago to Washington was as incongruous as his earlier move from cocoonlike Kansas to the inner city. "Making the pastoral rounds down glass-strewn streets, knocking on endless doors in dimly lit apartment hallways seemed a strange preparation for the assignment in the marble corridors of Capitol Hill," he explains.[110] Later, Franz adds, he recognized that his Chicago immersion in the lives of society's powerless, victimized people was an essential part of his formation for the director's role in Washington. "Faithfulness in my Washington assignment, more than anything else, means not to forget the disinherited of the earth while finding ways to sensitize the powerful to the impact of their actions on the world's powerless," he said shortly before his retirement. "To seek out witnesses to accomplish this is a crucial part of this ministry."

Franz was the office's sole employee when it opened on 1 July 1968 with a first-year budget of fifteen thousand dollars.[111] Within the first several months his spouse, Marian, began working part-time as a secretary and research assistant. Gradually, other paid staffers and volunteers were added as MCC Washington's issue areas broadened.[112] In the mid-1970s, Franz and two other persons, one of whom was an MCC service worker, tracked legislation for MCC Peace Section. By 1993, the office's staff included two-and-a-half salaried employees, two full-time service workers, and two part-time volunteers.[113] With increasing space needs, MCC Washington relocated twice, first into a two-room office and then in 1978 to the present nine-hundred-square-foot space.[114] The expansion and moves signaled changes within the Capitol Hill office as well as the larger MCC organization and opened MCC Washington to greater engagement with other religious lobbyists.

3

BEDDING AND BUNDLING
IN WASHINGTON

I mean, this is Washington. You're supposed to be able to form coalitions
with whomever you want, whenever you want, even if it's only for a few
minutes on a very narrow issue. Congresspeople do it all the time.

—Greg Goering

Within a year following Mennonites' formal entry into Washington, Director Delton Franz moved the fledgling Mennonite Central Committee office into the United Methodist Building, heart of the 1960s religious lobbying culture. There, where the office remains, Mennonite staffers began
sharing space and rubbing shoulders daily with secular and religious "peace
and justice" advocates. The growing interconnectedness of MCC with other
organizations with similar concerns disturbed some of MCC's constituents,
intensifying decades of criticism of cooperative peace efforts. "We fear that
there's too much hobnobbing with worldly peace groups," said one representative at the 1971 annual meeting of Mennonite Central Committee,
"and it is influencing the Peace Section."[1]

In the past several decades, and in the half century prior to the Washington office's opening in 1968, Mennonites have indeed engaged some unusual
bedfellows, bedfellows that make some Mennonites restless under the sheets.
Religious groups, particularly those with more sectarian, perfectionistic
understandings of faith and life, often resist these "outside influences," which

they fear may, in some sense, transform or corrupt the body of believers.[2] The fear is, in part, related to influences that may elicit changes in a religious group's institutions, beliefs, and practices, alterations that may require painful processes of reconfiguring identity and realigning commitments.[3]

However, within the Anabaptist tradition, the "bedfellows" metaphor evokes another metaphor with rich possibilities—that of Amish "bundling." Bundling consists of a courting couple's going to bed together—with their clothes on and sometimes with a board between them—purportedly for mutual edification and fuel conservation.[4] Apparently the practice is not always effective for edification or conservation, nor for prevention of intercourse. But in some cases, bundling may contribute to healthy, vital relationships. While sometimes one actor completely succumbs to the wishes and intentions of the bedfellow, on other occasions the parties involved are mutually influenced, and both are changed for the better in the process of interaction. In yet other situations the board reminds the relating partners that they are separate beings with their own histories and commitments, and that it is best to talk together about common goals and dreams without fully coupling. In this analysis of religious advocates on Capitol Hill, the MCC "bundling board" between the interacting parties can be viewed as the specific beliefs and practices of Mennonites—in particular, their emphases on pacifism, humility, and service. Complex associations among Mennonites and other religious and secular lobbying groups in Washington then provide opportunities for multiple outcomes, depending on the traditions of the organizations involved, the intensity of working relationships, and the demands of the political context.

BUNDLING IN THE UNITED METHODIST BUILDING

Housed within the imposing Italian Renaissance–style United Methodist Building—in addition to Mennonite Central Committee—are the headquarters for the United Methodist General Board of Church and Society, along with the Washington offices of the Episcopal Church, Presbyterian Church, United Church of Christ, Unitarian Universalist Association, Church of the Brethren, American Baptist Churches, U.S.A., and the National Council of the Churches of Christ in the U.S.A. Also, several dozen other nonprofit organizations—most of which are church-related—occupy the 100–110 Maryland Avenue building, sometimes known as the "God Box."[5] Among these are the National Peace Institute Foundation, Religious Coalition for Abortion Rights, American Agricultural Movement, the *Nation* magazine, National Coalition to Ban Handguns, Unemployed and Poverty Action Council, and United Nations International Children's Emergency Fund.

By virtue of their location, Methodist Building occupants find themselves at the geographical center of Washington's political institutions as
well. Directly across First Street is the U.S. Capitol, a stone's throw from the
main entrance of the United Methodist Building. Across Maryland Avenue,
within the view from MCC's fifth-floor offices, is the Supreme Court.
Three Senate office buildings are within a block, and three blocks away are
the three House office buildings. About a dozen former or present members of Congress have offices interspersed among the peace and justice
offices: immediately adjacent to MCC's office is Sen. Howell Heflin's (D–
Alabama) Washington residence, and former Sen. Al Gore Sr. (D–Tennessee), father of the vice president, lives on the floor below. At the Methodist
Building's dedication on 16 January 1924, Bishop William F. McDowell
said that the structure "will make our church visible and multiply its power
at this world's center." Another Methodist official, Clarence True Wilson,
said the building was "foreordained . . . to be the center of every good
movement in Washington."[6]

*The United Methodist Building, left, originally built for the Methodist Episcopal Church's
Board of Temperance, Prohibition and Public Morals, now houses the offices of many religious
advocacy offices and several dozen other nonprofit organizations. This view, from across First
Street in the Capitol lawn, also shows the proximity of the Supreme Court Building. MCC
Washington moved into the United Methodist Building, sometimes known as "the God Box,"
in 1969. Photo courtesy of the United Methodist General Board of Church and Society.*

Originally constructed for the Methodist Episcopal Church's Board of Temperance, Prohibition and Public Morals, the Methodist Building's activities expanded over the next several decades as temperance legislation waned, other Methodist social concerns broadened, and additional non-profit agencies rented what once were apartments. Although not part of the initial design, the oval-shaped lobby now features biblical inscriptions across the top of each side wall. Painted in bold, black letters are prophetic statements from Hebrew scriptures: "What does the Lord require of you but to do justice and to love kindness and to walk humbly with your God" and "They shall beat their swords into plowshares and their spears into pruning hooks."[7] Lining the lobby walls are labeled, sepia-tone burlap paintings. Among them are depictions of Andrezej, a Polish cartoonist resettled in Arizona; Elsa and her daughter, refugees from Ethiopia; Louis, a young Cuban seeking sponsorship; and the children of Xiong Ma, of Vietnam. A small bulletin board to the left of the lobby's elevators is plastered perpetually with flyers from diverse organizations. On one afternoon, the bulletin board promoted events sponsored by the League of Indigenous Sovereign Nations of the Western Hemisphere, Women Strike for Peace, and Women's Action for New Directions, along with information about a national march and rally for democracy in Haiti, a vigil at the South African Embassy commemorating the Boipatong Massacre, and a Wesley Theological Seminary course on "Black Perspectives on the Colombian Legacy."

During the 1960s, as the Methodist Board of Social Concerns (now the General Board of Church and Society) broadened its agenda, the Methodist Building became a base for civil rights activities.[8] It was used as a center for religious participation in Martin Luther King Jr.'s 1963 March on Washington, the 1968 Poor People's March, and multiple protests during the Vietnam War. Mennonite Central Committee entered Washington and then located itself in this volatile context in the midst of the unrest related to civil rights and Vietnam. In a more significant way than ever before, American Mennonites found themselves engaged with the political world, working alongside other peace and justice groups, and subject to constraints, demands, and possibilities they had encountered in only piecemeal fashion before. The ecumenical relationships MCC was forging in that highly charged context encouraged *some* Mennonites and made *others* wary. Such ambiguity continues today.

Following the Persian Gulf War, Levi Miller, then director of the Mennonite Church's Historical Committee, wrote about why he did not participate in antiwar activities. Although not referring specifically to Mennonite Central Committee or its Washington office, Miller "confesses" that he is "sometimes scandalized, sometimes confused, and sometimes even amused at the arrogance of Mennonite moderns who try in one generation to develop some warmed-over theology of humanistic Quakerism, pacifist Catholicism, and liberal Protestantism."[9] Miller claims he sat out the war because he is "trying to respect the centuries of pacifist teaching of the Mennonite church," which historically has "given more attention to what the church should do" and "not always tried to determine the wicked and the good for the state."[10] Miller's understanding is rooted in one strain of twentieth-century Anabaptist-Mennonite conceptions of nonresistance and two-kingdom theology, conceptions that in recent years have been *reinforced* by some and *reinterpreted* by other Mennonites.

Ironically, a related concern about theological "scandalization" came from a quite different perspective during the Persian Gulf War. Two political analysts writing in the conservative quarterly the *National Interest* publicly lament the position *mainline* denominations took on the Gulf War, citing the "de facto coalitions with traditional pacifist groups" as one source of mainliners' *critical* response to U.S. military action.[11] Robert P. Beschel Jr. and Peter D. Feaver write that the mainline Protestant churches' strong opposition to the war is remarkable because they have traditionally rejected pacifism in favor of just war theory. Beschel and Feaver note the consistency of peace churches such as Quakers and Mennonites, who opposed all phases of military operations in the Gulf, based on their long-standing rejection of the moral legitimacy of any form of organized violence, but blast the peace and justice leaders of mainline denominations who "never bothered to engage [traditional just war criteria] in a serious or systematic fashion."[12]

Mennonites always have been associated with the Christian pacifist tradition, while mainline churches historically have cast their lot with the just war tradition, as Beschel and Feaver suggest. As Mennonites have cooperated ecumenically with other denominations—both in Washington and elsewhere around the country and world—they no doubt have been shaped by their alliances, redefining what it means to be a peace church active in the world. Likewise, they may have contributed toward the reshaping of other denominational traditions related to violence and nonviolence, offering a quiet—and sometimes distinctive—voice in the political sphere. Mennonites have been talking for many decades about what it means to be a peace church, and the Presbyterians and Methodists and Catholics they meet on the elevator also converse about such issues. As other denominations move toward such notions as "just peace," Mennonites—especially those in Washington—find themselves working alongside others whose talk *seems* increasingly like their own, although some theological chasms still exist.

JUST WAR, CRUSADE, AND PACIFISM

Historically, most theologians and ethicists have referred to three classic strands of responses to warfare: just war, crusade (or holy war), and pacifism.[13] Theological sources for the three strands overlap somewhat, but to a certain degree they represent different understandings of God and of the nature of peace. All three approaches draw on and are present in other philosophical and religious traditions, but the following explication intentionally is limited to expressions within the Christian tradition. One should also note that, while the primary context in which these categories emerge is warfare, the principles may be applicable in other realms of social ethics as well. For instance, many strict pacifists consider all killing wrong—including, for example, capital punishment—not just killing in battle. A person who uses just war criteria may also apply the principles to such issues as abortion.

Just War

Proponents of the just war tradition long have argued that its intention is to *limit* rather than to *justify* war, as the term may imply.[14] In the just war tradition, war always must be judged twice: first regarding the *reasons* states have for engaging in warfare, and second for the *means* adopted in their fight.[15] As political philosopher Michael Walzer notes, "The two sorts of judgment are logically independent. It is perfectly possible for a just war to be fought unjustly and an unjust war to be fought in strict accordance with the rules."[16] Although the principles differ slightly from one interpreter to another, generally six conditions must be met before launching a war is considered just. These criteria include justifiable cause, legitimate authority, right intention, proportionality, probability of success, and last resort. Principles for *conducting* a war, the second tier of moral restraint in the just war tradition, generally consist of two principles: proportionality and discrimination.

During the Persian Gulf War, U.S. President George Bush adopted the language of just war theology as justification for "Operation Desert Storm," the U.S. name for the coalition action against Iraq. The president's staff submitted press releases listing just war criteria, claiming to meet all necessary requirements for a justifiable military operation. In his 28 January 1991 speech to the Annual Convention of National Religious Broadcasters, Bush said, "The war in the Gulf is not a Christian war, a Jewish war, or a [Muslim] war; it is a just war. . . . We will prevail because of the support of the American people, armed with a trust in God and the principles that make [people] free."[17] While throughout the speech the president referenced just war theology, some of his remarks evidenced slippage into what is generally perceived as crusade rhetoric: language labeling one's own position as undeniably right and just and denouncing the other's intentions and actions as wholly evil.

Crusade or Holy War

In his speech to the National Religious Broadcasters, Bush spoke of "good versus evil, right versus wrong, human dignity and freedom versus tyranny and oppression," language more closely aligned with the Christian crusade tradition than with just war theory. In this tradition, crusaders have absolute goals that they may relentlessly pursue against their entirely evil opponents.[18] The crusade approach draws on the Hebrew scriptures' narratives of conquest, especially those tales of utter destruction of enemies. Once the crusader's *intentions and objectives* are deemed morally justifiable, this tradition eliminates moral restraints on the *conduct* of war. The tradition was most clearly articulated, and most often explicitly practiced, during the Middle Ages, when the nations of Western Christendom sought to take back the Holy Lands from Islam. Both the Christians and their Muslim opponents adopted some version of a crusade ethic.

Within Western nations in this century, the crusade approach generally has been deemed morally indefensible, although the rhetoric and sometimes the practice of warring nation-states reflects a lingering crusade mentality. Absolutist claims during World War I led to immense loss of life and property on all sides. Two decades later the Nazis' systematic destruction of all opponents evidenced perhaps the clearest example of modern crusading—although the Allies' demands for Japan's unconditional surrender at the close of the war also expressed themes from the by-then discredited tradition.[19]

Pacifism

Unlike the crusade approach, the pacifist tradition often is considered, even by some of its critics, a legitimately *Christian* approach—although usually an *inadequate* one—to warfare. This tradition was preached and practiced during the first three centuries of Christianity, when the minority religion began to spread across Asia Minor. Prior to the legalization of the religion by Constantine, most Christian ecclesiastical leaders and theologians discouraged believers from serving in the military or participating in warfare.[20] In general, pacifists oppose all acts of violence, regardless of the intentions or outcomes of the action.[21] At the very least, pacifists uniformly refuse to participate in warfare, believing that their participation in such violence is always wrong, whether or not others have deemed the conflict "just."

Since the fourth century, when Christian involvement in military forces was legitimated, some *individual* Christians have chosen to renounce violence on the basis of their faith convictions. These persons often cite statements attributed to Jesus in Matthew's version of the Sermon on the Mount. In addition, some pre-Reformation religious groups—including the Waldenses and Albigenses in the thirteenth and fourteenth centuries, respectively—claimed pacifism as central to their faith and life. Surviving strands of the sixteenth-century Radical Reformation were among those carrying the Christian pacifist tradition into the modern era. In the United States, Mennonites, Quakers, and the Church of the Brethren have been considered the three historic peace churches.[22] Today it is probably more appropriate to speak of the "pacifisms" of such groups as Mennonites. Sorting through these "pacifisms" may help clarify some constituents' concerns for Mennonite Central Committee's "hobnobbing" with other peace groups.

In the third and fourth decades of the twentieth century, many Mennonite Church leaders desperately sought to differentiate their own commitments to nonviolence from the commitments of their peers.[23] This was especially true following the discrediting of the liberal pacifism touted earlier by many modern European and American theologians, who were perhaps influenced more by Enlightenment hopes than by biblical injunctions. Bolstered by years of limited international conflict, by belief in the realization of a warless world, and by religious liberalism's hopes in the good of humanity, early-twentieth-century theologians became proponents of pacifism. At the turn of the century, one could argue that a nationwide sentiment toward the appreciation of pacifism developed, even though the sentiment remained a minority view. For a short time, Mennonites began to feel more at home in a culture that seemingly supported one of its fundamental tenets. Although it is unlikely that Mennonites had any identifiable effect on this social movement toward pacifism, the pacifist trend did reduce the tension between Mennonites and their culture, and between Mennonites and other peace groups.[24] Two Mennonite Church leaders wrote in 1905 that "never has the church been in a better position to take her stand for Christ as an aggressive force in His earthly kingdom, than at present." The leaders claimed Mennonites had won the respect of their neighbors. "Those principles of freedom, which the church espoused in the days when the same meant persecution, have long been recognized by all civilized nations as being among the fundamental principles of free government," they said. "Even her doctrine on . . . non-resistance . . . [does] not meet the opposition [it] once did."[25]

However, most of the theologians and church leaders leaning toward pacifism prior to World War I abandoned their convictions just before, during, or following the war, no longer able to justify their hopes and claims.[26] Throughout much of this century nonpacifist theologians have viewed this era as evidencing the bankruptcy of the theological principles behind and the practical applications of pacifism. Some historic peace church theologians would agree that this particular type of pacifism, which emerged from religious liberalism's unrealistic hopes in humanity, is untenable.

Although it is an oversimplification, the clearest delineation of types of Christian pacifism is between "pacifism as a strategy" and "pacifism as obedient witness." The former "depends upon a particular reading of the morally relevant circumstances within which a decision is to be made about the use of violence," and the latter "depends upon a particular interpretation of the content of the basic moral standard of Christian ethics."[27] Pacifism as a strategy, then, can be altered or undermined depending on sociopolitical contexts and outcomes of particular conflicts. Pacifism as obedient witness, however, does not take into consideration "penultimate" consequences, but simply witnesses to the character and nature of God.[28] These pacifists may believe that somehow, in history, God is working out God's purposes, but only in that ultimate sense are consequences considered. The pacifist consistently rejects the use or sanctioning of violence, based on Christian principle.

Guy F. Hershberger, who for several mid-century decades was the Mennonite Church's leading scholar on peace issues, devoted two chapters in his classic *War, Peace, and Nonresistance* to the contrasts between "Biblical Nonresistance and Modern Pacifism."[29] Hershberger's text was published just after Mennonite Church scholar Harold S. Bender first presented his oft-cited address, "The Anabaptist Vision," an interpretation and synthesis of Anabaptism that became the "benchmark" statement to be reckoned with for the next three decades.[30] In his vision, Bender distilled what he considered to be the essence of Anabaptism, which included three elements: 1) the essential nature of Christianity as discipleship; 2) the church as a voluntary, nonconformed brotherhood; and 3) "the ethic of love and nonresistance as applied to all human relationships."

In reference to the ethic of love and nonresistance, Bender explains that the early Anabaptists "understood this to mean complete abandonment of all warfare, strife, and violence, and of the taking of human life."[31] This principle of nonresistance, Bender argues too sweepingly, "was thoroughly believed and resolutely practiced by all the original Anabaptist Brethren and their descendants throughout Europe from the beginning until the last century."[32] In his concluding remarks, Bender states, "Since for [the Anabaptist] no compromise dare be made with evil, the Christian may in no circumstance participate in any conduct in the existing social order which is contrary to the spirit and teaching of Christ and the apostolic practice." For Bender, that meant he or she "must consequently withdraw from the worldly system and create a Christian order within the fellowship of the church brotherhood. Extension of this Christian order by the conversion of individuals and their transfer out of the world into the church is the only way by which progress can be made in Christianizing the social order."[33] In Bender's synthesis, Mennonites' Anabaptist forebears had only one authentic response to violence: biblical nonresistance, which necessitated withdrawal from social orders—and, on the theological-ethical level, from systems of social ethics that may require compromise.

In Hershberger's first chapter "Biblical Nonresistance and Modern Pacifism" in *War, Peace, and Nonresistance,* he begins by noting that the terms "pacifism" and "nonresistance" both are based on Jesus' Sermon on the Mount. The latter is taken from Matthew 5:39, "Resist not him that is evil," and the former is from *pacifici,* the Latin translation of "Blessed are the *peacemakers*" in Matthew 5:9. However, Hershberger expresses discomfort with the term "pacifist" because of its contemporary, generalized usage for opposition to warfare, regardless of the philosophical or religious basis for that opposition. Nonresistant Christians, he said, expect the faith community to represent and embody the principles of God's kingdom, but do not expect the same of the state, nor of unbelievers.[34]

Hershberger also distinguishes *nonresistance* from various forms of *nonviolent* resistance, such as that espoused by Gandhi[35]—and, in later generations, by many Mennonites. The difference, says Hershberger, is rooted in the biblical question of social justice, and hinges around the scriptural emphasis on *doing* justice rather than *demanding* justice. Once one places the emphasis on demanding justice, no matter how admirable the cause, he or she "has taken the first step on the road which leads away from Christian nonresistance."[36] As is evident throughout Hershberger's chapter, doing rather than demanding justice has implications not only for individuals but for denominations and denominational agencies.[37] By 1968 Hershberger supported starting a Mennonite office in Washington, believing that it would enable the "Mennonite peace witness" to have an impact on Washington. "It is generally recognized that the Mennonite peace position has a more sound theological base than those of most peace groups," writes Hershberger in one church periodical, "and that those who speak for the Mennonite peace position can do so with a greater degree of corporate authority than most."[38]

Prior to and during the time Hershberger, Bender, and other Mennonite leaders were articulating clearly the sources for, intentions of, and theological and scriptural groundings for biblical nonresistance, Reinhold Niebuhr was developing his ethical system, which rejected pacifism on both pragmatic and theological grounds.[39] He said the normative nature of Jesus' law of love must be balanced against the impossibility of humans ever achieving it. Jesus' norm remains an "impossible possibility," in tension with historical reality.[40] Niebuhr's criticism of Christian pacifists is that they consider Jesus' demands for love a "simple possibility," achievable in the world. By not acknowledging that sin introduces an element of conflict into the world, says Niebuhr, pacifists end up with a "morally perverse preference."[41] He argues, "Most pacifists who seek to present their religious absolutism as a political alternative to the claims and counterclaims, the pressures and counter-pressures of the political order, invariably betray themselves into this preference for tyranny."[42]

As is evident throughout his repeated critiques of pacifism, Niebuhr is responding more to liberal Christian pacifism—a pacifism he embraced during his formative years as a young theologian—than to Mennonite nonresistance. He believed that liberal pacifism, which emphasized *doing good* through nonviolent action, was heretical, since it failed to take seriously biblical teachings about fallible human nature.[43] Niebuhr says the nonresistant form of pacifism, which stresses *not doing harm,* is not heretical: it simply is irresponsible.[44] But while critical of both pacifism as a strategy and pacifism as an obedient witness, Niebuhr was more sympathetic toward and appreciative of the latter, most evident in Mennonite-style nonresistance. Nonresistant persons, he held, could remind others that war is horrible and that they should strive toward the ideal of love. Without that reminder, more pragmatically oriented persons may become lost in the necessary compromises entailed in full social engagement.

The relevance of Niebuhr's criticism of liberal pacifism, and his perhaps backhanded praise of Mennonite nonresistance, is that he reinforced Mennonites' commitment to a distinctive "nonresistant" witness. Mennonites who accepted Niebuhr's construct sought to be different from some of their pacifist peers, who believed the law of love to be a realistic social ethic, even in an "immoral society." At a time when American Mennonites were clarifying their historical and contemporary identity, Niebuhr made his own contribution toward solidifying "nonresistance" as an authentic, valid, and somewhat legitimate position.

Mennonites' clarity about their identity as relatively uncompromised, nonresistant Christians—especially in terms of their associations with the state—underwent *some* transformation already in the 1950s and 1960s. Since the 1970s, however, Anabaptist-Mennonite nonresistance has undergone serious redefinition.[45] In his provocative 1972 text *Anabaptists and the Sword,* Radical Reformation historian James Stayer acknowledged multiple views regarding "the sword," both beyond and within "evangelical Anabaptism."[46] Through Stayer's text and another seminal article published three years later,[47] twentieth-century ancestors of Radical Reformers, long dependent on historiography for contemporary identity formation, were compelled to ad-

mit the pluralism within Anabaptism, a pluralism present from the beginning.[48] Bender and Hershberger's clear boundaries marking legitimate
Anabaptist peace attitudes moved out to encompass broader responses. "Traditional" nonresistance, perhaps as much a twentieth-century creation as a
sixteenth-century creation, was no longer the only normative response
possible for well-intentioned Mennonites.[49]

Stayer's historical redefinition coincided with considerable theological-
ethical revisions within Mennonitism, revisions prompted in part by greater
ecumenical engagement. John H. Yoder broadened definitions of pacifism
in *Nevertheless,* a book he dedicated "to the many friends, some still militant
and some triumphant, whose different styles of pacifist commitment have
judged and enriched my own."[50] Yoder contends that "[i]t is time for nonresistant Mennonites to move beyond their initial defensive reflex to the
recognition of a real degree of practical common conviction which they do
and properly share with non-Christian pacifists or (much more) with non-
Mennonite Christian pacifists." He also observes that "it would contribute
more to sober conversation if, instead of fixing upon an irrational avoid-
ance of the word 'pacifist,' Mennonites would recognize with more preci-
sion and responsibility the varieties of ways in which [people] are led, sometimes by intelligent analysis and sometimes by emotional revulsion, sometimes
by irrational optimism and sometimes perhaps by the Spirit of God, to
recognize the wrongness of war and to devote themselves to the service of
[others], even though in other ways or under other labels and with other
understandings than those a historic peace church has found adequate."[51]
Even as Yoder wrote his words of ecumenical encouragement, staffers in
Mennonite Central Committee's Washington office daily were engaged in
such "sober conversations" with their lobbying peers.

In the nation's capital, Mennonites discovered companions in peacemaking, persons who shared their commitment to international peace and
social justice. Mennonites' socially "liberal" concerns, combined with their
political involvement in Washington and the working alliances such involvement requires, began tugging Mennonites somewhat closer to a cluster of Protestant and Catholic churches, some of which also seemingly
were moving toward pacifistic Mennonites through espousal of such notions as "just peace." While Mennonites were working ecumenically elsewhere across the United States and around the world, the Washington office most clearly distills the institutional demands and benefits related to
"bedding down" with others.[52] Partly through rubbing shoulders with other
lobbyists, Mennonites were reshaping what it means to be a church and to
act in the world—especially what it means to be an engaged peace church.

WORKING TOGETHER WITH OTHERS

For the past half century, Mennonite Central Committee, MCC Washington's parent, has been involved more ecumenically than most other Mennonite and Brethren in Christ organizations. It has had working relationships with a variety of conservative organizations, including the German Baptists, Christian Apostolics, various independent or "faith" missions, the Christian Missionary Alliance, and the World Relief Committee of the National Association of Evangelicals. It also has worked closely with Church World Service of the National Council of Churches in dozens of areas abroad. Many non-Mennonite persons now work under MCC's umbrella, and MCC often has "loaned" its volunteers to other agencies. MCC has worked with Methodists, Wycliffe Translators, and the Andes Mission in Bolivia; with the Presbyterians in Korea; with the Greek Orthodox Church in Greece and Cyprus; with Near East Relief, Near East Foundation, Edinburgh Medical Missionary Society, Lutherans, and Anglicans in the Middle East; with Waldensians in Italy; with Kimbanguists and Baptists in the Congo; and with multiple other Christian and non-Christian service organizations around the world.[53] Still, MCC is aware of its constituent denominations' reluctance to fully engage with other organizations and has maintained sensitivity to those concerns.

From the beginning, Mennonite Central Committee's U.S. Peace Section was concerned that its Washington office join coalitions sparingly. In his Peace Section–sponsored study of Washington's religious lobbying offices, the study that eventually led to the establishment of MCC's capital office, Dwight King interviewed Mennonites in and around Washington, as well as constituents elsewhere around the country. King said, in his final report, "Desire for explicit and well-thought out objectives is intricately related to the future and identity of the denomination[s]." He said that among the frequently asked questions that revealed the need for clear objectives were: "How do we keep a Mennonite office from identifying us with every other 'liberal' group? How can we preserve our Mennonite distinctiveness and simultaneously concur with other groups in a prophetic witness to government?"[54] King's questions have resurfaced repeatedly throughout MCC Washington's history, sometimes emerging from troubled constituents, sometimes from Akron administrators uncertain of the ramifications, and sometimes from within the Washington staff. "To what extent this [reluctance to join] reflects an authentic concern for preserving our own vision and mission and to what extent it reflects an undesirable and unjustifiable stand-offishness is likely debatable, but it remains a fact," wrote U.S. Peace Section director Ted Koontz in 1976.[55]

Of course, Mennonites have been working cooperatively with other groups in Washington since at least 1940, with the founding of the National Service

Board for Religious Objectors (NSBRO). The board served as a testing ground for Mennonites interested in working cooperatively with others in Washington. The Civilian Public Service (CPS) program, for which the NSBRO provided oversight, may have appeared to be a mechanism for conscientious objectors to withdraw, but Mennonite Brethren historian Paul Toews argues that it was "more a mechanism for engagement than for withdrawal." He notes that "while [CPS's] legacies are numerous, three particularly fostered this engagement: 1) CPS engendered a new self-confidence; 2) it produced a missional and service activism; 3) it accelerated the Mennonite ecumenical movement."[56] This "acceleration" of ecumenism is verifiable, but the beginning speed was negligible, and for some years the engagement continued to be primarily with more like-minded denominations, such as others in the historic peace churches, who were also a part of NSBRO.

Long before the formation of NSBRO, Mennonites had monitored national legislation related to conscientious objection. This monitoring necessitated "continuous contact with other peace groups engaged in similar activity," says Guy F. Hershberger. He suggests that "[i]nterpreting the nonresistant faith to other Christians obviously required a frequent interchange of views with other Christians. It meant not only that others were learning from Mennonites; but also that Mennonites were learning from others." Hershberger claims that although this procedure was "natural and necessary," it involved certain dangers, "and this was disturbing to some members of the brotherhood."[57] Most of the early monitoring took place from a distance, outside of the "dangerous" whirl of Washington. Even later, in the involvement with NSBRO, Mennonite alliances remained confined to selected groups working on a narrow range of legislation specifically related to conscientious objector issues, limiting the conversation partners considerably. Such an involvement required less interchange with diverse groups operating in the nation's capital. MCC's official move to Washington in 1968 placed Mennonites in the context of more powerful political and religious organizations and institutions, which made their working relationships more intense and tugged in new ways at Mennonites' boundaries.

Religious lobbyists working within Washington readily admit the necessity of joining forces with other religious and nonreligious advocacy groups in order to gather information efficiently, analyze data, and speak with greater numbers—and perhaps greater impact—in the political arena. "We believe very, very much in working with others," says Robert Tiller, director of the Washington office of the American Baptist Churches, U.S.A. "It's practical, it's biblical, and it increases our values and accomplishments."[58] Joe Volk, director of the Friends Committee on National Legislation (FCNL), notes the tension between offering a distinctive witness and getting tasks accomplished. He contends that because part of FCNL's job is to represent Quakers, it is important for the office to say, "Our practice of faith compels us to say this or that, or moves us to speak to a problem in some particular way." On the other hand, says Volk, "We think nobody has access to truth by themselves, and the search for truth comes when we collect as many perspectives as possible." He adds that "a good division of labor needs group work in order to get work done."[59] This tension between offering something distinctive and getting the necessary work done is echoed repeatedly in the offices of Mennonite Central Committee, both in Washington and at the headquarters in Akron.

When MCC's office opened 1 July 1968, Delton Franz was the only full-time staffer, responsible for covering a wide range of issues about which his constituents were concerned, tracking legislative actions in both the House and Senate, and keeping abreast of developments and policy changes in the judicial and administrative branches of the federal government.[60] In order to adequately cover the political arena in Washington, Franz soon discovered the necessity of cooperating with various working groups already meeting in the capital. "It would be impossible for our staff, or the staff of most of the other . . . religious bodies with Washington offices, to do the necessary research and analysis of the legislative issues focused on peace and justice, if each office had to function autonomously," Franz states in an early review of the office.[61] MCC's new peers consisted of not only historic peace church representatives, but also members of Protestant denominations, who came with their own traditions and understandings of Christian peacemaking; Jewish advocacy groups, who operated with yet another framework of understandings; and nonreligious advocates for peace and justice, whose philosophical commitments made them allies on various legislative issues.

Often working on specific legislative issues helps in cutting through whatever theological and philosophical differences groups have. Regardless of the groups' histories and traditions, alliances readily can form around common causes. The fear of some Mennonite critics of MCC Washington is that such alliances could "act back" on Mennonite theological and ethical frameworks. One initial MCC Washington solution to the "problem" of joining coalitions was to provide a small amount of financial assistance to a coalition as a show of support, and then to participate fully in the coalition's policy discussions—without ever formally *joining* the group. In that way, MCC could glean essential information and provide some nominal input and direction to the groups' discussions without inviting serious criticism from constituents troubled by such alliances. To a certain extent, the practice—now used less frequently by MCC Washington, partly because of integrity questions—was effective. However, glitches sometimes resulted from MCC's nonmember participation in such alliances. In a 1971 *Congressional Record,* for example, MCC was listed among the religious groups opposing the Wylie Prayer Amendment, legislation that many Mennonites supported. Two weeks later the Washington office received a letter from a constituent responding to the supposed MCC Washington opposition, suggesting that "it is wrong to agree with other religions, when it means a surrender of our own Christian traditions." Delton Franz quickly responded, acknowledging that MCC's name was inadvertently included in the list of opponents through a misunderstanding resulting from his participation "on a number of the church agency discussions regarding the Prayer Amendment."[62]

By 1977, nine years after the opening of the office, MCC's U.S. Peace Section prepared a detailed set of guidelines for cooperative efforts. The guidelines offer helpful insights into the tensions MCC perceives and the organization's rationale for joining or rejecting certain Washington alliances.[63]

Guidelines for Joining Coalitions

Definition

Joining means permitting the MCC name to be listed as a member in printed materials of a coalition. Thus, to join means to subscribe publicly to the stated goals and strategy of the coalition. On the other hand, to permit the listing of MCC as a parallel organization from which information or assistance in dealing with the issue(s) in question is available is not considered joining a coalition.

Guidelines

1. Theological—Discipleship
   We can more readily make common cause with groups that are motivated and guided by a conscious Christian commitment. This commitment must include the peace and justice, as well as the grace, of Christ. In the choice between a Christian and a non-Christian group working on the same cause, the presumption is in favor of joining the Christian group. However, it is clear that working for peace and justice is not confined to persons or groups that are confessing Christians and there can be times for making common cause with those who are doing the will of Christ without calling it that.

2. Working relationships
   We would be more inclined to join a coalition where the Peace Section (U.S.) and MCC staffs have time and resource to be substantially involved in the issue addressed than where we would have relatively little involvement. Similarly, we would be more inclined to join where our voice on the policy-making body would be sought than where others make the decisions and we would simply endorse.

3. Financial Commitment

Our name is worth more than our money (although neither is worth very much if it is extended at the price of withholding the other), so we will not consider it a bargain to join a coalition which asks little or no financial commitment. If we join a coalition, it is implicit that we will support it financially. On the other hand, if we have reasons for not joining a coalition, we would not make any substantial financial contributions to it.

4. Constituency Response

We would not join a coalition to which an overwhelming adverse reaction could be expected from the constituency.[64] In general, we are more ready to take up unpopular causes than to join up with un-Christian organizations when it comes to risking criticism from the constituency.

5. Effectiveness Criterion

The coalition must offer a significant opportunity for prophetic witness, constituency education or legislative impact which goes beyond what is already available through MCC channels. In other words, there must be some promise of effectiveness in doing something more than is already being done by Peace Section (U.S.) efforts.

6. Basic Caution

In general, we will join rarely and slowly. The principle is more with less— more meaning and benefit will be found in fewer coalition memberships.

Decision-Making Procedures

A decision to join a coalition can be made only by the Peace Section or its officers. The staff can recommend to the Section or officers.

The guidelines, which have been subjected to interpretation in the years since they first were proposed, theoretically continue to serve as the basic principles governing MCC Washington coalition decisions.[65]

Among the capital's religious lobbies, the primary cooperative working relationships fall under the umbrella of the Washington Interreligious Staff Council (WISC), which functions as a clearinghouse for more than forty religious advocacy groups. Among WISC's member groups are most of the denominational and organizational offices in the Methodist Building, along with the American Friends Service Committee and Friends Committee on National Legislation, the American Jewish Committee, Catholic Charities U.S.A., Columban Fathers Justice and Peace Office, Church Women United, Jesuit Social Ministries, NETWORK (a national Catholic social justice lobby), Salvation Army National Public Affairs Office, the Union of American Hebrew Congregations, and a dozen other groups. Cooperating agencies include the AIDS National Interfaith Network, Bread for the World,

Churches' Center for Theology and Public Policy, Washington Seminar Center, Coalition to Stop Gun Violence, National Campaign for a Peace Tax Fund, Central America Working Group, and Churches for Middle East Peace. Of the cooperating agencies, MCC's Washington office has the closest links with the latter four, participating as founding members of three of the groups.

WISC meets in plenary sessions once each month, and task forces and working groups meet an additional one to four times each month. WISC members cover a wide range of peace and justice issues, but take no action on Middle East or abortion issues because of disagreement among members. MCC Washington staffers participate regularly in the task forces and working groups, including, for instance, the Foreign Policy and Military Spending Task Force and the International Development Policy Working Group. At these meetings, Mennonite workers share information and ideas with their Catholic, Protestant, Jewish, and other religious peers. Each religious agency office remains free to do with the research and analysis whatever their agency deems appropriate.

Interfaith Impact for Justice and Peace, another major coalition whose office is just down the hall from MCC Washington's, also pulls together most of the Mennonites' peers for cooperative work. Interfaith Impact includes Protestant, Jewish, Catholic, and Muslim organizations and individuals who seek to bring grassroots leaders to Washington to help coordinate local and Washington-based lobbying efforts. Among their primary issue areas are winning rights for women and families; improving civil, human, and voting rights; promoting international peace; fighting poverty; working for a more just economic policy; protecting and preserving the environment; and assuring health care for everyone. An Interfaith Impact brochure sent to individuals and organizations states: "Start translating your values into votes on Capitol Hill." After several years of encouragement by MCC Washington, MCC U.S. officially became a member of Interfaith Impact in 1993.

Churches for Middle East Peace (C-MEP) is a coalition of sixteen Washington religious advocacy offices. The organization acts as the churches' Washington liaison for advocacy on Middle East issues, organizing the collective work of the offices on such issues. Most other coalitions in MCC's network include Jewish groups, which made reaching consensus on Middle East issues difficult. As a result, for many years the church lobbies did not work on Middle East policy and legislation. C-MEP's founders, recognizing that religion plays a distinctive role in Middle East politics and conflicts, sought to fill that gap in the churches' advocacy efforts. Among the major issues the coalition addresses now are Israeli-Arab-Palestinian peace, Middle East militarization and arms sales, human rights abuses, foreign aid, and the status of Jerusalem.

Often three or four members of the various coalitions, task forces, and working groups go jointly to legislative offices for lobbying visits. Even more frequently, "sign-on" letters emerge from coalitional meetings. Sign-ons are brief letters written to legislative committees, groups of legislators, or administration branch officials recommending particular action on a bill or policy, expressing concern about an upcoming political decision, or affirming a new direction. Generally written by one advocacy group or by leaders of one of the task forces or working groups, the sign-ons are then circulated to other lobbying offices for their signatures. MCC Washington staffers regularly face decisions about whether or not their name should be attached to particular letters.[66] Because the letters sometimes are picked up by the media, or even find their way into the *Congressional Record,* signing-on publicly acknowledges an organization's agreement with the tone as well as the content of letters and aligns its view with that of all other signers. Because the letters are brief, and because they have greater impact if they speak with a clear, unified voice, noting nuanced differences between signers is impractical.

Mennonite Central Committee's original policy was not to act on an issue—including signing on to letters—unless some consensus had been reached among MCC's constituent bodies, or where specific requests for action had come from one or more constituent denominations. Many other denominational offices have similar policies, although the interpretation of the directives varies considerably between lobbying offices, and even within a particular lobbying office, depending on the nature of the issue. When questions arise about letters, MCC Washington staffers consult with their organizational peers at MCC's Akron base, faxing letters back and forth before attaching their names.[67] These intraorganizational conversations regularly remind Washington MCC workers of their connectedness not only to Washington's political culture, but also to a complex interdenominational organization with institutional demands from its constituent bodies.

As with other coalitional arrangements, MCC's Akron administrators generally subscribe to the "more-with-less" philosophy of sign-ons.[68] Titus Peachey, co-executive secretary of MCC U.S. Peace and Justice Ministries Cluster, says, "My sense is that, the more you join, the less your joining means because your name becomes so easily used that it's meaningless, or it doesn't have the meaning it does when you're more selective." Peachey says he believes sign-on letters have limited influence, especially in comparison with personal contact, "or the sharing of something that comes out of our own experience rather than out of a document that keeps everybody's interests in mind."[69]

At a September 1992 meeting of the MCC Washington Coordinating Council, several of MCC Akron's administrators asked Washington staffers about their practice of signing on to letters.[70] The questions have become a regular part of the Coordinating Council's biannual meetings. MCC Washington employees were asked how much influence the sign-ons have and how they might affect MCC's credibility. Some legislative aides in Washington suggest that church lobbyists do need to be discriminating in their sign-ons. Jacob Ahearn, Republican professional staff member for one House subcommittee, notes that MCC Washington's name sometimes appears alongside a wide variety of religious and nonreligious organizations. "Some of the sign-ons, to be honest, are absolute horseshit," claims Ahearn. "And to the extent that they sign on to things that are out of their expertise, it doesn't enhance their reputation."[71] Cynthia Sprunger, who has worked for Rep. Jim Leach (R-Iowa) and the U.S. Department of Education, suggests that "some religious groups may be perceived as being more knee-jerk liberal. It might be important for MCC to maintain enough of a distance from the larger groupings to maintain its credibility."[72]

Coordinating Council members also asked MCC Washington staffers how many sign-ons are done with church organizations versus secular ones, and how important they are for maintaining other relationships.[73] The latter question is the most pressing one for MCC Washington staffers, who are more deeply entrenched in Washington's political and lobbying culture than are their Akron peers. A healthy tension between the "different worlds" of Akron and Washington is apparent to visitors who spend sustained time in both cities. Earl Martin, one of few MCC employees who has had experience overseas as well as in both the Washington and Akron offices, observes:

> When I was in Washington, day after day, I did tend to think about specific legislation, or even specific personalities on Capitol Hill or in the administration, that I would want to engage. I did tend to think, in that context, that what happened in Washington was pretty important around the world. Now I'm in Akron. And I still do believe that. But I must confess that from this geographical setting I think much less about specific U.S. policies or legislation and I tend to think more now about peoples' movements or the influence of the church in other countries. I tend to think American policy is just one part of the bigger picture. . . . The people I bump into daily, my neighbors and people in the office, are not attentive to legislative action on a day-to-day basis, so [being in Akron] does produce a different reality.[74]

The amount of sign-ons MCC Washington does is one area where this tension between the two worlds emerges.[75]

Staffers in the Washington office, while sympathetic to Akron's concerns, also feel administrators there do not fully understand the constraints and demands of Capitol Hill lobbying. "I feel pressure personally to do sign-ons from colleagues that we work with," contends Keith Gingrich, a long-term veteran at MCC Washington. Gingrich acknowledges that he "can appreciate Akron's concern about not putting our name on every piece of paper that comes across our desk," but adds that "if we have significant involvement or leadership on an issue, not to sign on feels uncomfortable."[76] Franz, who says he understands why Akron administrators could feel some uneasiness about "whether we are sometimes going out on a limb without consultation," also mentions the pressure to sign on to letters after benefiting from the dialogue that prompted the letter.[77]

Gingrich and Franz both note that, during their tenures in Washington, coalition members have been open to altering sign-on letters if the language remedies problems with the letter. Franz argues that usually the hang-up is not MCC's concern alone, but that of other historic peace church representatives as well. Usually this occurs with military questions, and coalition members make a modification or deletion to satisfy the needs of pacifist groups. Gingrich adds that sometimes the requested change has more to do with tone than content. "I think the language fairly often comes across too strongly," observes Gingrich. "Again, it sort of comes out of the Mennonite experience, more of a conciliatory language, soft-spoken, which is often somewhat different than that the rest of the community feels is appropriate."[78] Gingrich claims that these discussions about sign-ons rarely result in an impasse—MCC and its allies can make sufficient compromises so that all can sign. "I guess I've had to learn that while I know Mennonites put more weight in actions than words," he observes, "when you're in Washington in this job, somehow you've got to make exceptions to that."[79]

There are a number of occasions when MCC Washington declines invitations to attach its name to coalition letters. In late 1992 and early 1993 the office and its Akron headquarters refused to sign on to several letters because of their military implications. They agreed *not* to sign a November 1992 letter from InterAction that called for increased armed intervention to deliver food aid in Somalia; a February 1993 letter from a group of nongovernmental organizations calling for the use of "all necessary means" to ensure peace and free elections in Cambodia; and a May 1993 letter from a Washington working group calling for intervention to oust dictator Mobutu in Zaire.

Franz says that sometimes, as director, he needed to reject sign-ons that other staffers were recommending.[80] "I think the hard part is when the sign-on includes a couple of labor unions and who knows what else, organizations that are not even a part of the church configuration," he explains. Occasionally letters with MCC's endorsement also include signatures from the American Civil Liberties Union, the American Humanist Association, or Amnesty International, along with other nonreligious organizations whose concerns overlap with MCC's. Even when MCC Washington's coalitions are limited to the religious community, which is more often the case, the signers generally represent the religious left, with few rightist organizations represented. Members of the Washington Interreligious Staff Council and organizations within the Methodist Building generally are perceived by both insiders and outsiders as left of mainstream American politics.[81]

MCC Washington staffers readily acknowledge that their primary associations are with liberal religious groups, rather than with more conservative, evangelical religious organizations—which some of their constituent members support. One MCC Washington staffer observes, "I think we [and other religious offices in the Methodist Building] are probably a little inconsistent in that we have no problem getting together with the Unitarians or the American Humanists, but much less often do we form coalitions with the National Association of Evangelicals or Concerned Women for America or some of these other ultra-right organizations."[82] The staffer admits, though, that his personal social critique is closer to a liberal than a conservative one, "and that's probably true for everyone in the office. And that's probably why we've tended in that direction."[83]

At an institutional level, MCC Washington's nonalliance with conservative evangelical groups is partly a result of its involvement with WISC activities, which take up considerable time and energy. Making connections outside of the already-present alliances would require additional hours of limited staff time. Franz notes that, in the 1980s, WISC sent a letter to the National Association of Evangelicals (NAE), inviting it to be a part of the umbrella organization. "This was a short-lived effort," he says. "They attended a few meetings, but I think after maybe a year they realized it just wasn't their cup of tea. . . . I think in part the rather broad agenda [of WISC] itself is intimidating to them, because much of that is just not on their agenda. And there is such a rather different theological perspective."[84] Franz admits that he always felt "sad and uncomfortable" when Mennonites asked him how his office related to the NAE. However, Franz and other Washington MCC staff accurately ascertain that usually MCC's faith-based social concerns have more affinities with the religious left than the right. Echoing MCC Washington staffers' views, one Mennonite observer states about the capital's religious lobbies: "If you have to make choices between [the left] and being swallowed up by right-wing think tanks, why, I'll take the left most of the time . . . but not flat out."[85]

Political scientist Guenter Lewy recently dealt pacifist organizations a blow in a book that selectively documents the activities of four groups since the 1960s.[86] Among those whose behavior and alliances Lewy critiques are the War Resisters League (WRL), the Women's International League for Peace and Freedom (WILPF), the Fellowship of Reconciliation (FOR), and the American Friends Service Committee (AFSC). In his preface, Lewy lays out the charge he set out to prove: "While at one time pacifists were single-mindedly devoted to the principles of nonviolence and reconciliation, today most pacifist groups defend the moral legitimacy of armed struggle and guerrilla warfare, and they praise and support the Communist regimes emerging from such conflicts."[87] The political scientist argues that, during their formative years, the organizations rejected options that involved them in cooperating with Communist governments and groups, but that the political climate during and after the Vietnam years has tugged them toward close association with Communists.[88] He cites extensively from the pacifist organizations' documents, seeking to concretely forge this link.[89]

Lewy, who occasionally draws on Reinhold Niebuhr and Max Weber in his critiques, also is concerned that such pacifist groups have tremendous influence on more mainline Protestant and Catholic denominations and on the political process. He claims that while the American pacifist movement never has been large, "its political influence has often been extensive and has always reached beyond the relatively small number of the movement's active members." When combined with their allies in the churches and numerous church-related social action groups, contends Lewy, "American pacifists today constitute a potent grass-roots network that can mobilize substantial voter sentiment and at times have considerable impact on Congress."[90] The author cites the United Methodist Council of Bishops' repudiation of the doctrine of nuclear deterrence as illustrative of the inroads the American pacifist movement has made on the religious community.[91]

The relevance of Lewy's critique is twofold: 1) He suggests that the face of American pacifism is undergoing a remarkable transformation; and 2) He argues that pacifist organizations have an effect, beyond what their numbers would indicate, on other denominations and on American politics. Both concerns—and much of the other material—are overstated in Lewy's text, but they evidence the complexity of contemporary pacifism as it takes shape in the sphere of national politics. MCC Washington, as one pacifist player in American politics, no doubt is shaped by its political context and its bedfellows, and likewise it contributes something toward the reshaping of its partners and American politics. The office's responses to two political crises in the last decade, the Persian Gulf War and the United States and United Nations intervention in Somalia, may illustrate the process at work. They illuminate the formation—and the breakdown—of Washington alliances, suggesting how MCC seeks to participate closely with its religious allies while also maintaining a voice faithful to its own tradition of peace.

HARMONIC VOICES, DISSONANT VOICES

During the buildup for the Persian Gulf War, religious advocacy groups with whom MCC Washington relates presented a unified front, criticizing the U.S. military response and calling for peaceful negotiations. From the earliest weeks, the Catholic, mainline Protestant, and peace church lobbyists sang a similar tune, and differentiating one voice from another was difficult, at least until the war began in January 1991.[92] MCC Washington, for the most part, sounded like its Capitol Hill peers. On the other hand, the intervention in Somalia met with a much more dissonant response, at least in terms of MCC Washington's relationship to its allies. While most of the advocacy groups, including nongovernmental organizations (NGOs) with workers in Somalia, supported the intervention, MCC and the American Friends Service Committee were among few organizations calling for a different response. Somalia was one example where the peace church advocates' "absolute" commitment to nonviolence drew a line between them and others committed to "just peace."

In general, churches came to oppose the Vietnam War late in the war's history. In the score of years between Vietnam and the Persian Gulf War, however, significant alterations had occurred in mainline Protestant and Catholic religious bodies—among leaders more so than among the laity—regarding the issues of war and peace. In the last two decades, representatives of several major Christian bodies have published texts espousing various versions of "just peace."[93] Although they do not use "just peace" language, the National Conference of Catholic Bishops made dramatic steps toward nuclear pacifism in *The Challenge of Peace*.[94] In 1985 the United Church of Christ's Fifteenth General Synod declared the denomination to be a "Just Peace Church" and followed up its declaration with a book by the same title.[95] In 1992 peace advocate and Southern Baptist Glen Stassen—although he clearly was not writing for his denomination—published *Just Peacemaking: Transforming Initiatives for Peace and Justice*.[96] Multiple, complex demographic and cultural changes contributed toward these shifts in using "just peace" language. But whatever the causes, many American religious bodies entered the dialogue about the fall 1990 Iraqi-Kuwaiti dispute with transformed understandings of war and peace, and with a commitment to speak quickly and "prophetically" to political decision makers.

One day after Iraq crossed Kuwait's borders on 2 August 1990, Churches for Middle East Peace—the Catholic, mainline, and peace church coalition—released a statement to the press that urged Iraq to withdraw immediately from Kuwait territory and called upon the United States to avoid any unilateral military action. "We further urge the United States to press for an immediate withdrawal of Iraqi forces and to actively support the efforts of the United Nations and the Arab League for a peaceful resolution of the conflict," the statement says.[97] "The Gulf War was different for us than I think it was for others who came into working on the Middle East only at that time," contends Corrine Whitlatch, director of C-MEP. "We started work right away. We were already involved and we continued to stay involved."[98]

While the religious community immediately pleaded for a peaceful resolution to the Iraqi-Kuwaiti conflict, they were not as united as C-MEP's statement may suggest. Joe Volk, newly appointed director of the Friends Committee on National Legislation, also provided leadership for the Washington religious lobbies' response to "Operation Desert Shield" and "Operation Desert Storm." Volk observes:

> I think the first thing, the short-term goal after August 2, was to try to persuade the other religious denominations and arms control and disarmament organizations to oppose U.S. military action. Because in those first weeks, there was an unbelievable number who were inclined in the other direction, and who were saying, "Hell, we could get some political currency by backing the administration, and then we could use that currency to eliminate the B-2, cut SDI, reduce the military budget. This is a chance for us to buy some credibility." And so I think it was the peace church groups who immediately were trying to say, "This is a bad idea."[99]

Of course, many of the religious organizations in Washington already were predisposed to see a quick U.S. military response as a "bad idea," based on their denominational statements restricting or qualifying their previous traditions of just war thought. If Volk's observations are correct, the historic peace churches simply helped move other religious bodies along the trajectories they had set for themselves in the post-Vietnam decades.

Throughout the fall of 1990 and January 1991, coalitions consisting of mainline, Catholic, and historic peace church bodies continued to express their opposition to U.S. intervention. They did so alongside nonreligious groups, who worked with their own coalitions or in tandem with religious organizations based in Philadelphia, New York, or Washington.[100] Between 4 August 1990 and 17 January 1991—the day after the Persian Gulf War officially began—the National Council of Churches of Christ (NCC) in the U.S.A. issued nine major statements to politicians, member bodies, and the press.[101] In each case, NCC leaders consistently called for measures to avert war.[102] Eighteen church leaders, including Orthodox, Catholic, and Protestant bishops and ministers, participated in an NCC-sponsored "Church Leaders Peace Pilgrimage to the Middle East" 14–21 December 1991. Upon their return, the church leaders released a statement entitled "War Is Not the Answer: A Message to the American People." Another umbrella coalitional body, the National Campaign for Peace in the Middle East, emerged in New York, serving as a clearinghouse and initiating center for the antiwar movement. The National Campaign coordinated the work of other local coalitions and national organizations into a common effort to stop a war in the Persian Gulf. The Fellowship of Reconciliation, SANE/ FREEZE, Operation Real Security, and the War Resisters League actively participated alongside other religious and nonreligious peace activists.[103] Another unexpected set of "peace" allies were former military officials, including former secretaries of defense, former chairmen of the joint chiefs of staff, and other national security figures, who argued until the war began for prolonged sanctions rather than offensive military action.

Obviously, these organizations and individuals based their criticism of the military response on differing foundations.[104] Some implicitly or explicitly used just war reasoning. Others—including some of those whose historic traditions were rooted elsewhere—argued on the grounds of one version or another of pacifism. Still others rooted their nonsupport in radical ideology; they believe all war is the result of a corrupt capitalist system, or a product of the military-industrial complex's hegemony over the American political system. Yet others used the traditional rationale of the political sphere—national interest, or *realpolitik*.[105] Some used combinations of the various frames of reference, perhaps basing their critiques on one set of understandings but publicly using the language of another. And some of the voices fell away by the time large-scale war began on 16 January 1991.

But before the war, the antiwar chorus—though slightly dissonant— sang with gusto. In the midst of such a chorus, the tenor of Mennonite Central Committee's voice was muffled, sounding in most ways precisely like its allies in various coalitions. MCC Washington signed onto every letter that C-MEP and other coalition bodies of which it is a member produced. The organization's primary coalition contributions came in its handling of sections of the sign-ons that dealt with sanctions on food and medical supplies. On this issue MCC Washington based its work on its parent organization's seventy years of humanitarian assistance around the globe. MCC Washington also facilitated Capitol Hill visits for a number of Mennonite groups that came to Washington during the fall of 1990 and winter of 1991. The office, like others in the capital, kept its constituents abreast of congressional and administrative branch actions during the tension-filled days leading up to the war. Mennonites and other Methodist Building religious advocates were close partners throughout the early months of preparation for war.

Less than two years later, another conflict garnered a different response from Washington's more liberal lobbyists, including both religious offices and other NGOs. The conflict was the famine and clan wars in Somalia, on the Horn of Africa. Over centuries of repeated water shortages, Somalis had learned to deal successfully with drought, but fighting between opposing clans after the collapse of the U.S.–backed Siad Barre regime in January 1991 complicated the food problem. Thousands were dying of starvation each week. In December 1992 President Bush, in cooperation with the United Nations, sent in thirty thousand U.S. troops to do, as he said, "God's work": stop the bloodshed and looting, get food to desperate people, and then hand the country over to United Nations peacekeepers.[106] Whereas an outspoken minority of U.S. citizens and organizations criticized the president's calls for a major military response in the Persian Gulf, public opposition to the Somali intervention, dubbed "Operation Restore Hope," was virtually nonexistent. Most U.S. citizens, and most Washington lobbyists and national relief organizations, saw military intervention as the only solution.[107]

At an NGO meeting in the capital in late November 1992, just before U.S. troops left for Somalia, a Department of Defense officer asked if any agencies would object to the U.S. military providing security for their food deliveries. Hershey Leaman, Mennonite Central Committee's disaster relief coordinator, was the only person present who immediately expressed disapproval. InterAction, a coalition of 143 U.S. private and voluntary organizations, circulated a sign-on letter to General Brent Scowcroft 19 November 1992, inviting MCC to add its name, even though MCC is not a coalition member. While affirming the "humanitarian concerns that obviously drive this NGO call for a strengthened mandate for a UN security force in Somalia," MCC did not sign the letter. In a response to InterAction, MCC's co-secretary for Africa, Eric J. Olfert, says the MCC decision was based on the "30 plus years of Mennonite experience in Somalia."[108] Olfert writes, "Again, we recognize that the urgent and imperative humanitarian needs must be responded to, but the approach advocated seems to us to be fraught with danger, unlikely to succeed and likely to have a very unhelpful impact on the even more important task of encouraging and enabling Somalis to rebuild their society."[109] Olfert also asks for more creativity in "seeking ways to respond to the humanitarian needs which do not close off the peace processes which offer hope for the longer term."[110] MCC's response to InterAction was a preliminary one, and it was followed up with a more comprehensive statement to the NGO community and political officials.

Several weeks later, on 18 December 1992, MCC and the American Friends Service Committee (AFSC) co-sponsored a Washington forum for the NGO community. Twenty representatives from ten international relief and development agencies attended. Led by Mennonite and Quaker representatives, the NGOs discussed the assertion that military intervention confuses humanitarian and political issues, wrestling with the impact the U.S. decision may have on their present and future efforts. The group unanimously agreed that the questions raised by military delivery of food aid are legitimate discussion points. One NGO representative said, "We expect the historic peace churches to have problems with military involvement. You have a history that gives integrity to this perspective and we need your voice to raise questions."[111] The impact of the MCC and AFSC representatives on other NGOs on the Somalia question is uncertain. Likewise, the long-term effects of U.S. and UN military intervention in the African country will remain unsettled for many years.

What the debate suggests, however, at least from the context of Washington's religious lobbies and NGOs, is that there may be a place for those whose advocacy is rooted in particular kinds of relief and service experiences, which in turn are grounded in particular understandings of peace. The Somalia discussion also suggests that, despite the tight alliances forged between Washington's peace and justice groups, sufficient space is allowed for peers to offer a distinctive voice, when experience and faith commitments call for a counter response. Such was the case for the Mennonite Central Committee—and for the Quaker lobbyists—on the issue of intervention in Somalia.[112]

KEEPING THE BOARD IN PLACE

During the past several decades, MCC Washington has sought to steer a path through the capital's political and religious lobbying culture, maintaining its historic peace tradition and adapting to the realities—and the necessities of forming alliances—that Washington's long-standing institutions demand. Those Mennonites concerned about MCC Washington's bedfellows fear, on one level, that such associations will alter the character, theology, and self-identity of Mennonites. On another level, some Mennonites are worried that cooperative efforts simply will affect their "good name." It is likely that some alterations are occurring, partly because of changing demographics among Mennonites, and perhaps also as a result of MCC Washington's alliances as well as ecumenical involvements elsewhere.

Behind the questions Mennonite and Brethren in Christ constituents ask about MCC's partnerships is, in part, a recognition of transformations occurring in previous understandings of rigidly separated kingdoms, or ethical realities: the world and the church. The lines between the two become less clearly demarcated in an organization such as MCC Washington. Mennonites are finding that they *can* work cooperatively with other religious organizations that have different frameworks of reference and fewer concerns about a separation between two kingdoms. By extension, Mennonites also are discovering that although it is difficult to do so, they can, to a certain degree, address and "participate" in the political realm without losing sight of their particular religious identity.

The MCC Washington office's relationship to its parent relief and service organization and Mennonite Central Committee's close ties back into its constituent denominations assist in keeping a necessary "bundling board" in place between MCC and its allies.[113] Such connectedness allows Mennonites to enter into Washington lobbying alliances that can be mutually beneficial. Whenever MCC Washington staffers attempt to roll over and get too cozy with their coalition partners, they are reminded of the nature of their relationship, which is more like a cooperative friendship than a marriage. The institutionally placed board they bump into as they move toward their conversation partners—a board that is firm but that does not prevent conversation—has enough substance to keep the relationship healthy and relatively "virtuous."

While MCC Washington's agenda does closely parallel that of its allies, the Mennonite office is—and rightly so—not entirely in line with its lobbying friends. MCC Washington and other historic peace church offices in the capital—including the Friends Committee on National Legislation and the Washington offices of the Church of the Brethren and the American Friends Service Committee—sometimes find themselves at odds with other religious and humanitarian lobbies because of their commitment to a more "absolute" pacifism. Pacifism then functions as one of several "traditional" components of the bundling board that separates MCC Washington from some of its peers.

4

SPEAKING THE TRUTH QUIETLY

In the vortex of power which whirls around the centers of political influence, the persons serving in the Ottawa and Washington offices need to
be fully aware of the reality of the temptations Jesus faced. The pressure
to try to establish the kingdom of God by selling out to the expedience
of political and military power is great. The offices need constant reminders that the task is first of all to be faithful, to be wise as serpents
and harmless as doves. If Mennonites can operate in Washington and
Ottawa with integrity to the history of nonresistance and nonconformity
which is a part of their heritage, the witness to that possibility may be
more important than any other accomplishments on particular issues of
militarism, war taxes, capital punishment, migration for religious freedom, or social injustice.

—William Keeney, "The Establishment"

In his careful review of Washington's religious lobbying organizations,
Allen D. Hertzke suggests that the need to be successful "moves groups
toward an accommodation with the system they are attempting to influence." Religious lobbyists, he contends, "do influence public policy, but
are themselves influenced by their participation in the national public
square."[1] If religious groups want to achieve success, they must grasp the
congressional system's norms, rituals, parliamentary intricacies, and multiple points of access, he writes. Hertzke observes that, in his interviews

with congressional staffers, the same theme repeatedly emerged: "To be effective, religious lobbyists must learn to play the game, to think strategically, and to understand the norms of congressional politics."[2] Through his treatment of how religious interest groups shape American *politics,* Hertzke then also sheds light on how the congressional milieu "channels, constrains, and in some cases alters that religious political 'witness.'"[3]

A similar notion, from the perspective of political Washington, was stated in its crassest form in a 1994 *Newsweek* article about former White House Chief of Staff Mack McLarty. "No wonder McLarty has fared badly in Washington. Unwilling to play by Washington rules—leaking, back-stabbing, self-promoting, etc.—he was never feared," said reporters Bob Cohn and Eleanor Clift. "Last week he was moved aside in a long-expected White House shake-up, proving once again that when outsiders come to Washington they either learn the local tribal customs or wind up in the pot for dinner."[4]

For some denominational offices in Washington, adapting to the local lobbying customs comes more easily than for others. Sociologist Mark Chaves develops the notion that denominations develop a dual structure—a *religious authority* structure and an *agency* structure. Chaves then argues that agencies that are increasingly autonomous from their denominational religious authority structures "are more apt to develop organizational forms and priorities that adhere to the functional organizational fields in which they reside rather than to the religious traditions whose names they bear." In other words, relatively *autonomous* religious agencies' lobbying—no matter what the denomination—will be indistinguishable from comparable secular activities.[5] And, Chaves implies, such work will be indistinguishable from the work of other denominations similarly involved. A closer look at the actual lobbying efforts of MCC Washington and its peers is needed to recognize the pervasiveness of certain established practices and the ways in which "humility" or "quietness" may make Mennonites' advocacy efforts somewhat distinct.

MONITORING AND INFLUENCING

In his entry under "lobbying" in the *Mennonite Encyclopedia,* Delton Franz holds that the term means "bringing citizen perspectives to bear on governmental policy," adding that this can be for either altruistic or self-seeking concerns. Among the means of "seeking to influence government decisions" Franz lists are letter writing, appointments with legislators and their aides, and testifying in congressional hearings, all of which Mennonites as individuals or denominational and agency representatives have utilized.[6] The fact that Mennonites would include an entry on lobbying in their encyclopedia illustrates a significant shift in church-state understandings in the past several decades. When the Washington office was founded in 1968, proponents of the office and official documents regulating its work scrupulously avoided the term "lobbying." In MCC's "Report and Recommendation Concerning a Washington Office," the functions of the new office were designated as: 1) to serve as an observer in Washington, analyzing and interpreting trends that affect Mennonite concerns; 2) to equip the constituent groups where they desire to make representation to the government; 3) to serve as a source of knowledge and expertise on peace and social issues related to government; and 4) to provide facilitating services for constituent groups.[7] A 1968 MCC news release notes that the office may, upon request, help interpret the position of Mennonite groups to government. "Concerns will not be pressed by using the political pressure methods of lobbies maintained by groups working in their own narrow interests," the release states.[8] Initially the key term used to describe the MCC Washington office was the relatively passive "listening post." In the following years the description—and the reality—changed subtly, suggesting a slightly more active role.

Letters from Washington staffers to constituents, and correspondence between MCC's Akron-based administrators and Washington workers, repeatedly have emphasized that the office was not set up as a lobby. In a letter to one constituent, Franz says the office's role is as a facilitator. "The emotionally freighted word 'lobby' is too sweeping to accurately describe the legitimate voice of Christians speaking on behalf of the disinherited," explains Franz, "while also characterizing the pressure tactics of labor unions and business corporations who approach government officials for their own self-interests."[9]

Washington Mennonites are not alone in their discomfort with being called lobbyists. The Friends Committee on National Legislation, the first registered religious lobby in Washington, is a notable exception. The FCNL office makes no disclaimers about its attempts to influence legislators. Most other denominational and parachurch organizations prefer to call their work "advocacy" or "witness." In many ways, the work of the religious offices might fall under the classification of "lobbying."[10] However, the means of lobbying for the religious organizations differs from that of corporations and other moneyed special-interest groups. Because of these differences, maintaining the terms "advocacy" and "witness" alongside "lobbying" may be appropriate. Whatever it is called, though, all of the religious offices understand their work as involving seeking to influence government officials and government policy.

This potential influence concerns not only some lay persons disturbed by their denominational office's work in the capital, but many philosophical liberals as well. Historically, the two "spheres" of "private" domestic life and the "public" life of politics and the marketplace were delineated sharply. Political theorists said the two spheres operated with vastly different principles, and the private should not be dragged into the public. This has functioned as a way of excluding certain voices from the public realm and of severely limiting the parameters of legitimate public discourse. In *A Theory of Justice,* John Rawls argues that in public life, concerns about what is "right" take priority over concerns about what is "good." Creating a just society, with a "thin" consensus on rights, will allow for multiple forms of "the good" to emerge, contends Rawls. Politics then becomes relegated to the narrow field of configuring procedural justice. Rawls worries that religious groups, with their strong versions of what constitutes "the good," will interfere with the political process by dragging into public life that which should be private. In his rendering, religion clearly fits into the realm of "the private."[11] Religious lobbying, then, would be an inappropriate—and perhaps dangerous—venture.

Political philosopher Michael Walzer builds on the notion that there are various "spheres" in which social goods are distributed. Walzer is not concerned about monopoly over any given sphere by certain persons or organizations, but worries about dominance of one sphere over another. Political power stands as one sphere among many—including those of kinship and love, free time, education, and money and commodities—but political power is a special sort of good. While it is like the other goods, notes Walzer, it is unlike them in that "however it is had and whoever has it, political power is the regulative agency for social goods generally. It is used to defend the boundaries of all the distributive spheres, including its own, and to enforce the common understandings of what goods are and what they are for."[12] Walzer severely limits the sphere of religion or "Divine Grace," however. Here, rather than speaking about somewhat permeable "boundaries" between spheres, Walzer notes the historic development of the "wall" between church and state. "Politics is not dominant over grace nor grace over politics," he states, adding: "I want to stress the second of these negative propositions. Americans are very sensitive to the first. . . . In any case, the monopoly of the saints is harmless enough so long as it doesn't reach to political power. They have no claim to rule the state, which they did not establish, and for whose necessary work divine assurance is no qualification."[13]

In light of Walzer's remarks it is worth noting that the "wall of separation between church and state" is not the language of the American Constitution nor the Bill of Rights. The language was used by Thomas Jefferson in his famed letter to the Danbury, Connecticut, Baptist Association. Martin Marty says students of the Constitution and the writings and concepts of the Founders and Framers have preferred James Madison's phrase: "the line of separation between the rights of religion and the civil authority."[14] However, in popular parlance, Americans often speak of Jefferson's "wall." Marty contends that Madison's line "deals more realistically with the American situation, for a line allows for more fluidity, viscosity, and adaptation than does the more concrete metaphor of a wall."[15]

Others besides Rawls and Walzer have been critical of the influence of religious organizations in the political realm. Addressing more specifically the influence of religious *pacifists,* critic Guenter Lewy claims that if American pacifists were to practice "clear thinking," they would acknowledge Weber's distinction between an ethic of ultimate ends and an ethic of responsibility. He writes: "Each has its place, but they should not be confused. In the best of all possible worlds, pacifist activity could be both morally pure and politically relevant. In the real world, that is usually not possible. . . . For the moral ambiguities of history and the world of politics, Niebuhr insisted, ambiguous methods and answers are required. 'Let those who are revolted by such ambiguities have the decency and courtesy to retire to the monastery where medieval perfectionists found their asylum.'"[16] In Washington, religious lobbyists who also are pacifists fortunately have not had such "decency and courtesy."

Although operating out of considerably different frameworks, Rawls, Walzer, and Lewy all make sharp delineations between religion and politics, or the church and state, or the public and private. They have much good company, including many Mennonites who speak about their ancestors' separation of church and state. However, this "separation" has gone through a metamorphosis over the centuries. Frank Epp, a theologian and journalist who also was involved with MCC's peace activities, argues that what "separation of church and state" meant to Mennonites' parents in the sixteenth century and what it means to Mennonites now is radically different. While "our pioneers in the faith had the highest respect for the state" and believed "that order and government came from God," Epp holds, they also "refused to acknowledge the state as sovereign in the life of the church, and they even refused to acknowledge for the state ultimate sovereignty in the affairs of humanity." Epp suggests that today "separation of church and state" has come to mean the opposite: "Thus, as time went on, we not only made the state sovereign, responsible not even to God, in its sphere, but we also accepted a great deal of what the state had to say with respect to the domain of the church. . . . Now we have the paradoxical situation that we invoke the same doctrine which our Anabaptist forebears invoked, but the meanings have been turned around completely. We have given to the state far more sovereignty and authority than the doctrine ever intended or that God ever intended, and we have removed ourselves, the church, and the divine revelation increasingly from the affairs of human society."[17] Epp, who was writing about nuclear disarmament in this context, concludes with an admonition to Mennonites to "lead the way, forcefully, completely, without delay, and not seek escape in the false separations which remove us from the moral responsibility that salvation requires."[18]

Robert Bellah and his associates also write about "false separations," highlighting particularly the modern American distinctions between the "public sector" and the "private sector." In *The Good Society,* they note that usually the distinction separates what is governmental from what is non-governmental. However, they suggest that biblical religion cannot be private. "Both Christians and Jews recognize a God who created heaven and earth, all that is, seen and unseen, whose dominion clearly transcends not only private life but the nations themselves," they state. The writers also point out that in one sense "public" does not mean governmental but is a *contrast* term to it. Building on critical theorist Jürgen Habermas's work, they say that during the second democratic transformation of the eighteenth century, "'public' came to mean the citizenry who reflect on matters of common concern, engage in deliberation together, and choose their representatives to constitute the government. . . ."[19] Bellah and his associates criticize those philosophical liberals who seek to remove religious groups from the public conversation. They suggest that organized religion can offer a genuine alternative to destructive tendencies in the United States's current pattern of institutions, and they point to Washington's religious advocacy groups as organizations that seek to embody the "public church."[20] "These groups want to bring religious and ethical insight to bear in defining America's vision of a good society and in making recommendations for public policy on specific issues," they contend.[21]

FAITHFUL OR EFFECTIVE?

Some critics would suggest that Walzer, Rawls, and Lewy need not worry about the religious advocacy groups influencing legislators or governmental policies. Sen. Mark O. Hatfield (R-Oregon), whom many religious advocacy organizations consider an ally, once told a meeting of religious representatives that they are "the least effective lobbyists in Washington." The senator said he does not look to the religious organizations for help, mainly because they do not understand issues and do not know how to deal with members of Congress.[22] On the other hand, on some issues the church groups collectively *do* have clout. When former President Ronald Reagan's administration was looking for support for its aid package for U.S.-backed "Contras" seeking to overthrow Nicaragua's Sandinista government, the church advocates were strong opponents. Langhorne A. Motley, assistant secretary of state for inter-American affairs, contended that Reagan's 1985 decision to compromise on Contra aid rather than risk a serious defeat in Congress had something to do with the religious voice in Washington. "Taking on the churches is really tough," observed Motley. "We don't normally think of them as political opponents, so we don't know how to handle them. It has to be a kid-glove kind of thing. They are really formidable."[23]

In actuality, Hatfield and Motley's comments may not be as divergent as they first appear. Both are suggesting, implicitly if not explicitly, that the religious advocacy groups can be confrontational and uncompromising. In Washington, legislators have become accustomed to confrontational encounters with their peers, constituents, and secular and religious advocacy groups. But in the capital, *compromise* also is part of the political game, a point which has not been missed by such critics of pacifist organizations as Niebuhr and Lewy. Compromise is part and parcel of interest group politics and the American tradition of pluralism.[24] A plaque in the entryway to the Dirksen (Senate) Office Building, located directly behind the Methodist Building, says of its namesake, Everett McKinley Dirksen: "His unerring sense of the possible enabled him to know when to compromise; by such men are our freedoms retained."

In some cases and by some people, religious advocacy groups are perceived as uncompromising, and therefore as unwilling to participate fully in the necessary give-and-take of politics. Legislative aide Nelle Temple Brown argues that the down side of Washington's religious community is obvious: not all, but many, of the religious lobbyists are "extremely inflexible." Temple Brown says a friend of hers calls it "the M.R. Factor," the Moral Righteousness Factor. "Because God is on their side, if you aren't going to do it their way, then the devil's in your camp," she explains. "And so some of the religious community are really hostile to the political process as a process because these are issues about which morally they feel there can be no compromise whatsoever." Temple Brown observes that such advocates "come up here carrying the snow-white banner of truth to the benighted politicians. You can't really have a dialogue with them. They don't respect the process."[25]

Bill Tate, top legislative aide for Rep. James Leach (R–Iowa), speaks about historian Sidney E. Mead's notion, developed in *The Lively Experiment,* that the establishment clause in the Constitution turned upside down the traditional understanding of the role of religion in communal life.[26] Tate notes that up until the American experiment, the power that connects or makes a state cohere as an entity flowed from the top down—the king or pharaoh was simultaneously the representative of the deity on earth.

We turned that around and said the power was going to come from the bottom up. This breakage of the link between the church and state meant that no peculiar faith would dominate, but all faiths would have to participate in the conflict of ideas that politics at its best should be. It's a peculiar role for people who take their faith seriously, because if you believe in God, you believe in the Absolute, that there is an absolute source of truth. And in the world in which I work, there is no such thing. All truths are relative, all are open to question and debate, and the most we can hope for out of this messy conflict is some approximation of the truth. And that's foreign territory to a religious person, or so it seems to me.[27]

Behind this question of compromise is the tension between effectiveness and faithfulness, an issue that frequently emerges in conversations with directors of religious lobbying offices. Hertzke's examination of religious advocacy organizations indicated that most religious lobbyists claim that legislative success is less important to them than being faithful to their calling to be "witnesses" or "advocates."[28] To a certain extent, as some religious lobbyists see it, being faithful *is* being effective. Further complicating the issue is the difficulty of measuring "effectiveness" for most religious lobbies.[29] "I can't count influence in terms of votes won and lost," observes Father J. Bryan Hehir, counselor on social policy for the U.S. Catholic Conference. "Long-term influence is through the vision someone grows up with as a member of the [Catholic] Church community. There is also the influence that comes from public opinion, which is expressed in a number of ways and sets a framework within which policy is set."[30] This is a different "effectiveness" test than that of other secular lobbyists representing various interests.[31]

In the Anabaptist-Mennonite tradition, as in many other religious traditions, faithfulness has long taken priority over effectiveness. Faithfulness is near the heart of Mennonite theological and ethical thinking, with the background hope that God has structured the world in a way that faithfulness also will be, eventually, effective. During his tenure at MCC Washington Keith Gingrich said: "I think when I first came here I tended to think in terms of effectiveness primarily and only, but more recently I've come to feel that this is a legitimate and important part of the church's ministry and therefore we should be doing it regardless of how effective we are—just because we need to do it, just because it's the right thing to do." Gingrich noted that he needs to keep reminding himself to "just to keep going."[32]

MCC-Akron's Titus Peachey says he is concerned that what the office does comes out of a desire to be faithful. "I think [Washington] and a lot of other towns—the whole world—operates a lot out of the principle of setting a goal and doing whatever you need to do to get that done," he observes. "But I guess I would very much feel that means and ends are part of the same cloth, and that a goal of being faithful always has to be kept in front of you." Peachey acknowledges that this belief does not make one's choices or decisions without dilemmas, "but I would think there are a number of methods of lobbying that are effective, but I wouldn't want to do them."[33] Peachey notes that applying a great deal of pressure would be one lobbying strategy he would want to avoid. As will be illustrated below, even if Mennonites *wanted* to apply major pressure in Washington, they would find themselves lacking in two major lobbying resources: numbers of constituents and money committed to effecting political change.

Although MCC Washington's lobbyists and those from other religious organizations often claim that faithfulness takes precedence over effectiveness in their work, one ought not assume that effectiveness—even by Washington standards—is not valued. As Gingrich's remarks suggest, specific legislative change often is desired and worked toward in the lobbying efforts of MCC. When Mennonite visitors come to the Washington office, staffers sometimes select files for their perusal: among these, in most cases, are several documenting the office's "success stories." When staffers speak to groups attending weekend conferences MCC Washington sponsors, the director has encouraged them to include such stories as part of their presentations. Franz's own speeches to visitors almost always included remarks about the several cases where MCC's fairly direct influence could be observed. Among the reasons MCC Washington staffers may want to include accounts of the office's influence in their public presentations is that for some of their constituents, they are still attempting to "justify the existence" of the Washington office. Since some constituents would think in terms of specific legislative influence, it makes sense to include some of these stories. MCC Washington staff members, like their constituents, are pleased when legislative or policy changes occur partly as a result of the office's work: effectiveness is indeed defined, in part, by the organizational field, and the actors cannot fully escape that definition.

Some researchers who have examined Washington's religious lobbying culture have *underestimated* the church lobbyists' concerns for effecting change. This is especially true for those researchers whose work is based entirely on interviews with the capital's religious advocates, neglecting the important dimensions of their efforts that occur in various task forces and working groups.[34] It is in these coalition groups where careful strategizing, goal setting, and even compromising take place in an effort to influence Washington's power brokers. Faithfulness may well be guiding participants' recommendations in working groups, but clearly the intention of allied actions is to influence legislators and other government officials in an effective way. At a meeting of the National Coalition to Abolish the Death

Penalty, representatives of various religious and secular organizations discussed strategies to "maximize the level of debate" around a Supreme Court death penalty case. For several minutes they considered conducting a worship service the night before the case was heard, possibly reading the names of those wrongly executed in the past. Finally, one participant said, "I think a religious service is OK, but that's not as effective in bringing people out." The idea was then dropped and the discussion turned toward getting a celebrity speaker or anti–capital punishment rock group, such as U2, to participate in some public event.[35]

In another meeting, which occurred just days after Bill Clinton's presidential election in November 1992, the religious community's Foreign Policy and Military Spending Task Force conducted an emergency meeting to discuss the task force's future in light of the changing administration. Together the representatives discussed what strategies they should pursue and what issues they should focus on, given the new situation. Although Clinton's White House would likely be more sympathetic to their concerns, they recognized that some of their international agenda would be placed on the back burner because of Clinton's intended "laser beam" on the domestic economy.[36] In another setting, Arms Transfer Working Group members asked whether the group should push hard for an amendment conditioning aid to the former states of the Soviet Union on nonproliferation of conventional weapons as well as weapons of mass destruction. The meeting's discussion centered on whether the amendment might raise the profile of conventional weapons issues in Congress and get weapons transfers on the legislative agenda even if it did not pass.[37] Another example of religious lobbyists' concern for effectiveness came at a meeting of the Central America Working Group (CAWG). CAWG was considering both a detailed listing of priority issues related to 1993 assistance for Central America and an action timeline for communications to the Senate about the Foreign Aid Appropriations Bill. Selections from CAWG's action timeline evidence careful strategizing:

> *July 3–20.* Grassroots activists of targeted senators should attend public events where their senator is speaking or will be present to ask him/her about Central America-related issues in the foreign aid appropriations bill.
>
> *All July.* Letter-writing campaigns and preparations for action alert phone response at time of votes need to be made *now* in order to be ready at time of full committee votes.
>
> *10–3 Days Prior to Mark-Up.* Editorial board work to produce editorials in newspapers favorable to our positions. CAWG staff will coordinate. National groups working with hard news journalists should also coordinate efforts.

Grassroots Call-In Day. When date of subcommittee and full committee action is more clear, choose a date for call-in to Washington office from constituents in all Democrats' and targeted Republican senators' states.

5–2 Days Prior to Mark-Up. Consider at least one high-power delegation in Washington attempting to meet with key targeted senators on full committee.[38]

Mennonite Central Committee participates in all of the groups mentioned above, some of which include secular as well as religious representatives.[39] By observing the careful, detailed, rationally organized work of the groups, one could hardly hold that they have little concern for effectiveness, nor that they are unwilling to make minor compromises for the sake of being heard.

Still, it seems true that the religious representatives are less willing to compromise than are some of their secular counterparts or paid staff members on the working groups. At the Central America Working Group meeting mentioned above, paid CAWG staffers—who make more of the direct contacts with congressional aides—were more ready to compromise language slightly in order to be more effective, while denominational and other religious representatives wanted to keep the language strong, even if that offended the legislators. Similarly, during the Arms Transfer Working Group (ATWG) discussion about aid to the former Soviet states, several persons mentioned that the time for proposing an amendment to the aid bill was not good, given Russian President Boris Yeltsin's precarious political situation and his need to sell arms to raise the funds necessary to run his embattled country. The director of one religious lobbying office then stated that he realized that the organizations in the ATWG have different goals and intentions, but that he was concerned with maintaining a clear witness. He noted that, as a member of a church group, he wanted to be able to say, "We want to urge both the U.S. and Russia to abide by these [arms transfer] restrictions." He added, only partially tongue-in-cheek, "For my office, I don't want to be constrained or overly shaped by the realities out there."[40]

James Matlack, director of the American Friends Service Committee's Washington office, recalls debates in the religious lobbying community over such issues as military armaments and Contra aid. Sometimes the Monday Lobby, a group consisting of both religious and secular organizations, has had difficulty reaching agreement on military reductions. "Many of the church offices, especially the peace church offices, can't sign a statement saying we support funding 50 MX missiles as opposed to 100," explains Matlack. In cases where some of the Washington Interreligious Staff Council groups disagree with their partners in the Monday Lobby, the WISC organizations have written their own separate letters rather than signing on to the Monday

Lobby's letters, which may allow for more compromise. Matlack also recalls a debate in the mid-1980s over aid to the Nicaraguan Contras. This time the issue split the religious community in a variety of ways. Congress was considering drastically reducing aid to the Contras, and the religious lobbyists were considering whether or not to get on board. The issue was that if the measure were not passed, then the Contras would get their *full* allotment. Some of the religious organizations believed they could not support *any* aid to the Contras, even if the reduced funding seemed to be a better alternative. "This didn't just split along peace church/non-peace church lines," notes Matlack. MCC Washington and the Quakers voted against supporting the reduction, while the Church of the Brethren cast its lot with the reduction. Some of the mainline churches sided with the Mennonites and Quakers over against their usual comrades.[41] For some of the lobbyists, having a clear, uncompromised witness means facing such bizarre dilemmas, unreasonable as they may seem in the rationalized world of politics.

A LOSS OF INNOCENCE?

For Mennonites, even the establishment of the MCC Washington office signifies a shift away from their earlier decades of decentralized and sometimes disorganized "witness" toward more carefully rationalized and institutionalized advocacy.[42] One of the clearest illustrations of the Mennonite transformation toward political rationalization is the denominations' responses to proposed alterations in military conscription. Mennonites' responses to conscription prior to the U.S. entrance into World War II and their efforts in recent decades evidence dramatic shifts in how Mennonite denominations engage the political realm.

By Autumn 1940 the Burke-Wadsworth conscription bill—which recognized conscientious objection to military service, but did not articulate specific applications of the C.O. exemption—had become law.[43] The various Mennonite peace committees were aware of the dangers of this unspecified exemption and were working to avoid the dire situation religious conscientious objectors faced in World War I.[44] In 1939, before the Burke-Wadsworth bill was introduced in the Senate, the Mennonite Central Peace Committee had adopted "A Plan of Action for Mennonites in Case of War." The plan proposed that Mennonite conscientious objectors could demonstrate their sincerity of purpose—i.e., that they were seeking to avoid fighting and killing, but were open to alternative humanitarian work—by devising a blueprint of "constructive service to the needy in the spirit of Christ." On 10 January 1940, historic peace church representatives met with President Roosevelt, followed by consultations with Attorney General Murphy and Secretary of War Woodring. Six months later the Burke-Wadsworth bill was introduced in the Senate, and the Mennonite Central Peace Committee authorized Orie O. Miller to represent the committee in Washington. Mennonites did not contest the legitimacy of military conscription, but wanted to be certain the bill recognized an alternative to noncombatant service under *civilian* direction.

When hearings on the Burke-Wadsworth bill began in the Senate Military Affairs Committee, Mennonites—even with their plan of action in place—were not adequately prepared. They failed to request permission to testify until 12 July, the final day of the hearings, and therefore were unable to speak. Mennonites did testify before the House Military Affairs Committee, which met from 10 July to 14 August. Amos Horst of Lancaster, Pennsylvania, represented Mennonites in the hearings. His testimony, remarks historian Albert N. Keim, was "an interesting combination of guilelessness and subtle contradiction":

> In answer to the question "Are you asking any different protection now than you were accorded during the World War?" Horst answered, "Not as to the handling of the C.O." The questioner persisted: "The people of your faith were satisfied with their treatment during the World War?" Horst answered, "Yes, Sir. We were." And then, in what must have been an equally astounding assertion, Horst went on to argue that the chief reason for seeking civilian control of the C.O. was that Mennonites did not want to create, as he put it, an "unpleasant experience for the officer or whoever it is" who would have to deal with the C.O. in the Army camp.[45]

Keim contends that the style of Horst's testimony was more important than its content, especially in comparison with that of Paul C. French and Raymond Wilson, who represented the Friends War Problems Committee and testified immediately after Horst. "French and Wilson were combative, self-assured and obviously a match for the Congressmen on the committee," writes Keim. "Horst was clearly uncomfortable and out of his element in the hearings."[46]

Forty years later—after Mennonites had passed through the 1967–68 proposed changes in the Selective Service System that prompted the founding of the MCC Washington office—Mennonites found themselves facing the return of registration for a possible military draft. This time, with more than a decade of Washington lobbying under their belts, MCC staffers on Capitol Hill were ready. MCC responded quickly to the Selective Service System's December 1980 "Concept Paper on Alternative Service," sending a three-page letter to government administrators. Franz and MCC's Edgar Metzler met with SSS Deputy Director James Bond in June 1981, and MCC mobilized two other delegations to Congress in the following year. In an article documenting a full decade of Mennonite activity in relation to proposed Selective Service System changes, former MCC Washington staffer James Amstutz observes that Mennonites wanted to be cautious about working out a "special deal" with selective service: "This was the mode of operation when General Lewis B. Hershey was at the helm of SSS," he says. "Personal contacts and arrangements often superseded official policy. The Old Order Amish, in fact, stated at the 1982 inter-Mennonite gathering to discuss alternative service that, 'When the time comes, we will work something out for our boys with the Selective Service.'"[47] In the intervening years since Hershey's leadership of the SSS, the agency had shifted to a more administrative, regulatory model, a model that disallowed such "under the table" arrangements. In contrast to the Amish naiveté of waiting to strike a deal "when the time comes,"[48] Amstutz notes that MCC staffers regularly were talking with government officials, sending letters, making phone calls, paying personal visits to members of Congress, mobilizing their constituencies, and providing indirect pressure through congressional channels. Among Amstutz's conclusions from the experience are that Mennonites demonstrated some experience and skill in Washington; that they have credibility in the capital because of their record of service and commitment; and that they can be "wise as serpents and innocent as doves," making systematic use of Capitol Hill but "not lobbying in the strict definition of the term."[49]

Not all Mennonites, of course, are comfortable with this "systematic use of Capitol Hill." In an article entitled "Innocence Lost?" one Mennonite editor writes about Keim's observations regarding the 1940–41 Burke-Wadsworth bill.[50] "We've come a long way since those days," notes Richard A. Kauffman, later a vice president at the Mennonite seminary in Elkhart, Indiana. "The question we must reflect upon is whether in becoming politically wise as serpents, have we now lost our dovelike innocence?" Kauffman explains that by innocence he means having a purity of heart, clarity of conviction, and certainty of purpose so that when Mennonites become politically involved, "we have in mind our ultimate goal and we've adopted means (and attitudes) appropriate to that end."[51]

BEING PROPHETIC

Related to the faithfulness-and-effectiveness and wisdom-and-innocence questions is that of "being prophetic." At a 1992 meeting of the Foreign Policy and Military Spending Task Force, the meeting's facilitator, Joe Volk, asked whether the religious advocacy organizations were called to be a "prophetic witness" or whether they were "to work on things which are more realistic and winnable." The concept of the prophet is evident through-

Although since 1968 Mennonites have rationalized and systematized their political advocacy efforts a great deal, they still are perceived by some as less sophisticated than other lobbyists on Capitol Hill. Such a perception is sometimes taken as a compliment. Cartoon by Joel Kauffmann, courtesy of the artist.

out the biblical texts, but earlier in this century sociologist Max Weber expanded and developed it as a sociological category. For Weber, the prophet and the priest were contrasting figures. The latter works within the context of an established organization, receiving official sanction from an authoritative group. For the prophet, a charismatic figure, there is no official certification process: she or he stands on the edge, exerting authority over existing traditions on the basis of a personal call.[52] Prophets challenge the present structure, while priests provide comfort. Prophets crystallize religion in an attempt to simplify the relationship of human beings to their world. Priests systematize the content of the prophets' message, codifying the sacred traditions and adapting them to the particular needs of a religious body.[53] In the classic sociological texts, prophets serve sects, while priests serve churches.[54]

While Weber's descriptions seem limited to dynamics *within* religious organizations, the concepts have carried over into understandings of how religious advocates function in the political realm. This, some would argue, is a legitimate understanding of the biblical prophetic tradition of speaking to the nations. In the context of Washington, one might hold that some religious advocates function as priests, working from within the system and adapting and compromising the given traditions as necessitated. Because this assumes common membership between advocates and legislators, one might consider this a more "churchly" mode of lobbying. Other religious advocates in the capital may function as prophets, perhaps tossing theologically fueled Molotov cocktails over the political wall. This would be a more "sectarian" mode of functioning—operating as outsiders who simply want to make a point. Senator Hatfield, in his critiques of religious lobbyists, has argued that they would benefit from "an incarnational approach of practicing what they preach": being more inclusive rather than so confrontational in their approach.[55] Hatfield also stated to a Princeton Seminary audience: "Prophetic words about the materialism destroying our society, about misplaced priorities as a nation, about war, about the injustice within our land will never be truly heard by those in the mainstream of society unless they know that the one speaking to them also loves them. The prophet who is not also a pastor goes unheard and unheeded."[56]

Although Capitol Hill Mennonites and many other religious lobbies fall somewhere between the "churchly" and "sectarian" categories, it seems MCC Washington stands nearer to the prophetic than the priestly tradition in the *content* of its messages. During Franz's tenure, the words "prophet" or "prophetic" popped up frequently in his explanations of the advocacy office's work. The public presentations also were punctuated with illustrations from Hebrew prophets such as Moses, Isaiah, and Micah. *Washington Memo* articles on the office's work often speak about the need for a prophetic voice. In 1978 Franz wrote: "It was in these Mennonite city churches that we began to hear sermons and engage in biblical discussion on the meaning of the prophetic task of seeking justice for all people; about the need for a Christian witness to people in power, not just to the powerless."[57] Even when MCC Washington staffers do not use the language of "prophecy," they use related language—such as "bringing an alternative consciousness to bear on the dominant consciousness" or "advocating for the poor and others who are locked out of the political structures."[58]

However, MCC's presence in Washington does evidence a willingness to work somewhat within the present system, complete with the compromises and adaptations—and relationship formation—necessary in Washington's political whirl. Franz nurtured strong working relationships with several long-term members of Congress. MCC administrators in Akron have urged Washington staffers to build relationships with legislators, partly because such relationships best represent conciliatory actions, one interpersonal Mennonite expression of nonviolence. MCC headquarters also is aware that in Washington, relationships are necessary for the trust building that may lead toward acceptance of policy recommendations.[59] Ironically, Mennonite traditions of nonviolence and humility may have contributed toward MCC staffers' functioning both faithfully and at times effectively—even by "worldly" standards—in the capital. As will become more evident, Mennonites' relatively humble and generally conciliatory approach has allowed them to gain a hearing, and to be taken seriously, in some congressional offices.

INDIRECT METHODS OF ADVOCATING

Most students of American political lobbying delineate between two lobbying strategies: 1) indirect or "outsider" methods, which involve bringing pressure on legislators from constituents in their home districts; and 2) direct or "insider" methods, which include personal contacts with legislators designed to influence specific legislation.[60] The latter may include recommending amendments to congressional bills during the mark-up stage, suggesting specific changes in bill language, feeding information to representatives and senators during legislative discussions, and assisting in the creation of political coalitions. The former method, mobilizing the grassroots, is the method to which Washington's religious advocates say they devote much of their energies, with varying degrees of success. The intention of grassroots mobilization is to shape the congressional agenda, create a favorable environment for a certain view, or to predispose members of Congress to respect an organization's power. MCC Washington employs most of the same techniques as do other religious lobbies. However, the office's relationship to the larger Mennonite Central Committee organization, which is based well outside the capital—both geographically and culturally[61]—provides concrete reminders and constraints that occasionally make the style of MCC Washington's advocacy distinct.

Lobbying studies of the 1950s and 1960s suggested that lobbying was primarily for insiders and that members of Congress discounted district pressure elicited by Washington lobbyists.[62] In the last several decades, the face of American lobbying has changed, with constituent contacts carrying considerable weight among legislators. New technologies—such as faxes and other communication systems—changing attitudes, the influence of the mass media, political parties' decline, and congressional decentralization all contributed to the increased influence of constituent contacts.[63] Most representatives and senators now feel they cannot discount constituent pressure, says Hertzke. The political scientist adds that, to be credible, even those Washington lobbies who play the insider game well must demonstrate that they can get the word out to voters in congressional districts or states.

In his study of Washington's lobbying culture, Daniel J. B. Hofrenning compared the methods used by religious advocates with those of other interest groups. The two dozen methods Hofrenning charted included everything from "helping to draft legislation" to "inspiring letter writing or telegram campaigns" to "filing suit or otherwise engaging in litigation." Hofrenning's work suggests that, in general, religious lobbyists use outsider tactics more frequently than insider ones—although like almost all lobbying organizations they use both. Hofrenning also reports that more than half of the religious advocacy groups he surveyed said they use nineteen of the twenty-four listed tactics *on some occasions.* One hundred percent said they sometimes enter into coalitions and talk with people from the press and media. More than 90 percent said they sometimes send letters to constituent members to inform them of their activities; contact government officials directly; shape the government's agenda by raising new issues; consult with government officials to plan legislative strategy; mount grassroots lobbying efforts; testify at hearings; and present research results and other information.[64]

Mennonite Central Committee, one of the religious lobbying offices Hofrenning examined, was among the more than 90 percent of organizations employing the strategies listed.[65] Much of MCC staffers' energies go toward the office's primary function: serving as a listening post by monitoring legislative and administrative actions and reporting those actions back to MCC headquarters and their constituent bodies. MCC Washington's guidelines, based on revisions of the 1968 "Report and Recommendation Concerning a Washington Office," state that the office a) monitors the Washington scene, particularly with reference to public policy developments in the federal government and in liaison with other church and nongovernmental agencies in Washington; b) analyzes and interprets pending domestic and international policy considerations; c) provides facilitating services for constituent groups, such as Washington seminars, workshops, and presentations in local congregations or at regional meetings; and d) arranges representation to government on issues identified by MCC and constituent groups. Here we will give attention to the first three of these directives, which fall most clearly into the "outsider" or "indirect" methods category.

Monitoring

MCC Washington staff members generally begin their working day by thoroughly reading the newspapers the office receives: the *Washington Post,* the *New York Times,* and the *Christian Science Monitor.* Stacks of clippings from these and other publications—sometimes attached to MCC memos, meeting notes, and correspondence with other religious lobbying organizations—perpetually covered Delton Franz's desk during his years at the office. The newspapers and other news publications still line the walls and work spaces of other staffers. While the uninitiated might expect that Washington lobbyists would spend many hours at the Capitol listening in on hearings and floor debate, most religious advocates have discovered that such monitoring is inefficient. While newspaper reports alone are insufficient to garner a true picture of what happens on Capitol Hill, they give religious advocates a broad view of what is happening in the legislative and executive branches of the federal government.

In addition to newspapers, MCC's capital office bookshelves are lined with other periodicals and books that allow the staff to keep one foot in Washington's political culture and another in the church. Alongside subscriptions to denominational periodicals such as *The Mennonite, Gospel Herald, Christian Leader, Mennonite Weekly Review,* and *Festival Quarterly* are the *Nation, Defense Monitor, Africa Report, Nuclear Times,* and *Worldwatch Magazine.* Other Christian periodicals MCC Washington subscribes to include *Christianity and Crisis, Sojourners, Christian Social Action,* and *Bread for the World Newsletter.* Mennonite texts from Faith and Life Press in Kansas and Herald Press in Pennsylvania are interspersed with copies of the *Congressional Quarterly Almanac* and the *Congressional Staff Directory.* Academic journals stand alongside issue-oriented books on hunger, poverty, homelessness, civil rights, and handgun control. MCC Washington's monitoring begins with keeping abreast of actions and trends both in Washington and in the office's constituent denominations.

Franz, whose issues area in his later working years included primarily Central and Latin America, the Middle East, and United Nations Peacekeeping Forces, read with an eye toward legislative happenings related to those regions and issues. When MCC Washington's office first opened in 1968, Franz was responsible for monitoring all the issues MCC wanted covered. Initially, four issue areas were prioritized for coverage: 1) the draft; 2) the urban crisis; 3) international development; and 4) arms control and disarmament.[66] While four issues may seem manageable, each included reams of reading material and sometimes scores of legislative actions. On the issue of draft reform alone, forty-two separate bills were introduced in Congress that year. Today four or five full-time paid and volunteer Mennonite staffers monitor legislation in Washington. However, as the staff has increased, so have the issues that Mennonite Central Committee monitors. Recently the issues covered have included—in addition to the areas and issues Franz monitored—Africa, Asia, aid/debt/trade, arms control, women's issues, Native American issues, the environment, poverty programs, health care reform, civil rights, and criminal justice. A host of legislation falls under each issue area in any given year. In recent years, the director and one other staffer generally have devoted full time to international issues, while two others have spent their energies monitoring domestic issues. Periodically, a fifth person, often a student from one of the Mennonite colleges, assists the other employees and monitors additional domestic or international actions.

The Washington office's Coordinating Council, which consists of the staff and MCC's Akron-based administrators, meets twice each year to formulate the office's priorities within the larger MCC context. At a 1987 Coordinating Council meeting, Washington staffers wrote in their presentation to the council:

> The four of us here in the D.C. office . . . are mindful of the importance of keeping our assignment in perspective. Roughly 70 percent of MCC's 1,000 workers are *in the field* with the disinherited. Approximately 30 percent are in administrative and support-staff assignments in Akron, Winnipeg, and the regional/provincial offices. As the -1 percent who are in Ottawa and Washington, we need to complement the larger interests and realities found by MCC workers in the field. The tail does not wag the dog. . . . Hopefully ours can be an appropriate role in facilitating the voice of interested constituents to "rulers and authorities" (Eph. 3:10), regarding the connection between much of the suffering in the world and policy actions of government. We need a *Coordinating Council* to test and re-test our task and our partnership.[67]

Washington staffers also consult regularly with MCC program secretaries for Asia, Africa, Latin America, and the Middle East as well as the Food Aid Program Office and MCC U.S. These connections back into the parent organization are essential for the office's functioning and for maintaining close linkages to the various constituent denominations and MCC's field workers.

The office's primary sources for monitoring the Washington political scene are the regular meetings of task forces and working groups of the Washington Interreligious Staff Council. WISC, which has no staff or budget, meets monthly as a total body, but its specialized task forces and working groups meet more frequently. MCC Washington also participates in other working groups consisting of both religious and secular representatives, such as the Central America Working Group, the Southern Africa Working Group, the Civil, Human and Voting Rights Issue Group, and the Energy and Ecology Task Force. At the meetings, religious and other advocates report their "findings" related to specific legislation and based on their own analyses. In addition, outside nongovernmental specialists and congressional committee staff specialists are sometimes invited to speak from their perspectives about legislative action. Religious advocates then are free to use this information as they deem appropriate. At least several times a week, one or another MCC staffer participates in working group and task force meetings.

Analyzing, Interpreting, and Informing

Washington religious advocacy groups, including MCC, then take information gleaned from their various sources and analyze and interpret it for their constituent members and bodies. In theory, the Washington Interreligious Staff Council—where much of the information sharing takes place—has no obligation to adhere to a particular political, ideological, legislative, or religious perspective. Most religious lobbyists would acknowledge, though, that the information selected and reported on at WISC meetings, as well as the interpretation given in the reporting of the information, have affinities with a more socially liberal worldview. WISC's concerns center broadly around peace and social justice issues—concerns and perspectives that MCC Washington typically shares. Participants in WISC working groups then take information from the meetings and conduct their own informational networking.

More so than some religious lobbying organizations, MCC Washington has a ready network for disseminating information to its constituencies. The Akron headquarters weekly pumps out news releases about its international service and relief work, as well as about Washington office events and actions. Mennonite periodicals frequently include such releases in their weekly, biweekly, and monthly publications. Periodically, the Washington office director writes articles and editorials for denominational publications; for a time Franz had a semiregular column that analyzed and interpreted legislation for readers of *Mennonite Weekly Review*. All of these sources reach the broader Mennonite constituency, some of whom follow MCC Washington's work and some of whom do not.

The most important organ for communicating to interested Mennonite constituents, however, is the *Washington Memo,* the office's newsletter. The *Memo,* published six times annually, was begun in January–February 1969, about six months after the office's opening. A 1976 news release promoting the publication acknowledges that "newsletters and the mimeograph were not known in biblical times," but adds that "calls to action" were. The release cites Ezekiel 33:6, where the prophet speaks about being God's watchman and his responsibility to warn people when he "sees the sword coming." "In a modest sense, the Washington Office has been called to function as a watchman," claims the release. "The *Washington Memo* is its trumpet."[68] The release also notes that it hopes the newsletter will allow constituents to move "beyond the handwringing stage" when they see another distressing news item; the newsletter will provide them with "timely alerts and background information that will facilitate an informed Christian witness and response to pending policy decisions of government."[69]

Initially the newsletter was mailed to denominational peace and social concerns committees, conference commissions, college peace club officers, and MCC board members and administrators. By the late 1980s, the *Memo* went to nearly six thousand homes, offices, and congregations. But in 1989, MCC headquarters culled mailing lists for all of its publications, dropping persons who no longer wished to receive their various newsletters or who did not respond to inquiries. Through this reduction and others since that time, the *Memo* list was reduced to about three thousand subscribers in recent years. MCC Washington staffers, however, can be relatively certain that their present subscribers—including many of the other religious advocacy offices in Washington—are interested in their work. Proportionate to the size of their supporting denominations, MCC Washington's newsletters have more readers than many mainline denominations' similar publications.[70]

The *Washington Memo* includes articles on specific legislation; biblical-theological reflections on church-state questions; announcements describing projected seminars; and analyses of trends and issues such as health care reform or UN Peacekeeping Forces. The breadth of the newsletter is remarkable, evidencing how expansive MCC Washington's monitoring has become. One twelve-page issue included pieces on arms sales abroad, Bolivia's drug production, campaign finance reform, international trade, American militarism, the Religious Freedom Restoration Act, and hope in the midst of despair in Africa, plus a one-page review of the recently published book *America: What Went Wrong?* Such breadth is typical rather than atypical in the bimonthly publication.[71]

Each year the *Washington Memo* also includes a "Voting Profile," which "may be used as a tool to evaluate candidates." The profile, staffers explain, "selects votes which indicate the stance legislators have taken on issues covered in *Washington Memo.*" The profile usually has several disclaimers about the complexity of the legislative process and the inadequacy of any profile, but says "the votes listed here provide a barometer of attitudes toward peace, justice and the environment."[72] The voting record includes all one hundred senators and all representatives' districts with a sufficient number of *Memo* readers. Beside each legislator's name, his or her votes on ten to twelve issues are noted. A darkened box indicates a "favorable vote," one which, "in the judgment of the Washington Office, moves toward our understanding of the biblical concerns for justice and peace as reflected in the work and statements of MCC U.S. Peace and Justice Ministries and the Mennonite and Brethren in Christ churches." An open oval indicates an unfavorable vote in MCC Washington's judgment, and a question mark indicates that the legislator did not vote or make her or his position known. Among the votes included in the 1994 Voting Profile were those regarding Trident missile production, UN Peacekeeping, military recruiting, CIA budget disclosure, the Vietnam trade embargo, an assault weapons ban, racial justice, Head Start reauthorization, and spending for women, infants, and children.[73]

The Voting Profile is as close as MCC Washington comes to applying pressure on legislators through votes.[74] This lobbying method, known as direct electoral mobilization, generally is not within the "tool kit" of Mennonites' religious lobbying allies either. Some of the other peace and justice advocacy offices publish a similar scorecard, but none seeks to apply significant pressure through state or district votes.[75] There are good reasons for Mennonites, and perhaps other religious lobbyists, not to attempt direct electoral mobilization. Ted Koontz, formerly director of MCC Peace Section, observes that when Mennonites testify at a congressional hearing they are not seeking to convince legislators that they will vote them out of office if they disagree with their position. Koontz writes: "This stance is dictated both by realism—the simple recognition that Mennonites are small and relatively powerless to wield major political impact—and by theology—the view that it is our calling as Christians to witness to the way of Jesus in all life, but not to seize control and shape the course of history through the exercise of coercive power."[76]

The nonuse of direct electoral mobilization is a sharp contrast to Washington's fundamentalist and conservative lobbies, who sometimes register voters in their churches, back candidates, and mobilize for them, and provide campaign contributions to friends. The fundamentalist and conservative lobbies generally *solicit* membership in their organizations, and therefore their members are committed to the lobbies' work and perspective. On the other hand, *presumed* constituents in the more liberal religious lobbies—especially the denominationally based ones—are not necessarily committed to the work of their advocacy office. Even if the liberal mainline lobbies wanted to mobilize votes, their "masses" would not necessarily respond.

Franz and others, throughout much of the history of the MCC Washington office, have written the *Memo* with a strident, confident, sometimes caustic tone, a fact Franz readily admits. Those who knew Franz only through their readings of the *Memo* had a considerably different impression of him than those who saw how the director functioned on Capitol Hill. In person, whether in dealings with his staff or lobbying peers or government officials, Franz was calm, humble, and sensitive in his approach. While his theological perspective and commitments were clear, they were presented less aggressively in person than they sometimes appeared in the *Memo*. In one issue of the publication, Franz wrote: "In this newsletter, we have dealt candidly over the past 15 years with the specifics that characterize the American Empire. In so doing, much of what we have said and will say has a negative ring. We plead guilty to not having enough pointed to some of the *signs of hope* to be found in the midst of darkness.... We will continue to be tough on issues, but—hopefully—gentle with people."[77] Franz's toughness came across in the newsletter, just as his gentleness was evident in his face-to-face dealings in Washington.

Both critics and supporters of the MCC Washington newsletter—as well as the staffers who write it—acknowledge its lean toward the political left. On the political landscape, being pacifist and politically engaged almost automatically categorizes a person or organization as liberal. Since the beginning, though, some Mennonites have criticized the *Washington Memo's* liberal bias. Emmett Lehman, then MCC's appointee to the National Service Board for Religious Objectors, supported the creation of the MCC Washington office. However, in early 1969 he sent Franz a cautionary seven-page memo. In the memo, Lehman reaffirms his support for the office as an observer, informer, and objective interpreter, but holds that he does not understand the purpose of the office to be to educate constituents or make partisan recommendations, either explicitly or implicitly. He writes:

> If the function of the Washington Office is to be by intent or practice only a facade, serving principally or disproportionately the political actionist elements of our constituency, or if its function is to attempt to persuade and educate the conservatives by excluding their interests or stacking the deck against their viewpoint, or if the office is secretly hoped to be a carefully disguised, but effective molder of policy rather than a channel, then I submit we have created a first class fraud as to its effect whose result will be to further divide our constituency along the line of our political positions.[78]

In his letter, Lehman also documents his disagreement with specific positions Franz takes in the March 1969 *Memo* on the Nuclear Nonproliferation Treaty, gun control, a Department of Peace bill, and even book recommendations.

Throughout the years since Lehman's letter, others have written periodically to complain about the *Washington Memo's* liberal or "anti-American" bias—and to cancel their subscriptions. "While I come down solidly on the side of nonresistance/peace, I do feel it is only reasonable to present both sides of issues," said one constituent. "There is no question that the United States Government has acted responsibly and peacefully (or with restraint) in a multitude of situations. Somehow you habitually manage to overlook such.... Your monotonously negative diatribe about our nation simply does not fit the big picture."[79] Another reader wrote: "I find your every issue to be predictably slanted to uncritically reinforce the image of a malicious, indeed malevolent, federal government, which government is supposedly cold to the 'sincere' pleadings for peace from the Soviet Union, and supposedly wholly callused to our own poor and disadvantaged. Surely you don't believe the real world to be this simple."[80] Yet another constituent called the *Memo* "anti-business, anti-free enterprise, pro-Democrat, knee-jerk liberal, pro every left wing movement around, anti-progress, anti-technology, etc. etc. ad nauseam."[81]

Other readers, of course, appreciate the *Memo*'s particular slant. One reader said, "I felt compelled to sit down to write and thank you for your untiring, exceptional work analyzing for us the situation in the world as you and your staff see it. . . . The lives of millions in the world depend on the kind of information we in North America are provided with. Your *Memo* is a great 'life saver.'"[82] Another wrote: "I hope you know that the Peace Section's *Washington Memo* is effective, well-written and needed, so much so that there are probably those who avoid it in order to protect their 'faith.' . . . The contents are clearly stated and objective."[83]

Few persons within MCC or in the constituency would agree that the *Washington Memo*'s contents are "objective." The question for most is whether such nonobjective reporting and interpretation is necessary. At the office's twentieth anniversary consultation in 1989, some participants emphasized the importance of balanced critique in the publication. Others emphasized the necessity of standing with the oppressed so that "a biased American media" would be balanced.[84] Objectivity—if that means not taking a position when staffers feel one is clear—is not the goal of *Washington Memo* articles. The intention of the MCC Washington newsletter is both to inform recipients and to prompt their response. Seeking to elicit mass response in this manner is part of grassroots mobilization.[85] Legislative articles typically end with tag lines such as "Urge your Senators and Representatives to support this much-needed reform. So much depends on it," or "Now until January, when Congress reconvenes, is a good time to contact your Representatives and Senators. Express your disappointment that the Religious Freedom Restoration Act didn't pass this year, and ask them for a commitment to work for swift passage next year." Each issue includes addresses for legislators as well as the president, and the Capitol switchboard number for all congressional telephone numbers. Occasionally subscribers are asked to fill out a response card indicating that they have contacted their appropriate legislators about an issue.[86] This generalized grassroots mobilization can be effective if readers respond quickly. However, the turnaround time on the newsletter is about three to four weeks from the day MCC Washington's originals leave the office to the time *Washington Memo* arrives in constituents' homes.

One way MCC Washington has remedied this delayed response, when immediate mobilization is desired, is by periodically publishing *Hotlines,* brief legislative alerts that are sent first-class to selected supporters. This practice, common to other religious lobbyists in Washington, is known as elite mobilization. These targeted contacts have committed themselves to responding with phone calls or letters after receiving a *Hotline*. Many of the *Hotline* recipients are MCC alumni who served in the regions for which they receive the legislative alerts. Each year MCC Washington sends between six and a dozen of the mailings to committed Mennonite advocates across the country.

Overall, MCC Washington's mobilization efforts are directed at the constituent bodies rather than at the general public. Some religious lobbies in the capital occasionally do radio, television, or newspaper campaigns that are directed far beyond their constituent bodies, although this is rare for MCC Washington's allies. During the Persian Gulf War, however, some advocacy offices did use mass media advertising. Jay Lintner, director of the United Church of Christ's Washington office, notes that he believed the debate on whether or not to respond to Iraq militarily would be "primarily won or lost in the media." Lintner claims, "The key was in the fighting match for the public mind, and it was essential to register the religious community as much as possible as positioned against this war and to try to make that point in the public media."[87] The United Church of Christ published full-page ads in the *New York Times* and the *Washington Post*. The ads, signed by two thousand national executives, conference ministers, and clergy, called on President Bush not to go to war with Iraq, but to work through the United Nations and with other nations for a "just and peaceful resolution of this crisis." MCC Washington did not run any advertisements, but an ad-hoc group of Lancaster County, Pennsylvania, Mennonites and Brethren in Christ ran a full-page ad in the *Lancaster Intelligencer-Journal*. Persons who had recently attended an MCC Washington–sponsored seminar on the Persian Gulf conflict were among those who participated in placing the ad. Such seminars are part of the "facilitating services" in MCC Washington's portfolio.

Providing Facilitating Services

Although the seminars, workshops, and speaking engagements that fall into the "facilitating" category of MCC's work in Washington cannot be identified easily as "lobbying," they are part of the "informing" that Washington staffers do. The programs also illustrate the ongoing dialogue between the advocacy office and its Mennonite constituencies. For some attendees, the events allay their fears and discomfort with the office's work, and they become more politically involved after participating. Mennonites who go to Washington often are exposed to government personnel as "real people" and learn concrete ways in which they may have a constructive impact on the perspectives and decisions of legislators and executive branch officials.

The office's seminars usually include presentations on MCC's work in the capital, including theological-biblical input, legislative updates, and explanations of how MCC Washington does its advocacy. Seminars also include visits to sites on Capitol Hill, and sometimes feature input from other advocates or legislative aides. While some seminars are geared more generally for pastors and interested lay persons within a given geographic region, others focus specifically on such issues as health care. The first MCC Washington seminar took place in October 1969, the second year of the office's operation. That initial seminar, scheduled for General Conference Mennonite Church ministers, was followed a week later by the first Washington Churchmen's Seminar. Representatives of four of MCC's constituent bodies—General Conference Mennonite Church, Mennonite Church, Mennonite Brethren, and Brethren in Christ—attended the latter event. Since then, the office has sponsored more than eighty major seminars with nearly forty-five hundred constituent participants.[88] These figures exclude scores of one-day student seminars and one-hour sessions with numerous Mennonite tour groups. In addition to bringing groups into Washington, MCC staffers also travel around the country to speak, as time allows. In one year the director and others spoke twenty-one different times in church settings from Maryland to Kansas.

A pastor-in-residence program, implemented in late 1992, has allowed a small number of Mennonite pastors to take short-term sabbaticals in the Washington office. In a *Washington Memo* article entitled "Connecting," Franz wrote about the impetus for the program. "MCC staff in Washington are mindful of the dangers of becoming isolated from our congregations, communities and conference bodies," he said. The new program would invite pastors to spend a month or more as part of the Washington staff "to sensitize us to the changes and challenges in Mennonite congregations and their communities. . . . Together we would reflect on the biblical questions and implications of the church's voice to government."[89] The pastor-in-residence program educates and informs pastors, who take what they have learned back into their congregations, perhaps making hundreds more people aware of and responsive to legislative actions. The program also serves as one additional reminder for office personnel of their rootedness in Anabaptist-Mennonite communities. The sustained presence of Mennonite ministers in the capital office supplements the briefer contacts MCC Washington has with seminar participants, and the more regular involvements it has with MCC headquarters in Akron. Such interconnectedness serves the office well in keeping abreast of the constituent bodies it, in part, represents.

REPRESENTING MENNONITES?

Representation, most political scientists would suggest, is a more complex notion than may be popularly perceived. By "representing" constituents in their state or district, members of Congress do not slavishly mimic the views of those constituents. Such representation would be impossible, given the diversity of the American electorate, even within a given geographical region. Similarly, religious lobbies—especially those that are denominationally based rather than issue-based—cannot represent their constituent bodies in a direct manner. Hertzke proposes that what is intriguing about the religious lobbies is "not that they mirror the intricacies of the concept of representation, which they do, but that in significant ways they demonstrate even greater complexity" than does legislative representation.[90]

In her classic writings, Hanna Fenichel Pitkin documents the development of the modern concept of representation. The concept, and modern representative institutions, began to emerge in the Middle Ages, and in many countries became institutionalized as a "right" following the American and French revolutions.[91] From among the multiple meanings associated with representation in democratic theory, Pitkin mentions three primary ones. The first is formalistic representation, in which a representative is one who has been given authority to act in the name of another, so that "whatever the representative does is considered the act of the represented."[92] In some church traditions with more hierarchical structures—e.g., the Roman Catholic Church—upper-echelon leaders such as bishops may be authorized to speak in the name of the church. Mennonites, and most other religious lobbyists in Washington, do not have this kind of authority to speak for their denominations, although they are sometimes allowed to speak for the particular organizations or committees that oversee their work.

A second meaning of representation in democratic political institutions is having a "descriptive likeness" between representatives and those for whom they stand. This is a "standing for something absent," a kind of mirroring of the people, and a faithful echo of their voice. John Adams said a representative body should be "a portrait, in miniature of the people at large, as it should think, feel, reason, and act like them."[93] Most employees and volunteers in denominational lobbying offices are members of that denomination, although this does not automatically imply that they are a portrait of the people in their churches. Given the diversity in most American denominations, this would be as improbable as legislators thinking, reasoning, feeling, and acting like their constituents.

A third usage of representation Pitkin identifies is standing as a symbol for something. With this usage, the symbol, if this is a human being or group, need not resemble what he or they stand for. Applied to politics, explains Pitkin, symbolic representation "tends to focus attention on those activities of political leaders which create charisma, enhance belief, [and] stimulate irrational and affective reactions in people." In this sense, representation is like Weber's sociological use of the term "charisma." This third concept of representation emerged in part from the medieval notions of priests and bishops symbolically representing the form of Christ to the people.[94] In today's political world, it may mean that a religious lobbyist or legislator stands for "God and country" or, as in 1990s presidential election campaigns, "family values."

A persistent problem that characterizes the literature on representation, says Pitkin, is the "mandate-independence controversy": Should or must representatives do what their constituents want or what they think best? Some stress the popular mandate a representative is given by those for whom she acts, a mandate that obligates the representative to do what constituents expect of her. Others maintain that the representative must act independently, using her own judgment, since she was selected for her special ability to adapt and enlarge the constituents' diverse needs into what is best for the local, state, or national welfare.[95] Edmund Burke's thought is at the heart of the controversy. Burke viewed the representative as a "trustee" who has an obligation to look after the constituents, but not to consult with or obey them. While the trusteeship must have a foundation in elections and consultation with the people, Burke envisioned an elite leadership that essentially represents not individual people but the major, ongoing interests that make up the national interest.

Washington's religious lobbyists live with this same tension between the needs and interests of their supporting bodies and their own perceptions of what is best for other persons and groups or for the national community.[96] Complicating their representativeness is their concern not only for national constituencies, but also for international ones—especially, as many religious advocates say, those persons otherwise unrepresented or underrepresented in U.S. policy decisions. In addition, religious lobbying organizations represent not only individual constituents, but also institutions such as denominations. In the case of Mennonite Central Committee, the organization is supported by multiple, diverse Mennonite and Brethren in Christ denominations, all of which participate in decisionmaking processes. Further complicating religious advocates' representation, say some Washington office staffers, is their representation of theological or biblical values, which sometimes conflict with other interests, including those of their individual constituents and denominational bodies.

In 1992 Mennonite Central Committee's headquarters, in consultation with the MCC Washington office, prepared a new brochure entitled "Faith,

Power and Politics: Questions and Answers." In the initial draft, written in Akron, the brochure posed the question "Does MCC accurately represent North American Mennonite and Brethren in Christ political opinions?" The proposed response was that, while church papers show that members of the denominations have a wide range of political views, "MCC needs to represent the views of these constituents, who are an integral part of MCC along with Christian partners around the world."[97] When MCC Washington staff members met to discuss the draft, they talked extensively about the response and the posing of the question. Franz said the reality is that Mennonite and Brethren in Christ views are so diverse and even contradictory that it would be difficult to represent all those views.[98] In their critique of the draft, MCC Washington staffers restated the proposed question about whether MCC represented constituents' political opinions, and then said:

> The answer to this question is obviously, "No." We agree that MCC's constituents hold a variety of political viewpoints. However, we don't believe that MCC tries to represent the range of political views nor that it should. MCC should recognize the variety of political views among our constituency, and MCC does represent some of the theological and political diversity in our constituency, but our views are not representative of our constituents' views. We don't "need," as the draft says, to represent the views of [some critics]. In fact, at times MCC has led its constituency on such critical issues as U.S. foreign policy towards Central America during the 1980s when Christian base communities with whom we partnered pleaded with MCC to appeal to the U.S. government on their behalf.[99]

The final brochure takes seriously the comments of the Washington office staff. The representation question is altered to read "Who does MCC represent when making statements or expressing political opinions to government?" The response says, in part: "A quick look at the letters and columns of church papers shows that Mennonites and Brethren in Christ have a wide range of political views. These constituents and Christian partners around the world are an integral part of MCC. The MCC boards and committees in the United States and Canada, which represent 18 member conferences, strive to take the diverse opinions of constituents and partners into account when making statements and determining the most appropriate and faithful ways of serving others. However, when political views are polarized, MCC cannot represent all Mennonite and Brethren in Christ viewpoints."[100] The brochure goes on to say that all MCC work is done "in the name of Christ" and that Christians must look to Jesus as the source for beliefs and guide for action. It acknowledges, in rather understated form, that even when looking to the gospel as a guide for actions, Christians sometimes disagree.

Whether or not they are using the gospel as the primary guide for their attitudes and actions, it is clear that Mennonites and Brethren in Christ do disagree on social and political issues. The "Faith, Power and Politics" brochure was correct in its assertion that letters and articles to denominational publications show a wide spectrum of responses on questions of homosexuality, abortion, women's issues, political involvement, religious freedom, and even warfare. J. Howard Kauffman and Leo Driedger's survey of five Mennonite and Brethren in Christ denominations illustrates this range. For instance, on the issue of whether state and national governments should exercise capital punishment, 34 percent of the respondents agreed, 40 percent disagreed, and 26 percent were uncertain.[101] Among those surveyed, 21 percent agreed with the statement that "[f]or the most part, people are poor because they lack discipline and don't put forth the effort needed to rise above poverty." In contrast, 28 percent said the government should guarantee a minimum annual income for all individuals and families who are unemployed or who receive incomes below the poverty line. With respect to national welfare programs, 20 percent thought the government should increase current levels of welfare benefits, 24 percent suggested decreasing them, and 56 percent thought current levels should be maintained.[102] "The Mennonite mosaic is very evident in the wide range of views among members on moral and ethical issues," state Kauffman and Driedger. "The sacred canopy covers views much more divergent *within* each Mennonite and Brethren in Christ denomination than between them. . . ."[103]

Further evidence of Mennonite diversity, and perhaps the contrast between members of the denominations and MCC's Washington office, are the voting patterns of most constituents. Mennonite ethicist Duane Friesen once said, "I suspect that the efforts of the majority of Mennonites working on issues of justice in the urban setting or in third world countries are largely canceled out by the voting patterns of the majority of Mennonites living in rural Mennonite communities."[104] Even though the director of MCC Washington and some other staffers have been registered as Independents, over the years the office's flavor has appeared, to most observers, to be more closely aligned with the Democratic Party. But among those Anabaptist-Mennonites surveyed by Kauffman and Driedger, 49 percent voted for Republican George Bush, 18 percent voted for Democrat Michael Dukakis, and 1 percent voted for someone else in the 1988 national election, while 32 percent said they did not vote or did not qualify to vote.[105] More than half of the American Mennonite survey respondents said their political preference was the Republican Party: 46 percent identified themselves as Republican Party conservatives, and 8 percent said they were Republican Party liberals. On the other hand, 19 percent identified themselves with the Democratic Party, almost evenly divided between liberals and conservatives in the party. Another 3 percent said they were Independent, or preferred some other party, and 23 percent said they take no position at all.[106]

MCC Washington workers recognize that the voting patterns of their constituent bodies differ from their own positions on many issues. "Because a very substantial percentage of the people in our churches consider themselves Republican, we still have that reality to understand and relate to," Franz observed during the time he directed the office. "That still has some frustrations for some of us, of course, but I think we try to be understanding, patient, affirmative, as best we can, to keep the doors of communication open."[107]

The strong Mennonite support for the Republican Party and its positions is especially remarkable when combined with another figure from the Kauffman and Driedger survey: 72 percent of the respondents said they favor the work of the MCC offices in Washington and Ottawa.[108] It is possible that many constituents are unaware of the work of the offices. Or constituents may suppose that the Washington office seeks to be consistent with the social concerns of the faith tradition, and therefore support its work, even though they vote differently. Some critics suggest that Mennonites, whatever their faith commitments, vote with their pocketbooks, like most Americans. In an article entitled "Why U.S. Mennonites Talk Democrat But Vote Republican," one former General Conference Mennonite pastor said the issue boils down to one's philosophy of government. "The Republican philosophy about government and its role in the life of its citizenry is more compatible with the Mennonite way of thinking and its history than the Democratic approach," he contends. "A fundamental difference between Democrats and Republicans is their understanding of the amount of influence the government should have in people's lives. Simply put, Democrats believe that the government should play a central and active role in citizens' lives, whereas most Republicans believe that the role of government should be secondary to the initiative of the individual. . . . Like good Republicans, most Mennonites are suspicious of government. A book on Mennonite politics could appropriately use the same title as our well-known cookbook: *More With Less.*"[109] The author goes on to explain that Mennonites have never been able to watch human beings suffer for long, as is evident from their relief and disaster programs. However, he claims Mennonite-sponsored social programs "reveal an implicit belief in people's ability to help each other and themselves without government help." Mennonite Disaster Service and other MCC programs are "living testimony of the redemptive actions that can take place when people, not their legislators, take the initiative."

Sociologist Driedger offers another theory for Mennonites' political conservatism: their early roots prompted them to "play it safe" with governments.

They were in the middle politically—a very precarious position to be. Their radical religious stand did not permit them to compromise; they had few opportunities to become involved in political processes until recently; their radical religious convictions were often strongly expressed, thus leading to many schisms; their delegations to governments sought to gain privileges for their own group, but seldom included appeals for the welfare of others; and their long rural isolation and conservatism often made them irrelevant politically. Indeed, politically they became very inexperienced and conservative.[110]

While the reasons for and origins of Mennonite social and political positions may be debatable, the actual voting patterns are more apparent.

Most legislative aides who know Mennonites only through the MCC Washington office, the churches' most public face, would be surprised to learn of denominational members' political leanings.[111] While a number of Mennonites have more conservative political leanings, there is no *rightist* Mennonite voice comparable to MCC Washington in the capital, nor is there strong evidence that the most fundamentalist Mennonites have dramatically increased their political involvement in recent decades. Kauffman and Driedger acknowledge that the overall shift in voting patterns in the denominations is slightly in the conservative direction, based on comparisons between a 1972 survey and the one completed in 1989.[112] However, the sociologists also report that those scoring higher on their fundamentalism scale tend to be *less* active politically than those low on the scale. James Davison Hunter has noted the increased political activism of conservative groups in recent decades, suggesting that evangelicals have a greater commitment to political activism than all other groups.[113] Mennonite ultraconservatives may counter the trend Hunter traces because of their rigid two-kingdom theological framework. Assuming they are faithfully representing the separatist spirit of early Anabaptism, they hold firm to the belief that Mennonites ought not be engaged in the political realm.[114]

MCC Washington clearly does not represent the views of these ultraconservative Mennonites, who generally are not in *denominational* leadership positions even though they are influential in congregations and the denominations themselves.[115] Nor does it consistently advocate for the positions its conservative Republican constituents would embrace. Nor, for quite different reasons, does the office represent its most radical constituents, who have given up on working through official government structures.[116] In most cases persons in each of these categories would not be in official leadership roles in the larger Mennonite denominations.

Occasionally an inside observer will note the distance between those working in various denominational offices and those in the pew. In his 1951 text on church lobbying, Luke Ebersole says, "As agents of the churches rather than representatives, church lobbyists promote the causes in which groups of church leaders are interested rather than the views of church members in general."[117] In Dwight King's 1966 report on the possibility of Mennonites starting an office in Washington, he writes: "If and when the office becomes a podium for prophetic voice to government, there is considerable concern that it should speak for the Mennonite church and not a few thinkers/leaders/specialists who have a vision of what the church and its message should be."[118] But already in 1969, just after the MCC Washington office opened, one critic argues, "During the last five to ten years there has been, in my opinion, a tremendous gap between the position and pronouncements of the leadership of the Mennonite church and that of the lay members."[119] A decade later an ad-hoc group of pastors and lay persons, meeting in Smoketown, Pennsylvania, decried the "widening gap in the Mennonite Church between the people who are doing the talking and the people in the pews."[120]

Social theorists also have commented on this gap in the mainline churches, sometimes attributing the division to education.[121] Among Mennonites, the split between denominational leaders and lay persons is sometimes apparent, although it does not always break down along educational lines. On the issue of political involvement, some Mennonite persons who are quite educated, and educated in liberal institutions, share views with less erudite members. Regardless of the cause for the split, however, such divergence can lessen the impact of those seeking to influence political processes in Washington.

MCC Washington already is working with a constituent base of fewer than 250,000 in the United States, so the appearance that it is not representing its denominational members could be detrimental to its effectiveness in Washington. "There aren't a hell of a lot of Mennonites up in Boston," explains Jim McGovern, press secretary for Rep. John Joseph "Joe" Moakley (D-Massachusetts). "With the U.S. Catholic Conference you have to think twice if you're going to disagree with them. We're not going to lose our election if we disagree with the Mennonites."[122] Legislative aide Marty Rendon contends that MCC is a power in Washington, and its work is respected but he believes it is perceived as an "inside the Beltway" kind of group. "It may help if there were a sense of Mennonites across the country who would write in and say, 'I am a member of the Mennonite church, or I support the work of the Mennonite Central Committee in Washington,'" suggests Rendon. "I think it might be more useful if there was a sense that [MCC] represented a grassroots constituency. Who are these people speaking for other than an informed opinion based on conscience and faith? Who are these people back home?"[123]

Based on the 72 percent of Mennonites who said they support the work of the Washington and Ottawa offices, we must presume that the majority of constituents feel represented in the capital offices. MCC's Earl Martin credits Franz with gaining respect for the office over its several decades. "I think Delton is a very careful communicator. He's just not reckless," observes Martin. "Some of us younger types with hotter blood would have opted for a bit more recklessness or a bit more of an unvarnished approach, but I think Delton has really seen the importance of not having the office become an orphan from the Mennonite church."[124]

Many of the office's constituents must realize that although the MCC office, in the broadest sense, represents them, it does not always represent their self-interests. Susan Goering, formerly chairperson of MCC's U.S. Peace Section and now a board member on MCC U.S., says representation is a function of which *interests* an office represents, not just which *people* it represents. "If we were talking about just representing our interests . . . boy, it would be a very different message [than we have now], because our interests would be with an unjust system that favors rich or middle-class North Americans," she contends. "I hope that [MCC Washington] represents our faith perspective as we best understand it. The Washington office shouldn't be for the economic interests or even the social welfare interests of Mennonites."[125]

On a few occasions over the years MCC Washington has been asked by Mennonite denominations or agencies to make political contacts that would benefit them directly. Franz expressed an uneasiness with these requests. In his presentations on the office's work, he often admitted that in earlier centuries, and in the first part of this century, Mennonites usually only addressed governments when their own religious freedoms were threatened. In the late 1970s, MCC Washington and MCC Ottawa did assist with an appeal from six hundred Old Colony Mennonites who were illegal aliens in Seminole, Texas, and Boley, Oklahoma.[126] The Mennonites, who had come to the United States from Mexico, were scheduled to be deported after they had purchased land in the states where they had settled. In a report submitted by MCC Akron, MCC acknowledges its discomfort with what might appear to be a special request based on self-interest: "It may seem unusual to make an appeal like this to the Congress of the United States. However, MCC in its 50-year history has been involved in a wide variety of refugee and immigration work. Even now it is working with refugees from Southeast Asia, with Hispanics who want to obtain immigrant status in the United States, and with some who are able to receive permission to leave the Soviet Union. Thus, the appeal is made not in the belief that Mennonites deserve special consideration but on the ground of the unique dimensions of the difficult situation in which these particular people find themselves."[127] Much to MCC's chagrin, after the Mennonite colony was granted residency, a lawyer told the commissioner of the U.S. Immigration and Naturalization Service, "I know how we can solve the problem of illegal aliens. Get them all to become Mennonites."[128] MCC Washington seeks to avoid such perceptions of representing self-interests.

If the Mennonites' Washington office does not represent Mennonite self-interests, nor even the political views of some of its constituents, whom does it represent? This question became especially acute during the 1993–95 national debates about health care reform. During that period, MCC Washington was not the only Mennonite organization "lobbying" in Washington. Mennonite Mutual Aid, an insurance and financial services agency, also made its own legislative contacts, hiring a professional "consultant" in Washington and spending more than MCC Washington's entire annual budget on its health care lobbying efforts. This is the first time two Mennonite agencies have, in effect, lobbied against each other on Capitol Hill, or at least provided such confusing "Mennonite" messages to legislators. On occasion MCC Washington would contact a key legislator, only to be told by an aide that the office already had spoken with "the Mennonites" about health care reform. MCC Washington was supporting a single-payer plan, while Mennonite Mutual Aid was asking for an exemption from whatever regional health alliances might be arranged so it could continue serving its Mennonite constituents as a fraternal benefits organization. Eventually the two agencies released a joint statement stressing the points on which they agreed, including such things as providing a basic level of care for all persons and recognizing limits.[129]

Most MCC staffers acknowledge that in personal contacts and sign-ons they represent the Washington office or the larger Mennonite Central Committee organization. As with most other denominational lobbying offices in the capital, MCC Washington has permission to formally advocate only for positions on which their parent organization or constituent denominations have official statements or policy. Prior to a 1982 change in the office's guidelines, personnel technically were restricted from communicating views to government officials unless instructed to do so by MCC or one of the denominations under its umbrella. The guidelines were updated and modestly revised in 1982. The principal adjustment in the revised guidelines reads: "Without pretending to speak for all Mennonites, the office may convey to government officials the peace and justice concerns of the Mennonite constituencies as reflected in the consensus of representatives to the U.S. Peace Section and other MCC bodies."[130] The change in guidelines was an acknowledgment and approval of the office's evolving practice.

In conversations and written articles, MCC Washington staffers repeatedly stress their concern for the poor and oppressed. "I think of my first constituency personally as folks within the jurisdiction of the criminal justice system, the environment, people of color, and impoverished people," remarks one employee. "I believe the constituent churches of MCC are also my constituents and I am their representative, but I definitely don't feel like the views I convey to members of Congress or their staff are necessarily representative of our constituency."[131] Franz's Washington Memo cover articles and presentations on the office often spoke of "acting with and on behalf of the oppressed," or effectively translating "the concerns of Jesus and the prophets for the poor and oppressed," or "lifting up the downtrodden, defending the weak, and protecting those who are vulnerable."

The language is far from unique for MCC Washington. Most of the office's Methodist Building peers use similar language to describe their primary goals or their constituencies. Partly by virtue of its embedment in an international service and relief organization, however, the Mennonites' lobbying office may have closer contacts with the disinherited, downtrodden, and oppressed for whom staffers advocate. Persons with whom Mennonite Central Committee service volunteers work, both domestically and overseas, become their primary resources, and in many ways, their primary constituents. Titus Peachey claims that increasingly the office represents those people in North America and overseas who are "deeply impacted by decisions that are made in Washington, D.C., and whom our workers become aware of and who have no voice back here." Peachey notes that there are times when MCC's two constituencies—its Mennonite supporters and the persons for whom MCC advocates—are almost contradictory or in tension.[132] Still, MCC Washington takes its cues, especially on its international agenda, from the organization's personnel on the ground in Third World countries and elsewhere. The following chapter will examine more closely the impact these working relationships have on the functioning of MCC's Washington office, and on the Washington legislative processes.

It would be impossible for the MCC Washington office to represent fully the diverse concerns and viewpoints of its Mennonite constituencies spread across the country. In contrast to many of their lobbying peers, the Mennonite staffers instead seek to represent the poor and oppressed. This, the Mennonite workers believe, is also a way of representing the best of their theological-ethical traditions. On occasion, speaking for and with "the poor and oppressed" appears to be an unsubstantiated rhetorical claim, for MCC and for other religious advocates. But broader connections into the worlds of those harmfully affected by U.S. policy help legitimate that claim.

ADVOCATING AS "INSIDERS"

MCC Washington, like most of the other religious advocacy offices in the capital, spends most of its time and energy on "outsider methods" of advocacy. Rather than making extensive contacts with legislators, the State Department, or the White House, Mennonite staffers monitor the federal government and encourage their constituents to respond. The *effectiveness* of constituent mobilization—when constituents actually respond—may be one reason religious organizations in Washington devote much of their efforts to contacts with their members and congregations. Legislative aide Bill Tate notes, "I pay a lot more attention to *constituent* contacts than a letter we would get from a national organization. I don't mean to say that MCC and these other groups are, what shall I say, predictable, but there are themes in which they're interested in which they have positions which are long-standing with which I'm familiar." Tate believes that "the role of the national offices is more in introducing us, or facilitating an office like ours, in getting in touch with constituents."[133] Other legislative aides agreed that contacts from "the folks back home" have considerably more impact than those from the Washington-based lobbying offices. Drumming up responses from the grassroots, even if these include only a few letters, generally has more impact on legislators than a letter or sign-on from national organizations, who may or may not represent lawmakers' constituents' views.

Political scientist Hofrenning suggests that religious lobbyists also prefer indirect lobbying—which involves informing their publics about *general* legislative goals and actions—over direct lobbying partly because working with specific legislative language often involves some form of compromise. Religious lobbyists, contends Hofrenning, are not willing to make the compromises necessary in the give-and-take of policy making.[134] Hertzke says insider lobbying is "mundane, technical, incremental, and does not lend itself to prophetic stands." Hertzke confirms that unwillingness to compromise is one reason religious lobbyists do not function well with "insider" methods.[135] He also adds a laundry list of reasons religious advocacy organizations are weak at the operational level: modest staffs of from three to eight full-time employees; insufficient focus, since "ethically minded, socially concerned religious leaders are tempted to take stands on a multitude of issues"; and lack of assertiveness in expanding access on the Hill.

Hertzke and Hofrenning are correct that religious lobbyists, including MCC, are generally unwilling or unable to work effectively as insiders in the political climate of competing interests, where compromise is part of the game.[136] That means the church advocates work only episodically "inside" the halls of Congress. The religious-advocacy organizations may come closest to insider strategies in their participation in coalitions with other humanitarian groups in the capital. In these working groups and task forces, issues are focused enough that members can devote time and attention to specific legislation. In the alliances, coalitions' paid staffers initiate most of the contacts with legislators regarding changes in bill language. Religious advocates then follow up the insider contacts on designated lobby days, with several church representatives visiting two or three key members of Congress to voice their support of the legislation or of specific alterations. MCC Washington itself does not routinely propose amendments to congressional bills, nor does it seek sponsorship of particular legislation. Conscription issues are one exception to this general rule, but even on this issue Mennonites' work is done in conjunction with other offices, especially the National Interreligious Service Board for Conscientious Objectors. The National Campaign for a Peace Tax Fund, which appears to be another exception because of its close connections with the Mennonite office, receives the support of MCC Washington but does not fall under its jurisdiction. Marian Claassen Franz, executive director of the National Campaign, aggressively pursues both outsider and insider methods to seek passage of the bill.

Another insider lobbying strategy is creating coalitions to impact specific legislation. MCC Washington has participated in forming politically powerful coalitions such as Churches for Middle East Peace. Founded in 1984, the organization is able to work inside congressional channels by concentrating its energies on specific regional issues. Insider methods also include waiting in rooms adjacent to the House and Senate floors and feeding information to senators and representatives during legislative debates. MCC Washington staffers usually are not among the lobbyists standing in the House and Senate wings. On more than twenty occasions, they have arranged for Mennonites to testify at congressional hearings on legislation about which they are concerned; these have included hearings on conscription, the U.S. Peace Tax Fund, capital punishment, world hunger, victims of crime, a nuclear weapons freeze, Vietnam, the West Bank, and the Philippines. Overall, though, Mennonite Central Committee has never functioned as an insider lobby. Some of the office's younger staffers, in their work on domestic issues, express more willingness to engage in the compromise necessary to effect meaningful, even if incremental, change. However, such a shift is unlikely, given the present orientation and constraints of the office.

Certainly MCC, as well as its peers, regularly makes known its views on legislation under consideration, but this is not so much insider lobbying as "witnessing." Most of the letters that MCC Washington signs on to and most of its legislative and executive branch visits could be classified as witnessing, which means that staff members do not engage the legislative process in a sustained and detailed manner. Staffers say they spend only 10 to 15 per-cent of their time in direct conversation with government personnel.[137] In one representative year Mennonite workers reported signing on to fifty-four coalition letters and writing eight letters of their own. Their personal letters, all on international issues that year, were sent to a total of 110 congressional offices. During the year MCC Washington personnel also made twenty-nine phone calls, clustered around three legislative actions, to congressional offices. In addition, they made one hundred congressional visits, most of them along with other coalition members, on issues from assault weapons to U.S. policy on Zaire. And, perhaps most important, they facilitated eleven sets of gov-ernment appointments for MCC personnel to visit congressional offices and State Department personnel, and two sets of appointments for con-stituent delegations. That year, like most years, they did not have any ap-pointments at the White House. MCC Washington, along with most other Methodist Building lobbying offices, was virtually shut out of the White House during the presidencies of Ronald Reagan and George Bush. Delton Franz said Jimmy Carter freely invited in the church organizations during his four years there, but during the following twelve years the opportunities to speak directly with the president or his aides were virtually nil.[138]

STILL THE QUIET

MCC Washington staffers, directors of other religious lobbying organizations, and legislative aides agree that MCC's style in Washington has been rather consistently low key. Because Franz oversaw the office's work during its initial decades and has been its longest-term public representative, it is difficult to separate out his personal style from that of the office. It is ironic that Franz, whose office reflected the Mennonite transformation *away* from being "the Quiet in the Land," was most often described by his peers as "quiet." Under Franz's leadership, perhaps *die Stillen im Lande* simply became *die Stillen in der Stadt* ("the Quiet in the City").[139] Robert Tiller, head of the American Baptist Church's Capitol Hill office, described Franz as "introverted," "very quiet," and "not as verbal as some of us."[140] The UCC's Jay Lintner characterized MCC's work, during the Franz years at least, as "cautious." "MCC has a dis-tinctive voice," he observed. "And a very *soft* voice."[141] Franz responded, "I am by temperament, I think, fairly low-key and I don't rush into very many initiatives with a gangbuster approach. I'm sort of a gradualist, I guess."[142]

One legislative aide, who is somewhat critical of religious lobbyists in the Methodist Building as well as of career politicians and aides, states, "I've come to the conclusion that people's minds alter—regardless of their politi-cal persuasion—when they are inside the Beltway too long. People lose a sense of reality here. It's not good."[143] Most observers agreed that, even though Franz worked in Washington for more than a quarter century, he managed to avoid being fully transformed by his work context, a fact that delighted some and confounded others. "Even though he's been inside the Beltway for [twenty-six] years, you'd never know it," said MCC Washington staffer Jalane Schmidt. "He hasn't picked up that slickness that some people find necessary to survive here. I think a lot of the reason some Mennonite constituents have a positive opinion of the office is because of him."[144] Staffer Keith Gingrich claims that he often found himself wanting to be more aggressive, but that he understood Franz's reluctance to be more pushy since Franz came "out of a period when [MCC Washington staff] had to walk very gingerly to not upset the constituency's apple cart."[145]

One might have expected that Franz would have adapted to the demands of Washington's lobbying culture, picking up the "slickness" of secular lobbyists or taking on the more aggressive, sometimes confrontational, occasionally sanctimonious style of some religious lobbyists. Certainly Franz was not alone in his conciliatory manner. Jean Schrag Lauver, a Republican professional staff member for the Senate Committee on Environment and Public Works, says many of the organizations in the Methodist Building have a "refreshing" lobbying style, in contrast to the religious right and secular lobbyists. "It's very clear that other lobbyists want something, or they let you know that if this or that isn't done, there will be consequences," observes Schrag Lauver. "The low-key approach is appreciated and is very different from what we're used to."[146]

Still, MCC's Franz appeared to take nonaggressiveness beyond the call of duty. His lobbying manner may have been largely a result of his self-described introversion. This "outside the Beltway" style, however, also seemed to be a conscious choice, rooted in his Anabaptist-Mennonite faith tradition, which has stressed humility, or *Gelassenheit* (yieldedness), over making demands of political leaders.[147] Whatever the source, legislative aides with whom MCC Washington works have taken notice. "Many lobbyists who represent foreign governments or other causes tend to be sort of aggressive and pushy," contends Tim Trenkle, legislative aide on Africa for Sen. Nancy Kassebaum (R-Kansas). "MCC is very low-key, not pushy, and it's nice because it's—I don't know how to phrase this—quiet, and allows you to sort of ask your questions of the person."[148] "They're certainly not confrontational," agrees legislative aide Marty Rendon. "They sort of present the facts, let you know what's going on. They're not strident. They don't have a chip on their shoulder."[149] Another legislative aide observes, "They're not pushy, but they're not wallflowers, either. . . . It's kind of a quiet, reserved style, but very determined."[150]

Bill Tate echoes others' observations about Franz and other MCC Washington personnel. "I don't know what goes on in their inner life, but there is a gentleness and respect for others that is exhibited in their outer life that makes them more effective than others we deal with—people who come in and say, 'It's our position or be damned.' Mennonites might think that, but they don't say that."[151] Speaking eloquently about the tensions of life in Washington, Tate continues:

> MCC is very good at non-confrontational lobbying, and I think that's essential. The use of coercion, whether it is through money, which is the bane of this world, or through the spiritual coercion that some groups use . . . I feel that's very destructive to the process. And I think Mennonites are better at avoiding that than any other group. I think it is that element of graciousness that is increasingly missing from our life here in all of its aspects. It's not a superficial thing. It's not simply a matter of tone. I don't mean to overstate the case, but we're not doing well right now at the moment in governing ourselves. And the reason we're not is that we don't respect one another enough. We confuse people with whom we differ as being evil or stupid instead of simply being different, and we can't find ways to communicate across these differences and in the process find a common ground. I think that the one thing that is essential, the one thing that is necessary if one is wanting to be a putative Christian, is that the end or ends *never* justify the means. And I think the Mennonites keep that in mind better than anyone else. There is not enough respect for the processes of governance, and I've always sensed from Delton and the Mennonites we've dealt with a respect for the processes we're all engaged in. It *is* possible for very principled people to disagree deeply about certain subjects. The Mennonites will grant you that. And it is not a small thing.[152]

Tate remembers a contact he had with Franz during congressional deliberations about authorizing force for the Persian Gulf War. He says Rep. Leach and his office staff reviewed treatises on just war theory before finally, with great difficulty, deciding to vote to authorize the use of force to push Iraqi troops out of Kuwait. Tate claims that of the many contacts he had with religious lobbyists opposed to the war during that period, Franz and the Mennonites he brought with him were the one group he "didn't feel judged by."[153]

Franz's graciousness, while appreciated by the legislative aides and by many Mennonites, also frustrated others. MCC board member Susan Goering accompanied Franz and other Mennonite denominational leaders on their 5 March 1991 visits to congressional offices.[154] Most of the fighting in the war had ceased by that point, but the inter-Mennonite delegation hoped to express compassion for war sufferers. Goering, Franz, and the five

Immediately following the Persian Gulf War, MCC Washington Director Delton Franz accompanied a delegation of Mennonite leaders on visits to White House, State Department, and legislative offices to express compassion for Iraqi war sufferers. The March 1991 delegation included, left to right, Vern Preheim, General Conference Mennonite Church general secretary; Arthur Jost, Mennonite Brethren Conference representative; Vernon Wiebe, Mennonite Brethren representative; Susan Goering, MCC U.S. Peace Section chair and General Conference Mennonite Church representative; Owen E. Burkholder, Mennonite Church General Board member; and James M. Lapp, Mennonite Church executive secretary. Photo by Delton Franz, courtesy of MCC Washington.

Mennonite denominational leaders met with White House and State Department officials, as well as with thirteen senators and representatives with large Mennonite constituencies. Goering, a lawyer who works with the American Civil Liberties Union in Baltimore, Maryland, remarks that she was struck that Franz and other church leaders were being kind to "these officials who had done nothing to stop the war and had been in cahoots with a government that had committed terribly outrageous and immoral acts there." This kindness is in stark contrast to Goering's secular work with the ACLU, she notes. "What I've found to be effective in the secular world is a more demanding posture," says Goering.

From what I've gathered, we [MCC] go at it in a different way. I mean, the Mennonites take great pride, and MCC especially takes great pride, in not being like the rest of the world in this respect, and being respectful of the individuals they are speaking to, being deferential, and trying to speak the truth in a quiet way. I don't even know that it's calculated. My sense is that the church leaders' response that day wasn't a strategy. This is the way they treat people in their lives, and they weren't treating these people any differently. But these men came from all different parts of the country and aren't used to speaking to government anyway. But when it comes to MCC, where there is more frequent contact with the government, I suspect there's more thought given to it, and that decisions have been made that we don't operate like people in the secular world—being demanding, going to the press, and sort of leveraging and playing our strong suit and all that, a kind of gamesmanship. And I think there's a conscious decision to not engage in that.[155]

Goering contends that while "the truth was spoken that day," she felt frustrated. "The difficulty for me was feeling very ineffective, like people were going to forget about us the next day. This egregious wrong had been done, and here we were stuck being ineffective." Goering also thought the legislators were being patronizing to the church leaders, "sort of patting them on the back and saying, 'We hear your concerns.'"

Goering speaks for a number of young, politically engaged Mennonites who are pushing at MCC's boundaries on the question of "speaking the truth in a *quiet* way." As is clear from her remarks—which are based on her experience both with the ACLU and MCC—Goering recognizes that not operating like "people in the secular world" has been, in part, a conscious choice on the part of Franz and others. Whether or not this choice usually results in greater or lesser effectiveness remains an open question. And, for some within the Mennonite churches—including Goering—it may not be the most important question.

Rarely do any of the church lobbies know whether they are being effective in any direct or immediate sense. Most of them, though—including MCC Washington—continue plugging away on Capitol Hill, at the State Department, and at the White House, hoping to be *faithful* if not *effective*. In many ways, the religious lobbies—those on the right and those on the left—work in similar ways: they monitor legislative and policy activity; they seek to mobilize their constituencies with newsletters and special alerts; they speak directly to elected and appointed officials; and they write letters, either independently or in partnership with others. Part of "being faithful" means communicating with U.S. government leaders about legislation and policies that religious lobbyists believe harm persons, both in this country and elsewhere around the world.

It is these harmed persons whom many left-of-center religious lobby-ists say they represent. The gospel, and the desire to legitimate their pacifist witness, drove twentieth-century Mennonites into action among suffering persons overseas and in the United States. In turn, living and working along-side these oppressed persons drove Mennonites to Washington to speak for those affected by U.S. policy or to help them find their voice. Over the years, then, and especially since the establishment of MCC Washington, Mennonites have moved dramatically toward "rationalizing" their lobbying efforts. Still, both by design and by the constraints of their traditions, Men-nonites remain perhaps less strategically sophisticated—by most objective lobbying standards—than many other religious lobbyists. Formerly *quiet* Mennonites still are perceived as *soft-spoken* proponents of peace and justice on Capitol Hill. Whether this is an asset or a liability—a kind of wisdom or foolishness, a form of innocence or simply naiveté—is a complex question. Legislative aides express their appreciation for MCC Washington's respect for them and their work. Some Mennonite critics may say staffers are avoiding their calling to be prophetic, while others may be pleased. What is impor-tant here is to note that Mennonite lobbying is sometimes differentiated from some of the practices of other offices with similar mandates.

MCC Washington has maintained strong ties back into its parent organiza-tion, which is linked to diverse Mennonites across North America and the world. Frequently, through letters or congregational visits or Washington semi-nars, MCC personnel hear directly from their constituents. Partly because the office has *not* become autonomous, it and its staffers continue to embody strands of the Mennonite traditions. "Not doing violence," whether through physical or verbal attacks, seems to be one of the guiding principles of MCC Washington's work. At the same time, Mennonites in Washington seek pas-sionately to reduce the violences attributable, in part, to their government.

"There are so many groups lobbying on Capitol Hill, and to pick some-one out of the crowd, or to get noticed in the crowd is difficult," states legislative aide Schrag Lauver. "You don't want to be like everyone else on the Hill—if you are, you'll never get noticed. You'll only be one more group shrilling at Congress. A different approach is what gets their attention."[156] In *small* ways, and in *some* settings in Washington, MCC has been different enough to capture the attention of persons and agencies making life-and-death decisions in the capital. What is perhaps most striking about MCC Washington's work is its regular practice of taking itinerating volunteers and overseas nationals through congressional and State Department offices. Here we can see most clearly the intermingling of service and politics.

5

REPORTING FROM THE FIELD

In trying to be faithful to the Great Commission, [Mennonites] have been forced into painful awareness of just how pervasive and determinative are the actions (or neglects) of government in affecting the lives of people we care about, next door or across town or around the world. It's not a partisan political act when overseas missionaries or service workers seek hearings with Congresspersons to testify about human rights or African famine, but an expression of justice and mercy. . . . It's simply been the result of efforts to respond faithfully to the needs of suffering human beings whom we have encountered in the amazing expansion of our mission and service activity.

—*John Richard Burkholder, "Talking Back"*

Perhaps more so than many other religious lobbies in Washington, Mennonite Central Committee's Capitol Hill office is rather directly "wired to the world." By virtue of being under the umbrella of a service and relief organization, the advocacy office has access to the perspectives of more than nine hundred workers in some fifty countries around the globe.[1] This interconnectedness with others throughout the world deeply affects the message and the messengers at MCC Washington, giving the office a distinctive character in a highly charged political setting where many voices seek a hearing. Working alongside those persons "on the ground" who are affected by U.S. policy provides MCC with difficult-to-obtain information often not otherwise accessible to legislators, who are eager for accurate and credible international reports. From its inception in 1968, Capitol Hill staffers have drawn on the national and international human resources available to them from the organization's headquarters in Akron, Pennsylvania. No doubt MCC Washington's "effectiveness" also has been bolstered by the strong reputation of its parent organization's service work.

A recent MCC brochure states: "As Mennonite Central Committee workers serve around the world, they often find that the human needs they work to meet—such as poverty, hunger, poor health and education—are caused by governments' political decisions and actions. Because of this, MCC sometimes calls on governments to change policies that harm people. . . . Relief and development work can be ineffective if the conditions that first created the needs—war, debt, greed, selfishness, materialism—are not addressed."[2] It was these contacts with suffering people in the United States and overseas that contributed to the opening of MCC Washington and that continue to give the office substance.

Former director Delton Franz contends that the degrees to which MCC Washington and its constituency can have an impact on Capitol Hill ought not be overestimated nor discounted. While votes, letters, campaign dollars, and industry contracts are one measurement by which change is enacted in the nation's capital, that is not MCC's contribution, explains Franz. "If we have a voice and an experience to convey, it should be out of our identification with the victims of war, of poverty, hunger and oppression," he says. "And it should be out of our concern for those who may yet become victims of an arms race, of economic exploitation and the destruction of the earth's ecosystem. This suggests the imperative of our coordinating the gifts, the calls, the experiences and the unique insights and exposure that our personnel and our constituents have as a result of the many locations in which we labor."[3] During his tenure in Washington, Franz often reiterated that the MCC Washington staff was never envisioned to function as Mennonites' principal spokesperson to government: the staff's role is to monitor and interpret, and to facilitate the voice of their constituency and MCC personnel. "The vacuum that continues to hinder many members of Congress and administration personnel, especially with respect to Third World countries and domestic poverty areas, is an accurate perception of the causal factors and the linkage of those factors to U.S. economic, political and military policy," argues Franz. That, he adds, is where some of MCC's service workers periodically can make meaningful contributions, facilitated by the Washington staff.[4]

MAKING THE CONNECTIONS

These "reports from the field" are where MCC Washington makes a contribution in Washington, and where it has the most impact, agree office staffers, their lobbying peers, and the legislative aides with whom they speak. At times these reports are communicated by MCC Washington staff passing on relevant information, gleaned from MCC workers or their associates, to appropriate government officials. For example, in October 1992 MCC Washington staffer Ken Martens Friesen wrote to Sen. Nancy Kassebaum (R-Kansas), stating that MCC has received "disturbing information concerning events taking place in southern Sudan." Those providing the information had written to MCC Washington just after the Sudanese government expelled them and other foreigners from Juba, Sudan. The MCC staffer then cites four paragraphs from the report, which provides detailed information about various fighting factions, dynamics in the conflict, and the unavailability of adequate food supplies. Friesen concludes by stating that this report and others noting the abduction, torture, and death of foreign-aid workers in southern Sudan, "trouble us greatly." Friesen continues, "We wish to express our concern for the increasingly violent situation in southern Sudan and encourage you to seek ways of promoting a peaceful end to the conflict in the region."[5]

On other occasions field reports simply provide MCC Washington advocates with the information they need to take a particular position. Washington staffers are careful that their public stances are consistent with what their field workers are saying, especially on volatile and complex issues such as military aid for Central America or using U.S. military power to provide security for food shipments to Somalia. Capitol Hill staffers are in regular contact with Akron-based MCC administrators, who keep in close touch with MCC's service workers. During the nongovernmental organization debates about military intervention in Somalia, Franz and Friesen were on the phone frequently with Eric J. Olfert, MCC's co-secretary for Africa. MCC Washington staffers provided facilitating services for Olfert to speak directly with other NGOs in Washington about MCC's concerns.

On-the-ground reports also are communicated directly to government officials. When articulate, politically concerned service workers assigned to one of the world's many "trouble spots" return from their overseas assignments, MCC Washington sometimes channels them through the State Department or other administration and congressional offices.[6] Usually an MCC Washington staffer accompanies field workers to their governmental appointments, but allows those with firsthand experience to do most of the speaking. At times these service workers give their reports when they are back for short-term North American assignments or sabbaticals, and then they follow up again later when they return more permanently from overseas. MCC's Akron office often suggests certain persons for Washington itineration. The Washington office also has made broad direct contacts of its own, with the approval of Akron headquarters. In 1984 Franz and other staffers wrote to MCC's country representatives, encouraging them to "try to decide whether you, or another MCC person in your country, should seek to communicate with U.S. officials or Members of Congress about any aspect of American military or economic involvement in your country." They add:

> Many of you scattered throughout 51 countries, are in a better position than most of us to see effects of U.S. and other foreign involvement in the world. Here in the Washington Office we have learned that most U.S. Members of Congress who vote on foreign military and economic aid also have an inadequate sense of the situation on the ground in the Chads, the Jordans, and the El Salvadors of the world. Perhaps there is, in some instances, a positive ministry for our vast network of MCC workers to express concern about the real impact of this foreign aid. . . . It is our belief from the Washington perspective that various legislators here have respect for the authentic grassroots involvements of Mennonites around the world.[7]

Another effort at making contact with MCC workers in the field took place in 1990 and 1991. Franz remarks in a 1990 memo that Washington office staffers "have the sense that we are not adequately connecting with many of our MCC alumni with significant 'on-the-ground' exposure to a wide range of domestic and overseas realities." Franz states that while MCC staffers recognize that coming to Washington or responding to *Hotlines* may not be a "calling" for every MCC worker, they assume many would identify with the biblical concept of being "advocates" with and on behalf of the victims of poverty, violence, and injustice.[8]

In at least one case, an MCC worker in Central America spent *nine months* in Washington doing advocacy work about the region where he had extensive experience.[9] Because of MCC's close ties with other Mennonite and Brethren in Christ mission and service agencies, both administratively in North America and overseas in cooperative efforts, MCC Washington also can draw on the larger mission pool represented by these organizations. In addition, on a number of occasions, the Washington staffers have scheduled appointments with visiting nationals whom MCC workers know from their contacts abroad. Also, MCC administrators based in the Akron office travel frequently to where their workers are placed in Africa, the Middle and Far East, Eastern Europe, South and Central America, and elsewhere. When they return from trips with new information relevant for legislators or the State Department, they also make a stop in Washington for a set of appointments with appropriate government officials.

Appointments with government leaders vary considerably, but a typical day in Washington for visiting MCC personnel may include conversations with six to eight influential or sympathetic persons. For example, in 1987 Franz scheduled a one-day visit for John Paul Lederach, then an MCC worker in Central America; Andrew Shogreen, superintendent of the Nicaraguan Moravian Church; and Rich Sider, MCC's Central America administrator in Akron. The day began with a meeting with Ruben Robles, deputy chief of mission at the Costa Rican embassy, followed by a conversation with Ronald Goddard, Central America director for the State Department. Six other appointments scheduled throughout the day were with legislative aides for Sen. Tim Wirth (D-Colorado), Rep. Dan Glickman (D-Kansas), Rep. David Skaggs (D-Colorado), Rep. Pat Schroeder (D-Colorado), Sen. John Kerrey (D-Maine), Sen. Edward Kennedy (D-Maine), Sen. Tom Harkin (D-Iowa), Rep. Tom Foley (D-Washington), Sen. Arlen Specter (R-Pennsylvania), and Sen. Nancy Kassebaum. Foley was House majority leader, Specter served on the Intelligence Committee, and Kassebaum was on the Foreign Relations Committee. In some cases the aides simply asked questions and took notes, and in others they made commitments to work at MCC's concerns. Kennedy's staff person said he would draft a letter for three key senators to sign, and then have it hand-carried within forty-eight hours to key official contacts in Managua, Nicaragua, urging them "to not drop the mediation ball." At the time MCC's Lederach, whose family had been threatened because of his work,[10] was involved in mediation between Sandinista government leaders and Nicaraguan Miskito Contra leaders.[11]

In August 1976, Franz arranged for an extensive set of appointments for LeRoy Friesen, who recently had returned from his MCC assignment in the Middle East. Friesen was in Washington for six days, considerably longer than most other service workers, and had meetings with a State Department official, White House staff member, three members of Congress, twenty-two congressional staff persons, seven Jewish organization leaders, and a variety of church personnel. "The significant (five-year) exposure of Friesen to a broad spectrum of Palestinian, PLO, and Israeli leaders and MCC's 26 years in West Bank lent credence to his analysis," claims Franz, "particularly because it is filtered through his perceptions as a Mennonite (not an Arab or Jew) representing an agency whose involvement in the Middle East is based on *humanitarian* Christian service, rather than *political* objectives." Franz contends that Friesen's "candid and thorough documentation of the violation of human rights in West Bank, his insightful analysis of the PLO, and his balancing statements confirming Israel's right to exist as a state, created respect for him and MCC as a credible interpreter of the Israeli–Palestinian conflict."[12]

The Washington office schedules both government appointments and congressional testimony for MCC workers and other Mennonites with special information about international or domestic issues. During the first several years of MCC Washington's work, MCC field workers' visits with congressional and State Department officials were quite limited. In 1969 only one service volunteer had government appointments. The following years also were sparse: in 1971 and 1972, three sets of appointments were scheduled in each year; in 1973, six sets; in 1974, two sets. The numbers, while still quite modest, increased considerably by the late 1970s and early 1980s. Since 1990 the Washington office has scheduled between ten and twenty sets of government appointments each year, mostly for MCC's overseas personnel. As has been true since MCC Washington's inception, MCC's representation to government has been far more heavily weighted toward international rather than domestic issues. During the first twenty years of MCC Washington's existence, office personnel arranged for a total of only nine sets of government appointments for visiting MCC personnel who were speaking about domestic issues.

Far less frequently, MCC Washington arranges for Mennonites and MCC personnel to testify at congressional hearings. During the office's first two decades, such testimony on international issues was scheduled on eight occasions: in 1971 on refugees and again on foreign operations; in 1972 on refugees; in 1975 regarding Vietnam; in 1977 on the West Bank; twice in 1981 on world hunger; and in 1983 on the Philippines. It should be noted that while MCC's government appointments are scheduled more regularly on international issues, testimony before congressional committees occurs more frequently on the domestic agenda. During the same period (1968 to 1988), MCC Washington scheduled congressional testimony fifteen times for MCC administrators, service workers, or constituents on domestic issues such as conscription, capital punishment, a nuclear arms freeze, criminal justice, and the World Peace Tax Fund. In a 1977 memo to MCC Peace Section administrators, Franz suggested that Peace Section had not sufficiently developed the mandate and mechanisms for tapping resource persons for congressional testimony. Franz suggested that Peace Section draft and reach consensus on several critical issue areas each year, then identify six constituents with expertise in each of the areas. The constituents would then write position papers and be available to present testimony at congressional hearings and to lead delegations in appointments with key government officials.[13] MCC Washington does identify primary issue areas each year, although it has not fully implemented Franz's proposal.

The congressional testimony on Vietnam, given by MCC's Robert Miller, who recently had returned from an assignment in Hanoi and Saigon, took place in the fall of 1975. "The insights of Mennonites, among the very few groups with ongoing humanitarian programs and contacts in Vietnam, are now considered noteworthy by those decision makers who have serious interests in normalizing postwar United States–Vietnam relationships," says Franz in a news release following the testimony. Franz says the testimony by Miller, along with lawmakers' conversations with MCC's Earl Martin, who also returned from Vietnam in 1975, contributed to a meeting between a twelve-member congressional delegation and Hanoi's ambassador in Paris in December 1975, with both sides seeking to reestablish friendly relations between the United States and Vietnam. At the time, except for Quaker and Mennonite involvement in Vietnam, MIA (Missing in Action) organizations were virtually the only other interest groups speaking out about concern for Vietnam. "The voice of Mennonites in interceding on behalf of Vietnam war victims represents a crucial witness in reawakening the conscience of a society and a government that carries heavy responsibility for untold hardships suffered by thousands of Vietnamese families," states Franz. Miller and Martin, who were part of a meeting of four MCC workers with the premier of North Vietnam, also shared their perspective with Rep. G. V. "Sonny" Montgomery (D–Mississippi), chair of the recently created congressional Select Committee on Missing Persons in Southeast Asia. The MCC workers encouraged a conciliatory approach rather than the stance of retribution exemplified by a trade embargo. Franz remarks that Mennonites, by continuing to assist the refugees of Vietnam, "have generated the good will of the leaders and people of Vietnam. Now we can also stimulate the conscience of decision makers in Washington."[14]

CITIZENS OF THE WORLD

A number of religious lobbying organizations on Capitol Hill take international field workers through Washington and provide persons with on-the-ground service experience for congressional testimony. On at least some occasions, nearly every mainline denominational office in Washington, not to mention the other peace church offices in the nation's capital, has lobbied in this way. Other nongovernmental organizations, such as Bread for the World, also take service workers to speak with members of Congress. Some of the Catholic orders with Washington offices offer information on countries where they have members. Former House Speaker Thomas P. "Tip" O'Neill, who effectively led the Democratic opposition to U.S. aid to Nicaraguan Contras during the 1980s, was deeply influenced by the lobbying of activist nuns. When his opponents argued that the Contras were fighting for democracy, O'Neill's frequent response was "That's not what the sisters tell me."[15] It is clear that many other religious advocacy groups in Washington have similar international interests and, at least episodically, function as MCC Washington does—by drawing on their human resources from abroad. Most of the denominational offices, however, are organizationally at some distance from their mission and service boards and therefore are not as in tune with their denominations' on-the-ground work in international settings. For example, the American Baptist Church's Washington office comes under a subdivision of the denomination's Board of National Ministries. Occasionally the office has contact with its Board of International Ministries, which has missionaries in twenty-two countries, but the linkage is far less direct than it is for MCC.

The American Friends Service Committee (AFSC),[16] MCC Washington's close ally, is one of few Washington advocacy groups similarly embedded in a service organization.[17] AFSC's presence in Washington began in 1947 with Davis House, a guest house that hosts international visitors, the staff of Quaker agencies, and representatives of other organizations working on peace and justice concerns. Gradually AFSC's presence expanded to include planning international affairs seminars and then public affairs programs, which brought in leading social scientists to meet with government officials. In the early 1980s, the office's mandate changed to maintaining "an effective presence in our nation's capital through bringing AFSC insights and advocacy to bear on policy-makers, opinion-shapers, and diplomats and through monitoring developments in Washington so as to inform affected programs and staff throughout the AFSC."[18] James Matlack, director of AFSC's Washington office, says he hosts visiting international delegations and AFSC field workers in Washington about once a month, on average, taking them through congressional, State Department, and National Security Council offices. The international delegations come together at Davis House, where they may meet each other for the first time, and then establish a coherent voice before approaching government officials. Because AFSC has only about eighty U.S. nationals serving overseas, AFSC hosts a higher proportion of study groups or delegations than field workers. Matlack, usually the sole worker in AFSC's Washington office, notes that in most cases AFSC also schedules press conferences so their service workers and visiting foreign nationals can speak directly to the media.[19] In the context of Washington's religious advocacy groups, AFSC most resembles MCC in terms of drawing on international field workers. Matlack says the Washington AFSC office *plus* the more activist Friends Committee on National Legislation, the other independent Quaker organization in Washington, serve the same function as does the MCC Washington office.

Because of the AFSC's work, and that of some other religious lobbies in the nation's capital, one certainly cannot consider MCC's international reporting unique. However, many Washington observers agree that, in comparison with other religious advocacy groups, MCC's international network is more extensive and more frequently drawn upon, giving the organization a distinctive voice. MCC Washington's religious lobbying peers frequently mention its international contacts as one of the organization's significant contributions in the capital. Walter Owensby of the Presbyterian Church U.S.A.'s Washington office contends that MCC has a major impact because of the service people it brings through Washington, providing "a perspective that some of the rest of us do not have."[20] Legislative aide Tim Trenkle observes that MCC "tends to bring by a different group than we see normally. Most of who we meet from foreign countries are people who are brought by our government or by governments of their own countries, visiting ministers or ambassadors, and MCC tends to bring people by from NGO communities. It's a perspective more closely related to people on the ground in these countries." Trenkle adds that while other NGOs bring people through his office, "MCC does more of that than anyone else in the crowd."[21] Aide Marty Rendon claims that MCC Washington's providing these firsthand reports is "a special thing that the Mennonites do that a lot of other groups don't do quite as well. Other groups do it occasionally, but they're not as consistent as the Mennonites."[22] Lori Murray, another Capitol Hill legislative aide, adds that what is distinctive about MCC's international reporting is that the office provides firsthand accounts even on issues that are not necessarily on the front pages. "I guess that's where the difference is. They're not just here to talk about Bosnia or Somalia," says Murray. She notes that MCC staffers are able to speak knowledgeably about many regions of the world. "And they're all top foreign policy areas, but they're not all hot spots, whereas I think the other church groups are more hot-spot focused," she suggests. "You know, whatever is the issue of the day, to get a specific policy decision out now. Whereas Mennonites are providing a constant source of insights about various parts of the world over the course of the year."[23] Other legislative aides agree that MCC Washington's international input is perhaps more frequent and more broadly based than the reports of some other NGOs or religious lobbies.

Visitors to MCC Washington's office quickly notice its international flavor. The front office features a Peters Projection world map, with countries shown in proportion to their relative sizes rather than with the oversized northern hemisphere found on most maps. During his years as director, Franz's office walls were lined with a map of the Middle East, one of the areas for which he was responsible; a burlap wheat bag from MCC

Bangladesh; a colorful poster from Palestine; and another poster in Spanish from the *XVI Jornada Mundial de la Paz*. A coffee table boasted two books: one was a Russian-language photo book, in recognition of the homeland of Franz's ancestors; the other was titled *Before Their Diaspora: A Photographic History of the Palestinians 1876–1948*. Full file drawers carried "Middle East" and "Latin America" labels. Another office, out of which two other MCC staffers worked on international issues, included posters on a Burmese war and an African peace tour, other African art, and a computer-generated map of Somalia.

Such symbols of international concerns are not all that atypical among the Washington religious lobbies housed in the Methodist Building. But although most of the left-of-center religious advocates have a concern for poor and oppressed persons the world over, some observers have suggested that perhaps pacifist organizations are more intentionally international in perspective than are some other religious groups. In a response to pacifist critic Guenter Lewy, John Richard Burkholder writes: "What [Lewy] refers to as 'anti-Americanism' could be better described as 'more-than-American-ism.' Pacifists identify with the entire human community and the long sweep of history. For the pacifist, citizenship in a particular nation-state is just not that important. He [or she] cares less about national interests than about the well-being of the people of all nations. Since most pacifist leaders are not parochial in their worldview, they do not see the U.S. national interest as paramount."[24] Burkholder adds that pacifists "consciously adopt a more global worldview than most Americans. They wear tribal identifications lightly and see themselves as global citizens."[25] Since its inception the Washington office has had both international and domestic issues on its agenda, but the longer-term staffers have nearly always worked on international and arms issues, with short-term workers concentrating on domestic issues. That means there has been greater continuity in and greater emphasis on MCC Washington's international agenda, a concentration that parallels the parent organizations' more extensive experience overseas than domestically.[26]

LOBBYING OUT OF EXPERIENCE

From the beginning, MCC Washington has sought to base its advocacy efforts in Washington on the gospel and Anabaptist faith traditions as well as Mennonite experience. This may appear to be a truism, but legislative aides suggest that some lobbyists advocate without the benefit of such experience. Congressional aide Jim McGovern, who has worked extensively on Salvadoran issues, notes that he was surprised to hear that some of the advocacy groups lobbying for Salvadoran causes "hadn't even been to El Salvador before their initial contacts." MCC's Blake Byler Ortman, who served many years in El Salvador and also worked at the Washington office during 1991, has been one of McGovern's primary resource persons on the Central American "hot spot."[27]

MCC Washington attempts to focus its lobbying on geographical areas where or issues on which MCC has done long-term work. In his 1965 report to MCC's Peace Section regarding whether or not to start a Washington office, Dwight King writes about choosing issues for prophetic witness. In addition to those issues on which Mennonites approach agreement, such as conscription, he says legitimate subjects for witness are those for which MCC has sufficient relief experience. He recommends looking at other examples, such as migrant worker problems, "where *urgency* and *experience* would coalesce, allowing 'legitimate' witness."[28] King adds that MCC's relief work abroad qualifies the organization for suggesting alternatives in foreign policy and in allocations for development and food monies. In a 1969 report to MCC's headquarters in Akron, Franz encouraged MCC administrators to seek means to speak to the government about reformulating U.S. economic assistance programs. "If firsthand involvement is one of the criteria which determines a church body's right to speak to government, then it would seem appropriate for our [denominations] to share insights and constructive concerns related to international development," he writes. Franz says that while economists and development specialists had worked at the issues from a theoretical standpoint, "Practical lessons from firsthand involvement, such as MCC workers have had, would still be regarded as valuable input."[29]

During Franz's tenure in Washington, he referred to this method of working as "orthopraxis," a term that has emerged in Latin American liberation theology. He observes that two dynamics characterize this movement: 1) creating solidarity and community among the marginalized poor in Third World countries; and 2) identifying with massive public suffering as the material reality and focus for biblical reflection on unjust systems.[30] Theologian Rebecca Chopp explains that praxis, while traditionally translated as action or doing, "has come to signify intentional, social activity and the need for emancipatory transformation." Chopp contends that if there is a paradigm shift going on in contemporary theology, praxis signifies the new paradigm. This manner of *doing* theology—or this way of *knowing*—has been developed extensively in European political theologies, Latin American liberation theologies, (African-American) womanist theologies, and feminist theologies.[31] To some extent, it also appears to be embodied in the Mennonite Central Committee's life and work.[32]

Delton Franz, left, and Marian Claassen Franz, right, met with Archbishop Dom Hélder Camara in 1974 in Recife, Brazil. The Franzes visited the archbishop during a four-week study tour of five South American countries. Photo courtesy of MCC Washington.

While Franz often was quiet at coalition meetings or in joint lobbying visits, when he did make a contribution, it often was related to what he heard "from our people on the ground." At a 30 June 1992 meeting of the Central America Working Group, coalition members were discussing their 1992–93 program plans, attempting to set priorities on Central American economic issues. Franz, who was silent through most of the meeting, made only one contribution. He said he would be traveling to Central America the following week to meet with MCC's representatives there, and he would get feedback from the organization's long-term workers on what directions would be best on these economic questions.

Franz, who did not have *international* service experience under his belt—though he had been an inner-city pastor and community worker—attempted to travel every few years to one of the areas for which he had responsibility.[33] While serving as director of MCC Washington, he actively participated in the peace and justice work of his congregation, Hyattsville Mennonite, and for a time he was chair of the board of the Washington-based Casa de Esperanza, a counseling and assistance center for Central American refugees.

Most of MCC Washington's paid staff members, and some of its other workers, come to the Capitol Hill office after having some type of service experience. Many of the Washington office workers who have covered international issues—and some of those who cover the domestic agenda—have had overseas experience; in fact, often such experience is necessary for obtaining a position in Washington. During Franz's last year as director, the staff included Franz, Keith Gingrich, Ken Martens Friesen, Greg Goering, and Jalane Schmidt. Gingrich had carried out MCC assignments for seven years in Sudan and for three years in Nigeria, the latter occurring during the country's civil war. Gingrich had also worked additional time in Nigeria loaned out to another mission agency, and in India for four years with Lutheran World Relief. Friesen had undertaken short-term assignments with MCC in China and Lebanon, and had been in Lesotho for three years. Goering had served with MCC briefly in Egypt before returning to the states and completing his term at MCC Washington. Schmidt, who grew up in an intentional Christian community in Kansas, had gone to Washington as a service worker directly from college, so she did not yet have the international experience of some of her working peers.

Several staffers note the unfortunate reality that once they are in MCC's Washington office, they are unable to have firsthand contacts with the persons

Keith Gingrich, right, later assistant director of the MCC Washington office, speaks with other relief workers in 1981 during the time he served in Sudan. Photo courtesy of Mennonite Central Committee Photograph Collection, Archives of the Mennonite Church, Goshen, Indiana.

for whom they advocate. Full-time positions usually do not allow time for additional service work, even in Washington where many opportunities to plug into existing ministries are available. Staff members are not completely removed from the realities of poverty, violence, and oppression, however. Washington office service workers stay in a group home owned by Mennonite Central Committee and live with other MCC volunteers who have assignments in more hands-on settings. The MCC house is located in the Mount Pleasant neighborhood, about two miles north of the White House. The interracial neighborhood, while usually quiet, was the site of a major riot in 1991 and a series of random, drive-by shootings two years later.

To get to work near the Capitol, the MCC Washington service workers leave their three-story, brick townhouse and walk two blocks down Killbourne Street, passing an open alley used as a rest room by homeless persons. Then they head south on Mount Pleasant, passing La de Todos, the Pan American Barber Shop, Distribuidores El Salvador Del Mundo, and a Seven-Eleven, where several Hispanic men typically wait for trucks to pick them up for the day's work. Before turning onto Irving Street, they see a burned-out and fenced-in Church's Chicken, the last remaining symbol of the 1991 riot. On Irving the MCC staff walk past abandoned buildings interspersed with social agencies: Centro Comunal Unidad and the Barbara Chambers Children's Center, where a subline says "Bilingual Multicultural." They may walk by several homeless men, some sitting in chairs on the sidewalk, and past Chuck's, a closed bar where a man with no legs sometimes sits in his wheelchair. Across the street, on the side of a block building labeled Mudrick's Liquor, scrawled graffiti proclaims: "$ FOR HOMES, NOT WAR, FROM D.C. TO EL SALVADOR." The MCC service workers board public bus number 54 at the corner of Irving and Fourteenth, taking the twenty-minute ride down to Capitol Hill.

The MCC Washington service workers usually have worked on domestic rather than international issues. Living in an economically and racially diverse neighborhood no doubt provides some firsthand knowledge of issues on which they advocate. However, because they still do not have time for the hands-on experiences that help authenticate their advocacy, some MCC service workers have sought to minimize the distance between themselves and the "poor and oppressed." Greg Goering chose to spend one month of his two-month sabbatical in 1991–92 working at the Open Door Community in Atlanta, Georgia. Open Door is an interdenominational house where formerly homeless persons live alongside others, provide meals for homeless persons, and work on poverty and criminal justice issues. In an exploratory letter to Open Door, Goering states that although he lives in a diverse neighborhood in Washington, his work with Congress allows "little contact with the people for whom I advocate." He writes: "Having worked on national criminal justice policies generally (alternatives to incarceration, victim's assistance, capital punishment), I am interested in prison visitation, deathrow work, and relating to families of prisoners and death row inmates. Of course, I am also interested in any political work involving criminal justice issues. Second, I would appreciate experiencing the personal dimensions of impoverishment and engaging in direct service ministries."[34] Goering spent December 1991 working at the Open Door and returned to MCC Washington with new inspiration and information, continuing in his advocacy work another eighteen months.

Goering admits that his experience at Open Door was more for his benefit than for direct experiential reporting to legislative aides or other government officials. It is the *international* experiences MCC reports that carry weight, says Goering, echoing the perceptions of other MCC staffers. "Everybody in the U.S. thinks they're an expert on poverty because they live here," he explains.[35] Indeed, on legislative or policy questions other than conscription, MCC's primary entree and primary influence in Washington is on selected international issues. A second look at MCC Washington's responses to the Persian Gulf War and the Somali famine and interclan conflict will illuminate how MCC Washington seeks to draw on experience in its advocacy efforts.

ADDRESSING THE CONFLICTS

At the time of the crises, Mennonite Central Committee's experience in both Iraq and Somalia was more limited than in some other countries. MCC has worked with persons from the Middle East since 1944, when trained volunteers went to refugee camps in El Shatt and Tolumbat in Egypt under the umbrella of the United Nations Relief and Rehabilitation Administration. After the establishment of the State of Israel in 1948, MCC began work in Gaza and Jordan over the following two years. Soon afterward MCC placed workers in Bethlehem and in other areas scattered across the Hebron/Nablus/Jericho triangle in the West Bank. MCC also has worked in Egypt, Lebanon, and Syria, at times combining forces there and elsewhere in the Middle East with other Mennonite and Brethren in Christ mission and service agencies in the regions.[36] Prior to the Persian Gulf War, however, MCC's direct involvement in Iraq was almost nonexistent. Only one volunteer, Carl Jantzen, had served there, and that was only a brief term when he was loaned out to International Voluntary Services. Jantzen had been on an MCC assignment in Europe, and was transferred to Iraq in 1953. Even though MCC did not have service volunteers in Iraq at the time of the war, the organization did have forty-three workers scattered elsewhere across the Middle East in health, education, and agricultural development assignments.

In his work on the Persian Gulf crisis, Franz was not able to draw on the organization's experience in Iraq or Kuwait, since MCC's firsthand experience in those countries was minimal. Instead, Franz based his Persian Gulf work on MCC's extensive experience more generally in the Middle East and on MCC's decades of providing humanitarian aid. Two areas in which MCC's experience may have helped the Washington office contribute to the religious lobbies' coalition efforts were 1) helping others see the interconnectedness between the Iraqi conflict and broader Middle East tensions; and 2) focusing energy on removing U.S. sanctions on food and medical shipments to Iraq. Other religious advocates in Washington were working with these same issues, although many of them had less experiential basis on which to ground their efforts.

Churches for Middle East Peace (C–MEP), of which MCC Washington was a founding member in 1984, "continued to address the gulf in connection with our whole larger body of work," suggests Corrine Whitlatch, staff person for C–MEP. Refugee issues and arms control issues were part of C–MEP's agenda related to the Persian Gulf. "You also may recall that during the Gulf War, whether or not it would be linked to the Israeli–Palestinian conflict became a big nationally debated issue," explains Whitlatch. "In our mind and work, the issues were always connected." Whitlatch contends that Mennonites' and others' work on the ground in the Middle East helped make C–MEP's work credible during the Gulf War. MCC and the American Friends Service Committee were C–MEP's two member organizations with the most experience in the Middle East prior to the war. This experience and C–MEP's long-term interests in the Middle East gave them a perspective different from that of other groups that sprang up in response to the conflict and war.[37]

Religious coalitions in Washington produced multiple background documents and sign-on letters in the months preceding the outbreak of the Persian Gulf War. C–MEP, like other coalition groups, prepared a September 1990 background paper for coalition members and government officials with whom they met. The background paper included a condemnation of Iraq's annexation of Kuwait as well as sections on, among other concerns, halting the U.S. military buildup, the War Powers Act, the use of chemical weapons, and Middle East arms sales. Franz was assigned the task of writing C–MEP's section on exempting food and medicine from the sanctions approved by the United Nations. Franz drew on MCC's resources and experience in preparing the paragraphs for the document. The final version in the background paper reads, in part:

The U.S. Administration currently argues that since Iraqis are not starving, food should not be exempted from the blockade. . . . However, even a policy of near-starvation of civilians is morally repugnant and unacceptable as a tool to achieve political ends. Civilians would be paying for the policies of Saddam Hussein and those who advocate such a price would stand accused of using them as pawns as well as contravening the UN resolution [Security Council Resolution 661] for which adoption the U.S. worked so hard.

Quite apart from the moral objections to such a policy there is the matter of timing. It can be a very long period from the recognition of danger to the actual arrival and distribution of food for 17 million people. There is no assurance that policy makers will get the calculations right. The global community is justified in resisting Saddam Hussein's actions, but the response ought not be without limits. Economic sanctions are appropriate to compel Iraq's withdrawal from Kuwait, the abandonment of its threats against other nations in the region, and release of hostages. Sanctions, however, must not be allowed to become a siege against the Iraqi and Kuwaiti people that endangers the life or health of the civilian population. Basic foods and medical supplies should be permitted to flow in keeping with international humanitarian law.[38]

The statement included in the C–MEP background paper closely resembles the tone and position of a Mennonite Central Committee statement adopted by MCC's Executive Committee in early September 1990. The statement says that as an organization responding to human need "in the name of Christ," MCC opposes the inclusion of food and medicines in the embargo against Iraq. "We believe Jesus' words, 'Give them something to eat' (Mark 6:37), are a call to share food with the hungry irrespective of race, religion or political persuasion," the statement says. "Much of our work internationally is aimed at improving poor people's access to food. Access to food is a basic human right enshrined in the United Nations Declaration of Human Rights. The withholding of food as a method of warfare is prohibited by international law (Article 54 of Protocol II Additional to the Geneva Conventions, 1977)."[39] The statement concludes by remarking, "We believe it is morally wrong to keep food from hungry people" and by urging the international community to ensure that the people of Iraq and Kuwait are not deprived of adequate food and medical supplies.

Prior to the outbreak of the war, MCC also sent personnel on two delegations to Iraq. John Stoner, then acting executive secretary of MCC's Overseas Peace Office, traveled to Baghdad with a Fellowship of Reconciliation (FOR) peace delegation in October 1990. The delegation carried vitamins and antibiotics across the embargo line, delivering medical supplies for evacuees in Jordan and the Red Crescent Society in Iraq. The FOR delegation also met with U.S. Embassy employees and saw fourteen hostages released while the delegation was visiting Iraq's capital. Several former MCC workers, including LeRoy Friesen, mentioned above in connection with MCC's Middle East program, and Betsy Beyler, formerly an employee at the MCC Washington office, participated in a twelve-member Christian Peacemaker Teams (CPT) delegation to Iraq in November 1990. Stoner, who went on the FOR delegation a month earlier, was MCC's representative on the Mennonite- and Brethren in Christ-supported CPT board. The group also took in boxes of medical supplies for the Red Crescent Society and discussed medical needs with the organization and with administrators at the Saddam Children's Hospital. Both the FOR and CPT delegations were designed to provide opportunities to communicate with Iraqi people, to assess the embargo's effects on Iraqis, to review the possibilities for concrete humanitarian assistance, and to embody a protest against preparations for a military confrontation.

Partly since MCC had not had sustained experience in Iraq prior to the 1990–91 conflict and war, after the war the organization sought ways "to have a presence with the Iraqi people and to assist in appropriate ways those who have returned to Jordan and the Occupied Territories." In response to the war and its aftermath, MCC created a "Bridge the Gulf" fund, which raised more than eight hundred thousand dollars for relief, reconstruction, and reconciliation work in the Middle East region. With the monies, MCC sent short-term relief workers to Iran, Iraq, and Turkey; shipped relief supplies to Iran, Iraq, Jordan, and the Occupied Territories; and brought Middle Eastern Christians to North America to inform U.S. and Canadian communities of the situation of Christians in the Middle East. During the conflict MCC volunteers served in refugee camps in Iraq's neighboring countries, assisting with some of the more than two million Iraqis who fled to Iran, Jordan, and Turkey. Following the war, MCC sent in Harry Huebner to assess the situation and the country's needs and, on his recommendation, sent an MCC public health nurse to Baghdad. The nurse, Carol McClean, spent six weeks in Baghdad assisting UNICEF and the Iraqi government in designing a supplemental nutrition program for Baghdad. In 1991 MCC sent a total of fifty-five hundred pounds of medical supplies and forty metric tons of powdered milk to Iraq. MCC also collaborated with the American Friends Service Committee in providing spare parts for wheat-harvesting machinery. MCC staffers and Quakers who worked in or visited Iraq concluded that, following the war, the most urgent issue was the lifting of nonmilitary sanctions to enable Iraq to sell oil and purchase the food, medicines, and other supplies on the world market that it needed to rebuild its basic infrastructure.[40]

Based on its wartime and postwar experiences in Iraq, MCC prepared a video and study packet entitled *Feeding the Enemy: The Christian Response to Hunger in Iraq*. In July 1991, Delton Franz sent a *Hotline* to persons on MCC

141

Washington's mailing list who had expressed interest in the Middle East. Franz urged recipients to write to their members of Congress and to Secretary of State James Baker and Thomas Pickering, U.S. ambassador to the United Nations. "Many of our church groups are now engaged in supporting relief programs inside Iraq," Franz wrote. "Relief workers on the ground tell us, however, that such relief efforts cannot possibly meet the civilian needs. Only a change in the sanctions regime that enables the Iraqi people to rebuild their own systems for health and nutrition can forestall tragic and large-scale loss of life." Franz suggested supporting the legislative initiatives taken by Rep. Tim Penny (D-Minnesota), who filed House Concurrent Resolution 168 for easing the nonmilitary sanctions to enable prompt response to the health crisis inside Iraq.[41] The organization also sent Carol McClean, the public health nurse who worked for MCC in Baghdad, to Washington to speak at a Middle East Forum sponsored by Churches for Middle East Peace. The 27 September 1991 forum, entitled "The War Is Not Over: A Report on Humanitarian Conditions in Iraq," included presentations by McClean and AFSC worker James Fine, who spent three months in Baghdad on special assignment as a Quaker representative. With McClean's short-term assignment in Iraq, MCC had its first sustained firsthand information on Iraqi conditions, and it provided opportunities for her to share those experiences with MCC Washington's coalition partners in the capital.

A second complex political and military issue in which MCC Washington became embroiled was the 1992–93 crisis in Somalia. While MCC had more experience in Somalia than it had in Iraq, the organization's experience was more limited there than in some other countries. During the Somali crisis, when U.S. and UN troops were sent into the war-torn country on the Horn of Africa to assist with food shipments, Mennonite Central Committee and the American Friends Service Committee were two of the few nongovernmental organizations to express objections to military intervention. For many months Somali warlords and their gangs had been hijacking shipments of food to the famine-stricken country, exacerbating the food shortage problem. InterAction, a coalition of 143 U.S. private and voluntary organizations working on a broad range of international humanitarian issues, sent a 19 November 1992 letter to General Brent Scowcroft expressing support for military intervention in Somalia. Although MCC is not a member of InterAction, MCC administrators were invited to attach their names to the sign-on letter sent to Scowcroft. MCC declined the invitation and instead responded with a 25 November 1992 letter to InterAction, expressing MCC's opposition to a military solution to Somalia's situation. The reasons MCC's Eric J. Olfert gave included the following: 1) an increased unnegotiated international military presence to protect deliveries was likely to exacerbate the difficulties and undermine the process of long-term reconciliation; 2) MCC had grave misgivings about the probability of success of an unnegotiated armed United Nations security intervention in being able to effectively facilitate relief aid to the destitute; and 3) MCC feared that if UN forces were deployed to protect NGOs, the reaction to their force would certainly include the NGOs as targets, and the result might be even greater insecurity and restriction of movement for those NGOs.[42] MCC's objections to the military intervention, and those of the American Friends Service Committee,[43] resulted in an 18 December 1992 consultation on Somalia hosted by the two organizations for other agencies with workers on the ground in Somalia.

MCC, like AFSC, based its nonsupport of military intervention on the organization's experience in Somalia and elsewhere in the Horn of Africa. After the military operation began in Somalia, three MCC workers in Mozambique, south of the Horn of Africa, wrote to one Mennonite periodical:

> A privilege of living in this part of the world is the opportunity to get glimpses of ourselves as North Americans as viewed from afar. Few Mozambicans accepted the sending of U.S. troops to Somalia as simply a humanitarian gesture. Opinions for the "real reason" ran from a desire by President Bush to leave office strongly to seeing this as a trial run for a future war against Muslim fundamentalists. . . . Perhaps the saddest part of the whole operation is that there is little solid evidence it will actually result in more food reaching the hungry. The food situation in many towns had improved and death rates had dropped in the weeks prior to the arrival of U.S. troops. Several organizations working in Somalia had warned that military force might make their work more difficult. They cited the "concentric circle" thinking by Somalis: if a Somali is killed by a foreigner, all foreigners become the enemy.[44]

At the time of the 1992–93 crisis, MCC did not have workers living in Somalia, although its programs in the country and with Somali refugees had continued. Mennonite Central Committee began its work in Somalia in 1980, when it assisted Ethiopian refugees who had fled there. MCC workers left Somalia in July 1989 when escalating violence made it difficult to continue their work. Bonnie Bergey, who coordinated MCC's and the Eastern Mennonite Missions' Somali programs at the time of the U.S. military intervention, worked from her base in Nairobi, Kenya. Bergey regularly traveled to Somalia to assess the situation and consult with Somali partners. In the twelve months prior to the crisis, MCC had sent 750 metric tons of food to Somali refugees in Kenya, along with four thousand school kits and fifteen cartons of bandages to northwest Somalia. Since 1990 MCC also had supported a group of Somalis living outside their country who had been gathering to discuss ways to bring peace to their country. MCC's international conciliation specialist, John Paul Lederach, had been working with this group, called Ergada, which included respected and well-connected Somalis from across the major family-based clans. Lederach also helped facilitate UN-supported regional negotiations in Somalia. In addition, MCC was working with other NGOs and Somali friends to find ways to disarm Somali gunmen. MCC gave ten thousand dollars, 10 percent of the total costs, to support a month-long meeting between three hundred clan elders and several hundred observers in northwestern Somalia in February and March 1993. Based on its extensive reconciliation and service programs in and around Somalia, MCC was able to speak authentically from its experience in the region. MCC's field workers also reported that the situation of people in southern Sudan and Mozambique was as desperate as the situation in Somalia. Since the international media had not reported on the situations of these neighboring countries, however, the world community had not responded with such intensity. MCC sent major food shipments to Sudan and Mozambique at the time the world's energies were focused on Somalia.

Tim Trenkle, Sen. Nancy Kassebaum's legislative aide, says he spoke with MCC's John Paul Lederach every month, if not more often, during the Somali crisis. At the time, Kassebaum was the ranking Republican on the Senate's African Subcommittee and was influential in congressional policy related to Africa. Trenkle notes that Lederach also stopped to see him whenever he was in Washington. "It was very helpful to me in learning a lot about Somalia from early on," Trenkle contends. "The information we've been getting on Somalia from MCC has had a big impact on the evolution of our position, even though we came to a different policy than MCC may have advocated." Trenkle says MCC's contacts with Kassebaum's office also contributed to the senator's decision to visit the country. In the Somali situation, as well as any other under consideration in Washington, what MCC brings to bear on policy or legislative decisions is only a tiny part of an expansive process. Among the multiple complex reasons MCC Washington may have had only *minimal* impact on Capitol Hill during the Persian Gulf War and the crisis in Somalia was the organization's lack of sustained experience in those settings. In Somalia, MCC had pulled most of its personnel and programs out of the country once ongoing work would have necessitated carrying handguns or requesting military escorts. In Iraq, MCC had virtually no experience. Because MCC Washington's distinctive value in the capital is rooted in the parent organization's firsthand observation, the lobbying office had less influence on other NGOs and on the U.S. government on these two crises than perhaps on some other issues.

HAVING AN IMPACT ON WASHINGTON

Not surprisingly, much of MCC Washington's impact in the nation's capital—along with the impact of other religious lobbying organizations—is neither measurable nor discernible. Policy and legislative decisions are made in the context of multiple competing interests, with diverse sources of information, intense political and monetary pressures, deal making, and well-intentioned compromising all having some effect on eventual outcomes. The stated primary concern of most Protestant and Catholic advocacy groups in the capital, as noted earlier, is not "effectiveness," but rather "faithfulness" to God and to those for whom they advocate. Still, MCC Washington keeps a record of its "success stories" or "diamonds in the rough." Franz observes in one summary of the office's work: "Because it is difficult to measure the effect of much of the letter writing and appointments which many of our people have initiated with decision-makers, perhaps there is some value in selecting some instances in which there is some empirical evidence that the message got through."[45] Following are three illustrations of where MCC's international work and connections had some rather direct effect on Washington and the world.

American / Laotian Relations

During a return visit to the states, Murray and Linda Hiebert, MCC workers in Laos in the mid-1970s, spoke with seven members of Congress, urging the release of U.S. food aid to a first drought-stricken and then flood-ravaged Laos. The seven representatives responded by obtaining the signatures of twenty-seven colleagues for a letter to then President Carter. A presidential aide disclosed that two factors finally had triggered the president's April 1978 decision to release the first humanitarian aid to Laos (or any country in Indochina) since the war: 1) the letter from twenty-seven House members, which was written by the Hieberts; and 2) a letter, written by an elderly woman and culled from the volume of White House mail, which opened by urging that postwar food aid be sent on the basis of observations by "[o]ur Mennonite workers in Laos." It is almost certain that the woman read an MCC news service release or that she had received MCC Washington's *Hotline* on Laos. Carter's aide told the Hieberts, "The president was moved."[46] Later the Hieberts met with the Laotian charge d'affaires in the Laotian Embassy in Washington, and their conversation resulted in or contributed toward the Laotian government's release of the bodies of four missing American airmen.[47] This in turn prompted a new openness at the State Department to review American-Laotian relations.

Argentinean Military Aid

In 1977 Franz accompanied Patricia Erb, the nineteen-year-old daughter of Mennonite Board of Missions workers in Argentina, to the offices of key senators and representatives. Erb, a university student in Buenos Aires, had worked in a social service assignment in a slum barrio as part of her study of sociology. As in other countries under authoritarian military control, such engagements can lead to arrest, imprisonment, and torture—without trial—for being "subversive." Erb was abducted from her parents' home in September 1976 and imprisoned and tortured for fifteen days, after which she was expelled from the country. Erb says that the last day she was tortured, the man torturing her told her he had been taught to torture in the Panama Canal Zone by U.S. officials in the army's School of the Americas. The man became angry when he was told to stop torturing Erb because she probably would be freed. "I don't understand," he told Erb. "After they teach us how to do it, they get mad at us and tell us to stop."[48]

When Erb returned to the U.S., MCC Washington arranged for forty appointments over several weeks for her to share her experience and to ask that U.S. military training assistance to Argentina be terminated. Prior to her congressional visits, Franz sent a *Hotline* on "Torture in Third World Countries" to 950 constituents, many of whom responded with letters and telegrams to members of Congress. When Erb arrived, two appointments were particularly influential. One was her meeting with Sen. Frank Church (D-Idaho), chairman-designate of the Foreign Relations Committee. Minutes after Franz and Erb returned to the MCC Washington office, Church's legislative aide told them Erb's testimony had caused Church to change his mind about military aid to Argentina. Although previously undecided, Church said he would be introducing an amendment to the pending Foreign Aid Bill to cut off all further military training funds to the country. In Church's Senate floor speech the following day, 15 June 1977, his presentation centered on Erb's account:

> The time has come to signal clearly to the rest of the world that the Congress does care about the kind of government to which she tenders military assistance. . . . Yesterday a young woman, Patricia Ann Erb, visited my office, accompanied by Mr. Delton Franz of the Mennonite Central Committee. She spoke movingly of the terrible torture she had personally experienced at the hands of the Armed Forces of Argentina. . . . Mr. President, we may not be able to persuade Argentinean and other morally bankrupt regimes to respect the rights of their citizens; but let us not train their soldiers, who then direct their new skills against innocent citizens within their own country. And let us not supply them with a steady flow of arms and ammunition. . . .[49]

A week later Reps. William Lehman (D–Florida) and Donald Bonker (D–Washington), whom Franz and Erb had visited on their rounds, also referred at length to her account in their congressional testimony. Franz claims that for many members of Congress, Erb's testimony was their first occasion to hear directly from a victim of an authoritarian military regime trained and aided by the United States.

The second influential contact was an interview Franz scheduled for Erb at the annual seminar of NETWORK, the Catholic sisters' lobbying organization in Washington. Patty Erb's input motivated the nuns to focus their energies on the congressional amendment up for another vote in the House. Earlier the amendment to terminate Argentinean military aid had been defeated in the House. After carefully doing their homework on the situation in Argentina, 450 nuns fanned out across Capitol Hill on 21 June 1977 to communicate Erb's message. The following 223–180 vote, coming one week after the Senate vote and eight weeks after a previous House vote had defeated the amendment, terminated U.S. military aid to Argentina. Amnesty International had reported that the number of those who had disappeared or been killed or imprisoned in Argentina numbered fifteen thousand at its peak in 1977. After U.S. military aid was cut off, the number dropped steadily, so that by 1981 Amnesty reported only fifty missing, imprisoned, or killed in Argentina.[50]

Ugandan Coffee Boycott

Several months after Franz took Patricia Erb through congressional corridors, he also accompanied Anglican Bishop Festo Kivengere of Uganda to meetings with State Department officials and members of Congress. Kivengere, whom Mennonites first related to when he was a teacher in an Anglican secondary school in Tanzania, went to Washington to plead on behalf of Ugandan refugees.[51] At the time, a bill that would give thirty million dollars for African assistance was before Congress. Kivengere sought to call Washington's attention to the fifty thousand refugees who had fled the increasingly brutal rule of Uganda's President Idi Amin. Kivengere himself had fled Uganda by night in February 1977 after it seemed clear that an attempt would be made on his life following his persistent appeals to Amin that he act according to law and reason and for the good of Uganda.

Franz scheduled seventeen appointments over a two-day period for Kivengere, including meetings with six career foreign service officers on East Africa at the State Department, representatives of the State Department Bureau of Human Rights, staffers from the House and Senate Subcommittee on Africa, and key members of the House and Senate. Rep. Donald Pease (D–Ohio) already had introduced a bill with twenty-three sponsors that placed an embargo on the U.S. importation of Ugandan coffee. Pease said he found helpful the information provided by Kivengere's documentation of Amin's atrocities and his armed troops' confiscation of most of the coffee crop for the dictator's treasury. Three months later MCC Washington convinced Kivengere to return to Washington because no Senate bill had been introduced regarding the embargo. When the bishop returned, Franz scheduled a crucial meeting with Sen. Mark Hatfield (R-Oregon), who had been reluctant to introduce an embargo bill because he believed an embargo would destroy the livelihood of Ugandan coffee farmers. In response, Kivengere told Hatfield that Amin's soldiers were taking the bagged coffee from farmers at a pittance of its real market value and that coffee exports to the United States were providing two-thirds of Uganda's hard currency. Virtually all of the funds were being used by Amin to pursue his genocidal killings and to purchase expensive automobiles and imported scotch whiskey to motivate his army officers to obey his orders, said Kivengere.

At the end of the meeting, Hatfield said he would introduce a Senate bill similar to that of Rep. Pease on the House side. The senator also asked MCC Washington staffers to consolidate the bishop's reams of information into a twelve- to fifteen-page summary for use in the senator's floor speech to introduce the embargo bill. MCC Washington provided Hatfield with the summary. Several weeks after he introduced the bill, the legislation was enacted, enforcing an embargo on the importation of Ugandan coffee. Just over a year after the embargo went into effect, Amin's regime fell. On 26 April 1979 Hatfield spoke on the Senate floor to reflect on the process. In that address, he remarked, "I cannot adequately express with words the elation I possess today to request that the trade restrictions invoked against Uganda by Congress be removed in joyous celebration of peace and democracy in East Africa . . . as the people of Uganda now emerge from eight years of rule by brutality and fear. . . . Less than two weeks after the U.S. trade embargo went into effect, reports began to come forth that Amin was facing serious discontent and division in his army. . . . U.S. withdrawal of purchases provided the psychological and practical ingredients necessary to . . . break Amin's survivability."[52]

With Amin's departure from Uganda, the number of massacres greatly subsided, although problems for Uganda did not end under the government of Amin's successor, Milton Obote. "Nevertheless," notes Franz, "a transition was beginning." Franz adds that when the phone rang from Eastern Mennonite Board of Missions requesting that he arrange for the bishop's Washington appointments, MCC Washington staffers canceled meetings and dropped everything. "We have no regrets," he says.

These three illustrations are among the few cases where MCC's role in world affairs can be traced rather directly. As is clear from the stories, both

MCC's personnel and workers from other Mennonite mission and service agencies contributed to changes in Washington, Laos, Argentina, and Uganda. Most of the time, however, MCC Washington's influence is less measurable, given the complexity of Washington. It is likely that often MCC Washington is not even aware of how its work factors into the legislative process or policy decisions. Legislative aide Nelle Temple Brown says she wrote a floor speech in January 1993 for her boss, Rep. Doug Bereuter (R–Nebraska), which cited MCC Washington as one of the religious organizations supporting the Select Committee on Hunger. "MCC has one of the best reputations, so I thought we might as well highlight the advocacy of the groups who are known to be effective, because that carries a message," notes Temple Brown.[53] The legislative aide also remembers that in 1992 and 1993 she was crafting legislation related to the relief and reconciliation work in Somalia. "We were trying to explain to members of Congress . . . why we were supporting aid for reconstruction, not just relief, and the level of commitment of voluntary groups. Although I didn't use it as an illustration, I had in the back of my mind [MCC's] John Paul Lederach's [mediation] work in Somalia and elsewhere."[54]

It is also difficult to ascertain the influence or effect MCC Washington has on specific legislators with whom they have developed long-term relationships. One example is MCC Washington's relationship with the office of Rep. John Joseph "Joe" Moakley (D–Massachusetts). In the early 1980s Moakley's legislative aide, Jim McGovern, was making a trip to El Salvador, and he called to schedule an appointment with MCC Washington personnel because he had been told he should talk to the Mennonites while in El Salvador. Franz arranged for MCC's Blake Byler Ortman to host McGovern during part of his visit to the Central American country. McGovern was in El Salvador seven days, and spent three full days with Byler Ortman. "That simply was a turning point for that office," claims Franz. Soon after McGovern's visit, Rep. Moakley was chosen by the Democrats to be the leader on Salvadoran issues. He also sent out a "Dear Colleague" letter encouraging other representatives and their aides to attend a briefing with Byler Ortman when he was in the United States six months later, and fifty persons attended.[55] McGovern claims that, of the hundreds of service workers he met in El Salvador, Byler Ortman was one of the two people he most admired, trusted, and respected. McGovern admits that Moakley's office has a predisposition in favor of the positions MCC Washington advocates and therefore is open to hearing their perspective, but adds that he believes Byler Ortman knows more about El Salvador than anyone else he knows. The information and stories Byler Ortman and MCC Washington provide continue to have influence on Salvadoran issues.

Other intangible effects of MCC Washington's international networking include the influence on their religious lobbying peers, who also hear the stories of MCC personnel in the field—and the influence on MCC Washington staffers themselves. Several staffers note that their contacts with MCC's field workers give them not only information but also incentive to continue their advocacy efforts, even when the direct results of their lobbying are unclear. MCC's Earl Martin, who has worked both in Washington and overseas, states:"The stories, the consciousness, the awareness that comes from the far-flung spread of MCC workers around the world is the life-blood and the integrity of the Washington office."[56] Franz speaks about how hearing the stories of MCC workers overseas empowered him and other Washington staffers to continue their lobbying. "It's that gut-level reality, and that powerful witness to it, that helps us want to continue addressing those questions." Franz contends that MCC Washington needs to identify with the exposures MCC's service workers have at a feeling level, as well as an intellectual level, in order to have "staying power" in Washington.[57] Staffer Keith Gingrich says his contacts with MCC workers abroad, both directly and through MCC's Akron office, help provide energy for his advocacy efforts. As with other MCC Washington staffers who have served overseas, Gingrich also draws on his personal relationships with "our Third World counterparts" to remember why he works in Washington.[58]

Several Methodist Building lobbying peers called attention to MCC's contributions to their knowledge of what is happening in countries about which they are concerned. Such storytelling is a factor in the positions the religious advocates take. Carol Capps, director of Church World Services/Lutheran World Relief's Washington office, claims that MCC Washington's contributions to nongovernmental organizations' meetings is "to raise something which hasn't been raised adequately, and especially to keep a focus on the peace and negotiation issues." Capps suggests that the mainstream aid organizations focus almost exclusively on how to get foreign aid in, especially in a case such as Somalia. The contribution MCC offers, she observes, "is having information to share about ongoing mediation efforts, focusing discussion on that dimension and on the need for political reconciliation efforts."[59] In addition, having firsthand information is important for the legislative and State Department contacts the religious lobbyists make. C-MEP's Corrine Whitlatch, a Unitarian, contends that Mennonites' work in the Middle East "gives them credibility that groups like the Unitarians don't have. It's very important for our work here, the fact that some of our groups have direct, on-the-ground experience with the peoples there." Whitlatch says when MCC Washington takes returned service workers to congressional and State Department offices, "That of course *enhances* our credibility when we come in with just ourselves, the fact that one of our member groups has had this person in, even if they might not remember which one of our groups it was, it gives *all* of us a little bit more integrity."[60]

NO "WILD-EYED DISCONNECT WITH REALITY"

Whitlatch's remarks suggest a key dynamic—credibility—in why State Department and congressional leaders give service workers a hearing and what effect those reports have on the reputation of MCC Washington as well as its coalition partners. "I think a lot of the reason why we are credible in D.C. is because of our name internationally," observes Ken Martens Friesen. "And I don't think we would have anything to say—very little to say—if we didn't have international volunteers, international experience, and an international perspective."[61] Franz remarks that in lobbying visits it was important for him to begin with a brief background about "how we're connected"—a small staff in Washington with headquarters in Pennsylvania, hundreds of workers spread across the world, and another couple hundred in domestic assignments. "It is from our connecting to the exposure of our people on the ground that we have a very important source on what's happening in the international domain." Providing this background, and being embedded in MCC as the Washington office is, "can make a big difference in their listening more carefully," contends Franz.[62]

MCC Washington staffers, other religious lobbyists, and legislative aides all speak about the limited resources government officials have in discerning how persons overseas are affected by U.S. government and their own governments' policies. Keith Gingrich suggests that elected leaders on Capitol Hill "have to rely mostly on the State Department for their information. Most of them know that that's generally colored, or at least doesn't represent a lot of folks out there . . . so getting the local flavor and experience is important."[63] Titus Peachey observes that when he was in Laos he was impressed with the disparity between the kind of access and information U.S. government officials had in comparison with what MCC workers knew. "Perhaps the differences between what MCC workers know or understand about a country and what U.S. government officials might know aren't always that stark as in Laos because of some of the political realities there," acknowledges Peachey. "But I would think generally speaking that that's one of the concerns MCC has."[64] Franz claims that even State Department officials rarely turn down MCC Washington when the office requests appointments for returning service workers.

"Historically, field representatives have been much more interested in social and economic conditions on-the-ground for ordinary people as opposed to sort of the geopolitics and geoeconomics that concern those of us in Washington," explains James McCormick, Republican professional staff for the House Subcommittee on Asian and Pacific of the Committee on Foreign Affairs. "So oftentimes [MCC provides] a healthy point of view to receive because it's not the kind of thing we always hear."[65] Lori Murray of Senator Kassebaum's office remarks that MCC provides "an American perspective, but it's not an official American perspective. It's an American citizen living there who has a lot more interaction with the community than I think our embassy staff do." Murray also says MCC's information provides a balance to information circulating in Washington, particularly on regions where strong, one-sided lobbies already have a voice in the capital. "In terms of the Middle East, [MCC] tends to lend a balance especially to policy where clearly the Israeli government's position has a very strong voice and a lot of listeners. You don't get as many people coming through to provide another perspective." Murray observes that once peace negotiations were kicked in, the Palestinian delegation was more visible on the Hill in meetings, "but prior to that we were somewhat at a loss to get information except from the Israeli government."[66]

"We're in the information business," acknowledges another legislative aide. "It's my desire to gather quality information whether it's from the U.S. government or wherever so that my congressperson can make credible decisions."[67] FCNL's Joe Volk says his perception is that members of Congress are "hungry for information." He adds:

> I think an awful lot of members [of Congress] here don't have much experience, and I think staffers and members can easily figure out who has experience, and who can authentically reflect the lived experience. There also are some members who have traveled just enough to know whether they're talking to tourists. . . . Members are hungry for every detail. I am persuaded that when you leave, their door opens, they go out to their colleagues as if they've done this. They say, "My source says this." And over here, that kind of information is power. So they're really hungry for it.[68]

MCC U.S. board member Susan Goering agreed with Volk's sentiments. "When you think about it in terms of power positions, which I don't think church workers typically do, I think some of the most effective lobbying is when the Washington office sets up meetings with MCC workers who come from the field because there the power imbalance shifts a bit," contends Goering. "The people speaking to the person in power have a better idea of what's going on, and can't be pushed into the corner and patted on the back as easily."[69]

AFSC's James Matlack also claims hands-on experience is much more credible than other advocacy efforts further removed from lived reality. "We're all just sort of secondary analysts if we [advocate] on the basis of field reports," says Matlack. "It's like listening to a constituent versus listening to a lobbyist in terms of congressional reaction."[70] Just as constituents' letters carry considerably more weight than contacts made by national lobbying offices, so do direct reports from service workers. "People who have on-the-ground, firsthand experience clearly have an impact on members or their staff that people who are involved just inside the Beltway do not have," contends Walter Owensby of the Presbyterian Church USA's Washington office. Because MCC Washington brings more service workers through than many other religious lobbying organizations, they may have a more powerful voice on some international issues than many of their associates, notes Owensby.[71]

According to those who work in government offices on Capitol Hill, service workers do have much more influence than religious lobbyists themselves. Legislative aide Jacob Ahearn observes that he differentiates the information he gets from MCC into two categories: that which field people bring in, and that which MCC Washington staffers give. The field people, explains Ahearn, have very detailed knowledge and recent information. "Generally, for folks *inside* the Beltway, they don't have the mastery of details and they tend to be more sweeping in their generalizations," he claims. "Everyone in Washington thinks he or she is a good strategist, Delton included. But when these folks come in from the field, they have a real ability to tell us how the world *is,* which is more useful than telling us how it *ought to be.*"[72]

Nearly every legislative aide interviewed stressed the importance of providing accurate and, to the extent possible, unbiased information. "As a rule of thumb, when I'm talking to NGOs, I tend to discount 10 to 20 percent of what they say," contends aide James McCormick. "Just for instance if you go to Cambodia and talk with NGOs as a group, their point of view is much more likely to be alarmist, critical of American policy, than perhaps others. They may be right on a fair amount, but not all."[73] Ahearn was even more firm: "If an organization gives me information that is sometimes accurate, sometimes inaccurate, I discount it all," he states. "Religious lobbyists and field workers should not provide information unless they're 100 percent absolutely sure of the accuracy of their information. If they're wrong, subsequent information will not be treated with much respect."[74] Cynthia Sprunger, who has worked for a representative and also for the U.S. Department of Education, agreed about the importance of quality information. "Some of these groups exaggerate," says Sprunger. "There are enough really genuine policy problems that one shouldn't have to exaggerate. And once a group starts to exaggerate, the people reading [or hearing] it are going to say, 'Well, what else are they exaggerating that I don't know about?'"[75]

In Washington, Mennonite Central Committee service workers garner high marks for providing reliable information. "I've perceived MCC's field workers as having good information," notes Ahearn, who is quite critical of the overall contributions made by religious lobbyists in Washington. "I also find these MCC people to be very refreshing. They have a less cynical view of life than people inside the Beltway." Ahearn also explains that it is useful to hear from MCC personnel because they have been working long-term in the settings for which they provide information, whereas many other groups have gone to a "hot spot" for only a couple of days. "The quality of information gets better if someone has been around for awhile," he contends.[76] "I haven't found in my conversations with MCC people any sort of wild-eyed disconnect with reality," adds James McCormick.[77]

Many legislative aides mention that MCC's credibility is strengthened because of the service work MCC does, or because of positive contacts with other Mennonites on their overseas trips. Lori Murray notes that on a trip to southeast Asia she met MCC persons who had been working there for many years.[78] Senate legislative aide Andy Semmel says on one staff trip to Bolivia he was impressed with the "very rich farms" on Mennonite settlements there. "The country wasn't working well," claims Semmel, "but Mennonites were."[79] James McCormick recalls that in August 1992 he and other staff persons on the House Subcommittee on Asian and Pacific were trying to get plane tickets from Bangkok to Hanoi. The government officials couldn't purchase tickets because of the United States's tenuous relationship with Vietnam. McCormick sought out the help of workers from MCC, which has four decades of experience in Vietnam, and the MCC personnel were able to obtain the plane tickets for them.[80] Marty Rendon, who worked on the House Select Committee on Hunger, says he met MCC workers in Haiti when the committee went there in 1991 to look at sustainable agriculture activities. The MCC worker, Martin Gingerich, told them how they were educating farmers and about MCC's other projects. "There were no strings attached, just good information," notes Rendon. Later, when Gingerich came through Washington, Rendon and others on the committee met with him again. "I think Mennonites have the reputation of being out to help humanity," Rendon states. "They don't have a certain political ax to grind. And I think that gives them a lot of credibility."[81]

Other legislative aides agree that MCC field workers generally are objective in their reporting. Jim McGovern suggests that some religious lobbyists and service workers "have a view that is so skewed by ideology that they're not objective. In Washington, D.C., credibility is the name of the game."[82] Cynthia Sprunger argues that it is important that persons providing information to members of Congress or the State Department stick to the standard that "[t]hese are the facts as we know them. If it turns out that that tends to put us into this camp or that camp, well, that's not the goal. These have been our experiences."[83] MCC personnel, she contends, generally have maintained that standard. Other congressional staffers acknowledge that they recognize MCC workers have a certain bias toward peace-and-justice issues and a bias against military responses. However, they also believe MCC operates within a "credible margin."[84] "Obviously they present a position they support, and there may or may not be some distortion there," observes Andy Semmel, "but it's well thought through, well-reasoned."[85]

MCC Washington and the service personnel the office brings through Washington attempt to show concern and bring about change for the people for whom they advocate, regardless of where that places them politically. Prominently placed on Delton Franz's office wall for many years was a framed quote from mid-century theologian Karl Barth: "The church stands for the human against all systems and ideologies. . . . Man has not to serve causes, causes have to serve man." The recently produced MCC brochure "Faith, Power and Politics: Questions and Answers," speaks with a similar voice:

> In some areas MCC workers have called for provision of land to the land-less poor or an end to the ways in which multinational corporations abuse local economies. While some do not see this type of advocacy as the work of relief, development and service agencies, MCC does advocate for such reform occasionally, as a way to prevent suffering and human need. MCC also continues its traditional ministries, such as helping farmers in Zambia grow soybeans, encouraging Burkina Faso farmers to dig wells by hand and helping people in many nations help themselves rather than depend on outside aid. MCC's agenda is to help poor people, whether the solutions are seen as traditional or non-traditional, political or non-political.[86]

Such a commitment, which the MCC Washington office also seeks to em-body—with varying degrees of success—is difficult to maintain. This is especially true in a political (and a religious) climate, where lobbyists and government officials are perceived as having particular political agendas— or where *not* having a political agenda can be suspect. Experience often does not fit into neatly delineated ideological or political categories, but instead crosses over such boundaries. Basing their advocacy on firsthand observation, as they often do, sometimes places MCC Washington on one side of a conflict, sometimes on another.[87] This is awkward for an office that sits smack in the midst of religious and political organizations that suggest, at least implicitly, "Either you're on our side or you're against us."

Jay Lintner of the UCC's Washington office expresses his discomfort with one of MCC Washington's long-term staffers. "When I was doing foreign aid," he explains, "I was aware of Keith Gingrich, and I had heard him talk many times. It was never clear to me where he was coming from ideologically. It wasn't clear other than I knew that he worked for MCC, but he seemed to have a very unique perspective which was very much grounded in what he had seen on the ground in the part of Africa he had been in."[88] Lintner acknowledges that he is ambivalent about whether this kind of nonideological information giving is a helpful or unhelpful style on Capitol Hill. MCC's Gingrich says he recognizes that "very much in our milieu working here, people are looking for something more clear-cut." Gingrich claims, however, that he would take Lintner's "nonideological" comment as a compliment, "as long as there was some sort of message getting through." The MCC worker adds, "We try to convey an unbiased position relative to politics, generally. That's not always easy to do, even when you say that's your intention. People who are just getting to know us for the first time almost automatically read into our bringing people around as meaning we have some one side to play over against another."[89]

Mennonite political scientist Mark Neufeld, who researched MCC's work in the Philippines in 1988, also criticized MCC—the parent organization, not the Washington office—for the seemingly "nonpolitical" and "nonideological" nature of its approach, which promotes "communication" and "understanding."[90] Neufeld draws on critical theorist Jürgen Habermas's delineation of three types of knowledge, all of which are integral for human development: the technical, hermeneutic, and critical. Each of these types is based on a particular "cognitive interest." Technical knowledge is based on the "technical interest," the desire to transform the physical environment. Hermeneutic knowledge is based on the "practical interest" of communication for the purpose of understanding, thus allowing for the organization of the social world. Critical knowledge is rooted in persons' "emancipatory interest" in understanding and liberating themselves from structurally generated *distortions* of human interaction.[91]

Neufeld says that technical knowledge, such as agricultural techniques and the health sciences, has a role to play in the work of church service organizations. He further claims that MCC's emphasis is on the *hermeneutic* approach, noting that MCC workers are encouraged to show "cultural sensitivity," to be "open" and in a "learning and listening mode" as they share their technical knowledge as well as their faith. MCC provides extensive language study so that its workers can communicate effectively. This may be fine as far as it goes, according to Neufeld. What is missing from this approach, though, and what can be found in *emancipatory* interest, contends Neufeld, is the means of assessing competing interpretations of social reality. "Simply put," he says, "those interpretations which enable the oppressed to develop an understanding of socially structured inequalities (knowledge) and empower them to struggle for justice in the face of organized opposition (action) are considered superior."[92] What MCC workers need, argues Neufeld, are skills not only in the technical and hermeneutic interests, but also a knowledge of the critical social sciences, which would guide them in "choosing sides," participating with the poor and oppressed in an empowering analysis.

Certainly not all of MCC's work is as blind to structural and ideological distortions as Neufeld suggests, nor is MCC as "neutral" as the political scientist implies. MCC's guiding principles seemingly weave together strands of the technical, hermeneutic, and emancipatory approaches. The organization's principles for guiding its mission state: "Our service is expected to incarnate the love of God by standing with needy people. Our skills, resources and influence will benefit others but we also expect to learn from and be changed by the people we relate to. . . . Our work, whether short or longer term, will be developmental in character. Development is a participatory, transforming process leading to greater dignity and self-reliance, greater vision and possibility, greater community and interdependence."[93]

MCC's international mediator, John Paul Lederach, often speaks about the "fallacy of neutrality."[94] Other MCC workers frequently are hassled by military authorities for helping the poor, which may be considered a communist act. Many volunteers take personal risks, by endangering their lives in their support of the oppressed, or institutional risks, by speaking publicly about siding with marginalized people over against established regimes, potentially alienating some of their constituents with their "political" acts. The same is true in Washington: those who watch MCC staffers work on Capitol Hill or read the *Washington Memo* could hardly describe their overall work as neutral. Because of their institutional constraints and style, MCC Washington staffers may not jump on ideological bandwagons as quickly, but their commitments to those with whom MCC works are clear.

In Washington and in other political power centers, Jürgen Habermas's critical theory actually may help us understand the work of religious lobbies such as MCC. Habermas is most concerned about technology and science dominating in the *political* as well as in the economic and other spheres. Science and technology are sources of "systematically distorted communication," he says, since they are rooted in a form of rational-purposive action that excludes values from the discussion.[95] The problem with the expanding modern state is that by intervening in the realms of economics and scientific research, it has taken on the rational-purposive orientation of these other spheres. No longer can the state be concerned with processes of consensus or conversation about common values: now technocratic consciousness dominates nearly everywhere, leaving a values-discussion vacuum. To remedy this dilemma, Habermas contends, what is needed is development of "the public sphere," a place where citizens can discuss political decisions free of the prevailing technocratic consciousness.[96] Habermas implies that the eighteenth-century bourgeois public sphere in England, France, and Germany comes close to his notion of an "ideal speech community."[97] As described by one group of scholars, the bourgeois public sphere "consisted of private persons without strong links to particular political parties or regimes, who engaged in critical discourse about the claims of the state and examined the assumptions on which political decisions were based. With increasing penetration of the state into the bourgeois economy, this sphere eventually lost its autonomy and its capacity to reflect dispassionately upon the interests of the state."[98]

It is unclear in Habermas's writing what could fill this role in the modern world, or who could disassociate themselves adequately from the technocratic consciousness that brings with it distortion and false consciousness. Habermas, who is not keen on religious organizations or movements, makes brief references to certain grassroots interest groups fulfilling this function—perhaps environmentalists, consumer-action groups, student activists, or consciousness-raising groups.[99] For these groups to function legitimately they would need to maintain critical distance from political institutions and enter into discussions about values. One might suggest that, in some ways, an organization such as MCC could be among the discussants in Habermas's "ideal" world, tapping into the basic value commitments of policymakers rather than seeking to apply pressure. On particular issues and regarding particular geographic regions, MCC Washington seems located on a trajectory toward the critical theorist's hopes. Although MCC's Capitol Hill office has been deeply influenced by its highly charged political context, its—and the larger organization's—language and practices remain linked back into their traditions of origin. Nor is MCC overly dominated by "technocratic consciousness." In addition, MCC service workers' long history of caring for human needs, regardless of the political persuasion of those with whom they work, and their method of reporting experiences with both authenticity and a commitment to certain values, may qualify them as a potential "public." Even when MCC Washington is not a dispassionate observer, one may want to argue that the office should be among the voices in a "plurality of competing publics."[100]

Capitol Hill Mennonite staffers say MCC's domestic and overseas service work—nonideological as it may or may not be—provides the foundation for MCC Washington's involvements. This lived experience, combined with the *relative* objectivity of service workers who speak with government officials, has allowed MCC Washington staffers to develop relationships over the past several decades, building on the international reputation of the parent organization. "It's a matter of trust-building over a period of time," explains Keith Gingrich. "It's not just a matter of putting the message in, but building up human relationships with others here."[101]

Gingrich and other staffers recognize, though, that without the international dimension of MCC, Washington staffers would not get their lobbying feet through as many doors and would not have the opportunity to build up the relationships that have allowed them to be effective in D.C. Congressional aide Jim McGovern remarks about MCC: "I think it's one of those rare cases where people look at the [service] work and say, 'This is good stuff. These people are credible. They know what they're talking about. And maybe they deserve our ear on some of these issues.' And that's where their influence and power comes from."[102]

In a 1976 review of MCC Washington, Franz argues that the key in MCC's representation has not been the resource of traditional secular lobbyists—for example, massive voting strength or campaign money. Instead, "It has been our long-standing service involvement in relation to human needs."[103] Legislative aides, MCC staffers in Akron and Washington, and MCC Washington's coalition partners agree that it is Mennonite Central Committee's global service network that makes the difference in its lobbying efforts. MCC's international service and relief work provide another component to the "bundling board" separating MCC Washington's efforts from those of some of its peers.

It is true that many legislators and other national policymakers have never heard of Mennonite Central Committee nor its Washington office. And it is likewise clear that some of the international reporting that MCC Washington oversees is handled less effectively—and perhaps less faithfully—than it might be. Some have suggested that MCC could push harder and earlier for reconciliation in conflict situations before the outbreak of wars. Also, thus far the office has not done regular follow-ups on service workers' Capitol Hill visits, checking to see if more information is desired or if government officials are pursuing some course of action. Nor have staffers circulated as many written reports as may have been possible. Nor have they taken full advantage of the experiences of the scores of MCC service workers who return from overseas assignments. MCC and MCC Washington have not wanted all of the organization's service workers to do explicitly "political" work, but it does seem that more storytelling could be done.

The ongoing service and relief ministries of MCC do continue to inform, shape, and inspire the message and the messengers in the MCC Washington office. Maybe more importantly, MCC's commitment to humanitarian assistance *legitimates* the capital office's work, allowing MCC's lobbyists to function with episodic effectiveness, and prompting legislators and State

Department officials to grant them a hearing both when field workers return and when Washington staffers visit on their own. In Washington, credibility is a scarce but necessary attribute. And it is an attribute which MCC appears to have, at least for now. As one former MCC Washington staff person observed, the office would have very little to say if it did not have international volunteers, international experience, and an international perspective. Without its connections to Akron and the world, MCC Washington's speech would not just be more limited, it seems. It is also likely that far fewer would listen.

6

SPEAKING MULTIPLE LANGUAGES

The conversation at the wall, conducted according to imperial rationality, is a poor, if not impossible, place in which to do the "night work" of dream and vision, of remembering and hoping, of caring and fearing, of compassion and passion. Many burned-out and cynical liberals have succumbed to this conversation when, in fact, it cannot by definition be serious about some matters.

—*Walter Brueggemann, "The Legitimacy of a Sectarian Hermeneutic"*

As American Mennonites have moved from service work into the political arena, they have encountered new *languages* as well as new practices. In earlier centuries they, like most other religious groups, had only one form of discourse: the communal or churchly. As they began speaking to the state, however, Mennonites recognized that they could no longer speak only in theological or biblical languages, the languages of "believers." Instead, they needed to learn something about political discourse; hence, the beginning of a public language, and the distinction between their communal and public ways of speaking. "We are learning a new language—the language of the military, of the international economic order, of civil liberty," wrote MCC Washington Director Delton Franz a decade after the office's opening. "Without understanding the discourse in these and other critical areas, we cannot effectively translate the concerns of Jesus and the prophets for the poor and oppressed to the present day leaders who are accountable to govern with justice and equity."[1]

The original intent of public language—for Mennonites and other religious bodies—is to express the convictions of the communal language. The risk, of course, is that once a denominational organization begins speaking public languages, it may forget the primary language of the church. The secondary language may feed back into the communal language and transform it, perhaps drawing it away from its theological and biblical roots. Needed yet is an examination of the possibilities and limits of speaking communal discourse in the political arena and of speaking public discourse in churchly settings.

FINDING SPACE FOR THE RELIGIOUS VOICE

Already I've discussed the critiques of several social philosophers who believe religious groups ought not be players in public discourse. Their criticisms are based on an understanding of the "public realm" as "shared rational space," a place where *reason* is the legitimating norm. From the limited perspective of John Rawls and some other philosophical liberals, religious faith is inherently nonrational—grounded in claims that are not commonly shared—and therefore illegitimate as a resource in public discourse. Reinhold Niebuhr and his followers, of course, offer a more targeted critique: they suggest that at least religious *pacifists* should not have a voice in determining public policy. On the other hand, other philosophical liberals and theologians believe church organizations should be among those participants discussing what "the good society" may look like in the U.S.

In "The Legitimacy of a Sectarian Hermeneutic," Presbyterian theologian Walter Brueggemann perceptively speaks about "sect truth" as an "alternative perception of reality" that may serve as "an act of identity, energy and power." Such truth, contends Brueggemann, exercises "an important critical function [in showing] that the large claims of the dominant reality cannot be taken at face value." Brueggemann argues that the dominant rationality needs to be criticized because its power actions often "are separated from the truth of human suffering and human hope and are therefore illegitimate."[2] In a similar vein, social theorist David Harrington Watt claims that "rationality, as a governing principle of public discourse, is somewhat parochial." Rationality, he notes, is related to social power, and telling the dispossessed that they must speak rationally is simply a way of silencing their voices. "Moreover, there are . . . aspects of our common life that cannot be fully explored rationally," Harrington Watt observes. "Telling people that they have to be rational to enter into public debate marginalizes all those people for whom life is finally about something—such as art, or serving God and enjoying [God] forever—other than rational discourse." Given these problems, he says, traditional arguments about excluding religion from the public sphere have lost much of their force. He writes: "The manner in which religious language and religious symbols can enrich our public debate is now open for exploration in a way that it had not been before."[3]

According to Brueggemann, an "alternative perception of reality" would not provide a monopolized claim, but would be shared in an accommodating way. "It can be a proposal to the larger community, a proposal of an interpretation (a reading of reality) in which the larger community can share and which will bear the scrutiny of the larger community."[4] Such a reading, and such a sectarian conversation—if properly kept open to its own language, experience, and reference—is not only legitimate but essential for serious public discourse, Brueggemann contends. The theologian's comments are set within the context of a discussion of II Kings 18 and 19, which chronicles a dramatic encounter between the eighth century B.C.E. Assyrians and Judah. The strong Assyrian army is at the city gate of the much weaker Jerusalemites, shouting at them over the wall to surrender. The language of international diplomacy, the language *at the wall,* is usually the more sophisticated Aramaic. The language *behind* the wall is a different one—Hebrew—spoken by a different set of people with a different worldview and different understandings of Yahweh. Aramaic is the public language, while Hebrew is the communal language, spoken out of hearing range of the imperial negotiators. "The conversation on the wall is crucial, because the Assyrians are real. They are dialogue partners and must be taken seriously. And they will not go away," states Brueggemann. "But unless there is another conversation behind the wall in another language about another agenda, Judah on the wall will simply submit to and echo imperial perceptions of reality."[5] Brueggemann holds that when imperial perceptions of reality prevail, then everything already has been conceded.

In their passionate analysis of religious social activists and advocates, Robert Bellah and his associates express a similar concern: "Perhaps in the process of learning the state's languages of legal rights, cost-benefit utilities, and justice as due process, they have forgotten the language of covenant and communion." Bellah and his partners lament the potential loss of the churches' "unique endowment, their biblical and theological heritage." "When they fail to cultivate that endowment," they write, "[advocates and activists] live, like so many other sectors of our society, on borrowed time."[6]

163

LEARNING OTHER LANGUAGES

Staffers at MCC Washington are aware of the tensions between political discourse in Washington and the languages of their faith traditions. Greg Goering says he recognized early on that he was living in a "bi-culture" in the capital. While his primary language comes from the church, he soon realized that this is an inappropriate parlance to use for public discourse. Goering observes that while he was not in an international MCC assignment, he faced some of the same challenges as international service workers because he had a new culture to learn in Washington. "Even the language was foreign—it's English, but it's a different language that I needed to learn to speak," says Goering. "And then I realized that sometimes I wasn't careful about which language I used. Sometimes when writing a newsletter article, I'll realize that, oh yeah, I'm speaking to people in the community of faith, but often I'm using in a newsletter article language drawn from public discourse."[7] Goering admits that after three years in Washington, he found himself thinking primarily in the language of public discourse.

MCC Washington workers also are aware of the diverse languages rooted in their faith traditions and embodied in different forms among their constituents. Some of their constituent members still speak only the language of faith, and consider public discourse anathema for Mennonites. "There are some who don't even want to communicate with the Assyrians, who say that's not our agenda," notes Franz. "[They believe] our agenda is to remain pure and obedient to the gospel as we understand it."[8] Some within their traditions speak in strict two-kingdom language regarding ethics for the church and the state. In this view, God never expected the state to live by Christian standards, and the church ought not tell governing authorities how to conduct their God-ordained affairs. Others speak of a modified two-kingdom ethic, which seeks space to speak to the state but yet recognizes political power realities and the "need" for coercive violence for maintaining order. Yet others emphasize "Christ's lordship over all creation," implying a shift toward one ultimate ethic for both the religious and political worlds. Others use the language of just war; some speak out of the "political realism" of their studies in political science or economics; and others promote a "realist pacifist perspective." MCC Washington's constituents do not speak in one voice but in many.

Even when Washington and Akron MCC personnel converse, they find a communication gap. Goering says when he attended a September 1992 Coordinating Council meeting at Akron headquarters, he was struck with the realization that he was "back in the church." "It's just a very different atmosphere in Akron around that table than there is here," he contends.

"And I was recognizing that when I was trying to interpret our agenda to our advisors there that I had to use a different language. And it wasn't easy for me to slip back into interpreting the issues I usually speak about in public discourse here into the language of our heritage."[9]

Likewise, multiple languages are spoken in the Washington milieu. MCC's Washington Interreligious Staff Council peers speak out of their own unique religious traditions, with varying understandings of "the powers" and of redemption, justice, and peace. MCC Washington's Jalane Schmidt says she sees the biggest gap between MCC and other advocacy groups on the issue of simple lifestyle—the challenge of living with fewer of the world's resources. "You work on an energy policy or environmental sorts of things, and I don't find a willingness or even an awareness of how North American lifestyles might be adversely affecting the planet or resources available to others," Schmidt remarks. "On the issue of health care, people just want the moon and the stars and aren't willing to talk about limits."[10]

The religious organizations do, however, have significant overlap in biblical if not theological language. "The difference [between our voice and that of others in the religious community] is fairly significant in theological terms, but the minute we begin talking about public policy, the minute we begin approaching 'the wall,' those differences seem to become minimized," notes staffer Keith Gingrich.[11] In other words, the nuanced distinctions between the various denominational offices located in the Methodist Building often become muted in the collective church lobbying voice.[12] In the search for a common language to offer a unified "witness," some of the tradition-specific diction is lost.

Mennonite staff members also mentioned the different voices of their secular partners. On Monday afternoons Gingrich meets with two groups: the Monday Lobby, a coalition of religious and secular groups concerned with arms and the military budget, and with the Foreign Policy and Military Spending Task Force of WISC. While the groups monitor precisely the same issues, Gingrich observes that they sometimes couch their discussions in slightly different languages.[13] Goering says he found distinctions when he talked about energy policy with the religious community as opposed to the secular community. "The environmental groups were saying they didn't think we could get American people to give up their cars easily. And I said, 'But that's what we as churches are about—transformation of ourselves and other people.'"[14] However, MCC Washington staffers agree that whatever walls there may be between their lobbying counterparts— short ones between religious groups and higher but scalable walls for secular lobbies—these differences are small when compared with the "Great Wall" between the peace-and-justice lobbies and the state.

Even *those* differences, though, are muddied by the realities that all parties are speaking English, and that many of the "governing authorities" *also* are Christians. "Here, where we share English as a language of negotiation, there are words and phrases that can be used in both contexts that have vastly different meanings," notes Goering. "When [some politicians] talk about justice, they mean giving people what they deserve, and giving it *to* them, but I'm talking more about giving people what they *need.*" On the other hand, many members of Congress and administration officials come out of Christian traditions, and know the languages of those traditions. How does one converse with the "Assyrian" who speaks "Hebrew" at the wall, even if it may be a crudely accented Hebrew? Or perhaps the question should be, How does one converse with the *"Hebrew"* at the wall whose first language has become that of the "Assyrian"?

Senator Mark Hatfield has criticized the Washington religious community for addressing him as a secular government representative rather than as a "brother within the fold." George Bush used the just war tradition—which has secular roots but has been developed primarily in religious contexts—to justify U.S. involvement in the Persian Gulf crisis. Goering says, "I've encountered situations where a member of Congress is a devout Baptist, for instance, and he says the Bible is central to his world. And I also claim that the Bible is central to my world." Goering suggests that this commonality does not lead to common assumptions or conclusions.[15] The reality of these overlapping and conflicting language grids—within the religious community, within various coalition partnerships, and between the religious lobbies and the state—makes effective communication difficult. Before looking more closely at how the office tries to find a middle ground—and at what "compromises" such a ground has necessitated—we need to examine places where MCC Washington seeks to draw explicitly on its biblical and Anabaptist traditions.

DRAWING ON SCRIPTURE AND ANABAPTIST FAITH TRADITIONS

MCC Washington, like nearly every other religious organization based in the Methodist Building, does not quote Scripture or dwell on its faith heritage in its written or oral communications to government leaders. "We don't try to preach to people. We don't try to do our theology explicitly," explains Franz. Brueggemann writes that he does not believe "that the Bible serves very often or very well directly for participation in the public discourse at the wall," since that is not its intent, purpose, or character: biblical languages simply *nurture* the conversation *"behind* the wall."[16] Public conversation generally is limited to the languages that are comprehensible to all participants "at the wall." Religious organizations in Washington intend for their faith understandings to be *implicit* in—not the focus of—their public communications. In reporting back to their constituent bodies, however, the religious lobbies such as MCC Washington make more of an effort to include biblical and theological rationale for their interpretations. Such an effort helps legitimate their work to "the folks in the churches" and keeps them conversant in the language "behind the wall."

Washington Memo, the office's bimonthly newsletter to its constituent subscribers, often includes biblical references in its lead editorials and occasionally in other articles. MCC Washington's supporters, critics, and parent organization often remind staff persons of the importance of a sound Anabaptist-Mennonite basis for their work. "We have learned something of the importance of incorporating biblical/theological perspective in a newsletter that is focused on the impact of governmental policy/actions on human beings," states a 1989 "Self-Study" prepared by MCC Washington staff. "While ours is not principally the task of 'teaching' Bible and Theology vis a vis the 'principalities and powers,' (our congregations, colleges and seminaries *should* be doing that), we cannot ignore this dimension of our work, a work that has important biblical/theological implications."[17]

Still, it is difficult to think in the language of the faith when one's life is conducted primarily in the political arena. Greg Goering acknowledges that when writing newsletter articles he often wonders whether he is using the logic and language public officials use or that which constituent Mennonites and Brethren in Christ would understand. He says the experience of putting together the newsletter reminds him of a friend's first sermon. After the friend had written his sermon, he went to his Bible professor and asked, "Do you have a Scripture passage I could base this sermon on?" "I wonder how often we do that," says Goering. "We write [an] article in public discourse, and then we think, Oh, how can I ground this in Anabaptist-Mennonite biblical theology?"[18] To facilitate inclusion of relevant faith texts, Goering and other staffers sometimes use QuickVerse 2.0, a kind of computerized Bible-o-Matic concordance program.

Even without direct biblical references, one can find strands of Anabaptist-Mennonite biblical theology in the *Washington Memo.* In a presentation at the 1989 "Twentieth Anniversary Consultation on the MCC Washington Office," Mennonite ethicist Duane Friesen suggests that the operative perspective of the *Memo* reflects the following principles: a redemptive view of the state ("it can do better"); the recognition of the basic humanity of one's enemy; suspicion and mistrust of the reliance upon violent force as a way of solving human political problems, and a commitment to using human imagination, ingenuity, and resources to solve conflicts nonviolently; a commitment to internationalism versus nationalism; a criticism of unrestrained private pursuit and a commitment to justice, defined particularly in terms of how policy affects the poorest and least advantaged members of society; and a commitment to human rights.[19] While most of these principles find kinship in the political left, many also can be found in Anabaptist–Mennonite theological traditions.

In addition to faith-based citations in the newsletter, MCC Washington staff persons make explicit reference to their faith traditions and to the Bible in other constituent contacts, such as seminars. The two contexts for explicit allusions to their biblical and historical roots are 1) justifications for their existence and their work, and 2) applications for the general direction of public policy. Making biblical and Anabaptist traditions relevant to these questions sometimes means staffers need to select carefully from the traditions or modify some of the historical material that does not fully fit their hoped-for parameters of lobbying or witnessing to the state. In applying the traditions to public policy, MCC workers may need to make enormous historical, cultural, and political leaps.

Nearly every MCC Washington seminar includes a biblically based section on "Why it is good (or justifiable) for us to be a voice on Capitol Hill." In his presentations, Franz typically spoke about *passages*: his personal ones, those of MCC, and those of the biblical character Moses. Franz had moved from the rural wheat fields of Kansas to inner-city Chicago to the corridors of Washington. MCC shifted from providing emergency relief to doing service projects to working with Third World development to addressing justice issues. Moses—initially motivated by witnessing an Egyptian beating a Hebrew—moved from a period of quietude to the courts of Pharaoh. Franz repeatedly cited the story of God telling Moses to go to Pharaoh and to bring God's people out of Egypt. At first Moses, perhaps like Franz himself, was reluctant because he was "slow and hesitant of speech" (Exodus 3:11; 4:10). Sometimes the former director referred to the Book of Esther, which speaks about "a copy of the writ for the destruction of the Jews [being] issued." The message conveyed to Esther, Franz told his audiences, was "If you remain silent at such a time as this, relief and deliverance for the Jews will appear from another quarter, but you and your family will perish."

Other biblical passages MCC Washington staffers cite include, among others: Ephesians 3:10 ("It is God's intent that now, through the church, the manifold wisdom of God should be made known to the rulers and authorities"); Luke 18:1–8 (the story of the persistent widow and the unjust judge who finally said, "Though I neither fear God nor regard humans, yet because this widow bothers me, I will vindicate her, or she will wear me out by her continual coming"); Matthew 5:13–16 ("You are salt to the world"); Jeremiah 22 ("Josiah did what is right and just. . . . He defended the cause of the poor and needy. . . . Is that not what it means to know me?"); and Jesus' explanation of his ministry in Luke 4:16–22 ("The Spirit of the Lord is upon me, because he has anointed me to preach good news to the poor. He has sent me to proclaim release to the captives and recovering of sight to the blind, to set at liberty those who are oppressed, to proclaim the acceptable year of the Lord"). In a more general sense, Franz's presentations referred to God's oft-mentioned concern for the inequities that create injustice. On occasion Franz and now other staff persons attempt to deal with passages that urge the church to be relatively silent in the political arena, for example Romans 13:1–7 ("Let every person be subject to the governing authorities") and I Timothy 2:1 (on praying for kings and all who are in high positions, "that we may lead a quiet and peaceable life, godly and respectful in every way").[20]

MCC Washington workers also draw creatively on their Anabaptist-Mennonite tradition to justify their presence in Washington. Sometimes Franz spoke about how God historically has used committed minorities to accomplish God's purposes. The most obvious biblical examples are the Hebrew people and the early church, but Franz suggested that God's purposes also may be worked out through contemporary Anabaptist-Mennonites. Staffers go back to the earliest months of Anabaptism, when sometimes rowdy young leaders defiantly refused to obey civil authorities who demanded that they baptize their infants. The Anabaptists' first response, staffers rightly note, was to *engage* political authorities, not to withdraw. On occasion Franz also cited the writings of early Anabaptist leader Menno Simons. The Anabaptists' rigid two-kingdom ethic and centuries of withdrawal are described as not fully representative of the early Anabaptist leaders, as rooted in the misguided eschatological perspectives of certain spokespersons, and as a response to the reality of oppressive monarchical rule. In his presentations, Franz would tell his listeners that even Michael Sattler, who wrote the seemingly quietistic Schleitheim Articles, affirmed the egalitarian emphasis of the German peasants who revolted, rejected the large landholdings and wealth of the monastery, and empathized with the peasant reaction to the long injustices they had endured.[21] Franz also often spoke about his Russian Mennonite ancestors pleading their case to the czar in the 1860s and 1870s, and again in the 1920s when famine and revolution hit. He suggested that the twentieth-century changes in Mennonites' relationship to the state were brought about as a result of MCC's own service workers observing—as Moses did—"Egyptians beating Hebrews."

Sharing concerns with a Senate legislative aide, left, in 1974 are, left to right, Martin Schrag, Messiah College representative; Walton Hackman, MCC Peace Section; John E. Lapp, Franconia Conference bishop; and Delton Franz, MCC Washington director. Photo by Burton Buller, courtesy of Mennonite Central Committee Photograph Collection, Archives of the Mennonite Church, Goshen, Indiana.

The intention of mentioning these biblical and historical allusions here is not to analyze whether such selective readings are historically or biblically accurate or "faithful," but to indicate that MCC Washington staffers see the importance of legitimating themselves through their history and faith traditions. This is a difficult task, whether one is drawing on first-century or sixteenth-century texts and experiences. While the biblical references cited may look like prooftexting when separated from the context of seminar presentations or newsletter editorials, they are not necessarily so, particularly when they are used for justifying the office's work. MCC Washington staffers speak more broadly about the overall witness of the prophets and of the historical Jesus, and of God's intentions for humanity and human institutions. Clearly staffers draw selectively on their Anabaptist-Mennonite roots, but they are forthright about their tradition's history of withdrawal. Rather than discount the centuries of silence, they admit the collective quietude, point back to the political engagement of some early Anabaptists, and propose that God may be calling for new (or renewed) responses in the twentieth-century American context.

If using the Bible and Anabaptist-Mennonite history for "lobbying legitimation" appears problematic, the difficulty is seriously compounded when seeking to apply the same to specific public policies. Most of the *Washington Memo* articles about specific legislation make no direct reference to Mennonite traditions and history, nor to Scripture. Many *editorials*—which usually are directed at legislative action or administrative policy but do not concentrate on specific legislation—do include some citing of Scripture. The number of scriptural allusions in the *Memo* increased dramatically following the 1989 "Twentieth Anniversary Consultation on the MCC Washington Office," at which staff persons were encouraged to be more explicit about biblical and faith linkages in their work. In the newsletter, the theologizing generally remained implicit throughout most of the years between 1969 and 1989, except when Franz wrote about the Washington office's work. In the 1990s, however, Scripture has popped up frequently—not as the *focus* of but as *support* for an interpretation of public policy.

In a 1992 editorial entitled "A New Historical Moment," Franz deals with four issues, and refers to Scripture to support each point. 1) On the "Idolatry of Military Might," he quotes Jeremiah 31:15 and the biblical admonition to "weep with those who mourn," including the fatherless children and bereft widows of Iraq, El Salvador, Yugoslavia, South Africa, and elsewhere. 2) Regarding the international debt crisis, he refers to Matthew 18:23–35, the parable of the servant who had been forgiven a great debt by a king but then refused to forgive a small debt owed to him by another servant. 3) On "Peacekeeping: A Noble Enterprise," Franz argues that "as a people with a peace tradition, we need now to urge Congress and the Administration to raise United Nations peacemaking and peacekeeping initiatives to a higher priority." He closes by mentioning I Peter 3:11: "Seek peace and pursue it!" 4) Regarding "Poverty and Wealth in America," which addresses the "inequitable tax structure," Franz alludes to the parable of the rich man and Lazarus. Lazarus, says the parable found in Luke 16, longed to eat scraps from the rich man's table. Ultimately a great chasm was fixed between the eternally suffering rich man and the rewarded Lazarus.[22]

One might forcefully argue that the passages quoted give little helpful guidance for specific policy recommendations. Among the four passages, perhaps the most malleable is the reference to seeking peace and pursuing it, since such a directive could be used to justify a host of military and nonmilitary options on multiple issues. It is also worth noting that in two of the following three issues of *Washington Memo,* Franz uses the parable of the rich man and Lazarus. The next publication draws on the story in a discussion of the fiscal year 1993 federal budget. The editorial also cites Matthew 6:21 ("Where your treasure is, there will your heart be also") and says that "Biblical standards of justice do not allow us to be satisfied with an economic system where some struggle for subsistence while others accumulate great wealth."[23] Two issues later Lazarus serves as a metaphor for the suffering Haitians who travel in unseaworthy boats to the shores of the United States. Franz concludes the Haitian article by urging readers to write to senators and representatives and to ask them "to dispatch a peacekeeping force to Haiti to restore democracy and order."[24]

Over the years most other passages were not used as frequently as the Lucan parable. Also, although many of the citations noted above are from the writings of the early church, most biblical references and allusions have been from the Hebrew scriptures, especially the works of the prophets. In a 1981 article about the federal budget, staffer Betsy Beyler mentions Ronald Reagan's intentions to slash social programs but increase military-related spending by 30 percent. She then quotes Isaiah 58: "Is not this the fast that I choose: to loose the bonds of wickedness, to undo the thongs of the yoke, to let the oppressed go free . . . to share your bread with the hungry, and bring the homeless poor into your house. . . ."[25] In a post–Persian Gulf War cover article, Franz argues that "from our biblical and Anabaptist roots and peacemaking principles, we as a peace church are called to advocate alternatives to humiliating the adversary." For biblical backing he cites Isaiah 3:15 and 42:3: "What do you mean by crushing my people and grinding the faces of the poor, declares the Lord. . . . A bruised reed he will not break, and a smoldering wick he will not snuff out."[26]

In a 1985 *Memo* article about violence in the Middle East, Franz speaks about specific negotiations between Israelis and Palestinians, and reasons for urgency in resolving some of the crises in the region. In a sidebar attached to the article, Franz calls attention to "Ancient Truth for Palestine Today":

> The timeless biblical requirement for those who would live in Palestine with the expectation of peace and longevity is that they must "keep His statutes and his commandments which I command you this day that it may go well with you, and that you may prolong your days in the land." (Deuteronomy 4:40) If the land becomes defiled by abominations against God's commandments "the land will vomit you out as it vomited out the nation that was before you." (Leviticus 18:28) The Hebrew Torah implored: "Justice, and justice alone shall you pursue, so that you may live and occupy the land which the Lord your God is giving you." (Deuteronomy 16:20) The ancient teaching of Jahweh regarding the Israelites' dealings with peoples of other backgrounds is also instructive for the current tensions and injustices experienced in Israeli-Palestinian relationships in Palestine. "When an alien settles with you in your land, you shall not oppress him. He shall be treated as a native born among you and you shall love him as a man like yourself, because you were aliens in Egypt." (Leviticus 19:33–34)[27]

Franz ends the article by encouraging readers to write to the president and urge him to support these goals: 1) to call for Israeli and Palestinian mutual and simultaneous recognition of the right of Israel to exist within secure borders; 2) to support the self-determination for the Palestinian people; 3) to support political forces in Israel that call for territorial compromise on the borders of the West Bank; 4) to revive a diplomatic strategy that involves Syria; and 5) to explore joint U.S.–USSR participation in the peace process.

One cannot move easily from the Pentateuch passages to Franz's recommendations. Nor can one readily glean from the parable of the rich man and Lazarus directives for the federal budget, treatment of Haitian boat people, and the federal income-tax structure. This is not news to MCC Washington staff persons. Although some articles do appear to be sermons in search of a Scripture, the Mennonite workers do not always apply the Bible as slavishly as it may seem in these selected references. They are aware that centuries and changing sociopolitical contexts necessitate significant reinterpretation and reconfiguration of the biblical texts' intentions. Basic to Christians' responsibility, they observe, is "the task of bridging the gap between the New Testament's application of the Gospel to the pre-industrialized–pre-modern society of first century Palestine and the highly technological, shrinking world" of the late twentieth century.[28] They also recognize that the state cannot live by the ethic of individual Christians or Christian institutions. What is needed is a way to mediate between what peace-loving Christians might hope for and what can be expected of the state.

AN ENGAGEMENT IN WHAT IS POSSIBLE

While some MCC Washington volunteers and paid employees go to Washington with a sense of clarity about what the government ought to do, life in Washington soon changes that. Greg Goering says he went to the capital assuming his task would be easy because he understood peacemaking from his biblically based Christology. For him, pacifism and nonviolence also could function as practical tools. "So it seemed very easy for me to say that the U.S. government should not engage in militarism and violence as a form of policy," he explains. "I think that over the last three years I've come to a politically more sophisticated position of understanding that the state cannot be expected to live up to the ideals that the church is called to live up to."[29] Working in Washington, contends Goering, has made him more politically conservative.

Ken Martens Friesen notes that he was heavily imbued with a two-kingdom approach during his years at a Mennonite college. However, he also took one semester of college "in a more Reformed environment" at American University in Washington, "and I think [that] exposed me to some very valid realities. . . . I function on kind of a one-kingdom approach. We work in the world and we're stuck in the middle of it, and there's no real sense of trying to be so idealistic that somehow we're above the crowd," claims Friesen. "And yet part of me wants to hold these [Anabaptist-Mennonite] ideals as true and say that there is an alternative and that we don't have to solve these international or domestic crises through age-old ways."[30]

This tension between the ethic of the church and the ethic of the state often led Franz to speak about "middle axioms," a theological-ethical mediating ground. Franz said, during his tenure on Capitol Hill, that MCC Washington makes no effort to hold the government to standards based on the Sermon on the Mount. "We have sensed that within the larger Mennonite and Brethren in Christ communities, the inclination would be neither to opt for an absolutist 'two kingdom' dualism, excluding any communication from the churches to government, nor to go the route of a 'single kingdom' theology with its unwarranted optimism of what can be expected of government," observed Franz. "We cannot expect government to function by Christian norms."[31] What the MCC Washington director hoped for was that political leaders would work toward a *more just* society. Franz suggested that MCC Washington's work is "an engagement in what is possible."[32]

In an early paper on "middle axioms," Franz explored how Mennonites might help government officials bring about a more just society. He mentioned three possible modes of speaking to government. These included 1) proposing only general principles without analysis of particulars and without specific recommendations, the preferred approach of official church bodies, and 2) the activist strategy of choosing a highly visible target to promote or protest. Neither of these, said Franz, is an appropriate mode of communicating in the legislative context, since both avoid the complexity of problems resolved in the public forum. So he proposed 3) "to be quite clear about ethical principles, but to tailor moral evaluations to the established contours of public debate." Franz stated: "Here the religious community or spokes[person] lets the contending interests determine the relevant questions on which to comment. The advantage of this third alternative is that the church's spokes[person] has easy entree to the legislative debate and is not rejected as a wild-eyed prophet with a heart-hardening message." Franz noted that the danger, of course, "is that compromise involves sacrificing ethical prophecy for political influence and betrayal of one's call 'You are the salt of the earth; but if the salt loses its strength, how shall it be salted.'"[33] Franz, who believed the opportunities in this third alternative were worth the risks, differentiated between compromise and middle axioms. The former is simply a kind of accommodation and acculturation, while the latter presupposes rootedness in Christian principles, which then are carefully applied.

The term "middle axioms" originated at the 1937 Oxford Conference on Life and Work and was developed further in the preparatory materials for the social ethics discussion at the World Council of Churches' Amsterdam General Assembly in 1948. A definition for the term was first set forth by J. H. Oldham, who argued that middle axioms provide a mode of discourse that mediates "between purely general statements of the ethical demands of the gospel and the decisions that have to be made in concrete situations." Oldham held that middle axioms give relevance to the Christian ethic. While they are not binding for all time, says Oldham, they are "provisional definitions of the type of behavior required of us at a given period and in given circumstances."[34]

Mennonite theologian and ethicist John H. Yoder devotes a chapter to middle axioms in his 1964 monograph *The Christian Witness to the State,* which provided a theological foundation for Mennonites' move into Washington. Yoder gives three meanings to the term: middle axioms are halfway between meaninglessly broad generalities and unrealistically precise prescriptions; their claim to authority is midway between absolute moral principles and mere pragmatic common sense; and they mediate between the norms of faith and the situation conditioned by unbelief.[35] "What we ask of the state is not the total elimination of all evils, but a possible elimination of evils which are presently identifiable and particularly offensive," states Yoder. "The world can be challenged, at the most, on one point at a time, to take one step in the right direction, to approximate in a slightly greater degree the righteousness of love."[36]

In an addendum to his paper on middle axioms, Franz listed three public policy issues, mentioned a normative Judaeo-Christian principle for each, suggested a middle axiom for the church and the government, and then took the further step of applying the axiom to a desirable government policy decision. For example, regarding the nuclear arms race, Franz cited three passages to ascertain the normative faith principle: "Thou shalt not kill," "If possible, so far as it lies with you, live at peace with all [persons]," and "Nations shall beat their swords into plowshares." The middle axiom for the church was that "as Mennonites, we do not anticipate, in a fallen society, that government will be nonresistant. We will, however, encourage government to pursue the least violent strategies possible." The middle axiom for public policymakers was that national security must be redefined in the nuclear age: "To speak of defending America with nuclear arms is a very inadequate stance in an era when a nuclear exchange would have global, not merely national consequences and when it is clear that there is *no* defense against a nuclear exchange." Franz's desirable government policy decision was ratification of a strategic arms limitation treaty that would limit and move toward reductions in nuclear weapons, and pursuit of security through multilateral substitutes for the arms race, such as economic justice programs and economic conversion of military industries.[37]

In a later *Washington Memo* article, Franz claims that asking for far greater restraint in reliance on military force is not an unrealistic request. He says, "The prevalent assumption is that international affairs can only succeed if armed force or the threat of its use is the principal engine driving U.S. foreign policy." That assumption can appropriately be challenged by the religious community, he asserts. Constructive alternatives he lists include: 1) a more energetic and creative use of diplomacy; 2) rectifying global and economic disparities; 3) undergirding rather than undermining international law; 4) greater use of UN Peacekeeping Forces in areas of persistent violence; 5) and seeing the world's problems from a South-North (poor-rich) perspective, not just from an East-West (communism-capitalism) perspective. "The people of our tradition can surely encourage the expanded use of such underused options," he notes, "as constructive alternatives to excessive reliance on the engines of war."[38]

KEEPING THE LANGUAGES IN TENSION

The rationale for moving from Franz's Judaeo-Christian principles to his middle axioms and then on to specific legislative policy or to constructive alternatives is not always clear. Policy directives do not emerge, fully developed, from even *well-interpreted* Scripture. Most *Washington Memo* articles about legislation—even those that refer to Scripture—draw on multiple other resources. Economists and political scientists are cited alongside Hebrew prophets. Political and social philosophers bolster policy recommendations proposed by Mennonite and other theologians. Greg Goering speaks about "feeling schizophrenic" in his usage of these various analyses. "At times I argued that we should live non-violently and invite others to do so as well out of our convictions as followers of the peaceable Christ (church)," explains Goering. "Other times I advocated peace because disarming seems like the only way to survive as a human race (secular). Similarly, I would urge Christians to live sustainable lifestyles and argue for the government to implement sustainable policies with regard to the environment because God is Creator and asks us to be faithful stewards of the earth (church). On the other hand I would advocate to curb environmental degradation because our security as a planet depended on it (secular)."[39] Usually the *Memo* speaks in the language of what Goering calls the secular, but even when the primary language is that of the church, articles *also* use the language of other specialists.

In the previously mentioned post–Persian Gulf War article about not humiliating enemies, Franz went both to Scripture and to the lessons of history found in the treatment of Germany after World War I and of Japan after World War II. On United Nations Peacekeeping Forces, Franz spoke not only of "seeking peace and pursuing it" but also of the relative bargain UN Peacekeeping is in comparison to warmaking. MCC veteran Earl Martin says that, in his contacts with Washington, he makes it clear he is coming from a perspective of pacifism, but then goes on to explain how "I believe practical interests of people would be enhanced by the more humane policies."[40]

Similarly, letters to members of Congress often make clear Mennonites' historic commitment to peace, but also offer other reasons for particular legislation. In a letter to Sen. Arlen Specter (R-Pennsylvania) regarding Senate Bill 32, "The Federal Death Penalty Act of 1989," Goering wrote: "The impetus for our commitment to speak out against the death penalty is derived from our religious conviction of God's love, forgiveness and reconciliation." He went on to say that the death penalty had not been applied fairly and evenly to white and black persons and that capital punishment's deterrent effect upon crime is "too infinitesimal to measure." He closed by stating, "For *moral* and *utilitarian* reasons and *in the interest of true criminal justice,* I urge you to oppose Senate Bill 32."[41]

While faith-based and other norms often may lead to the same conclusions, especially when speaking about broad policy areas, religious lobbying organizations often find themselves knee-deep in quandaries when they make specific policy recommendations. This is especially true for an organization such as Mennonite Central Committee, rooted in a tradition of absolute pacifism. How does a pacifist group affirm and encourage the state's not-quite-so-violent response when the governmental action still entails life-threatening coercion or violence? Once Mennonites have stepped beyond *absolute* pacifism, what concrete norms and criteria guide their specific recommendations? And why should anyone listen? On several occasions in the 1990s Mennonite personnel on Capitol Hill have found themselves on the horns of pacifist dilemmas—and on the horns of some constituents—when they have sought to offer specific guidelines to policymakers.[42] Three illustrative examples will suffice.

UN Peacekeeping Forces

While "peacekeeping" is not specifically described in the UN charter, the "policing" function has evolved over the past three decades as an internationally acceptable way of controlling conflicts and promoting peaceful settlements of disputes. Article 43 of the UN charter calls for "armed forces, assistance and facilities necessary to maintain international peace." The charter also stipulates that UN peacekeepers are forbidden to use force, except in extreme circumstances. In most instances, those wearing UN uniforms carry only sidearms that can be used only if there is a direct need for self-defense.[43] "Peacekeeping is not to win wars, it is to give negotiations a chance," claims Brian Urquhart, founder of the UN Peacekeeping Force. "The job of peacekeepers is to stay above the conflict, have no enemies, take a great deal of abuse, be rigidly impartial and not confuse self-defense with reprisals."[44] Over the past decade, UN peacekeepers have been called into conflicts in Somalia, Iraq, Bosnia, Haiti, and in other hot spots around the world.

One of MCC Washington's early mentions of UN peacekeeping efforts was in a 1984 *Memo* article on terrorism. After detailing a number of terrorist attacks, Franz begins detailing options. Among those he suggests is the use of nonaligned peacekeeping forces under United Nations auspices. He notes that their objective would not be to engage in combat, but to reduce tension and serve as a buffer to outbreaks of violence.[45] In response to Franz's article, one *Memo* reader and MCC Washington supporter said he was "truly shocked" that Franz had advocated the use of UN troops in the interest of peacemaking. "Whether or not a non-aligned peacekeeping force works or not is not the issue. The issue is that we cannot advocate the use or threat of force as a justified means to an end," the writer said. "We as Christians cannot affirm any action of the state that we as disciples of the living God cannot in good conscience do ourselves."[46]

Some other constituents also questioned Franz's public support of UN Peacekeeping Forces. The former director admitted that the issue is a tough one, but suggested that supporting a minimally violent alternative was far better than sitting on his hands in Washington. He sometimes compared the international mediators with the police function of a state. Mennonites generally have recognized the legitimacy of a police force, so long as it is "guided by fair judicial processes, subject to recognized legislative regulation, and safeguarded in practice against its running away with the situation."[47] This carefully restricted violence has been seen as part of the state's role of maintaining order, as directed in Romans 13. Whether or not the UN peacekeepers have a parallel function to a state's own police force remains an open question. For now, MCC Washington continues to endorse UN peacekeeping activities as one alternative in a conflict-ridden world. In a 1992 *Memo* article Franz wrote: "As members of a church body with an historic legacy of peacemaking, we Mennonites of the 1990's should convey to members of Congress our support for the use of our federal tax dollars to be authorized and appropriated for UN Peacekeeping work, forthwith!"[48]

Sanctions

Over the years MCC Washington and MCC's Akron administrators have repeatedly dealt with the issue of sanctions. Throughout history, sanctions—the refusal of a country or countries to trade or supply goods to another country—have been used as a tool of warfare. In a 1992 MCC Peace Office working paper, Co-executive Secretary Judy Zimmerman Herr notes that the increased use of sanctions "as a tool for international order" creates dilemmas for organizations such as MCC. "MCC stands in the tradition of the historic peace churches and eschews war or violent force as a method for solving conflicts. As an agency for relief and service, MCC works with victims of conflict and disaster and attempts to heal and bind up wounds," says Zimmerman Herr. She adds that "economic sanctions are clearly less overtly violent than warfare, and so may seem attractive to pacifists looking for alternatives to war. But . . . sanctions can also be used to cause suffering to innocent persons."[49]

Usually MCC has not complied with nor supported the sanctions imposed by the U.S. government. In many cases, the Canadian government did not impose the same sanctions, so MCC simply sent its humanitarian aid through MCC Canada. In a few cases, however, one of MCC's bodies or the Washington office has supported the use of sanctions. After the September 1991 coup in Haiti, the Organization of American States imposed comprehensive sanctions on coup leaders in an attempt to reinstate the government of President Aristide. The Latin American Department of MCC wrote to the U.S. State Department to commend U.S. involvement in the OAS action but also express the hope that Haiti's people would not suffer the consequences of the trade embargo. MCC was able to continue to send food and medical supplies, since they were exempted from the embargo. MCC staff persons said their support for sanctions against Haiti was based on MCC's Haitian contacts, who supported sanctions as a tool of pressure to return the duly-elected government.

MCC U.S. Peace Section and MCC Canada Executive Committee also publicly supported sanctions against the government of South Africa. The South Africa case "has been the longest and most divisive instance in which MCC wrestled with the sanctions issue," observes Zimmerman Herr. MCC's workers in the region of South Africa thought it would be good for Western governments to impose sanctions, but were unsure whether MCC should take action on the matter. Zimmerman Herr explains that MCC's workers, "who needed to deal on a daily basis with South Africa and who saw the plight of persons losing jobs as companies withdrew but also wanted to support the call of partners, felt unable to make strong statements of support." Back in the United States, both in Washington and elsewhere, MCC's coalition partners found it difficult to understand MCC's hesitation to speak loudly on the issue.

During the Persian Gulf War, Franz signed on to church coalition letters that said, "We support the sanctions approved by the United Nations in Iraq." In each case, however, the letters also said that food and medicine should not be included in the sanctions, as specified in UN Security Council Resolution 661. Following the war, MCC Washington was among those religious organizations asking that punitive sanctions—including everything except military supplies—be lifted. MCC also made preparations to ship infant formula to Iraq even if no license was granted.[50] While most of MCC's constituents were silent or supportive of MCC Washington's position on sanctions, some did register their concern. One person wrote to a Mennonite periodical: "Economic sanctions are part and parcel of a nation's system of imperialism, of forcing others to accede to its will through the creation of need, want, and, ultimately, terrible human suffering."[51]

In her paper, Zimmerman Herr acknowledges that sanctions fall within a gray area, somewhere between a "hot" war and nonviolent action or pressure. In what may be one of the clearest statements of contemporary Mennonite dilemmas brought on by service work and political engagement, she goes on to assert:

> A theology which categorically rules out war but allows for coercion or pressure in the form of nonviolent action must wrestle with the questions of where sanctions fit and when they may be used. It must be kept in mind that any intervention or action will not remain pure. That is, even an attempt to help people will result in change which may negatively affect the lives of some people in a given situation. Our discussion of theological issues and practical action regarding sanctions must always be couched in the acknowledgment of sinfulness and of the mixed nature of life in the world. This acknowledgment need not paralyze us and keep us from acting, but it should remind us that no choice is completely pure.[52]

Zimmerman Herr concludes the paper by noting that the fact that Mennonites are discussing sanctions evidences the extent to which they have come to consider themselves responsible actors in society. "Involvement forces us to acknowledge ambiguity and the impossibility of making pure choices," she writes. "That we must wrestle with acceptable coercion is a sign of our rejection of a separatist ethic, and of our need to define our stance of Biblical pacifism within a context of participation."[53]

Reductions in the Military Budget

From the beginning, MCC Washington has promoted major reductions in the U.S. military budget. The key article in Franz's first *Washington Memo* was entitled "Human Need and Military Demands" and dealt with the cost and development of the Sentinel Antiballistic Missile (ABM).[54] Since then, in addition to scores of updates on arms control, military training, arms sales, military aid, and chemical weapons, the *Memo* has included more than fifty articles addressing the military budget. For much of its history, MCC Washington staffers usually have recommended reductions in the military appropriations without specifying amounts. For example, a 1981 *Memo* piece states, "Without getting into arguments about the merits or faults of various proposed budget cuts, it is possible to protest the vast diversion of resources into the military. Questions need to be raised about the impact of military spending and what its aims are." The article concludes: "Now is the time to raise with [Congress] your concerns about U.S. priorities and stewardship as reflected in the federal budget, and to share with them your experiences which inform them of your care for all of God's creation."[55]

When MCC Washington does propose specifics, it meets opposition from some of its constituents. One *Memo* reader wrote Franz in 1978 to protest military-related recommendations in two consecutive issues. In the March–April *Memo* Franz said MCC Washington and other church agencies had studied the budget and recommended that a minimum of twelve billion dollars be transferred from the military budget to civilian and human needs. In the following issue he urged constituents to write to Jimmy Carter to suggest a six-month freeze on the sale of paramilitary equipment, including instruments of torture. In response to the freeze on paramilitary equipment sales, Jim Bowman, an MCC volunteer in Indonesia, wrote, "We don't want a six-month freeze—we want permafrost!" On the budget issue, Bowman asked, "What about the remaining $100 billion for military? By supporting this amendment we are in danger of being interpreted to be saying, 'If 10 percent of the military budget is transferred to social categories, we go along with the military budget.'" Bowman added that "[w]e don't want to play footsie with the politicians. We want to send Washington a message calling for peace and justice undiluted with compromise and political intrigue."[56]

MCC Washington has continued to struggle with making general statements or proposing specific amounts for reductions. In recent years the office was aware that former Pentagon administrator Lawrence J. Korb, now of the Washington-based Brookings Institute, testified before the Senate Budget Committee in 1989 and again in 1992 that a 50 percent cut in the military budget was feasible and necessary. In 1992 Rep. Ron Dellums (D-California), chair of the House Armed Services Subcommittee on Research and Development, made the same proposal for cuts over four years. In a 1991 *Memo* article Keith Gingrich writes that many analysts say a 50 percent cut in the military budget could be made by the year 2000. "Congress and the White House must hear a loud and passionate call over the coming months for deep military budget cuts, accompanied by a strong conversion program," concludes Gingrich, stopping short of recommending the 50 percent figure.[57]

In December 1991, at the prompting of MCC Washington, the MCC U.S. Executive Committee passed a detailed, three-part "call" for reallocating U.S. military funds for meeting human and environmental needs. "The cessation of the Cold War provides an unprecedented opportunity to turn swords into ploughshares," remarks the *Memo* article announcing the MCC U.S. decision.[58] The call included reducing the U.S. military budget by at least 50 percent (145 billion dollars) by 1995, reallocating these savings to several domestic and international programs, and establishing a Peace Tax Fund. MCC U.S. was even more specific about the reductions, which they said could be achieved through 1) bringing all U.S. foreign-based military troops home (saving 90 billion dollars), 2) seeking agreement with the Soviets to reduce strategic nuclear weapons to one thousand for each side (saving 17 billion dollars), 3) terminating the B-2 bomber and SDI programs (saving 10 billion dollars), and 4) commencing a comprehensive test ban treaty.

With the "at least 50 percent" recommendation, some constituents again raised questions. Why not 70 percent, 90 percent, or even 100 percent? Did the proposal mean that MCC would be happy with a military budget of 145 billion dollars? On what criteria does a pacifist organization base a recommendation such as that made by MCC U.S.? If 50 percent is considered a kind of "middle axiom," what was the process for arriving at such an application of biblical principles? What sources were drawn on? On a different level, if the goal is to promote justice and peace around the world, how can a pacifist be certain that it would not be best for the United States to increase its military spending in the short-term, with the hope that reductions could come later after more stable balances had been established?[59]

Gingrich admits he was a little surprised that MCC U.S. went along with the office's recommendation of a 50 percent reduction in the military budget. At the time, MCC U.S. Peace Section—which usually has been on the "cutting edge" in the organization—was being phased out and absorbed into MCC U.S. Gingrich says MCC U.S. may have been going out of its way to make the Peace Section feel more comfortable with the transition. But Gingrich contends that the logical consequence for pacifists working in the public arena is simply to "hack away" at military appropriations. "We don't really argue the need to cut the military budget or do something about arms control from a pacifist position as much as we do from how these arguments make sense in the secular debate," he explains.[60]

Titus Peachey expresses ambivalence about the military budget debate. He wonders "how low a cut in military spending can we realistically call for and still be in the game without compromising who we are and what we believe?" Peachey continues:

There is a sense in which you have to accept the reality of where you are and who you're talking to in order to get their attention and talk on the same wavelength. On the other hand, I think it's OK sometimes to be perceived as totally off the wall. If you really want to state who we as a people are and what we feel committed to, it's OK sometimes for that not to compute in terms of the structures and language [in Washington]. I remember a powerful statement by Mark Hatfield in relation to military spending, just anguishing that all of his efforts about reducing military spending have seemed so paltry, you know, just playing in the margins. And if we find ourselves always dickering just a little bit lower or wanting to make something *just a little bit* more humane in an effort to be more effective, without ever really baring our souls, then I feel like we can't do that. I think there's a real gift to knowing how to balance that.[61]

In response, Franz said, "While we work for the best possible outcome from our perspective as church offices . . . we know that there are going to have to be some compromises, but we try to make the best of them."[62]

As should be clear from the illustrative cases of UN Peacekeeping Forces, economic sanctions, and the military budget, MCC Washington has entered uncharted, conundrumlike territory when it has made specific recommendations to policymakers. Once a pacifist organization is making other-than-pacifistic policy proposals, one might suggest it must have at its disposal the best economic, social, and political analyses available. And what if Ronald Reagan was right in asserting that international peace could be achieved through military strength or that money actually "trickled down" from the successful rich to the middle class and then to the poor?[63] Church groups may still want to add "at what human cost?" to such assertions. They also may be able, in the long run, to chip away at the legitimacy of some political and economic theorists' conclusions. But in the meantime, they would need some way of legitimating their own specific recommendations. What does a faith perspective contribute to public discourse once remedies enter the realm of technical analyses? And how much would gaining this technical expertise, and speaking as technocrats, draw the churches away from their own traditions and discourse?

In *Religion in American Public Life*, A. James Reichley claims churches risk "squandering their moral authority on questions on which their technical competence will usually be slight." Reichley rightly observes that nearly every decision made by government touches on moral concerns at some point. Some issues, such as civil rights, nuclear war, and abortion, are fundamentally but not exclusively moral in nature. At the other extreme are issues of administrative reform or choices of government contractors. In the middle are a wide range of issues that raise moral questions, "but on which persons operating on similar moral assumptions may come down on different sides because of differing technical or empirical judgments."

> The recent propensities of many churches to take detailed positions on issues on which they possess little technical competence were probably what chiefly provoked Peter Berger's expression of exasperation. [Berger, says Reichley, has asked, "Why don't the churches just shut up?"] Advocacy of one side or another, Berger has pointed out, by no means exhaust and may actually inhibit the useful and appropriate functions the churches may perform on such issues. By very reason of their broad and varied membership and the moral standing they should naturally possess, the churches are well suited to act as mediators or fact-finders on many issues over which technical experts disagree. But to perform such roles, the churches would have to cultivate reputations for objectivity and openmindedness as to means.[64]

Reichley suggests that these qualities are not compatible with the positions some churches have taken as "partisan combatants or propagandists for the political left or right."

David Harrington Watt counters Reichley's argument that one of the reasons religious groups should be careful about entering public debates is that they often lack the technical competence prerequisite for speaking authoritatively on matters of the public good. Harrington Watt says this competence seems to be "almost precisely the same as a mastery of technical rationality."[65] This domination of technical rationality is what critical theorists such as Jürgen Habermas are seeking to avoid, as discussed in the previous chapter. Habermas fears society's reliance on instrumental logic in contrast to communicative action—open, free, undistorted communication about society's goals and values.

What are the limits, and what are the possibilities, for the churches' engagement in public discourse? How much technical knowledge must church organizations gain before entering the debates about nuts-and-bolts policymaking? How fully can they participate in public discourse without this expertise? Is the churches' role something other than nitty-gritty legislative work and, if so, how much value can be placed on the churches' words? In the case of Mennonites, with their limited experience in governing, how much can they say without undermining their legitimacy?

Brueggemann, who would never suggest that the churches simply "shut up," nevertheless cautions religious groups against going beyond certain limits in public discourse. He cites Isaiah's quite specific words to King Hezekiah as recorded in II Kings 19:32–33. Here Isaiah leaves the realm of proposing a *vision* for transformation and mediation, saying to the unbelieving king: "Therefore thus says the Lord concerning the king of Assyria, he shall not come into this city or shoot an arrow there, or come before it with a shield or cast up a siege mound against it. By the way that he came, by the same he shall return, and he shall not come into this city, says the Lord." Brueggemann notes that "the conversation behind the wall departs from the legitimacy we have expected when it enters into policy formation that ignores primal language, shifts focus from God to the Jerusalem establishment, and makes a concrete political claim." The concrete claim becomes as self-serving as the claims of Assyria, Brueggemann argues, and is no longer legitimate since it cannot be received in public discourse.[66]

Brueggemann contends that, in terms of legitimacy, the conversation behind the wall is judged "not by its power to form policy but by its capacity to transform imagination, which makes a differently textured policy possible." He adds that in order for "sectarian readings of reality" to be legitimate, they must acknowledge administrative necessity, speak in energizing symbols, and stay close to experience.[67] "Acknowledging administrative necessity" will always be the point on which church groups will be

A Mennonite Central Committee delegation that visited Selective Service System officials, members of Congress, and Department of Justice officials in June 1980 to discuss Mennonite concerns about military registration pauses in front of the Department of Justice. Pictured are, from left, Dan King, Beachy Amish representative; Paul Landis, chair of MCC U.S.; John Stoner, executive secretary of MCC U.S. Peace Section; Atlee Beechy, MCC Executive Committee; Delton Franz, director of MCC Washington; and James Longacre, chair of MCC U.S. Peace Section. Photo by Reg Toews, courtesy of MCC Washington.

most vulnerable to criticism, Brueggemann suggests. From the point of view of "Assyria," it will always seem that the communal conversation is not "realistic" about power realities. This is not all bad, Brueggemann implies. As one Methodist Washington lobbyist says, "You can stand against the tide of realpolitik, but you can't ignore its force. On the other side of the coin, when a society loses its way, realpolitik can't tell it which way to turn. It doesn't know anything about good ends or the right direction to go. That's where the public church steps forward."[68]

Brueggemann's concern in "The Legitimacy of a Sectarian Hermeneutic" clearly is not only the conversation at the wall but also the conversation behind it. He worries about the church constituency of middle America that supports inhumane policies of government. The theologian observes that the church's primary educational access is not so much to government leaders who form policy but to the public that permits, authorizes, and embraces policy. "In a liberal church, so captured by laudable goals and imperial methods, the story that has lost power is the one behind the walls," Brueggemann writes. "And so, we end up with more knowledge about what to do, but without the will, courage, energy, or self-knowledge to act." Brueggemann says he is not making a plea for withdrawal or obscurantism, nor is he disregarding the conversation at the wall where policy must be formed in the presence of power-wielders. He is concerned, though, that at the moment, "we have forgotten our primal language."[69]

One of the problems Mennonites face is that they have never fully worked out how they may draw on sources outside the faith when speaking in public discourse. Mennonite ethicist Duane Friesen has long argued that Mennonites need to develop an adequate theology to affirm the use of human reason in ethical thinking. How does one relate a Christological norm with the insights of human reason and wisdom? Friesen contends that in practice Mennonites have been doing this integration throughout this century. For example, they have appealed to the state to preserve freedom, protect conscience, and engage in dispute settlement through arbitration—all normative principles that reflect the values of the Kingdom of God. Mennonites also have drawn on general humanistic wisdom and moral insight when they use secular language. "Though Mennonites have had good reason to be cautious about affirming human reason in ethical thought lest authorities other than Jesus Christ gain prominence, nevertheless, how can the Christian be obedient without using his [or her] God given mind to the fullest by drawing upon all the human wisdom and moral insight that is available?" asks Friesen.[70]

Friesen's question is a valid one. The ethicist also acknowledges that, even without a theology fully worked out, Mennonites have borrowed from humanistic wisdom and moral insight when speaking in public. Certainly this is true in MCC Washington's work. Faithful, authentic, life-giving theology takes into account one's sacred texts and traditions, and then is worked out in the dynamic interaction of "living out" those texts and traditions and reflecting on that experience. One need not have the theological puzzle entirely in place before participating in public discourse. By the same token, one ought to take care that a greater public engagement does not so transform communal discourse that it becomes vacuous, bereft of its traditions. Maintaining this dynamic tension is among the tasks for MCC Washington and its constituent bodies.

Throughout this century, and especially with the formation of MCC Washington in 1968, Mennonites have been learning a new language—that of public discourse. The intention of learning and speaking the new language— as should be the case for learning any second language—has been to communicate more sensitively and effectively with others in that context. The tension has been that the secondary language may wholly usurp the primary one. One may begin to converse—and even dream—in the secondary language, forgetting the primal parlance that provides the foundation and passion for engaging in public discourse. Unless words are chosen carefully, religious groups' utterances also may appear illegitimate in public discourse. Although they have not always had great clarity about "acknowledging administrative necessity," Mennonites and MCC Washington historically have done well at "speaking in energizing symbols" and "staying close to experience." The office has been at its best in the capital when it has drawn on the experience of MCC's domestic and overseas workers, and when it has spoken public language with an Anabaptist accent.

In an earlier day, when Mennonites addressed Washington from outside the city, they usually recognized "administrative necessity" by not denouncing the U.S. government's military involvements as long as Mennonites and other conscientious objectors were not required to fight. A two-kingdom approach, which generally granted the government the God-given role of maintaining order, allowed the state to operate on its own ethic. In recent decades, with the recognition of the interdependence and interconnectedness of persons, institutions, and nations, Mennonites' distinctions between the two kingdoms have become blurred. Now those entering the public conversation in Washington have sought ways of mediating between the Christian ethic and "what is possible" in the national political realm, hoping to bring to bear a vision of nonviolent alternatives while acknowledging political realities. Some Mennonites consider this the legitimate use of middle axioms. Others refer to MCC Washington's proposals as compromise or as a kind of troublesome accommodation to political realism. Most problematic has been MCC Washington's middle-ground position taking on specific legislative or policy issues that involve forms of coercion or violence. The difficulty for Mennonites and other religious lobbies is knowing what the limits and possibilities are for their faith-based analyses once specific remedies are proposed. One would hope the churches need not cease talking once policy discussions become technical. Perhaps MCC Washington could do better at drawing on the human resources within their traditions, inviting to Washington Mennonites with training—and experience—in various public policy areas.

On the other hand, the office *itself* need not—and ought not—be comprised of technical experts, nor ought the Mennonite workers be conversant *only* in political languages. They, and the denominations they represent, must continue to reflect on their new experience of being bilingual and consider carefully what implications this has for their theology and ethics. In the meantime, MCC Washington staffers' primary task is to remain engaged in the conversations about policy directions, allowing their dreaming and visioning to help transform public discourse. Earlier we referred to one legislative aide's appreciation for MCC service workers, who tell policymakers "how the world is, not how it ought to be." Perhaps MCC Washington's role is *both* to explain how the world is *and* to suggest how it ought to be, but *not* to provide a blueprint of how to rebuild it.

7

ENGAGING WISELY AND INNOCENTLY?

Be wise as serpents and innocent as doves . . .
you will be dragged before governors and kings
for my sake, to bear testimony before them.

—*Jesus, Matthew 10:16–17*

Never in its founding documents—nor in any later, official directives—is
Mennonite Central Committee's Washington office charged to be "wise as
serpents and innocent as doves." Nonetheless, Delton Franz and other Capitol
Hill MCC staffers have felt pressure to be both, pushed along by their
constituent bodies, the agency in which they are embedded, and their lobbying peers in Washington. Precisely what this kind of "wisdom" and this
kind of "innocence" would look like, and what group is demanding which
attribute, is unclear. One might argue that some Mennonites are most concerned about the dovelike innocence, while MCC's lobbying peers are
more keenly interested in serpentine wisdom. Or it may be that constituents, MCC's administrators, and the religious advocacy offices all expect
MCC to be both wise and innocent, although they have differing definitions of what these terms might mean.

Whether or not MCC Washington *achieves* both wisdom and innocence is an open question, then, depending on what criteria and understandings one brings to the discussion. The *value* one places on seeking to

be wise and yet innocent also depends on how one interprets the terms. Wisdom in a "technical/rational" sense would mean, in the spirit of Max Weber, a "rational, systematic investment of time and resources toward the expectation of future chances of profit."[1] This kind of technical rationality implies a movement toward efficiency, cost-benefit analyses, and a focus on specialization. In the case of MCC Washington, such "wisdom" would imply that staffers could speak the parlance of the technocrats with the best of them. It may mean that the Mennonites in the Capitol Hill office were fully integrated into the lobbying culture, adopting the languages and practices of political Washington, focusing only on effectiveness, and making all judgments according to means-end rationality. It would mean the office functioned smoothly and was perceived as politically sophisticated.

If this is the kind of wisdom that is meant in MCC staffers' allusions to Matthew 10, one would need to admit that MCC Washington is not wise. However, Weber himself may have been pleased to hear that such wisdom was lacking. The sociologist concludes his oft-cited essay on the Protestant ethic by introducing the notion of modern societies moving toward an "iron cage" of instrumentality, a situation that he finds frightening. Weber writes: "For of the last stage of this cultural development, it might well be truly said: 'Specialists without spirit, sensualists without heart.'"[2]

On the question of MCC's "innocence" in the midst of "the whirl of Washington," one again must ask what kind of innocence is meant. Is this "harmlessness"—as the term is sometimes translated—a benign presence? Does the usage mean innocence in the sense of unsoiled by the world, untouched by other pressures or "outside influences"? Does it suggest a form of clean-handedness maintained by total disengagement from the dirtiness of political Washington? If so, then MCC Washington's innocence must be denied. With such renderings of the key terms, it is unambiguously clear that MCC's office on Capitol Hill has been neither wise nor innocent. And perhaps that is all right. For a religious lobby, the wisdom and innocence described above would not do the world—nor the church—much good.

The type of innocence and wisdom Capitol Hill Mennonite staffers seek to embody, and the type intended in the creation of MCC Washington, has more to do with other, more commonsense notions of the terms. Franz once said that, because of the critical problems of suffering MCC Washington addresses, it is important that staffers have a sense for what is going on in the world, for what is achievable, and for what is beyond the office's grasp. "To be really naïve is not going to help you build a kingdom," he said.[3] Keith Gingrich observes: "The practical aspect of being wise as serpents may mean taking into account what our people in the field are saying, and what our nationals are saying, and being wise in using that information. We also use those stories to raise some questions or concerns about the approaches and strategies used here." Gingrich contends that while there is a need to be "street-smart" in terms of how political Washington functions, "there's also a certain amount of respect given to offices or individuals who work quietly but are seen to be doing good work."[4] So the wisdom that MCC Washington strives for is one of balance between understanding the languages and practices of Capitol Hill, but selectively choosing how the office participates in those languages and practices.

This interpretation overlaps with that which Mennonite workers in Washington give for "innocence," suggesting that "wisdom" and "innocence" are not incompatible concepts but differing strands woven together in the same cloth. "There are some problems with the word innocent, because obviously we're not innocent," acknowledges Greg Goering. "There's blood on my hands from the Gulf War because I'm a citizen of this country." Goering suggests that the meaning of the term more nearly approximates "not harming," although he does not interpret this as *passivity* but political *activity*. "The thrust of that part of the phrase would be to not participate in evil as far as we're able," he contends, "not to be pure and separate, but to reduce [our] participation in evil"—in a way which brings about social and political change.[5] Franz notes that "innocence" connotes that the office is not trying to move from a position of power or intimidation, but that it simply offers a trustworthy word and a trustworthy presence. "We are a transparent people," he once claimed. "We're not here to posture or anything like that—to intimidate or threaten. We're here to be vulnerable."[6]

In short, MCC Washington's *intentions* for its work during the office's first several decades of existence may come closest to the Matthew 10 interpretation proposed by biblical commentator Eduard Schweizer: the disciples' attributes are not seen in "clever diplomatic moves" but in "the purity of a life that is genuine and wears no masks."[7] With varying levels of commitment and success, MCC staffers have sought not to perfect their diplomatic moves but to evidence a "purity" of life that is genuine and maskless in the way Schweizer describes. This form of "purity" recognizes that one's hands may become soiled. It recognizes that engagement with people in the field and on Capitol Hill necessitates sometimes messy involvements. It refuses to believe that purity can be found only in distance, disengagement, and disassociation. Instead, innocence and wisdom in the Washington context may mean providing an authentic and consistently credible word—an open, engaged, passionate, and genuine masklessness.

The extent to which MCC Washington has *achieved* this genuine masklessness, and the desirability or effectiveness of such a posture, will be answered differently by differently located observers. My perception is that MCC

Washington personnel *should* strive for the kind of wisdom and innocence described above, and that—in some ways, on some occasions—the office *has* embodied such traits. What is certain is that the Capitol Hill office has provided a laboratory for examining the discourse and practices of contemporary Mennonites. The office also has provided a lens through which we can observe the denominational and more "public" tensions occurring partly as a result of the political engagement of a previously withdrawn people. Mennonite Central Committee began with the gospel as its primary authorizing agent. That gospel, combined with the motivation to do constructive peacemaking rather than simply "not resist," then propelled the service and relief organization into action among the oppressed. In turn, this experience of working among the oppressed prompted Mennonites to speak to national political powers—and provided the legitimation for that speech.

Mennonite ethicist Duane Friesen and others have noted the significant impact world events and varied experiences have had on Mennonite peace theology as well as practice. He suggests that some of the major differences between earlier (i.e., Hershberger's) and later peace theologies have occurred as a result more of contextual than theological factors—"the long period of the cold war and its disastrous impact on third world countries such as Vietnam and Nicaragua, the increasing utilization and success of nonviolence all over the world as a strategy of social change, the rise of the academic study of peace and conflict resolution, the growing awareness of the gap between rich and poor, and the environmental crisis." Mennonites have been affected by recognizing domestic violence and problems of sexual oppression within their homes and communities, by their work in urban environments, and by their overseas travel and service experiences.[8] All of these experiences, Friesen contends, contribute to breaking down walls that separate "us" from "them" and make Mennonites aware of the need for active engagement in the world. Encounters with others around the globe have made a rigid two-kingdom understanding of the church and world problematic.

MCC Washington's advocacy efforts do not fit neatly into a more "churchly" model of church-state relations, a model that may see significant overlap between the roles and functions of the church and the state. MCC staff persons do not believe the church—Mennonite, mainline, or otherwise—will be the primary factor in how political decisions are made, nor do they expect the state to live fully by the church's ethics. On the other hand, the office's work also does not square with a truly sectarian two-kingdom position, which cares *only* about the nature and role of the church, thus leaving the state to its own business. It is striking that both theologians within the Mennonite "fold" and outside theologians, such as Reinhold Niebuhr, have used some form of two-kingdom model to suggest that "nonresistant" persons and denominations should be silent in the realm of politics. In other words, Mennonites, whose nonresistance is rooted in a biblical but "impossible" or publicly "unpragmatic" ethic, should live out their lives pacifistically—and passively—not making "unrealistic" demands on the state.

Those who would wish to silence Mennonites, whether on theological or philosophical grounds, fail to recognize what they may contribute to public discourse. Organizations such as MCC, which work both in and beyond the world's "hot spots," can bring to policymakers' attention significant concerns that otherwise may not be heard. Critical theorist Nancy Fraser has argued that there is a need for such smaller groups, or "counterpublics," to help make the broader public more cognizant of relevant issues.[9] She says observers, participants, or recipients of a particular kind of violence, for instance, may see violence or oppression as a matter of concern for all, while others may not share that conviction. Her particular example is domestic violence against women, which until recently was not seen as a matter of common concern, except by some feminists, and was not considered a legitimate topic for public discourse. Her point is that various "minorities" in society should be guaranteed opportunities "to convince others that what in the past was not public . . . should now become so."[10] Fraser likely would agree that the poor and oppressed persons with whom MCC service personnel work and whom MCC Washington seeks to represent may constitute such "counterpublics." MCC Washington itself also becomes an important discussant as it carries the concerns of these persons, who experience the effects of U.S. domestic and overseas policies, back into the national political arena.

My observation is that the cautious, gentle, informative prodding practiced by MCC Washington staffers indeed challenges traditional, static models of how the church and state may legitimately interact. As the American state has expanded its involvements at home and abroad and as organizations such as MCC have broadened their service and relief work, the church and state increasingly have found themselves working in overlapping spheres of influence and concern. At those points of overlap, at least, church organizations must speak to the political powers when they see their detrimental effects, or when they see them as one harbinger of hope. A traditional two-kingdom perspective does not explain how Mennonites on Capitol Hill could be *both* faithful *and* effective, encouraging and bringing about positive change without expecting pacifism from the state. MCC Washington staffers need to remember—and usually do—that government initiatives are not the primary locus of God's activity in the world, and that the reign of God will not be implemented through political powers. However, that recognition should not keep them from engaging the state.

Delton Franz cuts a piece of cake for Senator Mark Hatfield (R-Oregon) during the July 1993 celebration of MCC Washington's twenty-fifth anniversary. Hatfield was among the speakers at the event, and he praised MCC Washington for its work on Capitol Hill. Photo by Dave Schrock-Shenk, courtesy of MCC Akron.

For organizations such as Mennonite Central Committee's Washington office, then, a new and yet *faithful* praxis is emerging in the realm of politics. The intent of this thick description of the office's work has not been to fully resolve how this praxis fits into Mennonite theological models. Other ethicists, including Friesen and Ted Koontz, already have proposed church-state models that merit further attention. Koontz expresses a "renewed appreciation for some sort of 'dualism' or two kingdom ethic," and thereby tentatively proposes a "modified" two-kingdom construct. Central notions in his conceptualization are that 1) "The church is the primary vehicle of God's action in history"; 2) "The church's integrity in its own life and mission is essential to its direct 'political' witness"; 3) "The appropriate overarching norm for the life of the church is *agape*"; 4) "An appropriate ethic for the state is different from an appropriate ethic for the church"; and 5) "The proper norm for the state is to protect the good by restraining evildoers with the least possible coercion or violence."[11] Koontz says he is drawn to this kind of model because it is congruent with the biblical material, "which does not . . . either implicitly or explicitly call the state to the same standard which it calls Christian disciples"; it does justice to his sense of the "dilemmas which states[persons] sometimes face and does not ask them, as states[persons], to follow the norm of agape in a fallen situation"; and it "allows plenty of room for prophetic critique of government." The latter reason for proposing his model, contends Koontz, is "radically differ-ent from the church/world dualism in Mennonite ethics which many re-cent writers have criticized, a dualism which saw the world as fallen and therefore sometimes appeared to feel there was nothing to say to the state by way of prophetic critique."[12] In short, Koontz's alternative model would allow the church to speak to the state on many issues, yet maintain some notions of dualism.

In *Christian Peacemaking and International Conflict: A Realist Pacifist Per-spective,* Friesen assiduously avoids the language of dualism. Friesen suggests that overlapping circles can illustrate the relationship between the political community and the community of faith. "The area in the middle where the two circles overlap reflect[s] the arena where the church can involve itself creatively in cooperating with the larger political community for common ends," he writes. "Even where the two circles do not overlap, the church plays an important role in initiating critical action and words of judgment within the political community that, if heeded, will make politics more hu-mane and more likely to endure."[13] The latter phrase is suggestive of Friesen's "realist pacifist perspective." In his view, "realist" means 1) a pacifism that "takes seriously the nature of human sinfulness as it expresses itself in the egoistic self-interest and exploitation of political and economic systems," and 2) a pacifism "that is political, that seeks to apply its ethic to resolution of practical, economic, and political issues within human institutions."[14]

My impression is that MCC Washington's lived reality falls somewhere between Koontz's and Friesen's rather distinct proposals. Staffers consis-tently express some level of discomfort with Mennonites' traditional dual-ism in church-state ethics. During his tenure, Franz admitted that in some sense there are two kingdoms, but said it was problematic for MCC Wash-ington to work from that theological premise because it has made for a "great chasm of separation." Franz said a two-kingdom ethic "makes things too simple, too pat."[15] On the other hand, Franz and other Mennonite workers seem unconvinced that a perspective such as Friesen's "realist paci-fist" one is sufficiently realistic, given the constraints of the democratic political process and the nature of present-day conflicts around the world. Several MCC Washington staffers speak about becoming more cynical about the possibility of effecting change through the federal government after working in Washington. These superficial critiques do not invalidate the alternatives proposed by Koontz and Friesen. The Washington experience does suggest, though, that ongoing theological refinement is needed regarding church-state interaction.[16] What can emerge out of observing Mennonites' new, tentative political engagement is a historically based practical theology. Theologizing about kingdoms or realms can be a secondary reflection on this experience of attempting to live out the gospel faithfully in the nation's capital.

For MCC Washington, such faithful living always is threatened by several hazards. First of all, Mennonite staffers may be tempted to adapt too much to the "instrumental rationality" of the state. Secondly, in the midst of coalitional work, they may become so much like other advocacy offices that they lose the credibility that comes from their distinctive traditions. When organizations work together in the same setting—or talk together about common concerns—the practical need for common languages and practices quickly whirls new partners into an orbit of similitude. My argument has been that MCC Washington has, to some degree, resisted this constraining process, due partly to its ongoing interconnectedness with its sponsoring agency, which is located well outside the Beltway. It is true that the Mennonite office has been relatively free to participate in various coalitions on Capitol Hill and indeed has adopted *many* of the practices and *much* of the language of those lobbying peers. In many ways, the office would be indistinguishable from others with which it works, especially the other peace-and-justice lobbies in the Methodist Building.

However, MCC Washington's "bedding down" in the organizational field of religious lobbying is only one dimension of the office's reality. The office has been keenly aware of the "bundling board" between it and its coalition partners, a board whose substance has been Mennonite theological-ethical traditions of pacifism, humility, and service. It also should be clear that while the materials out of which the bundling board are constructed are religious and cultural, the board's *placement* is the result of institutional influences. In other words, the traditions that help shape MCC Washington's distinctiveness may have only minimal influence were it not for the office's location in a larger service and relief organization that makes its own institutional demands. The office participates in at least two "organizational fields," then: the *lobbying* field and the *Mennonite* field. The bundling board's source, and the force which holds it in place, is simply a different field in which the Mennonite office is embedded.[17]

The tensions about Capitol Hill lobbying, both in Mennonite Central Committee's Akron and Washington offices, can be interpreted as a struggle over the boundaries of the two fields within which MCC Washington resides.[18] One might expect, from a distant glance, that longer-term staffers in the capital office would be more deeply influenced by the demands of the lobbying culture and that shorter-term staff persons would be more influenced by the Mennonite organizational field. As legislative aide Jacob Ahearn says, when people are inside the Beltway too long, their "minds alter" and they "lose a sense of reality." However, the reverse appeared to be true for Mennonite staffers. This may be a function of age, education, personality characteristics, or the initial "seduction" of political Washington, which is tempered by time and experience. It also can be attributed, in part, to institutional influences. Long-term Washington personnel are more directly accountable to the authority structure of MCC headquarters in Akron, Pennsylvania, and are more keenly aware of the forces of the Mennonite organizational field. Short-term staffers may have less invested in MCC itself, and therefore they may more quickly embrace the more aggressive, rationalized Washington culture and style.

John A. Lapp, former MCC executive secretary, acknowledges that MCC spends a good deal of time debating how aggressive and forceful an office like MCC Washington should be. Mennonite and Brethren in Christ constituents have diverse views of how much the Capitol Hill office should "engage" official Washington, given its Anabaptist-Mennonite traditions. Lapp suggests that one of the factors that keeps the office from being more aggressive is the *fragility* of Mennonite unity. "The irony is that that fragility may make the office a better one—a less vocal one," he says.[19] This fragility keeps Capitol Hill Mennonite staffers more attuned to the collective voice of the churches that they, in part, represent. Many of those churches and denominations are quite cautious about political work, and their discomfort with this and other aspects of MCC's peace, reconciliation, and mediation work sometimes threatens the organization's stability. Because of this discomfort, MCC Washington is less vocal and less demanding than it might otherwise be. As Lapp suggests, however, that does not mean it has not played a role in the nation's capital, nor that it is less effective than other religious advocacy offices.

MCC Washington has had its greatest impact on Capitol Hill when it has drawn on the experiences of service workers based outside of Washington. MCC Washington's most effective—and most important—work has been bringing itinerating MCC service workers or nationals with whom they work through the capital's marble corridors. In nearly every case these conversations with legislators and their aides consist of persons telling stories about their own and others' experiences. Superficially, these experiences may seem to be "private" ones—the death of a son, the rape of a daughter, lack of adequate food or medical care, loss of a job or home. However, they are inherently "public" concerns, partly because they often result from interventions or policies of the U.S. government or other governments, partly because they are shared by many, and partly because they have legal, social, or political ramifications. My hope is that MCC Washington's work, which begins with the "public" reporting of these experiences—experiences that some would like to ignore or keep out of public debate—can contribute to the recognition that essential public voices ought not be silenced, and legitimate issues ought not be discounted.

My perception is that, at this juncture, the danger to Mennonites lies not so much in dialogue with the state (as long as such dialogue is conducted *carefully*), nor in forging coalitions with other "peace and justice" organizations (as long as such coalitions are *modest*). If MCC Washington maintains its deep-rootedness in the organization that birthed it—and the Mennonite bodies and congregations that formed MCC—the churches should not fear these conversations and relationships. Such relationships, when entered into with caution, can enrich Mennonite discourse and assist Mennonites and Brethren in Christ in carving out their own identity in a pluralistic world. The danger, rather, may be in pulling back from participating in the public discourse that shapes the world *in* which the church lives and *for* which it lays down its life. This is not an argument for a "public church," as it is conceived in its most activist forms; it is an argument *against* a withdrawn church.[20] Anabaptist-Mennonite churches still are finding their way in this new world—a world that pushed them into hiding and silence centuries ago, but which is now willing to hear a word from them. In this world, a world in which the church already is embedded at so many levels, Mennonites need to continue speaking that word.

In the last decade, several "outsiders" have praised modern Anabaptists for providing an "alternative community" that speaks more loudly to "the powers" than does political activism. Allen Hertzke says, "Effective political witness flows, ultimately, from vital churches. To the extent that political activism undermines that vitality, it saps its own future."[21] Stanley Hauerwas, a Methodist who claims his "ecclesial preference is to be a high-church Mennonite," has been one of the most vocal spokespersons for modern Anabaptists, as he understands them.[22] In a book Hauerwas co-wrote with his Methodist colleague William H. Willimon, they state, "We argue that the political task of Christians is to be the church rather than to transform the world."[23] They contend that they "would like a church that again asserts that God, not nations, rules the world, that the boundaries of God's kingdom transcend those of Caesar, and that the main political task of the church is the formation of people who see clearly the cost of discipleship and are willing to pay the price."[24]

Shortly after Hauerwas and Willimon's book *Resident Aliens* was published in 1989, at least two Mennonite leaders cited it in articles written for *Gospel Herald,* the main denominational publication of the Mennonite Church. Wayne North, a pastor and former executive secretary of the Mennonite Church General Board, writes, "Unfortunately a lot of North American Christians seem to think that the church really doesn't matter and if we want to get things done it must be done with a lot of glitz and that governmental coercion and resources [are] necessary for success." North then quotes Hauerwas and Willimon regarding the churches' failing "to do justice to the radically communal quality of Christian ethics" when they pressure Congress "to pass laws and spend tax money." North notes that Hauerwas and Willimon point out that "the Sermon on the Mount ethics are so radical that they can be lived out only in a redeemed community and made credible only by the redeemed community."[25]

In "Why I Sat Out the Gulf War," Levi Miller also refers to *Resident Aliens,* which he describes as "a protestant appropriation of two kingdom theology." Miller explains why he remained silent during the Persian Gulf War: he "wanted to express our historic Mennonite Christian beliefs" and try "to respect the centuries of pacifist teaching of the Mennonite church." Miller rightly notes that "Mennonites have historically given more attention to what the church should do. We have not always tried to determine the wicked and the good for the state." He then mentions Hauerwas and Willimon's reference to how their own Methodist bishops had written a statement on nuclear arms, which the *Resident Aliens* authors describe as "a rather pontificating gesture to the political left-of-center . . . something not too unlike what might be said by the *New York Times.*" Miller agrees with Hauerwas and Willimon that "this now conventional message-to-Congress-approach is too easy."[26]

The basic thrust of the North and Miller articles was to stress, with Hauerwas and Willimon, that Christians should focus on "being the church" rather than trying to "change the world." This has, indeed, been the basic posture of Anabaptist-Mennonite churches since the sixteenth century, when persecution drove the Radical Reformers into relative obscurity. In other words, Mennonite energies *already are*—and *rightly so*—concentrated on creating redeemed people and forming alternative communities. And that is both representative of and faithful to the churches' traditions. It is only in recent decades that Anabaptist churches again have begun to reach *beyond* those church boundaries into the world in which they are located. It is only since Mennonite Central Committee was formed in 1920 that this Christian humanitarian outreach, a mission designed to lessen oppression and suffering around the globe, has been institutionalized among Mennonites. It is only since 1968, when MCC opened an office in Washington, that contacts with the federal government and participation in public discourse have become more routine. But even now, several decades after the founding of MCC Washington, only a tiny fraction of Mennonite Central Committee's budget goes toward advocacy on Capitol Hill. Moreover, only a small portion of the churches' overall time and efforts goes toward the work of Mennonite Central Committee. At most, "political" work is one digit on the hand of the Mennonite body of Christ, not the trunk—nor even a limb. MCC does, perhaps more than any other Anabaptist organization, seek to "transform the world." But it appears to do so—often even in the nation's capital—in ways consistent with its Anabaptist heritage.

The point is that Hauerwas and Willimon's call to "being the church rather than changing the world" may have more relevance for the mainline denominations for which they write.[27] Based on my observation of how Mennonites work in Washington, I am unconvinced that those Anabaptist churches need to pull back significantly from their minimal efforts at "world transformation." Anabaptists constantly need to remind themselves that "changing the world" does not happen simply in the national political arena; in fact, it may happen only minimally at the federal level. World changing also occurs at the state and local level, and it comes about as a result of alterations in other social, economic, and religious institutions, and it happens when the character of individuals is changed through Christian communities. But my fear, in part, is that Anabaptists will retreat from their "political" engagement, perhaps partly because they misunderstand what such thinkers as Hauerwas and Willimon are saying to the church.

If they wish to follow in the stream of their Anabaptist heritage, Mennonite churches *do* need to maintain their primary focus on creating alternative communities. But that is not the end of the story. These living, breathing alternative communities can then have an impact on the political process, partly because they are "witnesses" to an alternative way. MCC's Titus Peachey says he believes it is wrong for the church to expect the government to take positions and actions in areas the church itself has not been willing to take positions. "If we don't want the government to be racist, the church shouldn't be racist," Peachey contends. "If we want the government to be more accessible and diverse in terms of the people who operate there, then we ought to be doing the same. . . . It's that kind of parallel that we need to hold in tension if we're going to have any integrity."[28] It is this kind of integrity that may allow a church organization—even a pacifist one—to have some impact in the public arena. The task, then, may be understood as *both* being the church *and,* perhaps in moderate ways, changing the world.[29]

Even Hauerwas does not argue that Christian pacifists ought to avoid the political arena. "Once one disavows the use of violence, it means one has a high stake in developing political processes through which agreement is reached without the necessity of coercion," he writes in another article. He says Christians "want to make our societies as open as possible to the voice of dissent, exactly because we believe so profoundly in the necessity of politics—politics understood as the discussion of peoples necessary to discover the goods they have in common."[30]

Calling this conversation with political leaders "lobbying" sometimes is problematic—and perhaps misleading—for denominational outposts in Washington. The religious offices in the Methodist Building, throughout most of their shared history, have not been "insiders" in Washington, schmoozing with legislators and having direct access to legislative changes. Nor have they been fully "outsiders," simply uttering prophetic condemnations from outside the political wall. At their best, they function neither like self-interested lobbyists nor like indignant prophets: they simply inform in a way that they hope will provoke change. For *some* advocacy groups, at *some* level, this informing taps into value systems that resonate with selected legislators' convictions and experiences. Certainly, because of the small Mennonite constituency, the office's work does not seriously threaten any politicians' futures—as some more powerful lobbying organizations, secular and religious, might.

For many years the religious lobbies referred to themselves as "advocates" or "advocacy offices." Most of the denominational office directors and staffers with whom I spoke said that, according to their denominations, "advocacy" is still the preferred term. However, in common Washington parlance, religious advocates seem to use the term "lobbying" as frequently or more frequently than the earlier nomenclature. For that reason, I have freely moved between the language of "lobbying" and "advocacy" in this text, even though I believe religious "advocacy" and business or special-interest "lobbying" still are worlds apart. The shift toward "lobbying" language is likely the result of religious advocates' increasing adoption of long-established lobbying practices. Many of the offices began largely as observer posts for their denominations, but gradually took a more active role in Washington. Now, with few exceptions, the religious advocacy offices send out voting scorecards, stimulate the grassroots, write letters and position statements, take concerns directly to legislators and administration officials, and form coalitions to empower their positions. These advocacy practices approximate many of those of other secular and self-interested lobbies. However, *motivations* for their efforts still differentiate most of the religious "lobbies" from self-interested lobbies. Because of those different motivations and orientations, it may be prudent for religious lobbyists to maintain the language of "advocacy" or to come up with a more descriptive term for their work. This is especially true for those advocacy groups whose style and tone, if not their practices, dramatically diverge from those of many self-interested lobbies. To keep these different styles and functions clear in the minds of those both inside and outside the Beltway, denominational and other religious offices may do well to maintain the linguistic distinction between "lobbying" and "advocacy."

During his years as MCC Washington's director, Delton Franz sought to temper his advocacy for marginalized and oppressed persons with faithfulness to Mennonite traditions, traditions that have long included such concerns but have—until the latter part of the twentieth century—rarely voiced them to those in political power. Franz's humble and quiet manner, his passion for peace and justice, and his consistent presence over more than a quarter century clearly shaped MCC Washington's public personality. Franz gave the office a public face; he also established close working relationships with many lobbying peers, legislative aides, and political officials; and he embodied Mennonites' shift toward national political engagement more than any other figure within the denominations.

Most Akron administrators believe Franz was "the right person for the job," especially in the formative years of the office. Since 1994, the office's second director, J. Daryl Byler, has been forging his own way through the Capitol Hill thickets. With increasing distance from Franz's tenure, it may be easier to isolate Franz's particular influences in creating MCC Washington's public aura. Many persons—including Mennonites as well as legislative aides and lobbying peers—are watching with interest during these years of transition. Some observers would like to see the office less vocal and less engaged than it was during the Franz era. Others hope Franz's style and manner are being continued. Still others hope the office is becoming more active than it was under the first director's leadership—anticipating that Byler has more "fire in his belly." Partly because of institutional constraints from MCC's Akron headquarters and the constituent denominations, Byler has not guided the office in a dramatically different direction. Mennonite political trajectories have been established and institutionalized in ways that will be difficult to alter. However, within the two organizational fields of Mennonite denominations on the one hand and Washington's political advocacy culture on the other, sufficient fluidity exists for considerable pushing and pulling at the boundaries.

Regardless of what other directions the office may take, it should be clear that, for Mennonites, continuing to view Washington—and to speak to it—through the lens of on-the-ground service experiences is essential.

MCC needs to have a regular presence on Capitol Hill so that staffers might not only keep their constituencies informed, but also might create working relationships with legislators and policymakers. With those relationships established, the office can facilitate bringing itinerating service workers—or their stories—to the capital. As has been said repeatedly here, this is where faithfulness coincides with effectiveness. This reporting works because it emerges out of credible, lived experience, and MCC ought to be doing more of it.

From my conversations with legislative aides and MCC Washington's coalition partners, I am convinced that MCC's name carries a kind of integrity and credibility on Capitol Hill. This credibility is worth hanging on to, even if it means giving up something else—for instance, not speaking to every issue and being cautious about some alliances. In Washington, credibility is the name of the game. As congressional aide Jim McGovern says, "It's not so much that we have to listen to MCC because there are 20 million Mennonites out there and we're going to lose our election if we don't listen. They don't have that kind of voting power. I think it's one of those rare cases where people look at the work and say, 'This is good stuff. These people are credible. They know what they're talking about. And maybe they deserve our ear on some of these issues.'"[31] McGovern contends that MCC's power and influence in Washington are based on that credibility. Mennonites have long been skittish about power and have never fully developed a theology of power. However, McGovern describes a form of "power" in which Mennonites have long believed. And in a town where influence and power are hard to come by, even *episodically* having *this kind* of impact, and having *this kind* of credibility, is high praise.

1

MENNONITE CENTRAL COMMITTEE: PRINCIPLES THAT GUIDE OUR MISSION

"My children, love must not be
a matter of words or talk;
it must be genuine, and show itself in action."

—*I John 3:18 (NEB)*

MCC MISSION STATEMENT

Mennonite Central Committee is an agency of the Mennonite and Brethren in Christ churches in North America. MCC seeks to demonstrate God's love through committed women and men who work among people suffering from poverty, conflict, oppression and natural disaster. MCC serves as a channel for interchange between churches and community groups where we work around the world and the North American churches who send us, so that all may grow and be transformed. MCC strives for peace, justice and dignity of all people by sharing our experiences, resources and faith in Jesus Christ.

These guidelines and principles were approved 25–26 January 1991 at the annual meeting of MCC in Archbold, Ohio. The statement concluded with a list of references, including historical/theological texts, MCC documents, and biblical passages "which inspire MCC mission."

The following principles that guide Mennonite Central Committee are an expansion of MCC's mission statement. They serve as a guideline for planning and implementing program and provide some criteria for ongoing evaluation. The document updates a similar statement approved at the January 1976 Annual Meeting and at the January 30, 1988, Annual Meeting.

WHAT WE BELIEVE

1. We minister "in the name of Christ." Our work is rooted in the compassionate God who calls us to be compassionate people. We understand the fullest revelation of God to be Jesus of Nazareth, who invites all people to be made whole, through the redemptive work of his life, death and resurrection and to follow his example as one who serves. We believe the loving God wills the well-being of all people and the healing of creation; that the first fruits of the new creation, the Kingdom of God, are manifest in the peoplehood called church.

2. We accept our weakness and failures which underscore our need to be led by God's Spirit and to be taught by the people with whom we interact. Helping others is most effective when the "helper" learns from the wisdom and experience of the people in the immediate situation.

3. We are an inter-Mennonite organization which includes persons from a variety of Christian traditions. We strive to embody the values and insights of this faith community in our ministries. We believe the Kingdom of God is good news to be proclaimed, an invitation to conversion from a life of sin, and to be lived out in lives of discipleship in community. We seek to reflect a biblical view of Christian life as the wholeness of word and deed, body and spirit, faith and life, worship and proclamation.

4. We have been established by the constituent churches as a service ministry for inter-Mennonite work among the disadvantaged peoples of the world. The broadly defined functions include: emergency relief; rural, community and organizational development; refugee assistance; peace, justice and ecological concerns; education, health and technical support; encouragement of local churches; and nurturing the gospel vision of reconciled people in a reconciled world.

5. We seek to be sensitive to the times in choosing priorities as a church agency. A primary source for such understanding is learning from the people with whom we work. We want to be particularly sensitive to the voices and hopes of local partners, churches and agencies. We endeavor to become a communication link between the people with whom we work and the people who support our ministries.

6. We are aware that human suffering is frequently due to unjust social situations and various forms of exploitation. To relieve human suffering is to be concerned for social justice. Our work for justice recognizes that substantial societal change will be authentic only if it includes the product of local energy and struggle. As North American Christians we confess our involvement in the imbalance of privilege between our societies and much of the rest of the world.

7. We want to be responsible in the use of resources—personnel, financial, material aid—and to be self-critical and subject to evaluation. In order to avoid duplication and provide greatest coordination we expect to be in continual consultation with constituent bodies, local church bodies, Mennonite and Brethren in Christ mission boards, the Council of International Ministries, the Inter-Mennonite Home Ministries Council, the Council of Moderators and Secretaries in Canada and the United States, and Mennonite World Conference.

WHAT WE DO

1. Our service is expected to incarnate the love of God by standing with needy people. Our skills, resources and influence will benefit others but we also expect to learn from and to be changed by the people we relate to. We want to incorporate the vision, concern and participation of the poor in planning and implementing program, and to find ways to transmit their voice to our constituents.

2. Our ministry is rooted in the non-resistant, peacemaking example of Christ. We seek to understand the different points of view on violence but our own commitments to justice in social and political relationships will be as non-violent missioners of peace and reconciliation.

3. Our ministry will demonstrate and articulate the good news in solidarity with local partners through healing, feeding, clothing, creating, planting, building, teaching, listening, advocating, visiting, organizing, encouraging.

4. Our work, whether short or longer term, will be developmental in character. Development is a participatory, transforming process leading to greater dignity and self-reliance, greater vision and possibility, greater community and interdependence. Development cannot be done in isolation from the local and global milieu; it includes the spiritual as well as the material, the corporate as well as the individual.

5. Our work will be directed toward the most needy situations which are often scenes of conflict. Our service will attempt to be without racial, sexual, religious or political qualification. We strive for an identity with God's community that rises above national, racial, cultural or ideological affiliations.

6. Our most important resource is dedicated people willing to immerse themselves in difficult situations. Major effort must be made to recruit and nurture people who are willing to "fall into the ground and die" in life and service, so that the gospel of the Kingdom may bear fruit.

7. Our ministry recognizes the reality of the church in nearly every land. We expect our work and witness to be based on this reality and wherever possible to be done in partnership and mutuality with local churches. Our goal is to strengthen local structures and leadership. We will give priority to program with Mennonite and Brethren in Christ churches and missions.

8. Our service cannot escape the realities of power in the world system. The political, economic and cultural impact of North America is a major issue all over the world. Responsible action in today's world includes humbly "speaking truth to power" which includes a concern for the public policies of government but especially of Canada and the United States. Our experience, especially the reporting of returning workers, can be a helpful witness in local communities, churches and at various levels of government.

FUTURE DIRECTIONS

Priorities at MCC grow out of our mandate and experience. Most of what MCC does has much continuity: emergency relief; community development; refugee assistance; job creation; peace, justice and ecological concerns; education, health and technical support; encouraging the church. New themes come to the forefront. These five are growing edges we want to give increased attention.

1. Strengthening the program and placement of people within Islamic contexts.
2. Improving the level of educational activity within our North American constituency.
3. Expanding the conciliation dimension of overseas program.
4. Enhancing the exchange element with our partners, especially south/south networking.
5. Exploring new program among indigenous and pastoral peoples in Latin America and Africa.

2

REPORT AND RECOMMENDATION
CONCERNING A WASHINGTON OFFICE

In recent years constituent groups have become aware of an increasing need for more knowledge, service, and representation related to the federal government. The mandate of the Peace Section includes under "Scope and Areas of Interest" an item 3, Church and State Relations. Furthermore, under "Functions" items bearing specifically on the needs for a Washington office are #7, "Service in connection with representation to the federal government for any or all constituent groups as may be desired and authorized"; and #2, "Study and research in the assigned areas, including assembling of information on current trends." Other items bear less directly on the need for a Washington office, such as items Nos. 1, 3, 5, 6, and 9.

As a consequence urgings have come from two constituent groups that the Peace Section establish a Washington office, and the Board of Christian Service of the General Conference Mennonite Church has appropriated $4,000 specifically designated for such an office. At the Annual Meeting of the Peace Section on January 19, 1967, the following action was taken, "That we favor in principle increased representation in Washington

---

This document was drafted by MCC Peace Section chair William Keeney following a conference between Keeney, Stanley Bohn, and Ivan J. Kauffman, executive secretary of the Section. It was approved at the MCC Peace Section Executive Committee meeting 18 January 1968, and is available in the Archives of the Mennonite Church.

and that the Peace Section Executive Committee be instructed to work out a recommendation for implementation." (Item 13, Action VI)

The Peace Section Executive Committee has studied the issues involved and would propose the following for consideration to implement the principle:

I. FUNCTION

The Washington office shall be set up to carry out the following functions, with priority given in the approximate order of the listings.

A. The office shall serve as an *observer in Washington,* particularly with reference to developments in the federal government but also as a liaison with other church, welfare, and professional agencies in Washington.

  1. As an observer the office shall seek information and inform the constituent groups on developments in areas affecting the life and work of the Mennonite churches.
  2. The office shall analyze and interpret trends which may affect peace, religious liberty, social welfare, education, and related fields.

B. The office shall *equip the constituent groups* where they desire to make representation to the government.

  1. Primary responsibility for representation to government remains with the constituent groups, but the office may serve to educate and sensitize the constituencies in areas where requested by them.
  2. In accord with the "Guiding Principles for the MCC Peace Section," Section D., item 4, "The Section will speak for the constituent groups in a representative capacity only when and so far as it is requested and authorized to do so by the groups," the office shall not make pronouncements or resolutions. It may upon authorization and request, interpret the position of Mennonite groups to government.
  3. The office may interpret by counseling with government officials the spiritual and ethical concerns of the Mennonite groups as they relate to government programs and legislation, especially as the help is solicited by persons in government.

C. The office shall serve as a *source of knowledge and expertise* on peace and social issues related to government.

  1. The office shall be aware of what issues are being studied and discussed by the federal government and the implications they may have for interests of the Mennonite churches.

2. The office shall help the churches know when presentation of their concerns may be most helpful and shall help in identifying persons with expertise and competence on issues involved, such as the services rendered on drafting legislation affecting conscientious objection to military service, concerns of the Amish about insurance aspects of Social Security, war taxes, impingement of government on religious liberties.
3. The office shall seek to understand how our history, understanding and experience with the Biblical teachings on nonresistance and love may aid the government in better establishing justice and order, to restrain and minimize the effects of evil, and to allow the church to function in obedience to God and the state.

D. The office shall provide *facilitating services* for the constituent groups.

1. Where groups desire such services as education programs for their constituencies, or aid in participating in programs conducted by other agencies, the office shall provide such assistance as it can.
2. Due to its location in Washington, the office may be called upon to do a variety of tasks, such as picking up visas, assisting in setting up visits unrelated to official peace and social concern activities. These functions may be undertaken so long as they do not detract from other functions and the costs are borne by those benefiting from the services.
3. The office shall be ready to negotiate extension of its services to other interests of the churches, such as missions, education, hospital and homes.

II. LOCATION

The office shall be located in the Friends office building. Several locations have been surveyed with advantages and disadvantages weighed. The Friends building appears to have a decided advantage on several points:

A. It is located in the Capitol Hill area so that time and cost in maintaining close contact with a variety of government and church agencies are conserved.
B. The Friends are a peace church with considerable experience and can provide many resources which we would not need to duplicate. They have a comprehensive library and fact file on some of the issues where we share common interests.
C. They operate seminars similar to those which some of our constituent groups have requested.
D. A room is available at a reasonable cost and the Friends are eager to have us present.

III. PERSONNEL AND ADMINISTRATION

The Washington office shall begin initially with the following personnel and administrative relationship.

A. The personnel will be a director and an office secretary, the latter probably only part-time at the beginning.

    1. The Director should be a person with a deep interest in the life and work of the church, preferably with pastoral experience or theological preparation.

    2. The Director should be skilled in both oral and written communication in order to serve in a liaison role between the churches and government officials.

    3. The Director should have sufficient administrative experience and skill to manage the office and its related functions.

B. The Office shall be responsible to the Peace Section Executive Committee for policy and program, but an advisory committee shall be appointed by the Executive Committee to give greater attention to the development of the office. Included on the committee should be persons appointed annually and from such representation as the following: Mennonite lawyers and political scientists, Peace Section Executive Committee members, the staff executives of constituent peace committees, and the Peace Section Executive Secretary ex-officio.

IV. FINANCES

The annual cost of the office is estimated at approximately $15,000. Since the office will likely be in operation for at most six months in 1968, funds already allocated cover FY 1968 needs. The following sources of funds are projected for a further period of 2–3 years: General Conference Board of Christian Service, $4,000; Schowalter Foundation (renewable twice), $2,000; Peace Section regular budget, $6,000; other designated contributions (not needed during first part year operation, but it is hoped other groups might follow pattern of Board of Christian Service for the initial stages of the office), $3,000. Total: $15,000.

V. BEGINNING DATE

The office shall be established as soon as possible in 1968, hopefully no later than June.

NOTES

1. ENGAGING THE QUIET

1. Guy F. Hershberger, *The Mennonite Church in the Second World War* (Scottdale, Pa.: Mennonite Publishing House, 1951), 248.

2. Hershberger, "A Mennonite Office in Washington?" *Gospel Herald,* 27 Feb. 1968, 186.

3. The language is from Robert N. Bellah et al., *The Good Society* (New York: Knopf, 1991), 184.

4. Most references to Mennonites here are meant to be inclusive of (at least) the Mennonite Church (MC) and the General Conference Mennonite Church (GCMC), two of the primary North American Mennonite bodies and strongest supporters of Mennonite Central Committee (MCC).

5. Martin E. Marty, "On 'Being Prophetic,'" *Christian Century* 97 (18) (14 May 1980): 559. See also political scientist Allen D. Hertzke's critique of "cheap prophecy," which he says "allows religious leaders the luxury of not having to concern themselves with the actual consequences of tough choices and tradeoffs, as political figures must, but instead enables them to speak from Olympus about the injustice of this or that, content in the knowledge that they are pure and politically correct, even if often ineffective" (Hertzke, "An Assessment of the Mainline Churches Since 1945," in James E. Wood Jr. and Derek Davis, eds., *The Role of Religion in the Making of Public Policy* [Waco, Texas: J. M. Dawson Institute of Church-State Studies, 1991], 44–45).

6. John Richard Burkholder, "Talking Back to Caesar: The Christian Witness to the State," unpublished paper presented at C. Henry Smith Lecture, Bluffton

College, 26 Mar. 1985, 6. Available in Mennonite Historical Library, Goshen, Ind. (hereafter referred to as MHL). See also Donald B. Kraybill, "From Enclave to Engagement: MCC and the Transformation of Mennonite Identity," *Mennonite Quarterly Review* 70 (1) (Jan. 1996).

7. Mennonite Central Committee, "Faith, Power and Politics: Questions and Answers" (Brochure published by MCC's Akron office, 1992).

8. Richard K. MacMaster, *Land, Piety, Peoplehood: The Establishment of Mennonite Communities in America, 1683–1790* (Scottdale, Pa.: Herald Press, 1985), 250–51.

9. Ibid.

10. Jean-Paul Sartre, *Dirty Hands,* in *No Exit and Three Other Plays* (New York: Vintage, 1955), 224. In his argument with Hugo, Hoerderer says earlier, "How you cling to your purity, young man! How afraid you are to soil you hands! All right, stay pure! What good will it do? . . . Purity is an idea for a yogi or a monk." The Hoerderer remark also is cited in Michael Walzer, "Political Action: The Problem of Dirty Hands," in *War and Moral Responsibility,* ed. Marshall Cohen et al. (Princeton: Princeton Univ. Press, 1974): 62–82.

11. For example, see John Rawls, *A Theory of Justice* (Cambridge, Mass.: Harvard Univ. Press, 1971).

12. Max Weber, *From Max Weber: Essays in Sociology,* trans. and ed. H. H. Gerth and C. Wright Mills (New York: Oxford Univ. Press, 1946), 120. Weber adds: "You may demonstrate to a convinced syndicalist, believing in an ethic of ultimate ends, that his action will result in increasing the opportunities of reaction, in increasing the oppression of his class, and obstructing its ascent—and you will not make the slightest impression upon him. If an action of good intent leads to bad results, then, in the actor's eyes, not he but the world, or the stupidity of other men, or God's will who made them thus, is responsible for the evil. However a man who believes in an ethic of responsibility takes account of precisely the average deficiencies of people; as Fichte has correctly said, he does not even have the right to presuppose their goodness or perfection" (120–21).

13. Ibid., 126.

14. See, e.g., Reinhold Niebuhr, "Why the Christian Church Is Not Pacifist," in *The Essential Reinhold Niebuhr: Selected Essays and Addresses,* ed. Robert McAfee Brown (New Haven: Yale Univ. Press, 1986), 106–7.

15. On Mennonite responses to Niebuhr, see especially John H. Yoder, *Christian Attitudes to War, Peace and Revolution: A Companion to Bainton* (Elkhart, Ind.: Co-Op Bookstore, 1983), 343–418.

16. Mennonite historian Cornelius J. Dyck often notes the irony that "it takes a good war to bring out the best in Mennonites." Throughout this century, from World War I to the Persian Gulf War, major United States conflicts have served to remind American Mennonites of their identity, have compelled them to reiterate for themselves and the public their reasons for not participating in warfare, and have prompted them to contribute something—short of taking up arms—to the societies in which they live.

17. MacMaster, *Land, Piety,* 257. MacMaster rightly observes that this plea evidences the first stirrings of "alternative" service.

18. See James C. Juhnke, *Vision, Doctrine, War: Mennonite Identity and Organization in America, 1890–1930* (Scottdale, Pa.: Herald Press, 1989), 29.

19. Juhnke, *A People of Two Kingdoms: The Political Acculturation of the Kansas Mennonites* (Newton, Kans.: Faith and Life Press, 1975), 115–16. On this subject, see also Juhnke's *Vision, Doctrine,* especially chaps. 8 and 9.

20. P. C. Hiebert and Orie O. Miller, *Feeding the Hungry: Russia Famine, 1919–1925* (Scottdale, Pa.: MCC, 1929), 29. Parts of this also were cited in Juhnke's *A People,* 115–16.

21. Juhnke, *A People,* 156–57. On 192, Juhnke says a corollary to his argument is that the Mennonite relief program would *not* have arisen had there been no contact with American culture and no desire to be good Americans. He suggests that a comparison with the Amish, who remained isolated and uninterested in relief programs, would be instructive. Acculturation among the more progressive Amish has led to relief and mission work in recent years. Juhnke also notes that the link between American nationalism and Mennonite discipleship again could be seen in the early 1970s, when the number of Mennonites volunteering for church-related service declined, partly in response to the end of the military draft.

22. The following illustrations of "feeding and clothing" can be found in a variety of sources, including Frank H. Epp, *Partners in Service: The Story of Mennonite Central Committee Canada* (Winnipeg, Manitoba: MCC, 1983), 10.

23. Documents related to this spontaneous relief effort and the 1756 formation of the Friendly Association for Regaining and Preserving Peace with the Indians by Pacific Measures can be found in Richard K. MacMaster et al., *Conscience in Crisis: Mennonites and Other Peace Churches in America, 1739–1789* (Scottdale, Pa.: Herald Press, 1979), 130–44.

24. Juhnke, *Vision, Doctrine,* 254–55.

25. Peter Dyck, "A Theology of Service," *Mennonite Quarterly Review* 44 (3) (July 1970): 262.

26. M. C. Lehman, *The History and Principles of Mennonite Relief Work: An Introduction* (Akron, Pa.: MCC, 1945), 41. See also Ted Koontz, "The Theology of MCC: A Christian Resource for Extending God's Blessing," *Mennonite Quarterly Review* 70 (1) (Jan. 1996); Hershberger, *The Mennonite Church,* 194–95; Cornelius Krahn et al., "Altruism in Mennonite Life," in *Forms and Techniques of Altruistic and Spiritual Growth,* ed. Pitirim Sorokin (Boston: Beacon, 1954), 309–28; Albert Gaeddart, "Christian Love in Action: An Essential Aspect of Nonresistance," in *Proceedings of the Fourth Mennonite World Conference, 3–10 August 1948* (Akron, Pa.: MCC, 1950), 257–62; and Harold S. Bender, "Mennonite Peace Action throughout the World," ibid., 262–69.

27. For a concise summary of the origins of modern concerns for "responsibility," see Albert R. Jonsen, "Responsibility," *The Westminster Dictionary of Christian Ethics,* ed. James F. Childress and John Macquarrie (Philadelphia: Westminster, 1986), 545–49. See also J. Lawrence Burkholder, *The Problem of Social Responsibility from the Perspective of the Mennonite Church* (Elkhart, Ind.: Institute of Mennonite Studies, 1989), especially chap. 2, "The Meaning and Scope of Responsibility."

28. I am cautiously using the traditional term "mainline," even though I am keenly aware that many recent scholars refer to Methodists, Presbyterians, and other such religious groups as the "oldline" or even the "sideline" in order to accurately reflect their significant declines in influence and membership in the last half century. For analyses of this trend, see, e.g., Dean M. Kelley, *Why Conservative*

Churches Are Growing (New York: Harper and Row, 1972); Lloyd Billingsley, *From Mainline to Sideline: the Social Witness of the National Council of Churches* (Washington: Ethics and Public Policy Center, 1990); and Roger Finke and Rodney Stark, *The Churching of America, 1776–1990: Winners and Losers in Our Religious Economy* (New Brunswick: Rutgers Univ. Press, 1992).

29. Found in a variety of places, including the brochure "Mennonite Central Committee: Principles That Guide Our Mission," a statement approved at MCC's annual meeting, 25–26 Jan. 1991, in Archbold, Ohio. The full text is in appendix 1.

30. See below on Canadian Mennonites' Ottawa office. It also should be noted that, in recent years, United States Mennonites have had an additional "office" in New York with a mandate similar to that of MCC Washington. Off and on since 1981, MCC has assigned someone to monitor the United Nations. See, e.g., John D. Rempel, "Work by the Church Does Make a Difference," *Gospel Herald,* 10 Nov. 1992, 8, and the entire issue of *Peace Office Newsletter* 25 (1) (Jan.–Mar. 1995), which was titled "Mennonites Working with the United Nations." From 1985 to 1991, a group of North American and European Mennonites also observed the North Atlantic Treaty Organization (NATO) from Brussels, Belgium. See an unpublished paper by J. Robert Charles and Frederic Fransen, "On Watching NATO," available from the authors.

31. Mennonites who have served in Congress, all in the House of Representatives, include Benjamin Welty of Ohio, 1917 to 1921; Christian Ramseyer of Iowa, 1915 to 1933; and Edward C. Eicher of Iowa, 1933 to 1938. In recent years only three Mennonites even ran for Congress: James C. Juhnke of Kansas in 1970; LeRoy Kennel of Illinois in 1980 and 1982; and Eric Yost of Kansas in 1992. Among other sources, see John H. Redekop, "Politics," in Cornelius J. Dyck and Dennis D. Martin, *Mennonite Encyclopedia V* (Scottdale, Pa.: Herald Press, 1990), 711–14; Juhnke, "A Mennonite Runs for Congress," *Mennonite Life* 26 (1) (Jan. 1971): 8–11; Rich Preheim, "Mennonite Candidates Feel Called to Political Action" and "Mennonite Politicians May Face Challenges When They Take Beliefs into Politics," *Mennonite Weekly Review,* 22 and 29 Oct. 1992, 1–2, of each issue.

32. The best listing of Mennonites involved in electoral politics, both in Canada and the United States, is in John H. Redekop, "Mennonites and Politics in Canada and the United States," *Journal of Mennonite Studies* 1 (1983): 96–99. For other analytical accounts, see two articles by Koontz, "Christian Ethics and Political Ethics: An Irreducible Conflict?" in *Prophetic Vision Applied to One's Academic Discipline,* ed. John Rempel and Robert Charles (Elkhart, Ind.: Mennonite Board of Missions, 1979), 11–25; and "Reflections on American Mennonites and Politics," *The Window* 10 (1) (Oct. 1982): 1–2. See also Harold S. Bender's critique of Mennonites in politics in "Church and State in Mennonite History," *Mennonite Quarterly Review* 13 (2) (Apr. 1939): 90–91.

33. This tension has not gone unnoticed by those within the Mennonite fold. Mennonite ethicist J. Lawrence Burkholder, one insider who more than thirty years ago critiqued his denomination for its lack of social responsibility, has been among the most vocal critics. Burkholder's 1958 dissertation at Princeton Theological Seminary expressed such views and outraged Mennonite Church leaders Guy F. Hershberger and Harold S. Bender. The dissertation remained unpublished until 1989. Burkholder's wide range of experiences while doing relief work in China contributed to his theological broadening during the 1950s. His theology was formed primarily on the mission frontier.

34. Paul Toews, "Mennonites in American Society: Modernity and the Persistence of Religious Community," *Mennonite Quarterly Review* 63 (3) (July 1989): 228.

35. The full MCC constituency includes General Conference Mennonite Church, Mennonite Church, Brethren in Christ, Mennonite Brethren Church, Lancaster Mennonite Conference, Conservative Mennonite Conference, Fellowship of Evangelical Bible Churches, Old Order Mennonite, Beachy Amish Church, Evangelical Mennonite Church, Independent Mennonite, Emmanuel Mennonite Church, and Church of God in Christ Mennonite. At a joint conference in July 1995, delegates from the Mennonite Church and General Conference Mennonite Church voted to "move toward the integration of our two denominations." At this printing, no date has been set for the merger.

36. Toews, "Mennonites in American Society," 229.

37. Mennonite Central Committee Canada, based in Winnipeg, Manitoba, was formed in 1963. Already in 1944, Mennonite Central Committee had an office in Kitchener, Ontario, for channeling Canadian funds to the organization and communicating with the Non-Resistant Relief Organization and the Canadian Mennonite Relief Committee. The best sources on this are Frank H. Epp, *Partners in Service*; and Esther Ruth Epp, "The Origins of the Mennonite Central Committee Canada," (M.A. thesis, University of Manitoba, 1980).

38. Don Ratzlaff, "Ultimate Church Committee Knows Message," *Mennonite Weekly Review,* 9 Feb. 1989, 1.

39. Hertzke says mainline lobbies' effectiveness is "too often muted by a blend of naiveté and sanctimony. . . . One example is the pervasive language of 'peace & justice,' uttered as one, unambiguous phrase, as if to imply that no tradeoffs exist between the two, or that opponents somehow favor injustice and war" (Hertzke, "An Assessment," 44).

40. It should be said at this early stage that the Mennonite office in Washington was part of a much larger movement in Protestant and Catholic churches toward establishing monitoring or lobbying posts in the capital. Between 1951 and 1985, for example, church lobbies in Washington grew fivefold, from sixteen to more than eighty. See Hertzke, *Representing God in Washington: The Role of Religious Lobbies in the American Polity* (Knoxville: Univ. of Tennessee Press, 1988), 5.

41. Every reference here and below to numbers of Mennonites is based on a count of *baptized members,* and excludes thousands of children and adult attenders who have not formally "joined the church." The Old Order Amish are not institutionally affiliated with Mennonite Central Committee, although most other large Mennonite bodies are. The figures are from James E. Horsch, ed., *Mennonite Yearbook 1995* (Scottdale, Pa.: Mennonite Publishing House, 1995); Doris Mendel Schmidt, ed., *Handbook of Information, General Conference Mennonite Church* (Newton, Kans.: General Conference Mennonite Church, 1992); Dieter Goetz Lichdi, *Mennonite World Handbook* (Carol Stream, Ill.: Mennonite World Conference, 1990); Mennonite World Conference, "Mennonite and Brethren in Christ World Directory 1994," *Courier* 9 (1) (First Quarter 1994): 9–15; Larry Miller, "Global Mennonite Faith Profile: Past, Present, Future," *Mennonite Weekly Review,* 9 Sept. 1993, 1–2; and J. Howard Kauffman and Leo Driedger, *The Mennonite Mosaic* (Scottdale, Pa.: Herald, 1991). The latter text, which is based on a survey of 3,000 North American Mennonite and Brethren in Christ respondents who speak for some 232,000 members of their denominations, is the best recent source for Mennonite demographic information.

42. Kauffman and Driedger, *The Mennonite Mosaic,* 27.

43. For a thorough analysis of these changes, see Kauffman and Driedger, *The Mennonite Mosaic,* and Leo Driedger and Donald B. Kraybill, *Mennonite Peacemaking: From Quietism to Activism* (Scottdale, Pa.: Herald Press, 1994). For a careful look at twentieth-century Mennonites, see also Paul Toews, *Mennonites in America, 1930–1970: Modernity and the Persistence of Religious Community* (Scottdale, Pa.: Herald Press, 1996).

44. See, e.g., James M. Stayer, *Anabaptists and the Sword* (Lawrence, Kans.: Coronado Press, 1972). Because the Anabaptist movement coincided with the Peasants' Revolt of 1524–25, and because of unclear delineations between the various persons and groups seeking social and religious change in sixteenth-century Europe, "Anabaptist" became a derisive term covering a wide range of persons responding to Europe's unrest.

45. More thorough descriptions of these Mennonite bodies can be found in J. Howard Kauffman and Leland Harder, *Anabaptists Four Centuries Later: A Profile of Five Mennonite and Brethren in Christ Denominations* (Scottdale, Pa.: Herald Press, 1975), 31–45. These brief snippets are drawn in part from their descriptions.

46. Juhnke, "Mennonite History and Self Understanding: North American Mennonitism as a Bipolar Mosaic," in Calvin Wall Redekop and Samuel J. Steiner, eds., *Mennonite Identity: Historical and Contemporary Perspectives* (Lanham, Md.: Univ. Press of America, 1988), 84. In the same text, see also Rodney J. Sawatsky's broadening but sympathetic critique, "Beyond the Social History of the Mennonites: A Response to James C. Juhnke," 101–8. Among Sawatsky's on-target critiques (106) is that "the bi-polar ethnic model is too limited to embrace all those other ethnicities around the world which in the last century have chosen the name 'Mennonite.'"

47. Juhnke, *Vision, Doctrine,* 34.

48. Ibid., 35–37.

49. On other differences between the two major Mennonite denominations, see also Rodney J. Sawatsky, "History and Ideology: American Mennonite Identity Definition Through History," (Ph.D. diss., Princeton University, 1977), especially 89–121.

50. The following points in this paragraph are from John H. Redekop, "A Perspective on Anabaptist Pacifism in Canada," in John Richard Burkholder and Barbara Nelson Gingerich, eds., *Mennonite Peace Theology: A Panorama of Types* (Akron, Pa.: MCC Peace Office, 1991), 60–61. For another insightful analysis of Canadian differences, see Reginald W. Bibby's section subtitled "We Are Not Like the Americans" in *Fragmented Gods: The Poverty and Potential of Religion in Canada* (Toronto: Irwin Publishing, 1987), 214–22.

51. See William Janzen, "Mennonites in Canada: Their Relations with and Effect on the Larger Society," an unpublished presentation at an interchurch conference on "Christianity and Canadian Culture," Toronto, 20–22 Oct. 1988, revised in 1988. Available from MCCC's Ottawa office.

52. From John H. Redekop, "A Perspective," 61. See also Redekop's "Mennonites and Politics." In the Nov. 1988 Canadian general election, seventeen Mennonites were candidates for House of Commons seats. Four of the candidates won seats, including three for the Progressive Conservative Party and one for the New Democratic Party. See John H. Redekop, "Mennonite Politicians," *Mennonite*

Brethren Herald, 23 Dec. 1988, 8. See also John Duek, "Forsake a 400-year-old Tradition: Mennonites Enter Politics by the Dozen," *Mennonite Reporter,* 12 Jan. 1976, 10–11; and William Janzen and Freda Enns, "Canadian Mennonites and Politics," an unpublished overview written for the 1990 Mennonite World Conference, 10 Nov. 1989, available from MCCC's Ottawa office. Janzen and Enns note that persons with "Mennonite names" on the list of provincial candidates per decade in this century number as follows: 4, 4, 6, 11, 6, 34, 64, 82, 85.

53. Most of the observations in this paragraph are from John H. Redekop's "A Perspective," 62–65. See also Stephen D. McDowell, "Mennonites, The Canadian State, and Globalization in International Political Economy," *Conrad Grebel Review* 12 (1) (Winter 1994): 21–42.

54. I am, of course, referring to civil religion, a notion that has roots in the writings of eighteenth-century French philosopher Jean-Jacques Rousseau and was popularized in the United States by Robert N. Bellah. See Bellah's article "Civil Religion in America" in *Beyond Belief: Essays on Religion in a Post-Traditional World* (New York: Harper and Row, 1970): 168–89, and his subsequent critiques.

55. The comments were made by William Janzen, longtime director of MCCC's Ottawa office. Janzen's remarks are from my transcription of his 13 Feb. 1992 presentation at Associated Mennonite Biblical Seminaries in Elkhart, Ind.

56. In contrast, Canada has had no draft since World War II and was involved more as a peacekeeper than as a combatant in Vietnam. William Janzen says the draft has always reminded United States Mennonites of their separatism, whereas most Canadian Mennonites have not experienced conscription.

57. The best source on this progression is Monique Enns, "A History of the MCC Ottawa Office as Drawn from MCC files," unpublished paper for a course on Mennonite studies, 7 Apr. 1986, available in MCCC's Ottawa office. See also Robert S. Kreider and Rachel Waltner Goossen, *Hungry, Thirsty, a Stranger: The MCC Experience* (Scottdale, Pa.: Herald Press, 1988), 320–31.

58. See J. M. Klassen, "Statement Regarding an MCC (Canada) Office in Ottawa," a paper presented at the 1974 annual meeting of MCC. See also Siegfried Bartel's paper by the same title, distributed at the same meeting, which urged that an Ottawa office *not* be established. The "Functions" section of Klassen's paper was drawn extensively from the "Report and Recommendation Concerning a Washington Office," written in 1967. The Washington "Report" is included in my appendix 2.

59. Chris Derksen Hiebert, who was interim director of the Ottawa office, says that "in terms of like-minded advocacy groups, MCC is one of only three Christian religious bodies with government relations offices in Ottawa." Ottawa simply hasn't become the "mecca for lobbyists" that Washington has, says Hiebert. See his response to my article "Whirling Toward Similitude" in *Conrad Grebel Review* 13 (1) (Winter 1995): 102–6.

60. Janzen's familial political heritage bears mentioning in this context: years ago, one of his uncles was excommunicated from (formally kicked out of) his Mennonite congregation for voting in a political election.

61. See William Janzen, ed., *Mennonite Submissions to the Canadian Government: A Collection of Documents Prepared by the Ottawa Office of Mennonite Central Committee Canada, 1975–1990* (Ottawa: MCC Canada, 1990).

62. From my transcription of Janzen's 13 Feb. 1992 presentation at Associated Mennonite Biblical Seminaries.

63. While the larger passage in which Matthew's account is contained has parallels in Mark and Luke's gospels, neither adds the charge about being "wise" and "innocent."

64. Eduard Schweizer, *The Good News According to Matthew,* trans. David E. Green (Atlanta: John Knox, 1975), 240.

65. This same brass serpent was used in John's gospel as a metaphor for the way in which the "son of Man" was to be lifted up (crucified), so that "whoever believes in him may have eternal life" (John 3:14–15).

66. Schweizer, *The Good News,* 235.

67. W. F. Albright and C. S. Mann, *Matthew* (Garden City, N.Y.: Doubleday, 1971), 123.

68. Max Zerwick and Mary Grosvenor, *A Grammatical Analysis of the Greek New Testament* (Rome: Biblical Institute Press, 1981), 30.

69. William Keeney, "The Establishment of the Washington, D.C. and Ottawa Offices (first draft)," 1977, 17–18. Available in MCC Washington files.

70. Hedrick Smith, *The Power Game: How Washington Works* (New York: Ballantine, 1989).

71. Greg Goering, "Learning to Speak Second Languages," 5 May 1991. Unpublished paper available from the author.

72. Atlee Beechy, "First They Make Enemies," *Peace Office Newsletter* 21 (2) (Mar.–Apr. 1991): 3.

73. James F. S. Amstutz, "Dialogue with Washington: Mennonites and the Test of Faith," *Mennonite Life* 47(1) (Mar. 1992): 33–34.

74. J. Lawrence Burkholder, *The Problem,* 3.

2. BUMPING INTO THE STATE

1. As always, attention should be drawn to the different experiences of Swiss and south German Anabaptists and the Dutch-North German-Russian Anabaptists. Although the latter generally were not involved in *national* politics, they did take more responsibility for life in the local community than did the Swiss and south German Anabaptists. Mennonites who remained in the Netherlands also became quite acculturated, taking on a variety of governmental roles in the country.

2. Mennonite sociologist Leland Harder, who in his 1962 dissertation works with sect-cycle theories to interpret contemporary Mennonite experience, speaks about the inherently contradictory goals some social or religious groups have. These contradictions lead to a kind of disequilibrium for the group, which moves them toward certain social and theological responses. In the case of sects, these responses can be one mark of the shift toward becoming a denomination, says Harder. For Mennonites, the contradictory goals were separation for the sake of purity on the one hand and evangelism or outreach on the other. Social theorist Bryan Wilson identifies this as the tension "conversionist sects" experience. See Wilson's chapter entitled "An Analysis of Sect Development" in his edited volume *Patterns of Sectarianism: Organisation and Ideology in Social and Religious Movements* (London: Heinemann, 1967), 22–45. For Harder's analysis, see his "The Quest for

Equilibrium in an Established Sect: A Study of Social Change in the General Conference Church," (Ph.D. diss., Northwestern University, 1962). The outreach or service Mennonites did beginning earlier in the twentieth century necessitated dealing with this sort of disequilibrium and elicited a more socially and politically engaged—though still cautiously so—response.

3. Richard C. Detweiler, *Mennonite Statements on Peace, 1915–1966* (Scottdale, Pa.: Herald Press, 1968). Detweiler's analysis was only of Mennonite Church and Mennonite Central Committee documents, not those of other Mennonite denominations. My reference to "up through at least the 1960s" is not meant to suggest that thereafter there was a major change in the tone of Mennonites' public statements. Although the humble approach may have more of an edge in today's communications from MCC Washington, most of their own missives remain within that genre.

4. On this tone, see Driedger and Kraybill, *Mennonite Peacemaking*. It also should be noted that the tone of Mennonite statements may have as much to do with their "theology of humility" as their misunderstanding of democratic governance. In other words, perhaps Mennonites historically have spoken not only to the government but also to one another and their neighbors in a humble fashion. On this idea, see Theron F. Schlabach, *Peace, Faith, Nation: Mennonites and Amish in Nineteenth-Century America* (Scottdale, Pa.: Herald Press, 1988), especially 95–105.

5. In addition to the Detweiler text, two other sources on twentieth-century Mennonite statements to government are helpful: Urbane Peachey, ed., *Mennonite Statements on Peace and Social Concerns, 1900–1978* (Akron, Pa.: MCC U.S. Peace Section, 1980), and Duane Friesen, *Mennonite Witness on Peace and Social Concerns, 1900–1980* (Akron, Pa.: MCC, 1982). The Friesen booklet provides an analytical overview of the documents in Peachey's text.

6. This story is told in many places, among them Cornelius J. Dyck's *Introduction to Mennonite History* (Scottdale, Pa.: Herald Press, 1981), 37–49.

7. Walter Klaassen, *Anabaptism: Neither Catholic nor Protestant* (Waterloo, Ontario: Conrad Press, 1973), 60–63.

8. Thus far I have resisted addressing the "sectarian" designation frequently placed on Anabaptist-Mennonites and other marginalized groups. It seems essential, however, to say something about the sociological distinctions made historically between "churches" and "sects" and between those two and "denominations." Sociologist Max Weber first proposed the delineations just after the turn of the century, and they have been expanded and altered repeatedly since then, beginning with Ernst Troeltsch and H. Richard Niebuhr. Differentiations have been made using the following criteria: scale, boundaries, entry, social organization, leadership, type of authority, commitment level, relationship to society, social composition, and doctrinal ideas. Churches are perceived as accommodated to their culture, while sects are considered either actively opposed or passively withdrawn from their world. According to the theory, churches require a low level of personal commitment, are conservative in stance, have many members, are hierarchically organized, and are composed of the respectable majority of persons in society's center. Sects are exclusive, demanding a high level of personal commitment from those who voluntarily join—usually the disinherited at the bottom, edges, and cracks of society. They often are critical of society and small in numbers, and their

leadership is based more on a "priesthood of all believers." Most theorists have suggested that sects go through a process of social mobility and routinization and eventually become denominations. Denominations, in contrast to churches, do not enjoy a monopoly in their culture and, in contrast to sects, do not *mind* the resulting pluralism. One historical overview of the use of these terms is Russell Richey, "Institutional Forms of Religion," in Charles H. Lippy and Peter W. Williams, eds., *Encyclopedia of the American Religious Experience* (New York: Scribner's, 1988), 31–50. A helpful theoretical overview is Rodney Stark and William Sims Bainbridge, *The Future of Religion* (Berkeley: Univ. of California Press, 1985).

In her chapter in Russell Richey and R. Bruce Mullin, eds., *Reimagining Denominationalism* (New York: Oxford Univ. Press, 1994), 111–33, Nancy T. Ammerman notes that the biggest problem with these definitions, in particular "denomination," is that their empirical referent has often been unclear. "It is primarily a conceptual category (an 'ideal type'), and the constellation of factors constituting the definition rarely occurred so neatly in the real world," she writes. James Beckford has argued that sociology of religion's dependence on the Weberian-Troeltschian-Niebuhrian formulations has impeded theorists' understanding of the ways in which religious groups organize. See his "Religious Organizations," in *The Sacred in a Secular Age,* ed. Phillip E. Hammond (Berkeley: Univ. of California Press, 1985), 125–38. For Mennonite wrestlings with this theory, see Calvin Redekop, "Sectarianism and the Sect Cycle," in Leo Driedger and Leland Harder, eds., *Anabaptist-Mennonite Identities in Ferment* (Elkhart, Ind.: Institute of Mennonite Studies, 1990), 59–83, and the articles and texts cited in Redekop's bibliography at the end of the essay.

9. Leo Driedger, *Mennonite Identity in Conflict* (Lewiston, N.Y.: Edwin Mellen, 1988), 15. See also Bender, "Church and State," especially 87–91.

10. Schlabach, "Mennonites, Revivalism, Modernity—1683–1850," *Church History* 48 (1979): 399.

11. George W. Forell, ed., *Christian Social Teachings: A Reader in Christian Social Ethics from the Bible to the Present* (Garden City: Anchor, 1966), 184.

12. Claus-Peter Clasen, *Anabaptism: A Social History, 1525–1618* (Ithaca: Cornell Univ. Press, 1972).

13. Space does not allow for a full discussion of Anabaptism and the state here. One of the standard sources is Stayer, *Anabaptists and the Sword.* For many years, one brief source for understanding the church-state relationship was Hans J. Hillerbrand, "The Anabaptist View of the State," *Mennonite Quarterly Review* 32 (2) (Apr. 1958): 83–110. Recent historiographical works, such as Stayer's, have amplified and revised considerably Hillerbrand's summary. See, e.g., John H. Redekop, "A Re-Assessment of Some Traditional Anabaptist Church-State Perspectives," in *Essays on Peace Theology and Witness,* ed. Willard M. Swartley (Elkhart: Institute of Mennonite Studies, 1988), 61–72. For an overview, see Ted Koontz, "Church-State Relations," in *Mennonite Encyclopedia V,* 159–62. For a helpful listing of recent Mennonite writings on the church and state, see Willard Swartley and Cornelius J. Dyck, eds., *Annotated Bibliography of Mennonite Writings on War and Peace* (Scottdale, Pa.: Herald Press, 1987), 128–77.

14. A third classic understanding not dealt with here is the state's *redeeming* function, a view usually attributed to the Calvinist-Puritan heritage and found in the writings of Karl Barth and other more contemporary writers.

15. See Mennonite scholar Tom Yoder Neufeld's distinctions between "happy dualism" and "sad dualism" in "Varieties of Contemporary Mennonite Peace Witness: From Passivism to Pacifism, From Nonresistance to Resistance," *Conrad Grebel Review* 10 (3) (Fall 1992): 247–50. In "God in Public: A Modest Proposal for a Quest for a Contemporary North American Anabaptist Paradigm," *Conrad Grebel Review* 4 (1) (Winter 1986), Scott Holland criticizes Mennonite dualism. Holland proposes, without fully clarifying what such a Mennonite church might look like, "that the church learn to celebrate God in public through the medium of a truly public church."

16. Exceptions to this Anabaptist position of nonparticipation include Menno Simons, Balthasar Hubmaier, Hans Denck, and Pilgram Marpeck. Denck, Marpeck, and Menno all believed, though, that the tensions in being both a Christian and a magistrate would make life difficult for the true believer. The "outside the perfection of Christ" language is from the "Brotherly Agreement" written by Anabaptist leader Michael Sattler and others at a Feb. 1527 gathering in Schleitheim, near the Swiss-German border. Excellent sources on what has become known as the "Schleitheim Confession" include John H. Yoder, trans. and ed., *The Legacy of Michael Sattler* (Scottdale, Pa.: Herald Press, 1973), and C. Arnold Snyder's *The Life and Thought of Michael Sattler* (Scottdale, Pa.: Herald Press, 1984).

17. This is a distillation of Marpeck's "Defence," which is excerpted in *Anabaptism in Outline: Selected Primary Sources,* ed. Walter Klaassen (Scottdale, Pa.: Herald Press, 1981), 263.

18. Menno Simons, "A Pathetic Supplication to All Magistrates," in *The Complete Writings of Menno Simons,* ed. J. C. Wenger (Scottdale, Pa.: Herald Press, 1956), 523–31.

19. Detweiler makes this point in *Mennonite Statements,* 17.

20. Other *scattered* Mennonites were known to be in the New World as early as 1652.

21. See MacMaster, *Land, Piety,* 34–35.

22. Schlabach, "Mennonites, Revivalism," 404.

23. The antislavery document was sent to the regional Monthly Meeting, which then sent it on to the higher Quarterly Meeting, where it was forwarded to the Yearly Meeting. There the document was tabled. MacMaster says the document was "one of the earliest and clearest antislavery statements in American history—and indeed in the whole history of slavery's abolition in Western culture." See his *Land, Piety,* 42–43.

24. Ibid., 235–36. Mennonites did end up providing wagons, food, and supplies to the military in subsequent years.

25. MacMaster writes that "the efforts of American patriots to form a new national peoplehood had not worked well with Mennonites. Quite a few Mennonites had turned back to being subjects more than citizens. The American revolution had made Mennonites more than ever a people apart." See his *Land, Piety,* 280.

26. Schlabach, *Peace, Faith, Nation,* 171–72. Schlabach's chap. 6, "Politics and Pacifism," is a nuanced examination of Mennonite and Amish political activity from 1800 to 1900. Schlabach says, on 148, that when American Mennonites and other German pacifists voted, they usually favored the Democrats' opponents—the Federalists, then Whigs, then Republicans.

27. Information gleaned from Peachey, *Mennonite Statements*. Conferences within the various denominations also sent communications directly to national leaders, numbering from one to six, during those fourscore years. By far the most communications to government have come from Mennonite Central Committee itself. MCC's statements between 1940 and 1978 number more than *all* of the Mennonite and Brethren in Christ denominations and their conferences combined. Between 1978 and 1996, this trend has continued.

28. Not only the denominational statements but also the inter-Mennonite statements from MCC focused on conscription, up through about 1970. Detweiler writes in *Mennonite Statements,* 53–57, that between 1915 and 1950 Mennonite Church communications on disarmament and other policies do not provide sufficient theological rationale. "In other words, peace witness that goes beyond explanation of the church's own nonresistant position does not appear to altogether fit the concepts of church and state that were assumed by the Mennonite Church in that period." Detweiler says Mennonites' theological concept of the witness to the state was not clearly worked out, so when Mennonites moved beyond their nonresistant witness, they "had the appearance of moving into alien territory without sufficient awareness of the implications." Duane Friesen, in *Mennonite Witness,* 7, rightly suggests that Mennonites' practice was ahead of their theology: in 1950 Mennonites essentially had no theology of witness to political and economic structures.

29. Most of MCC's overseas workers and those in the United States and Canada are volunteers, serving two- to three-year renewable terms. Volunteers are provided only with food and housing and a subsistence-level monthly allowance. The major portion of MCC's 33.5-million-dollar annual budget goes toward material aid. From the time of its inception until 1996, more than twelve thousand workers had had domestic or overseas assignments with MCC. This figure does not include many thousands more who have volunteered with Mennonite Disaster Service or worked in Civilian Public Service units.

30. Originally a spontaneous outgrowth in the midwestern United States during the 1950s, Mennonite Disaster Service was institutionalized and placed under MCC's umbrella in 1962. For more on MDS, see Katie Funk Wiebe, *Day of Disaster* (Scottdale, Pa.: Herald Press, 1976). Helpful synopses of other MCC programs are Kreider and Waltner Goossen, *Hungry, Thirsty,* and Calvin Redekop, "The Organizational Children of MCC," *Mennonite Historical Bulletin* 56 (1) (Jan. 1995): 1–8. On the history of MCC, especially stories and key documents, see also Cornelius J. Dyck's four edited volumes, all published by Herald Press: *From the Files of MCC,* 1980; *Responding to Worldwide Needs,* 1980; *Witness and Service in North America,* 1980; and *Something Meaningful for God,* 1981.

31. Juhnke's *A People* and *Vision, Doctrine* (especially chap. 8) are among the best sources on this wartime guilt. See also Toews, "The Impact of Alternative Service on the American Mennonite World: A Critical Evaluation," *Mennonite Quarterly Review* 66 (4) (Oct. 1992): 615–27; and Sawatsky, "History and Ideology," especially 122–39 and 211–60. It should be said that while American Mennonites prospered economically during World War I, they also suffered various forms of harassment and persecution during the war. About 138 of the 2,000 Mennonites drafted were court-martialed and sentenced to federal prisons for refusing

to obey military orders, and others were ridiculed for being pacifists during their time of service at stateside military camps. About a thousand Mennonites and Hutterites (the communal Anabaptists) fled to Canada. Mennonites in local communities who refused to buy war bonds were taunted by their local peers; sometimes they were tarred and feathered or stripped and painted yellow.

32. The Wilson memo and remark about patriotism are from Kreider and Waltner Goossen, *Hungry, Thirsty,* 25. Much of the information in these paragraphs is gleaned from Kreider and Goossen's text, as well as the many other sources that tell about the founding of MCC. See, e.g., John D. Unruh, *In the Name of Christ: A History of the Mennonite Central Committee and Its Service, 1920–1951* (Scottdale, Pa.: Herald Press, 1952); Hiebert and Miller, *Feeding the Hungry*; and Guy F. Hershberger, "Historical Background to the Formation of the Mennonite Central Committee," *Mennonite Quarterly Review* 44 (3) (July 1970): 213–44.

33. John A. Lapp, "The Peace Mission of the Mennonite Central Committee," *Mennonite Quarterly Review* 44 (3) (July 1970): 281.

34. Cited in Kreider and Waltner Goossen, *Hungry, Thirsty,* 26.

35. Cited in Unruh, *In the Name,* 15.

36. The figures are from Kreider and Waltner Goossen, *Hungry, Thirsty,* 24.

37. Cited in Unruh, *In the Name,* 35.

38. In addition to the other sources already cited, on this period see also Irvin B. Horst, *A Ministry of Goodwill: A Short Account of Mennonite Relief, 1939–1949* (Akron, Pa.: MCC, 1950).

39. Robert Kreider, "The Impact of MCC Service on American Mennonites," *Mennonite Quarterly Review* 44 (3) (July 1970): 245–46. Up until 1940, says Kreider, MCC's office was simply wherever the executive secretary lived—either in Scottdale or Akron, Pa. MCC began with seven affiliate groups, including some denominations that no longer exist. In 1944 several large *Canadian* Mennonite bodies cast their lot with MCC, making the organization an international (or at least binational) one.

40. Cited in Unruh, *In the Name,* 43.

41. Even during the 1940s, most of the material aid MCC distributed in Europe and other parts of the world went to non-Mennonites. Now only a tiny fraction of MCC's budget would provide direct assistance to Mennonites.

42. See the story of Civilian Public Service told in Melvin Gingerich, *Service for Peace: A History of Mennonite Civilian Public Service* (Akron, Pa.: MCC, 1949), and in Albert N. Keim, *The CPS Story: An Illustrated History of Civilian Public Service* (Intercourse, Pa.: Good Books, 1990).

43. Mennonites' experiences in mental health work and reform are discussed in *If We Can Love: The Mennonite Mental Health Story,* ed. Vernon H. Neufeld (Newton, Kans.: Faith and Life Press, 1983).

44. These figures are from Unruh, *In the Name,* 262.

45. From *Twenty-Five Years, The Story of the MCC, 1920–1945* (Akron, Pa.: MCC, 1946), 20.

46. The NSBRO was formed 26 Nov. 1940 as the agency through which the peace churches would work in dealing with the Selective Service System. It was later renamed the National Interreligious Service Board for Conscientious Objectors (NISBCO).

47. Lapp, "The Peace Mission," 291. Other helpful sources for understanding the emergence and development of the Peace Section include the Sept.–Oct. 1992 issue of *Peace Office Newsletter,* entitled "Fifty Years of Peacemaking." The newsletter is available from MCC's Akron office. See also Frank H. Epp and Marlene G. Epp, "The Progressions of Mennonite Central Committee Peace Section," an unpublished "topical history in outline form," 1985. Available in MHL.

48. Between 1950 and 1969 MCC's work expanded into another thirty-one countries, more than doubling the number the organization had served since 1920. Until 1950, MCC had begun work in twenty-six countries, most of which had ongoing units. One program not mentioned in the text is the significant Pax program, which provided a place for conscientious objectors to serve during the 1950s and 1960s. On Pax, see Urie A. Bender, *Soldiers of Compassion* (Scottdale, Pa.: Herald Press, 1969).

49. Kreider, "The Impact," 253–55.

50. One source on the Winona Lake conference is the Nov.–Dec. 1991 *Peace Office Newsletter,* entitled "New Inter-Mennonite Peace Statement." The newsletter includes memories of the conference as well as the declaration itself. MCC's board adopted a new peace statement entitled "A Commitment to Christ's Way of Peace" at its 19–20 Feb. 1993 meeting at Niagara-on-the-Lake, Ontario. The new statement is intended to be an update of the Winona Lake document, reflecting changes in the church and world since that time. Among other additions and alterations, the new "Commitment" recognizes that violence occurs not only in warfare but through economic structures, and that violence has reached into Mennonite and Brethren in Christ churches and families.

51. One of the best sources on the Puidoux conferences is Donald F. Durnbaugh, ed., *On Earth Peace: Discussions on War/Peace Issues Between Friends, Mennonites Brethren and European Churches, 1935–1975* (Elgin, Ill.: Brethren Press, 1978).

52. These conferences and the documents, pamphlet series, texts, and statements they spawned have been covered extensively in a variety of other places. Although these meetings and writings are extremely important for understanding the fuller social and theological backdrop for this analysis, the focus here on MCC and its movement toward establishing the Washington lobbying office disallows adequate development of this material. The milieu of the 1950s and 1960s was fertile ground for the changes that were occurring in the various Mennonite churches on issues related to the church and state and to war and peace. Among the best recent sources that provide an overview of twentieth-century theological conversations among Mennonites are Driedger and Kraybill, *Mennonite Peacemaking*; Perry J. Bush, "Drawing the Line: American Mennonites, the State, and Social Change 1935–1973," (Ph.D. diss., Carnegie Mellon University, 1990); and Hope Renae Nisly, "Witness to a Way of Peace: Renewal and Revision in Mennonite Peace Theology, 1950–1971," (M.A./M.L.S. thesis, University of Maryland, 1992). For a viewpoint on Mennonite social changes during this period from the perspective of rhetorical analysis, see Ervin R. Stutzman, "From Nonresistance to Peace and Justice: Mennonite Peace Rhetoric, 1951–1991," (Ph.D. diss., Temple University, 1993). Briefer sources include Beulah Stauffer Hostetler, "Nonresistance and Social Responsibility: Mennonites and Mainline Peace Emphasis, ca. 1950 to 1985," *Mennonite Quarterly Review* 64 (1) (Jan. 1990): 49–73;

John Richard Burkholder, *Mennonites in Ecumenical Dialogue on Peace and Justice* (Akron, Pa.: MCC, Aug. 1988); and John Richard Burkholder, *Continuity and Change: A Search for a Mennonite Social Ethic* (Akron, Pa.: MCC Peace Section, 1977). For information on the Concern movement, which published numerous pamphlets between 1954 and 1971, see the *Concern* publications housed in MHL. The Mennonites involved in the Concern movement deserve much more than a footnote here. The American Mennonite graduate students, MCC workers, and missionaries who participated in the Concern dialogues, all of whom lived in Europe after World War II, prompted a reform movement among their denominational peers in their home country. For more on the movement, see the Spring 1990 volume of *Conrad Grebel Review* and J. Lawrence Burkholder, "Concern Pamphlets Movement" in *Mennonite Encyclopedia V,* 177–80.

53. Kreider, "The Impact," 254.

54. Contemporary liberation theologians, including those in Latin America and some feminists, as well as others, have developed this notion of theology as a secondary reflection on experience. This is sometimes referred to as "praxis."

55. James Stayer suggests that the move to Latin and South America contributed to the "quick and painless death of the normative vision of sixteenth-century Anabaptism." The cause of death was "a virus brought back by Mennonite missionaries and volunteer workers from the Third World, a different assessment of the Christian potentialities of a social revolutionary climate." See Stayer's "The Easy Demise of a Normative Vision of Anabaptism," in Redekop and Steiner, *Mennonite Identity,* 114.

56. John Boli-Bennett, "The Ideology of Expanding State Authority in National Constitutions, 1870–1970," in John W. Meyer and Michael T. Hannan, eds., *National Development and the World System* (Chicago: Univ. of Chicago Press, 1979), 228–38. Even MCC Washington, which periodically finds itself in tension with the American government, would not describe the federal government as "universal" and "omnivorous." The Mennonite office supports many of the programs of the activist American state. For several MCC Washington statements on "the role of government," see the Mar.–Apr. 1995 *Washington Memo.*

57. See, e.g., Robert Wuthnow's *Between States and Markets: The Voluntary Sector in Comparative Perspective* (Princeton: Princeton Univ. Press, 1991), and his *The Restructuring of American Religion: Society and Faith Since World War II* (Princeton: Princeton Univ. Press, 1988).

58. David Harrington Watt notes that the expansion of the American state in comparison with that of many other modern states is quite modest. He says that in 1983, e.g., governmental revenue in the United States accounted for only 37.3 percent of the Gross Domestic Product, considerably less than comparable figures for West Germany (45.7), the United Kingdom (45.9), France (47.4), and Sweden (62.7). See Harrington Watt's "United States: Cultural Challenges to the Voluntary Sector," in Wuthnow, *Between States,* 247.

59. Bellah et al., *The Good Society,* 112–13. Critical theorist Jürgen Habermas sees these changes in the modern state as the root of their "legitimation crises." Governments in developed countries are expected to buffer individuals against the ill effects of capitalism, but that places them in inevitable conflicts. See his *Legitimation Crisis* (Boston: Beacon, 1975), and *Communication and the Evolution of Society*

(Boston: Beacon, 1979), 178–206. "The problem encountered by the modern state in attempting to perform these tasks is not so much that the tasks themselves are difficult (although they may be), but that they engage the state in a fundamental contradiction of roles," says one analysis of Habermas's texts. "On the one hand, the state is expected to fulfill these functions; on the other hand, it is expected to respect the autonomy of private enterprise. State and economy are sufficiently interdependent that the state is 'damned' if it does not intervene, but 'damned' also if it does because of classical free enterprise ideology. Furthermore, when the state does intervene, it is confronted with conflicting norms. As representative of the public good, it is expected to base decisions on consensual values; as economic actor, it necessarily bases decisions on instrumental interests." See Robert Wuthnow et al., *Cultural Analysis: The Work of Peter L. Berger, Mary Douglas, Michel Foucault and Jürgen Habermas* (London: Routledge and Kegan Paul, 1984), 220.

60. All of the figures are from Harrington Watt's "United States," 248, and are based on data from the United States Bureau of the Census.

61. Ibid. Data sources include the Arms Control and Disarmament Agency.

62. David H. Kamens and Tormod K. Lunde, "Institutional Theory and the Expansion of Central State Organizations, 1960–1980," in *Institutional Patterns and Organizations: Culture and Environment,* ed. Lynne G. Zucker (Cambridge: Ballinger, 1988), 171.

63. On the negative effects for developing countries of cultural, economic, and political dependency, see, e.g., Lawrence Alschuler, "Satellization and Stagnation in Latin America," *International Studies Quarterly* 20 (1) (Mar. 1976): 39–81; Richard Rubinson, "Dependence, Government Revenue, and Economic Growth, 1955–1970," in Meyer and Hannan, *National Development,* 207–22; J. Delacroix and C. Ragin, "Modernizing Institutions, Mobilization and Third World Development: A Cross National Study," *American Journal of Sociology* 84 (1) (1978): 123–51; and J. Delacroix and C. Ragin, "Structural Blockage: A Cross National Study of Economic Dependency, State Efficacy and Underdevelopment," *American Journal of Sociology* 86 (6) (1981): 1311–48.

64. Lapp, "Missionaries and the Political Process," in "Missionary Retreat 1976," a collection of papers from the June 1976 General Conference Mennonite Church Committee on Overseas Ministries Retreat, 5. Available in MHL.

65. Franz et al., "Self-Study," prepared for "20th Anniversary Consultation on the Washington Office," 12–14 Jan. 1989, 3.

66. From "Mennonite Central Committee: Principles That Guide Our Mission."

67. Hershey Leaman, "MCC Thoughts on Food and Hunger After Seven Decades," an unpublished presentation at MCC's 1993 annual meeting. A synopsis of the paper can be found in Emily Will, "Twenty Years Experience Brings New Views of Hunger," *Gospel Herald,* 1 June 1993, 6–7.

68. Cited in an undated, untitled, anonymously written four-page paper on the MCC Washington office. Available in MCC Washington files.

69. Cited in Dyck, *Responding,* 61–63. It is worth noting that Byler's response to the crisis was to undertake a material-aid distribution project for the refugees in Syria. No effort was made to contact the United States government or United Nations about their roles in the refugee problem. This is unlike the response to Vietnam's war a decade later.

70. Cited in Steve Clemens, "Charity and Justice," an unpublished paper prepared for a June 1975 seminar at the MCC Washington office. Ken Martens Friesen, an MCC overseas service worker who worked at the Washington office from 1992 to 1994, tells the story of a 1980s experience in his assignment in Lebanon. While walking down a street he heard what sounded like a gun going off around the corner. By the time he arrived on the scene, several persons were taking a woman away on a stretcher. The woman had been wounded by an exploding bomb fragment she had swept up with other trash and attempted to burn. Another woman—after seeing Friesen, identifying him as an American, and recognizing that the United States had supplied the region's arms—shouted at him, "Why did you do this? Why did you do this? It's your fault." Later, when Friesen discovered his blood matched the injured woman's rare type, he donated blood for her survival. Experiences such as this one are part of what shape MCC's perspectives, and those of MCC Washington personnel. Interview with Friesen, 2 Sept. 1992.

71. Both MCC and the Eastern Mennonite Board of Missions (EMBM) had volunteers in South Vietnam. EMBM's mission program was initiated in 1957.

72. Story told in James Metzler, *From Saigon to Shalom* (Scottdale, Pa.: Herald Press, 1985), 30.

73. Mennonite theologian John H. Yoder compared MCC's relief work in this context to German Christians sending social workers to concentration camps without objecting to the camps themselves. See Yoder to Paul Peachey, 29 Nov. 1965, CPSC files, 1-3-5.13, box 69/3, AMC. Cited in Nisly, "Witness to a Way," 87–88. Nisly notes in the following pages that Mennonites faced the dilemma of knowing that they were "simply smoothing the path behind the upheaval of the military and its operations. Because relief work partially pacified the people whom the military displaced, it had political implications." Nisly's thesis, especially 83–98, is an excellent source on Vietnam and its effect on Mennonites. See also the more thorough treatment in Bush, "Drawing the Line," 242–81, and chap. 13 of Toews, *Mennonites in America.*

74. See Hershberger, "Washington Visitation on Vietnam," *Gospel Herald,* 15 June 1965, 520.

75. Luke Martin et al., "A Missionary Concern," *The Mennonite,* 25 Jan. 1966, 63. That issue of *The Mennonite* and the following day's *Gospel Herald* were special issues devoted to Vietnam concerns. See also David Leamon, "Politicized Service and Teamwork Tensions: MCC in Vietnam, 1966–1969," *Mennonite Quarterly Review* 70 (1) (Jan. 1996).

76. Cited in Dyck, *Responding,* 111–13.

77. The text of the letter can be found in "MCC Presents Vietnam Letter," *Gospel Herald,* 21 Nov. 1967, 1069–70.

78. John K. Stoner, "A Theology of Development Beyond Relief and a Theology for Witness to the State," unpublished discussion paper presented to a 13–14 May 1977 meeting of conference moderators and secretaries. Available in AMC, MCC files IX-12 (Data Files #7), file "Development, 1975–79."

79. The quote is from Peter L. Berger and Richard John Neuhaus, *Movement and Revolution* (Garden City: Doubleday, 1970), 13. Notes from most seminar presentations by MCC Washington Director Delton Franz and Keith Gingrich cite the Berger remark.

80. Hershberger, *The Mennonite Church,* 248.

81. Hershberger, "A Mennonite Office," 186.

82. It is worth noting that during the period from 1940 to 1967, before the opening of MCC Washington, Mennonites testified before Congress a total of fourteen times. In each case, the testimony was related to conscription.

83. MCC Peace Section's appointees who served in significant roles at NSBRO during this period include Paul Goering (1945–50), Elmer Neufeld (1951–54), Edgar Metzler (1954–56), John R. Martin (1956–58) and J. Harold Sherk (1958–69). To this day, MCC routinely assigns one of its Washington-based Voluntary Service workers to NISBCO. This is in addition to, but separate from, the work of MCC Washington.

84. Precursors to the religious lobbies include the Anti-Saloon League, which was founded in 1895 and sought to destroy the entire traffic in liquor. The National Woman's Christian Temperance Union was founded in 1874, but did not move its headquarters to Washington until 1895. Other denominations and issue-focused ecumenical organizations had Washington offices prior to the 1940s, but these were not registered lobbies. Among them were the National Council for the Prevention of War (1921) and the Methodist Episcopal Church Board of Temperance, Prohibition and Public Morals (1924). See Luke Eugene Ebersole, *Church Lobbying in the Nation's Capital* (New York: Macmillan, 1951), 1–23, for more on these early movements. See also A. James Reichley, *Religion in American Public Life* (Washington: The Brookings Institution, 1985), 168–242. Reichley traces American church political action from 1790 to 1985.

85. Registering as a lobby is significant, partly since it means contributions to Friends Committee for National Legislation are not tax-exempt. Nearly all of the other religious lobbies in Washington still are not registered as lobbies.

86. J. Harold Sherk to Irvin B. Horst, 19 Sept. 1955, available in AMC IX-6-3-77, MCC Correspondence, file "Horst, Irvin B., 1955." Horst, then a young professor at Eastern Mennonite College, had prior service experience with MCC.

87. Irvin B. Horst to Orie O. Miller, 14 Apr. 1956, available in AMC IX-6-3-84, MCC Correspondence, file "Horst, Irvin B., 1956."

88. Horst provided a one-page report on the explorations in New York and Washington in late 1956. "This project is unfinished," he wrote. "I would estimate that it is about half completed. Possibly a summer or three months of full-time work would be sufficient to finish it. Something more on the doctrinal basis and historical background of our witness to the State needs to be done." The report was Exhibit III at the 27 Dec. 1956 annual meeting of MCC Peace Section. Available in AMC IX-12-4, file "MCC Peace Section Minutes, 1946–1956."

89. From minutes of MCC Peace Section Executive Committee meeting, 1 Mar. 1957, available in AMC IX-12-4, file "MCC Peace Section Minutes, 12/29/54 to 12/13/58." One forward-looking paper presented at the conference was former MCC worker Elmer Neufeld's "Christian Responsibility in the Political Situation," published in *Mennonite Quarterly Review* 32 (2) (Apr. 1958): 141–62. On 161, Neufeld writes: "The simple point of this paper is the conviction that when we are thoroughly motivated by the love of the Christ of the cross—when we all actually take our neighbors' interests as seriously as our own—our concerns will appropriately find expression in actions that do have political relevance."

90. From minutes of the MCC Peace Section Executive Committee meeting, 6 Sept. 1958, available in AMC IX-12-4, file "MCC Peace Section Minutes, 12/29/54 to 12/13/58."

91. *The Christian Witness to the State* (Newton, Kans.: Faith and Life Press, 1964). Yoder also did a series of articles titled "Questions on the Christian Witness to the State" for *Gospel Herald* from Apr. to Aug. 1963.

92. The projection turned out to be prophetically accurate, almost to the month.

93. The five-year projection was Exhibit 4 at the 9–10 Aug. 1963 MCC Peace Section Executive Committee meeting, available in AMC IX-7-8, file 3/1.

94. The quote is from Unruh's 6 Sept. 1963 report to the MCC Peace Section Executive Committee, labeled Exhibit 6, available in AMC IX-7-8, file 3/1. Unruh was in Washington from 29 July to 24 Aug.

95. All of these remarks are from Unruh's seven-page report dated 6 Sept. 1963.

96. William Keeney, "The Establishment of the Washington, D.C., and Ottawa Offices" (First Draft), 2–3. Unpublished paper prepared as background for Kreider and Waltner Goossen, *Hungry, Thirsty.* Available in MCC Washington files.

97. Information in this paragraph is gleaned from "The MCC Peace Section Washington Office: A Review," Attachment II to the MCC Peace Section minutes, 29–31 Mar. 1973, available in AMC IX-7-8, file 3/8. The Mennonite Church action read, in part: "In view of the discussions of a Washington Office on an inter-Mennonite basis over the years, we urge [that the] General Council of Mennonite General Conference and Mennonite Central Committee seriously consider the establishment of such an office."

98. The following quotes from King are taken from his "A Report, Including Recommendations, to the MCC Peace Section on an Investigation of the Washington Scene in Order to Illumine Further Consideration of a Mennonite Office in the Nation's Capital," an unpublished paper dated 1 Sept. 1966. Emphases in original. Available from MCC Washington.

99. King also said a Washington office would be better than separate offices in selected state capitals. When the report was presented to MCC Peace Section Executive Committee, Canadian Frank Epp suggested several reasons why it might be better to have Mennonites' initial effort in this direction in Ottawa rather than Washington. See the minutes of the 1 Sept. 1966 MCC Peace Section Executive Committee meeting, available in AMC IX-7-8, file 3/4.

100. Dwight Y. King, "A Report," 19. Earlier, on 3–4, King writes about various Washington agencies' "Mandates and Resolutions from Governing Bodies." At the time, the Presbyterian Office of Church and Society was one of the organizations most dependent on its governing body.

101. Available in AMC IX-7-8, file 3/5. In the same file, see also "A Message to Mennonite and Brethren in Christ Church Leaders and Peace Committees," a three-page paper adopted by MCC Peace Section 19 Jan. 1967. The Peace Section was attempting to interpret sensitively its mandate regarding the Christian witness to the state. Shortly after the decision was made public, some more theologically and politically conservative Mennonite constituents who learned of Peace Section's intentions communicated their concerns to MCC leaders. In March the Capitol Hill office, now near fruition, was almost sidetracked when the Peace Section executive committee discussed the possibility of holding seminars for laymen and laywomen,

youth, and pastors in governmental centers such as the United Nations, Ottawa, and Washington. The seminars would be an *alternative* to the establishment of an office. The committee made no decision on the proposal. From MCC Peace Section meeting minutes, 8 Mar. 1967, available in AMC IX-7-8, file 3/5.

Throughout these months MCC administrators continued to hear from their Vietnam service workers, who called attention to the United States government's contributions to the bombing and destruction they were witnessing. In April they also received a commitment of support of two thousand dollars a year, increasing to at least four thousand dollars in several years, from the General Conference Mennonite Church's Peace and Social Concerns Committee, which had continued to push for a Washington office. Noted in the minutes of the MCC Peace Section Executive Committee meeting 10 June 1967, available in AMC IX-7-8, file 3/5.

102. Hershberger, "A Mennonite Office," 186.

103. John E. Lapp and Guy F. Hershberger were among the peace church leaders who went to Washington to explain that if Congress made the bill law, many of the young people from the peace churches would go to jail in violation of the law. The senators with whom they spoke said they were unaware of the consequences of their action and did not want to put Mennonites and other conscientious objectors in jail. The story of this incident is told in many places in Mennonite writings. Among them is Keeney, "The Establishment," 8–9.

104. Hershberger, "A Mennonite Office," 186. Hershberger's comments, as quoted here, suggest that more direct self-interest was involved in establishing the office than I have been proposing. I would suggest that the 1967 selective service incident added *urgency* to MCC Peace Section's decision, but that the *direction* had been established long before. The hope was to help others speak by bringing Mennonite overseas experience to bear in Washington. Later in the article Hershberger also broadens the reasons for opening MCC Washington.

105. Minutes of the 10 June 1967 MCC Peace Section Executive Committee meeting, available in AMC IX-7-8, file 3/5.

106. Available in AMC IX-7-8, file 3/6. The full "Report and Recommendation" can be found in my appendix 2.

107. William Keeney later wrote that the "listening post" language indicated that the office was to be the eyes, ears, hands, and feet for the churches, "not primarily the mouth except as specifically asked to speak for them." See his "The Establishment," 8.

108. From Franz's Mar. 1968 resume.

109. Most of this biographical information was gleaned from Franz's resume, his presentations at MCC Washington seminars, my interviews with him, and two other sources: Franz, as interviewed by Robert Kreider, "Planting a Church in a Changing City," *Mennonite Life* (Mar. 1988): 23–27; and Alan J. Beitler, "The Impact of Social Context on Theological Belief and Political Involvement: The Life Stories of Three Mennonite Men," (M.A.P.S. thesis, Associated Mennonite Biblical Seminaries, 1985).

110. Quotes in this paragraph are from Franz's draft copy of a 1977 "testimonial" prepared for *The Mennonite*. Available in MCC Washington files.

111. Franz's first-year salary was 7,320 dollars, and the office space at FCNL rented for 27 dollars per month.

112. Franz obviously is the longest-term employee of MCC Washington, with a total of just over twenty-six years of service. Several dozen other persons, including student interns from the Mennonite colleges, have served one- to ten-year terms in the office.

113. Considering the number of employees and the price of Capitol Hill office space, MCC Washington's annual budget, about 175,000 dollars, is remarkable.

114. While the capital office was evolving into its present form, MCC Peace Section in Akron also was experiencing structural change. In 1974 the Peace Section began a split into two distinct national committees, by 1979 becoming the MCC U.S. Peace Section and the MCC Canada Peace and Social Concerns Committee. The Washington office then fell under the umbrella of the U.S. branch. At the same time, a binational International Peace Section, now known as the Peace Office/ International Conciliation Program, was added to resource MCC's overseas programs. Another significant change occurred in 1979. Until that time, conferences funded MCC U.S. Peace Section's work directly. In other words, constituent bodies could choose to support MCC without providing any financial or representational support to the Peace Section. With the change, the Peace Section was fully integrated into MCC's budget and did not need to solicit its own contributions. By late 1973, the Church of God in Christ, Emmanuel Mennonite Church, and Conservative Mennonite Church had stopped sending representatives to Peace Section meetings. In Aug. 1973 the Evangelical Mennonite Church formally withdrew from MCC Peace Section. Several years earlier the Evangelical Mennonite Brethren had officially withdrawn from MCC entirely. On these withdrawals, see Walton Hackman to Delton Franz, 29 Nov. 1973, available in AMC IX-7-13, file 1/3.

Over the years, MCC U.S. Peace Section also added several "desks" or programs related to specific peace and justice issues. In addition to MCC Washington and the part-time office at the United Nations, other MCC U.S. Peace Section programs and their dates of origin include Mennonite Conciliation Services (1979), Peace Education (early 1980s), and Women's Concerns (1982). In 1992 the Section and its board were dissolved, with its programs being subsumed directly under MCC U.S. All of the Peace Section's programs were continued under the unwieldy designation of MCC U.S. Peace and Justice Ministries Cluster. After the dissolution of MCC U.S. Peace Section, the Office on Crime and Justice became a part of the cluster, and a Racism Awareness Office was added in 1993.

Many board members, administrators, staffers, and constituents had ambivalent feelings about the dissolution or absorption of MCC U.S. Peace Section. For many years the Peace Section was considered the radical wing of MCC, capable of being on the cutting edge without threatening constituent support of the larger service and relief organization. When the change was first proposed, representatives of the more conservative constituent bodies argued that MCC "can probably best maintain strong support by keeping its relief and service ministries under a separate part of its organization than the peace and social action ministries." On the other hand, progressive supporters questioned whether Peace Section staff "will not find themselves under great pressure to abandon prophetic stances and initiatives for justice and peace, and whether MCC U.S. can indeed be counted on to support the hard choices that need to be made for the peace and justice agenda." Too few years have passed to provide empirical data on the effects of the absorption. Whatever its outcome, the move embedded MCC U.S. Peace Section's programs, including the Washington office, even more deeply into the Akron-based organization. See Lynette Youndt Meck to MCC U.S. Board, 17 Jan. 1992, and the attached "Proposal to Dissolve the MCC U.S. Peace Section Board and to Transfer Those Responsibilities to the MCC U.S. Board." Available in MCC Washington files.

3. BEDDING AND BUNDLING IN WASHINGTON

1. The comment was made by Harry Wenger of Hesston, Kansas, representing the Church of God in Christ Mennonite, one of the smaller bodies in MCC's constituency. Cited in "Peace Churches Polarized by Peace Witness," *The Mennonite,* 16 Feb. 1971, 102.

2. On "outside influences," see, e.g., Harold S. Bender's "Outside Influences on Mennonite Thought," *Mennonite Life* 10 (1) (Jan. 1955): 45–48.

3. Mark Chaves's work on denominational dual structures—the *religious authority* structure and the *agency* structure—is relevant here, as it also will be in the following chapter. Chaves suggests that this division "provides a straightforward way to investigate what is perhaps the least well-theorized and least empirically-supported claim within the secularization literature: the claim that United States denominations have undergone internal secularization" (Chaves, "Denominations as Dual Structures: An Organizational Analysis," *Sociology of Religion* 54 [2] [Summer 1993]: 158).

4. William M. Kephart, *Extraordinary Groups: The Sociology of Unconventional Lifestyles* (New York: St. Martin's, 1976), 31–32. Historically, of course, the practice of bundling has not been limited to the Amish.

5. As Hertzke notes in "An Assessment," 48, this is "not necessarily a term of endearment."

6. Cited in "The United Methodist Building," a brochure published by the United Methodist General Board of Church and Society.

7. The former is found in Micah 6:8, and the latter in Isaiah 2:4 and Micah 4:3.

8. Hertzke notes that religious leaders played a key role in the passage of the Civil Rights Act of 1964, and he identifies civil rights legislation as the high water mark for the mainline. "It was a heady experience," he writes, "to be morally right, politically effective, and at the center of it all. The civil rights struggle thus stands at the hinge of a transformation that politicized mainline churches, especially their ministers and national leaders." See Hertzke, "An Assessment," 49.

9. Levi Miller, "Why I Sat Out the Gulf War," *Gospel Herald,* 5 May 1992, 3.

10. Ibid.

11. Robert P. Beschel Jr. and Peter D. Feaver, "The Churches and the War," *The National Interest* 23 (Spring 1991): 72. For a longer critical review of the mainline churches' involvement in Persian Gulf War debates, see James Turner Johnson and George Weigel, *Just War and the Gulf War* (Washington: Ethics and Public Policy Center, 1991), especially the section by Weigel. See also Reichley, *Religion in American Public Life,* 353–54. Sociologist Benton Johnson has written that "it is sometimes forgotten that the sect's interaction with its environment can be a two-way process. The world may compromise the sect, but some sects are able to com-

promise the world by having an impact on it." Johnson, "Church and Sect Revisited," *Journal for the Scientific Study of Religion* 10 (2) (1971): 129. Even if one rejects the sectarian categorization, Johnson's observation may be valid in this case: a minority position can transform a majority one, as history repeatedly shows.

12. Beschel and Feaver, "The Churches," 72–73. Joe Volk, director of the Friends Committee on National Legislation, contends, "I think MCC and other peace churches probably have more influence than we realize, partly because of the authentic experience situation. I think some of the influence we have is not directly with members of Congress or with the administration but with other lobbyists—environmental groups, some of the political action committees, and it would be an interesting thesis to see how those informational perspectives make their way somewhere" (Interview with Joe Volk, 9 Nov. 1992).

13. One of the classic texts expositing these positions is Roland H. Bainton, *Christian Attitudes Toward War and Peace: A Historical Survey and Critical Re-Evaluation* (New York: Abingdon, 1960). For a quick overview, see Joseph L. Allen, *War: A Primer for Christians* (Nashville: Abingdon, 1991).

14. Cicero (106–143 B.C.E.), a Roman jurist and political philosopher, is credited with offering the earliest statement on limiting war through criteria developed from natural law. Later Ambrose of Milan (339–397 C.E.) and especially Augustine of Hippo (354–430 C.E.) built on Cicero's views. Augustine brought Christian concepts of sin and love to bear on Cicero's understanding of just war. The tradition assumes the reality of a fallen, sinful world whose fallenness is most particularly expressed in economic and political institutions.

15. Among the many sources explicating just war theory are Allen, *Love and Conflict: A Covenantal Model of Christian Ethics* (Nashville: Abingdon, 1984); Childress, *Moral Responsibility in Conflicts: Essays on Nonviolence, War, and Conscience* (Baton Rouge: Louisiana State Univ. Press, 1982); J. T. Johnson, *Ideology, Reason and the Limitation of War: Religious and Secular Concepts, 1200–1740* (Princeton: Princeton Univ. Press, 1975), and *Just War Tradition and the Restraint of War: A Moral and Historical Inquiry* (Princeton: Princeton Univ. Press, 1981); Paul Ramsey, *Speak Up for Just War or Pacifism: A Critique of the United Methodist Bishops' Pastoral Letter "In Defense of Creation"* (University Park: Pennsylvania State Univ. Press, 1988); L. Walters, "Five Classic Just War Theories," (Ph.D. diss., Yale Univ. 1971); and Walzer, *Just and Unjust Wars: A Moral Argument with Historical Illustrations* (New York: Basic, 1977).

16. Walzer, *Just and Unjust,* 21. Walzer acknowledges that the dualism is puzzling and is "at the heart of all that is most problematic in the moral reality of war." Two sources of Anabaptist-Mennonite critiques of just war theory are Duane K. Friesen, *Christian Peacemaking and International Conflict: A Realist Pacifist Perspective* (Scottdale, Pa.: Herald Press, 1986), 157–72; and John H. Yoder, *When War Is Unjust: Being Honest in Just War Thinking* (Minneapolis: Augsburg, 1984). Yoder directs his critique to churches within the Reformed tradition in "The Historic Peace Churches: Heirs to the Radical Reformation," in Thomas D. Parker and Brian J. Fraser, eds., *Peace, War and God's Justice* (Toronto: United Church, 1989), 105–22. Yoder applies the criteria to the Persian Gulf War in his postwar article "Just War Tradition: Is It Credible?," *Christian Century,* 13 Mar. 1991, 295–98.

17. Jack Nelson-Pallmeyer, *Brave New World Order: Must We Pledge Allegiance?* (Maryknoll, N.Y.: Orbis, 1992), 135.

18. Some analysts, such as J. T. Johnson, argue against making such a sharp delineation between the just war and crusade approaches. Johnson claims that the "holy war" of the early modern period "is both in derivation and intention a just war doctrine." Johnson blames the misunderstanding of the tradition partly on Roland Bainton's typological framework in *Christian Attitudes*. "Bainton does not take into account that those whom he terms 'crusaders' understood themselves to be squarely within the just war tradition. . . ." he writes. See Johnson's *Ideology, Reason,* 9–10, 81–133.

19. Allen, *Love and Conflict,* 187.

20. While for many years few scholars questioned the early Christian Church's nonsupport of military service, a vast literature debating this point has developed in recent years. All sides would agree that some Christians did serve in militias. Some suggest those in church leadership sanctioned this service.

21. Various liberation theologians, including feminists and Latin Americans, have made North American theologians and ethicists aware of various types of *violences.* See, e.g., the discussion of direct and indirect, institutional and insurrectional, conscious and unconscious violences in Jose Miguez Bonino, *Doing Theology in a Revolutionary Situation* (Philadelphia: Fortress, 1975), 106–31. Mennonites sought to come to grips with the reality of these violences in Urbane Peachey et al., "Anabaptism, Oppression and Liberation in Central America," *Mennonite Quarterly Review* 58 (Aug. 1984). The entire issue of *Mennonite Quarterly Review* is devoted to questions raised by Latin American liberation theology. Among many other sources, see also C. Arnold Snyder, "The Relevance of Anabaptist Nonviolence for Nicaragua Today," *Conrad Grebel Review* 2 (2) (Spring 1984): 123–37; John S. Oyer, ed., "Anabaptist Dialogue with Liberation Theology," *Mennonite Quarterly Review* 63 (2) (Apr. 1989): 150–209; Robert J. Suderman, "Liberation Pacifism," in Burkholder and Nelson Gingerich, *Mennonite Peace Theology,* 69–77; and Daniel S. Schipani, ed., *Freedom and Discipleship: Liberation Theology in an Anabaptist Perspective* (Maryknoll, N.Y.: Orbis, 1989). In addition, feminists speak about various levels of domestic oppression and violence. See, e.g., Joanne Carlson Brown and Carole R. Bohn, eds., *Christianity, Patriarchy, and Abuse: A Feminist Critique* (New York: Pilgrim, 1989). In the 1990s, Mennonites have begun to acknowledge domestic violence within Mennonite homes. See, e.g., Elizabeth G. Yoder, ed., *Peace Theology and Violence Against Women* (Elkhart: Institute of Mennonite Studies, 1992); Carolyn Holderread Heggen, *Sexual Abuse in Christian Homes and Churches* (Scottdale, Pa.: Herald Press, 1993); Jim Coggins, ed., "Family Violence," in *Mennonite Brethren Herald,* 20 Jan. 1989, 1–9, 17; Ron Geddert, ed., "The Church and Sexual Abuse," in *Mennonite Brethern Herald,* 7 Dec. 1990, 1–9; Hedy Martens, "Peace-making within the Family System," and "Personal Peacemaking," papers presented at the Association of Mennonite Psychologists Conference, Fresno, Calif., 16 Apr. 1989; and Mary Anne Hildebrand, "Domestic Violence: A Challenge to Mennonite Faith and Peace Theology," *Conrad Grebel Review* 10 (1) (Winter 1992): 73–80. It is an understatement to say that these broadening definitions and understandings of violence will continue to challenge Mennonites in the coming decades.

22. The term "historic peace churches" gained prominence at a fall 1935 conference of the denominations at Newton, Kansas. Around 1917, some main-

line churches could have been identified as types of "peace" churches, although their roots were more in liberal pacifism. See, e.g., John Whiteclay Chambers, ed., *The Eagle and the Dove: The American Peace Movement and the United States Foreign Policy, 1900–1922*, 2d ed. (Syracuse: Syracuse Univ. Press, 1991). Goshen College, a Mennonite liberal arts school in northern Indiana, hosted a November 1992 conference recognizing the historic peace witness of *other* denominations.

23. This was true more for the Mennonite Church than for the General Conference Mennonite Church. One excellent source for understanding the tensions Mennonite Church peace committees lived with during this era and the following decades is Guy F. Hershberger, "The Committee on Peace and Social Concerns, Dissent: Past and Present," a twenty-three-page unpublished, confidential paper dated Nov. 1966. Available in AMC I-3-7, Box 7, file 13, labeled "General Correspondence, Yoder, Peachey ca. CPSC."

24. In the last several decades, B. Johnson and others have redirected the discussion of sects and denominations by the proposal of and, for some, the adoption of a "single-variable property" for differentiating between sects and denominations: "the extent to which a religious body accepts the culture of the social environment in which it exists." See "Church and Sect," 127–28. Bainbridge and Stark attempt to operationalize this "tension" criterion by considering it equivalent to "subcultural deviance," which is then marked by difference, antagonism, and separation. They also add direction to their triadic construct. "When [religious bodies] move toward less tension with their sociocultural environment they are church [denomination] movements. When groups move toward the high tension pole they are sect movements." See "Sectarian Tension," *Review of Religious Research* 22 (2) (Dec. 1980): 105–24. Ammerman cautions against this criterion, however: "Because American society is so varied in its accepted ways of life, a sign of tension in one location may be a sign of membership in another." See *Baptist Battles: Social Change and Religious Conflict in the Southern Baptist Convention* (New Brunswick: Rutgers Univ. Press, 1990), 165. Similarly, a sign of tension in one *era* may be a sign of membership in a different period.

25. J. S. Hartzler and Daniel Kauffman, *Mennonite Church History* (Scottdale, Pa.: Mennonite Book and Tract Society, 1905), 372. The General Conference Mennonite Church, more than any other Mennonite group, engaged in dialogue with others in peace movements. In 1905 the denomination sent a delegate to the Peace Congress in Lucerne and sent representatives to the founding of the Federal Council of Churches. At the beginning of World War I, General Conference Mennonite leaders wrote to President Wilson, encouraging him in his efforts toward peace. The letter to Wilson can be found in Urbane Peachey, *Mennonite Statements*, 215. See also Sawatsky, "History and Ideology," 118–120; and Schlabach, *Gospel Versus Gospel: Mission and the Mennonite Church, 1863–1944* (Scottdale, Pa.: Herald Press, 1980): 45.

26. In Aug. 1914 Karl Barth referred to this transitional period as a "dark day" and a "twilight of the gods," referring specifically to the time when ninety-three German intellectuals, including most of his venerated teachers, publicly proclaimed their support of the war policy of Wilhelm II. George Hunsinger, ed., *Karl Barth and Radical Politics* (Philadelphia: Westminster, 1976), 204.

27. Allen, *Love and Conflict*, 191.

28. Contemporary ethicists often cite John H. Yoder, the Mennonites' foremost theologian in the 1960s and 1970s, as an example of the "pacifism as obedient witness" position.

29. *War, Peace, and Nonresistance* (Scottdale, Pa.: Herald Press, 1944), 202–67. The text was revised in 1953 and 1969.

30. "The Anabaptist Vision," originally Bender's presidential address at the Dec. 1943 meetings of the American Society of Church History, was first published in *Church History* 13 (Mar. 1944): 3–24. Among other places, it also has appeared in *Mennonite Quarterly Review* 18 (Apr. 1944): 67–88, and in Hershberger's *The Recovery of the Anabaptist Vision* (Scottdale, Pa.: Herald Press, 1957), 29–54. For other analyses of Bender's statement, see Paul Toews, "Mennonites in American Society," especially 240–243; Duane K. Friesen, "Review of *Mennonite Peace Theology: A Panorama of Types*," *Conrad Grebel Review* 10 (3) (Fall 1992), 341–49; and Stephen F. Dintamin, "The Spiritual Poverty of the Anabaptist Vision," *Conrad Grebel Review* 10 (2) (Spring 1992): 205–8.

31. Bender, "The Anabaptist Vision," *Mennonite Quarterly Review*, 85–86.

32. Ibid., 86–87.

33. Ibid., 88.

34. Hershberger, *War, Peace*, 213–14.

35. One of the more interesting historical twists in separating out types of pacifism relates to a mid-nineteenth-century tract by Daniel M. Musser, *Non-Resistance Reasserted: or the Kingdom of Christ and the Kingdom of this World Separated* (Lancaster, Pa.: Elias Barr and Co, 1864). Musser was a member of the small Reformed Mennonite Church in Lancaster. Leo Tolstoy, in *The Kingdom of God Is Within You*, trans. Constance Garnett (Lincoln: Univ. of Nebraska Press, 1984 [1893]), devotes several pages to a discussion of Musser's tract. A recent article on this connection is Levi Miller, "Daniel Musser and Leo Tolstoy," *Mennonite Historical Bulletin* 54 (2) (Apr. 1993): 1–7. Musser therefore had some influence on Tolstoy, and Tolstoy, in turn, contributed to Gandhi's pacifism. Although this is hardly a direct line of influence, it does indicate that the lines between types of pacifism are much more permeable and complex than may be initially supposed.

36. Hershberger, *War, Peace*, 216–17.

37. Ibid., 211–12.

38. Hershberger, "A Mennonite Office," 186.

39. Among the most relevant writings here are *Moral Man and Immoral Society: A Study in Ethics and Politics* (New York: Charles Scribner's Sons, 1932); *An Interpretation of Christian Ethics* (New York: Harper and Brothers, 1934); "Why the Christian Church"; and *Christianity and Power Politics* (New York: Charles Scribner's Sons, 1940).

40. Niebuhr does assume the ongoing relevance of the law of love. See his "Why the Christian Church," 113–18.

41. On this, see John H. Yoder, "Reinhold Niebuhr and Christian Pacifism," *Mennonite Quarterly Review* 29 (2) (Apr. 1955): 111. See also G. H. C. MacGregor, *The New Testament Basis of Pacifism and the Relevance of an Impossible Ideal: An Answer to the Views of Reinhold Niebuhr* (Nyack, N.Y.: Fellowship, 1954).

42. Niebuhr, "Why the Christian Church," 110.

43. Ibid., 103–5.

44. In response to this charge, John H. Yoder writes in "Reinhold Niebuhr," 114: "The fact that these concepts—impossibility, necessity, responsibility—are used by Niebuhr in such a way as to introduce new norms into ethics which, because of the existence of sin, are allowed to cancel out love may lead us to suspect a deeper error in Niebuhr's approach to morality."

45. In a recent two-year period, three major texts dealing with Mennonite identity were published. See Driedger and Harder, eds., *Anabaptist-Mennonite Identities in Ferment* (Elkhart, Ind.: Institute of Mennonite Studies, 1990); Driedger, *Mennonite Identity in Conflict* (Lewiston, N.Y.: Edwin Mellen, 1988); and Redekop and Steiner, *Mennonite Identity.* These were forerunners to Driedger and Kauffman's *Mennonite Mosaic,* which further pluralized Mennonite identity through a detailed sociological survey.

46. Stayer's and others' reinterpretations appear to blend well the sixteenth- to nineteenth-century outsiders' understandings of Anabaptists as *Schwärmer* (fanatics) with the mid-twentieth-century Mennonites' more glowing self-definitions, acknowledging some truth in each position, and then nuancing the space between the poles considerably.

47. Stayer et al., "From Monogenesis to Polygenesis: The Historical Discussion of Anabaptist Origins," *Mennonite Quarterly Review* 49 (2) (Apr. 1975): 83–121.

48. See, e.g., Snyder, "Reflections on Mennonite Uses of Anabaptist History," in Burkholder and Nelson Gingerich, *Mennonite Peace Theology,* 84.

49. On Stayer's surprise that his pluralizing challenges to the established normative Anabaptist vision were not denounced at the time of his publications, see, e.g., Sawatsky, "The One and the Many: The Recovery of Mennonite Pluralism," in *Anabaptism Revisited,* ed. Walter Klaassen (Scottdale, Pa.: Herald Press, 1992), 141–54; Juhnke, "Mennonite History and Self Understanding"; and Stayer, "The Easy Demise of a Normative Vision of Anabaptism," in Redekop and Steiner, *Mennonite Identity,* 109–16.

50. *Nevertheless: The Varieties of Religious Pacifism* (Scottdale, Pa.: Herald Press, 1971), 4.

51. Ibid., 131–32.

52. This language shows up occasionally in critical letters to MCC Washington's office. After reading the Mar.–Apr. 1971 *Washington Memo,* one writer said: "You are willing to whitewash an Angela Davis, and 'go to bed' with an Alan Cranston, while throwing out the biblical teachings on the punishment of crime, etc." See Wesley A. Neufeld to Delton Franz, 24 Mar. 1971. Available in MCC Washington files.

53. Information gleaned from Kreider, "The Impact," 245–61.

54. King, "A Report," 28.

55. See Koontz, "Peace Section Experience Regarding Coalition and Lobby Efforts," a five-page paper presented at the MCC U.S. Ministries meeting, 15–16 Mar. 1976. Available in MCC Washington files.

56. Toews, "The Impact," 622.

57. Hershberger, *The Mennonite Church,* 247. On Mennonite wariness to enter into interchurch peace dialogues during the 1930s, see also Toews, "The Long Weekend or the Short Week: Mennonite Peace Theology," *Mennonite Quarterly Review* 60 (1) (Jan. 1986): 38–57. See also Beulah Stauffer Hostetler, "Nonresistance and

Social Responsibility: Mennonites and Mainline Peace Emphasis, ca. 1950 to 1985," *Mennonite Quarterly Review* 64 (1) (Jan. 1990): 49–73; and Donald F. Durnbaugh, ed., *On Earth Peace: Discussions on War/Peace Issues Between Friends, Mennonites, Brethren and European Churches, 1935–1975* (Elgin, Ill.: The Brethren Press, 1978).

58. Interview with Robert Tiller, 6 Nov. 1992.

59. Interview with Joe Volk, 9 Nov. 1992.

60. During the early years, Delton's wife, Marian Claassen Franz, also worked part time at the office as an administrative assistant. She later became director of the National Campaign for a Peace Tax Fund, serving as a vocal lobbyist in her own right.

61. Franz et al., "Origins of the Washington Office," 1981, a five-page summary of MCC Washington's work, 4. Available in MCC Washington files.

62. Paul M. Nolt to MCC, 19 Nov. 1971, and Franz to Nolt, 24 Nov. 1971. Available in AMC IX-7-13, file 1/17.

63. The guidelines were adopted at the 1 Dec. 1977 meeting of MCC U.S. Peace Section. Available in MCC Washington files.

64. On this, see Koontz, "Peace Section Experience," 2.

65. It is worth noting that recent MCC Washington staffers said they did not realize such guidelines existed, so the document's present functional value is questionable.

66. The MCC name on sign-on letters varies, depending on the scope of the letter. Often the signature is from MCC, Washington Office, but sometimes MCC U.S. or MCC International is the signer. In some cases MCC's area secretaries in Akron sign letters on international issues. The Akron office is most sensitive about those letters the Washington office asks the broader MCC organizations to endorse.

67. One of the reasons MCC Washington needs to consult with the Akron headquarters about sign-ons is that Akron administrators are more in touch with the organization's workers in the field. For instance, MCC service workers in some countries say no advocacy related to their country should have the MCC name attached to it for fear of indigenous government crackdowns on their work or on Mennonite churches there.

68. "More-with-less," a phrase used above in the "Guidelines for Joining Coalitions," also is the title of a popular MCC-sponsored cookbook. See Doris Janzen Longacre, *More-with-Less Cookbook* (Scottdale, Pa.: Herald Press, 1976).

69. Interview with Titus Peachey, 9 Nov. 1992.

70. The MCC Washington Coordinating Council was set up in 1983 as an advisory board for the Washington office. The council, which meets twice a year, includes a variety of Akron administrators as well as Washington office staffpersons.

71. Interview with Jacob Ahearn (pseudonym), 26 Feb. 1993.

72. Interview with Cynthia Sprunger, 25 Feb. 1993. Sprunger's parents were General Conference Mennonite Church missionaries for many years.

73. Participant-observation notes, 2 Sept. 1992.

74. Interview with Earl Martin, 2 Dec. 1992.

75. Betsy Beyler, who worked at the MCC Washington office from 1975 to 1985, observes that the number of coalition sign-ons increased dramatically during her years at the office. The sign-ons were a natural outgrowth of the proliferation of coalitional groupings, she contends. Interview with Betsy Beyler, 24 July 1993.

76. Interview with Keith Gingrich, 9 Nov. 1992.

77. Interview with Delton Franz, 10 Nov. 1992.
78. Interview with Keith Gingrich, 9 Nov. 1992.
79. Ibid.
80. My observation is that younger MCC Washington staffers, educated in Mennonite institutions after the breakdown of the Bender synthesis of the "Anabaptist Vision" and after Mennonites had become more politically engaged, are more ready to enter fully into coalitions with their Washington partners. They consciously seek to avoid being viewed as "sectarian" by their lobbying peers. Greg Goering once used the provocative metaphor of a balloon for Delton Franz: the other, more temporary staffers provided the air pressure which filled the balloon and pushed out the boundaries, but Franz kept them somewhat contained.
81. Under the boxed heading "Arm of the Religious Left," an article in the *National Journal* listed forty-four members of WISC, "the principal coordinating arm for religious groups that take predominately liberal positions on policy issues." MCC was among those listed. Richard E. Cohen, "Getting Religion," *National Journal,* 14 Sept. 1985, 2081.
82. Interview with Greg Goering, 1 Sept. 1992.
83. Ibid. This left-leaning tendency is not only a matter of staffers' personal preference, but is also part of MCC's organizational "personality." Because of its attention to peace and justice concerns in impoverished settings in the United States, Canada, and overseas, the organization finds itself most often aligned with the religious left.
84. Interview with Delton Franz, 1 Sept. 1992.
85. Interview with John Richard Burkholder, 1 Oct. 1992. Burkholder, who has long been active in church-related peace activities both locally and internationally, worked for the MCC Peace Office and MCC U.S. Peace Section in the mid-1980s.
86. Guenter Lewy, *Peace and Revolution: The Moral Crisis of American Pacifism* (Grand Rapids: Eerdmans, 1988). Although MCC did not come under Lewy's close scrutiny, Lewy does make two references to the organization, on 118 and 138.
87. Ibid., vii. See also Hertzke's criticism of "mainline" church leaders who underestimate the "evil of communism" in "An Assessment," 63–67.
88. Occasionally readers of MCC's *Washington Memo* also have charged MCC with communist sympathies. One person wrote: "Karl Marx predicted that well-meaning religious 'peace' groups would serve as 'useful idiots' for the Communist Revolution. After several years of reading your newsletter or position paper, this prediction makes perfect sense" (Chet Beiler to Editor, 3 Feb. 1988). Another writer sent an undated, unsigned postcard that read simply: "MCC. Mennonite Communist Committee. Get your heads out of the sand." Both the letter and the card are available in MCC Washington files.
89. Two years after Lewy's 1988 publication, fifteen persons responded to his charges in *Peace Betrayed? Essays on Pacifism and Politics,* ed. Michael Cromartie (New York: Univ. Press of America, 1990). Among the respondents was Mennonite John Richard Burkholder, "Pacifist Ethics and Pacifist Politics," 193–206.
90. Lewy, *Peace and Revolution,* ix.
91. United Methodist Council of Bishops, *In Defense of Creation: The Nuclear Crisis and a Just Peace* (Nashville: Graded, 1986).

92. It should be noted that at least one Jewish organization, the Religious Action Center for Reform Judaism—which is the Washington office of the Union of American Hebrew Congregations—also was an ally in the initial Persian Gulf War lobbying. By December 1990, the union itself passed a "Resolution on the Persian Gulf Crisis," which was more hawkish than the organization's usual statements. Most of the Jewish groups, from the beginning, agreed with Fundamentalists and conservative evangelicals that a military response was necessary.

93. "Just peace" positions are not to be confused with historic peace church pacifism. On this, see, e.g., Jay Lintner, *Just Peace Theology and the Gulf War* (Washington, D.C.: United Church of Christ Office for Church in Society, Feb. 1991), 1, 3.

94. National Conference of Catholic Bishops, *The Challenge of Peace: God's Promise and Our Response* (Washington: U.S. Catholic Conference, 1983).

95. Susan Brooks Thistlethwaite, ed., *A Just Peace Church* (New York: United Church Press, 1986).

96. *Just Peacemaking: Transforming Initiatives for Peace and Justice* (Louisville: Westminster/John Knox, 1992).

97. Corrine Whitlatch, "Churches for Middle East Peace Issues Statement on the Invasion of Kuwait by Iraq," 3 Aug. 1990. Press release available in C-MEP files.

98. Interview with Corrine Whitlatch, 10 Nov. 1992.

99. Interview with Joe Volk, 9 Nov. 1992.

100. Since the context for this analysis is Washington's *religious* lobbies, less attention is given here to nonreligious organizations who actively opposed the Persian Gulf War. For synopses of this work, see, e.g., Leslie Cagan, "Reflections of a National Organizer," in *Collateral Damage: The New World Order at Home and Abroad,* ed. Cynthia Peters (Boston: South End, 1992), 373–85; and Max Elbaum, "The Storm at Home: The U.S. Anti-War Movement," in Phyllis Bennis and Michel Moushabeck, eds., *Beyond the Storm: A Gulf Crisis Reader* (New York: Olive Branch, 1991), 142–59.

101. No Mennonite denomination is part of the NCC, although MCC is a member of Washington coalitions that also include the NCC—e.g., WISC and C-MEP. MCC also participates as an observer on some subcommittees of the NCC.

102. See the postwar booklet prepared by the NCC, *Pressing for Peace: The Churches Act in the Gulf Crisis* (New York: National Council of Churches Middle East Office, 1991).

103. Among the other helpful books on the Persian Gulf War not yet mentioned are Phyllis Bennis and Michel Moushabeck, *Beyond the Storm*; U.S. News and World Report, *Triumph Without Victory: The Unreported History of the Persian Gulf War* (New York: Random House, 1992); and Dennis Menos, *Arms Over Diplomacy: Reflections on the Persian Gulf War* (Westport, Conn.: Praeger, 1992). Postwar books emerging from an explicitly religious/ethical perspective include Alan F. Geyer and Barbara G. Green, *Lines in the Sand: Justice and the Gulf War* (Westminster: John Knox Press, 1992); Nelson-Pallmeyer, *Brave New World Order*; Johnson and Weigel, *Just War*; Charles A. Kimball, *Religion, Politics and Oil: The Volatile Mix in the Middle East* (Nashville: Abingdon, 1992); and Kenneth L. Vaux, *Ethics and the Gulf War: Religion, Rhetoric, and Righteousness* (Boulder, Colo.: Westview, 1992).

104. Geyer and Green do a good job of laying out the various "alternative frameworks" used to critique the war in their *Lines in the Sand,* 20–22.

105. Among the classic texts on political realism are Hans J. Morgenthau, *In Defense of the National Interest* (New York: Knopf, 1951); Robert Osgood, *Limited War: The Challenge to American Strategy* (Chicago: Univ. of Chicago Press, 1957); Henry A. Kissinger, *Nuclear Weapons and Foreign Policy* (New York: Harper and Row, 1957); and Raymond Aron, *Peace and War: A Theory of International Relations* (Garden City: Doubleday, 1966). See also Mark Neufeld, "Responding to Realism: Assessing Anabaptist Alternatives," *Conrad Grebel Review* 12 (1) (Winter 1994): 43–62.

106. Cited in Russell Watson et al., "It's Our Fight Now," *Newsweek*, 14 Dec. 1992, 31.

107. In "Reshaping Pacifism to Fight Anguish in a Reshaped World," *New York Times*, 21 Dec. 1992, 1, reporter Peter Steinfels quotes several prior antiwar activists who supported the Somali intervention. Steinfels claims that among intellectuals and pacifists concerned with warfare's ethical issues, "There is a widespread re-examination of the morality of military intervention to deal with events like the 'ethnic cleansing' in Bosnia or the politically induced starvation in Somalia." The reporter contends, "Some of these people say that as the world reshapes itself in the wake of the cold war many more such conflicts are inevitable, as are the agonizing questions they raise." In support of his thesis, Steinfels cites the Rev. William Sloane Coffin Jr., the Rev. J. Bryan Hehir, Ann McCarthy, and Jeane Bethke Elshtain, all of whom acknowledged their support of the military intervention in Somalia. The writer also quotes a joint statement from leaders of the major Protestant, Catholic, Jewish, and Muslim groups calling for firmer action by the United States in both Bosnia and Somalia. The United States "is not policeman to the world," the resolution acknowledged, "but the mass murder of innocents is unacceptable." It should be noted that not all of the "reshaped" persons Steinfels cited had previously considered themselves "pacifists."

108. MCC itself began programs in Somalia in 1975, assisting Ethiopian refugees there. Olfert's comment about thirty-plus years is a reference to MCC's work as well as that of other mission organizations lodged in MCC's member denominations.

109. Olfert to Peter J. Davies, 25 Nov. 1992. Available in MCC Washington files. It is striking that the letter makes no reference to Mennonite theology or pacifism, but bases its position on more pragmatic considerations.

110. Within Mennonite denominations, among academics, ministers, and laypersons there were mixed reviews of the military response. One editorial by J. Lorne Peachey was entitled "Feeding the Hungry with Messy Theology" (*Gospel Herald*, 12 Jan. 1993, 16). In the same issue, J. R. Burkholder and Koontz said that "this may be a time for silence. It may be a time to neither condemn nor advocate this particular use of military force" ("When Armed Force Is Used to Make Relief Work Possible," 6–7). This is a modified version of the dualism evident throughout Mennonite history. The Burkholder and Koontz article sparked a remarkable number of letters, several other articles, and extensive inter-MCC dialogue. Two articles that followed were J. L. Burkholder, "The Dark Side of Responsible Love," *Gospel Herald*, 16 Mar. 1993, 6–7; and J. Denny Weaver, "We Must Continue to Reject Just War Thinking," *Gospel Herald*, 27 Apr. 1993, 6–8. Perhaps the fiercest response to Burkholder and Koontz came from MCC Canada administrators Marv Frey and Ed Epp in an article entitled "Are We Being Swayed by a 'CNN Theology' of Peace?" *Mennonite Reporter*, 8 Feb. 1993, 7. Epp also prepared "Military

Intervention in Somalia: A Case Study," an unpublished eight-page document that rebutted Burkholder and Koontz's call for silence; it is available in MCC Washington files. Koontz responded with an insightful *nine*-page rebuttal. See Koontz to Frey and Epp, 1 Mar. 1993. Available from the author. For yet other perspectives, see Mark W. Charlton, "Pursuing Human Justice in a Society of States: The Ethical Dilemmas of Armed Humanitarian Intervention," *Conrad Grebel Review* 12 (1) (Winter 1994): 1–20, and Ernie Regehr, "Response to Mark W. Charlton," *Conrad Grebel Review* 12 (2) (Spring 1994): 217–21. The articles and letters evidence the peace pluralism among North American Mennonites, even among educated leaders and among persons working with Mennonite Central Committee.

111. Cited in Pearl Sensenig, "Military Role in Relief an Issue: Somali Situation Prompts Forum on Humanitarian Aid," *Mennonite Weekly Review,* 31 Dec. 1992, 1–2.

112. Much of the Mennonite leadership in providing this dissonant response came directly from MCC headquarters in Akron rather than from MCC Washington itself.

113. In "Response," Derksen Hiebert says that the key difference between the MCC Washington office and the MCCC Ottawa office is the political cultures in which Mennonite staffers work. "In Washington, the strongest pull towards conformity seems to come from the community of religious advocacy groups, as well as from the 'lobbying culture' which has developed there." In Ottawa, he says, "our 'bundling board' needs to be strongest and highest when we interact with government" (106).

4. SPEAKING THE TRUTH QUIETLY

1. Hertzke, *Representing God,* 93.

2. Ibid., 3.

3. Ibid. John W. Meyer and Brian Rowan write that "organizations are driven to incorporate the practices and procedures defined by the prevailing rationalized concepts of organizational work and institutionalized in society." When organizations do so, claim Meyer and Rowan, they "increase their legitimacy and their survival prospects, independent of the immediate efficacy of the acquired practices and procedures." See "Institutionalized Organizations: Formal Structure as Myth and Ceremony," in Walter W. Powell and Paul J. DiMaggio, eds., *The New Institutionalism in Organizational Analysis* (Chicago: Univ. of Chicago Press, 1991), 41. In "The Iron Cage Revisited: Institutional Isomorphism and Collective Rationality in Organizational Fields" in the same text, 63–82, DiMaggio and Powell build on Max Weber's arguments about rationalization and modernity in *The Protestant Ethic and the Spirit of Capitalism.* The "iron cage" image is, of course, from Weber's concluding remarks in *The Protestant Ethic,* trans. Talcott Parsons (New York: Charles Scribner's Sons, 1958), 181. On 64–66, DiMaggio and Powell suggest that the engine of organizational rationalization has shifted from capitalist firms and states' competition and bourgeois demands for equal protection under the law—which Weber had emphasized—to the structuration of organizational fields. Organizational field, for DiMaggio and Powell, means "those organizations that,

in the aggregate, constitute a recognized area of institutional life: key suppliers, resource and product consumers, regulatory agencies, and other organizations that produce similar services or products." Isomorphism is "a constraining process that forces one unit in a population to resemble other units that face the same set of environmental conditions." DiMaggio and Powell state that "at the population level, such an approach suggests that organizational characteristics are modified in the direction of increasing compatibility with environmental characteristics; the number of organizations in a population is a function of environmental carrying capacity; and the diversity of organizational forms is isomorphic to environmental diversity." The authors then note the homogeneity of organizational forms and practices within a given organizational field. See also Amos Hawley, "Human Ecology," in *International Encyclopedia of the Social Sciences,* ed. David L. Sills (New York: Macmillan, 1968), 328–37.

4. "Shaking up the Snake Pit," *Newsweek,* 11 July 1994, 16.

5. Chaves, "Denominations," 165.

6. *Mennonite Encyclopedia V,* 528. One concern of religious organizations related to lobbying is the Internal Revenue Code, which states that a civic organization can be tax-exempt if it is "not organized for profit but operated exclusively for the promotion of social welfare." Par. 501 (c) (3) of the code says the status can be maintained if "no substantial part" of the organization's activities are carrying on propaganda or otherwise seeking to influence legislation. In the courts, "no substantial part" has been interpreted to mean less than 5 percent of the organization's time and energies. MCC Washington's budget is less than half of one percent of MCC's 33.5-million-dollar total budget.

7. Keeney, "Report and Recommendation."

8. "Peace Section Opens Washington Office," *Gospel Herald,* 13 Aug. 1968, 733.

9. Franz to Sanford Shetler, 17 Oct. 1974. Available in AMC IX-7-13, file 1/15.

10. During many of my interviews with heads of denominational offices, the directors would use the word "lobby," and then catch themselves, smile, and say something such as, "I mean *advocacy.* We're supposed to say that what we do is advocate, not lobby."

11. Rawls, *A Theory.* In addition to his classic 1971 text, see Rawls's "Justice as Fairness: Political Not Metaphysical," *Philosophy and Public Affairs* 14 (3) (Summer 1985): 223–51; and "Kantian Constructivism in Moral Theory: Rational and Full Autonomy," *Journal of Philosophy* 77 (9) (Sept. 1980): 515–72. See also Richard Rorty, "The Priority of Democracy over Philosophy," in *The Virginia Statute for Religious Freedom,* ed. Merrill D. Peterson and Richard Vaughan (New York: Cambridge Univ. Press, 1988), 257–82. For counterviews, see Michael J. Perry, *Morality, Politics, and Law* (New York: Oxford Univ. Press, 1988), 57–63, 82–90; Kent Greenawalt, *Religious Conviction and Political Choice* (New York: Oxford Univ. Press, 1988); and Michael J. Sandel, *Liberalism and the Limits of Justice* (New York: Cambridge Univ. Press, 1981), 1–12, 55, 58–59, 172–73.

12. Walzer, *Spheres of Justice: A Defense of Pluralism and Equality* (New York: Basic, 1983), 15. The open-ended distributive principle that guides his work is that "No social good x should be distributed to men and women who possess some other good y merely because they possess y and without regard to the meaning of x."

13. Ibid., 246–47.

14. Marty, "Church, State, and Religious Freedom," in *Religion and the Public Good: A Bicentennial Forum,* ed. John F. Wilson (Macon, Ga.: Mercer Univ. Press, 1988), 81–82. Marty suggests that historian Sidney E. Mead resurrected Madison's phrase and gave it new life in *The Nation with the Soul of a Church* (New York: Harper and Row, 1975), 79.

15. Marty, "Church, State," 82.

16. Lewy, *Peace and Revolution,* 247. The last quote is from Niebuhr, *Christianity,* 28.

17. Frank H. Epp, *Visions: Speeches and Articles by Frank H. Epp* (Winnipeg: MCC Canada, 1991), 31–32.

18. Ibid., 38.

19. Bellah et al., *The Good Society,* 179. Jürgen Habermas, *The Structural Transformation of the Public Sphere: An Inquiry into a Category of Bourgeois Society,* trans. Thomas Burger (Cambridge: MIT Press, 1989 [1962]).

20. Bellah et al. say it could be argued that the greater public role of religion in the United States, in comparison with its western allies, "compensates for the narrow spectrum of our political parties, which often act as congeries of interest groups that seek the center for the sake of electoral victory. Frequently, issues that parties would not touch were raised first by religious groups and only after a long process of public debate and education taken seriously by the political parties." The authors offer the Civil Rights Act of 1964 as an example. See *The Good Society,* 180–81.

21. Ibid., 184.

22. Richard E. Cohen, "Getting Religion," *National Journal,* 14 Sept. 1985, 2080. Hatfield has been kinder to the religious lobbies in other settings. For instance, he attended the twenty-fifth anniversary celebration of the MCC Washington office 23 July 1993. "[MCC's] Washington office, along with many other groups, has become the center of the conscience of public policy in Washington by focusing on the moral, ethical and spiritual dimension of the issues we're dealing with," Hatfield said at the event. "I want to thank the Mennonites and their colleagues for keeping these issues alive." Cited in David Schrock-Shenk, "25 Years of Washington Witness," *Mennonite Weekly Review,* 12 Aug. 1993, 3.

23. Cited in Gerry Fitzgerald, "Religious Groups Orchestrate Opposition to 'Contra' Aid," *Washington Post,* 23 Apr. 1985. In *Representing God,* Hertzke contends that the church lobbies collectively have been able to generate respectable constituent pressure only on hunger and "peace" issues. "Were it up to the mainline Protestant churches alone, the impact would be considerably less than it is," states Hertzke, 56. "Thus the very limited mobilization efforts of the mainline churches are fortified greatly by the activities of smaller 'peace churches,' some Catholic groups, and the work of direct-mail groups such as NETWORK and Bread for the World."

24. Many political scientists have written about this reality. Among them is David Truman, *The Governmental Process* (New York: Knopf, 1951).

25. Interview with Nelle Temple Brown, 26 Feb. 1993. At the time, Temple Brown was a minority professional staff person on the House Subcommittee on International Development, Finance, Trade and Monetary Policy of the Committee on Banking, Finance and Urban Affairs. Her comments about the M.R. Factor were

directed at some organizations and individuals on both the religious right and the religious left in Washington. Temple Brown's husband works at the Presbyterian Church U.S.A.'s Washington advocacy office. See also Hertzke's "An Assessment" on the mainline churches' "sanctimonious" speech.

26. Mead, *The Lively Experiment* (New York: Harper and Row, 1963).

27. Interview with Bill Tate, 24 Feb. 1993.

28. Hertzke, *Representing God,* 69–79.

29. On the difficulty of measuring the effectiveness of religious lobbies and other public interest groups, see Jeffrey M. Berry, *Lobbying for the People: The Political Behavior of Public Interest Groups* (Princeton: Princeton Univ. Press, 1977), 272–85.

30. Cited in Cohen, "Getting Religion," 2084.

31. In his work, political scientist Daniel J. B. Hofrenning speaks of both the conservative and liberal religious lobbies as "purist" as opposed to "pragmatic" lobbying organizations. Hofrenning claims that a major exception to most religious advocates' definition of effectiveness were the Jewish lobbyists he interviewed. "Each Jewish lobbyist stated clearly that winning specific legislative victories was their first priority," Hofrenning observes. They avoided the "amateurish definition of effectiveness" he heard from other religious advocates. Hofrenning spoke with representatives of the American Jewish Congress and the Union of American Hebrew Congregations. See *In Washington But Not of It: The Prophetic Politics of Religious Lobbyists* (Philadelphia: Temple Univ. Press, 1995), 120.

32. Interview with Gingrich, 9 Nov. 1992.

33. Interview with Peachey, 9 Nov. 1992.

34. Hofrenning's study was based primarily on interviews with and surveys completed by lobbyists. In response to my inquiry, Hofrenning acknowledged that he did not attend any Washington working groups in drawing his conclusions. My impression is that this lack of observation of the setting where much of the lobbying work occurs may have skewed slightly his conclusions about the "purist" nature of religious lobbying.

35. Participant-observation notes, 31 Aug. 1992.

36. Ibid., 9 Nov. 1992.

37. Ibid., 30 June 1992.

38. "Basic Outline of Work Plan for Mark-Up of FY93 Foreign Aid Appropriations Bill in Senate Appropriations Committee Before August 13th/Labor Day Recess," document circulated at the 30 June 1992 CAWG meeting. Available in researcher's files. "Mark-up" means going through a bill, usually in committee, taking it section by section and revising language, adding in new phrases, and otherwise making adjustments. Mark-up gives the bill its final shape before a committee votes on it.

39. Bellah et al., *The Good Society,* 181, suggests that there is more of an "overlapping consensus" among diverse religious and secular constituencies than some theorists realize. "Few if any issues in the history of the United States have pitted the churches against the secularists," they write. "Usually we find different denominations on different sides, disagreement within denominations, and religious and secular people joined on one side or the other."

40. Robert Tiller, American Baptist Churches, U.S.A. Participant-observation notes, 30 June 1992.

41. Interview with Matlack, 26 Feb. 1993.

42. I am using "rationalized" here in the sociological sense of being rooted in explicit means-ends reasoning. One sets one's goals and engages in a rational process to reach them. Weber sees the engine of social change going in the direction of increasing rationalization, which at times he suggests is a giant step forward and at other times recognizes as ambiguous. Weber's *Protestant Ethic and the Spirit of Capitalism* is about how values become rationalized.

43. Much of this retelling of the 1940–41 interaction between Mennonites and government officials is from Keim, "Service or Resistance? The Mennonite Response to Conscription in World War II," *Mennonite Quarterly Review* 52 (1978): 141–55.

44. Religious conscientious objectors during World War I suffered immensely in military camps. Examples of this abuse can be found in Keim, *The CPS Story: An Illustrated History of Civilian Public Service* (Intercourse, Pa.: Good Books, 1990), 10–12; Gingerich, *Service for Peace*, 7–12; Juhnke, *Vision, Doctrine*, 208–42; and E. J. Swalm, comp., *Nonresistance Under Test: A Compilation of Experiences of Conscientious Objectors as Encountered in Two World Wars* (Nappanee, Ind.: E.V. Publishing House, 1949).

45. Keim, "Service or Resistance?" 148–49. See also *Congress Looks at the Conscientious Objector* (Washington: NSBRO, 1943), 8–10.

46. Keim, "Service or Resistance?" 149. Mennonites recognized that their Quaker allies had more effectively testified, and expressed their gratitude to them.

47. Amstutz, "Dialogue," 29.

48. It is not insignificant that even the Amish have rationalized and bureaucratized themselves in the last several decades. Marc A. Olshan traces the development and formation of the Old Order Amish Steering Committee, which emerged in 1966. Amish communities, contends Olshan, "share a normative stance directly antithetical to organization." It is remarkable, then, that the community-based religious group now has a committee that speaks to government officials when necessary, representing virtually all Amish in the United States. See "The National Amish Steering Committee," in *The Amish and the State,* ed. Kraybill (Baltimore: Johns Hopkins Univ. Press, 1993), 67–84. Journalist Tom Price says, "Old Order Amish bishops are testifying in the Indiana statehouse, writing letters to Congress and checks to Christian-right lobbyists." See his "Conservative Mennonites, Amish Raise Voices in Political Arenas" and "Old Order Amish Flex Political Muscle," both in *Gospel Herald,* 29 Mar. 1994, 10–11.

49. Amstutz, "Dialogue," 33–34. Amstutz also contends that the experience "illustrates the critical necessity of keeping a Mennonite presence in Washington to play a permanent 'watch dog' role."

50. Kauffman, "Innocence Lost?" *Gospel Herald,* 6 Mar. 1984, 16.

51. An interchange of letters between Delton Franz and Kauffman followed publication of the editorial. See Kauffman to Franz, 21 June 1984, and Franz to Kauffman, 2 July 1984. Both letters are available in MCC Washington files.

52. Weber's understanding of "charisma" builds on Christian scriptures' use of the Greek term, meaning "gift of grace." Charisma functions as a source of social change. The charismatic person is extraordinarily gifted, placing him or her above normal expectations and endowing the person with authority to challenge others. Charisma is a relational concept, since it emerges only within the context of a group willing to be led by the charismatic leader. On charisma, see Max Weber,

From Max Weber, 245–52. Regarding prophets' standing on the edge, "exerting authority over existing traditions," see, e.g., Gene M. Tucker, "The Law in the 8th-Century Prophets," in *Canon, Theology, and Old Testament Interpretation: Essays in Honor of Brevard S. Childs,* ed. Tucker et al. (Philadelphia: Fortress, 1988), 201–16.

53. One source for Weber's discussion of prophets and priests is his *The Sociology of Religion,* trans. Ephraim Fischoff (Boston: Beacon, 1963 [1922]), 46–59.

54. From the inside of a sect, it may appear that the leader is a priest, but to outsiders, she or he sounds like a prophet, or the group collectively appears to be prophetic.

55. See Cohen, "Getting Religion," 2080.

56. See Marian Claassen Franz, "Pastors, Prophets, and Politicians," *Mennonite Life* 37 (1) (Mar. 1982): 24–25.

57. Franz, "The Washington Office: Reflections After Ten Years," *Washington Memo* 10 (4) (July–Aug. 1978): 1.

58. Interviews with Greg Goering and Jalane Schmidt, 1 Sept. 1992.

59. See, e.g., Claassen Franz, "Pastors, Prophets."

60. See, e.g., Ronald J. Hrebenar and Ruth K. Scott, *Interest Group Politics in America,* 2d ed. (Englewood Cliffs: Prentice Hall, 1990); and Kay Lehman Schlozman and John T. Tierney, *Organized Interests and American Democracy* (New York: Harper and Row, 1986).

61. In the midst of the conscientious objector and alternative service discussions of the 1980s, Selective Service System administrators traveled from Washington to Akron, Pa., to meet with MCC employees on their own turf. At the historic 8 June 1983 meeting, MCC Executive Director Bill Snyder welcomed the SSS staff by observing, "You must feel like a lion in a den of Daniels!" (Cited in Amstutz, "Dialogue," 30).

62. See, e.g., Lester Milbrath, *The Washington Lobbyists* (Westport, Conn.: Greenwood, 1963), and Raymond A. Bauer et al., *American Business and Public Policy* (New York: Atherton, 1963). This paragraph owes much to Hertzke's discussion in *Representing God,* 44–49.

63. See chaps. 2 and 3 of Berry, *The Interest Group Society* (Boston: Little, Brown, 1984).

64. Hofrenning, *In Washington,* 130–31.

65. Franz, "Self-Study," 1.

66. Franz, "Report of the Peace Section Washington Office," 10 July 1969. Available in AMC IX-7-8, file 3/7.

67. Franz et al., "Washington Office Coordinating Council," 8 Jan. 1977. Available in MCC Washington files.

68. Since the early 1990s the *Washington Memo*'s regular legislative update has been labeled "Sound the Trumpet."

69. Franz, "*Washington Memo* Enables Constituency Voice to Government," news release dated 19 Apr. 1976. Available in MCC Washington files.

70. MCC Washington has a comparatively small constituent base, with under three hundred thousand Mennonites and Brethren in Christ in the United States. Some of the mainline denominations' Washington office newsletters have eight thousand or fewer subscribers.

71. The book reviewed is by Donald Barlett and James Steele (Kansas City: Andrews and McMeil, 1992).

72. One *Memo* reader sharply criticizes the 1992 Voting Profile for, among other things, being "strangely silent on the issue of abortion." The reader, an MCC community service worker in Lancaster, Pa., challenges MCC Washington's "assessment that legislation related to the hiring of replacement workers for striking employees is—but reducing the number of abortions (now at 4,000 per day) is not—an issue which Anabaptist Christians might want to consider before entering the voting booth if, indeed, they see voting as an appropriate Christian behavior." The MCC worker also claims the record is partisan in nature, strongly favoring Democrats. See Mark A. Roy to Sue Shirk, 2 Nov. 1992. Available in MCC Washington files. MCC Washington rarely deals with the abortion issue, even though MCC and some of its constituent denominations have statements on the issue. Between 1969 and 1996 *Washington Memo* carried only six articles on the subject (1974, 1977, 1981, 1985, 1990, and 1993). A May 1993 MCC Washington seminar entitled "Faith and Public Policy: When and How Should Government Be Involved in Our Lives" also included a discussion of abortion.

73. For comparison purposes, among the main issues listed on the right-wing Christian Coalition's "Congressional Scorecard" the same year were parental notification for abortion, banning immigrants with HIV/AIDS virus, lifting the ban on gays in the military, criminalizing pro-life free speech, cutting government waste, the Balanced Budget Amendment, government-sanctioned homosexual marriages, school prayer, and abstinence-based sex education.

74. In his 1963 report to MCC Peace Section, John Unruh Jr. states: "The presence of Mennonites is well known to most legislators and should Mennonites in their states and districts suddenly begin to vote in large numbers Congressmen would realize this and perhaps more carefully listen to a Mennonite witness. Kansas' Representative Garner Shriver commented that he hadn't experienced much voting from the Mennonites in his district—the inference being that therefore he didn't feel it necessary to pay much attention to their interests on the civil rights questions because most of them don't go to the polls anyway. Might the Peace Section office sometime do a study on Mennonite voting belief and practices? Would we want to go so far as to encourage our people to vote?" Unruh was being naively optimistic about the potential for getting Mennonites to vote—and getting them to vote with a consistent voice. The voting profiles Unruh hoped for were done later by Kauffman and Harder, *Anabaptists,* and by Kauffman and Driedger, *The Mennonite Mosaic.*

75. Bread for the World has sent questionnaires to candidates and provided election kits to district organizers. See Hertzke, *Representing God,* 65. It is not surprising that various peace and justice lobbyists have similar scorecards, since they freely share their ratings with one another and draw from others' profiles.

76. Koontz, "Peace Section Experience," 3. Koontz contends that the issue of conscription may be an exception to this general pattern. On that issue, "Mennonites *have* exercised considerable influence simply because government officials knew that if Mennonite leaders said that Mennonites would refuse service under certain conditions, many of them would in fact refuse such service, regardless of the consequences."

77. Franz, "On Speaking to Government," *Washington Memo* 16 (3) (May–June 1984): 2. I suspect that another reason for the strong tone in the newsletter is the responsibility MCC Washington staffers feel to be a prophetic voice to their constituents.

78. Lehman to Franz, 11 Mar. 1969. Available in AMC IX-6-3, file "DF 1969," 6.

79. David L. Shank to Franz, 4 Sept. 1986. Available in MCC Washington file "Correspondence (Samples), Critical . . . Complementary." The following letters are available in the same file.

80. Glen A. McGrath to Franz, 29 Sept. 1985.

81. John G. Tiessen to Franz, 1 June 1985.

82. Menno Klassen to Franz, 31 May 1991.

83. Ruth Eitzen to Franz, 14 May 1985.

84. Franz et al., "Summary Report of the 20th Anniversary Consultation on the MCC Washington Office," 12–14 Jan. 1989, 10. Available in MCC Washington files.

85. The term "grassroots mobilization" may conjure up images of major demonstrations on the Mall or at the Capitol. In general, the religious advocacy offices in Washington do not plan such major demonstrations, although occasionally some of the working groups or task forces in which MCC is involved plan minor demonstrations.

86. Since the founding of the office, MCC administrators have hoped that Mennonites' primary voice to government would come from individuals, congregations, and conferences, not from the Washington office. In a note to John A. Lapp, Franz writes in 1988: "We would like to believe that the Peace Section (Akron/ Washington) had some part in the shift in that direction. Through seminars, the newsletter, and constituency meetings a growing number of people in the pews are writing letters and meeting with their representatives in Congress. This, it appears, marks a shift from the preceding historical period when testimony, letters to government, etc. were primarily delegated to a limited number in church leadership positions." See the blind P.S. to Lapp in Franz to Michael L. Yoder, 23 Nov. 1988.

87. Interview with Jay Lintner, 4 Sept. 1992. UCC agencies and ministers responded to Lintner's proposal to place the ads by contributing sixty thousand dollars, much more than was needed for the newspaper ads. Twenty percent of the UCC's ministers signed the ad.

88. There were more of these seminars—many focused on particular topics—in the early years of the MCC Washington office's existence than in recent years. This is probably partly because the office was establishing its identity in the early 1970s, and partly because MCC personnel were trying to inform their constituents of their work.

89. Franz, "Connecting," *Washington Memo* 23 (4) (July–Aug. 1991): 1. Citing Bellah et al., *Habits of the Heart: Individualism and Commitment in American Life* (New York: Harper and Row, 1985), Franz also suggests that Mennonite communities provide the office with a significant legacy as "communities of memory."

90. Hertzke, *Representing God,* 100. This paragraph and the next draw extensively on Hertzke's work as well as on Hanna Fenichel Pitkin's.

91. Pitkin, ed., *Representation* (New York: Atherton, 1969), 4. Enlightenment social philosopher Jean-Jacques Rousseau, writing before either revolution, concluded that representation is a fraud, since political liberty presupposes universal participation. See his *The Social Contract,* trans. G. D. H. Cole (London: J. M. Dent and Sons, 1973 [1762]). Pitkin notes that Rousseau draws his ideal from the city-state of Geneva, and from the limited polis of classical Greek democracy. "Our age is cut to a different scale," writes Pitkin, 6. "Its touchstones are organization and mass, megatonnage and megalopolis."

92. Formalistic representation is rooted in Hobbesian understandings. In Hobbes's case, this gets carried to an extreme so that the sovereign's authority becomes unlimited. Whatever the sovereign does or decides automatically becomes the people's action by which they are bound. See Thomas Hobbes, *Leviathan*, ed. Michael Oakeshott (New York: Collier, 1962 [1651]). Pitkin holds that this misses the very essence of representation: "that above all a representative is someone who will be held responsible to those for whom he acts, who must account to them for his actions. What defines representation is not an act of authorization that initiates it, but an act of holding-to-account that terminates it" (Pitkin, *Representation*, 9).

93. Pitkin, *The Concept of Representation* (Berkeley: Univ. of California Press, 1967), 60.

94. Hertzke, *Representing God*, 96, notes that it is curious that Pitkin omitted a second sense in which representation was used in the medieval context: reversing the direction and viewing priests and bishops as representing the people to God or before God as intermediaries. This notion, of course, was challenged by the Protestant Reformation.

95. Pitkin, *Representation*, 18.

96. Hertzke, *Representing God*, 98–99, speaks about the delegate-trustee division among religious lobbyists. Representatives of established church denominations, he contends, tend to see themselves as "trustees" of the faith, while leaders of direct-mail membership organizations often see themselves as "delegates" who articulate their constituents' concerns. My research, primarily among denominational lobbyists, would confirm Hertzke's observation.

97. Memo and attached first draft of a brochure, Charmayne Denlinger Brubaker to MCC staff in Akron and Washington, 19 June 1992. Available in MCC Washington files.

98. See, e.g., Franz, "The Relationship of the Church to the State: Diverse Perspectives Within the MCC Family," *Washington Memo* 19 (6) (Nov.–Dec. 1987): 1–2.

99. Washington Office Staff to Denlinger Brubaker, 7 July 1992. Available in MCC Washington files.

100. "Faith, Power and Politics: Questions and Answers," brochure available at MCC Akron.

101. The issue is one on which MCC Washington has had a consistent voice for the last three decades, lobbying against capital punishment.

102. These figures include both Canadian and United States Mennonites and Brethren in Christ. See Kauffman and Driedger, *Mennonite Mosaic*, 205–6.

103. Ibid., 209. This is consistent with the findings of many contemporary sociologists, including Robert Wuthnow. See, e.g., his *The Restructuring of American Religion: Society and Faith Since World War II* (Princeton: Princeton Univ. Press, 1988). Wuthnow suggests that within denominations there is more difference than between denominations. He sees in recent years a pattern of convergence *between* denominations and polarization *within* denominations.

104. Duane K. Friesen, "Mennonites and Social Justice: Problems and Prospects," *Mennonite Life* 37 (1) (Mar. 1982): 20. Kauffman and Driedger, *Mennonite Mosaic*, 208, suggest that "[o]n the average, liberal [social] views were more typical of members who were young, urbanized, more highly educated, and more involved in community organizations. Those retaining the more conservative attitudes on personal morality and social ethics scored higher on scales measuring religious orthodoxy, personal piety, and church participation."

105. Whether or not to vote is still an issue, even among some educated Mennonites. In the Kauffman and Driedger survey, 84 percent of the respondents agreed that members of their denomination should vote in state and national elections, although only 65 percent had voted in most or all recent elections. It is worth noting that this 65 percent is an increase of 19 percent over a similar survey in 1972. In an earlier article, Kauffman concluded that Mennonites vote in proportions similar to those of other Americans. See his "Dilemmas of Christian Pacifism Within a Historic Peace Church," *Sociological Analysis* 49 (4) (Winter 1989): 376. For contemporary Mennonite debates on voting, especially in the Mennonite Church, see Merle Good, "Why I Haven't Voted," *Gospel Herald,* 11 Oct. 1988, 698–99; and J. Lorne Peachey, "If I Were a Voting Mennonite," *Gospel Herald,* 27 Oct. 1992, 16. Whether or not to vote is not such an issue in the more politically engaged General Conference Mennonite Church.

106. Kauffman and Driedger, *Mennonite Mosaic,* 141. After Mennonite voters helped sweep Newt Gingrich and his fellow Republicans into congressional leadership in 1994, MCC Washington's J. Daryl Byler wrote a piece entitled "Do Mennonites Want to Send a Message to Washington?" The response to Byler was mixed in church publications, but a good number of respondents said, in effect, "Yes, we *do* want to send a message . . . and we just *did.*" See *Gospel Herald,* 20 Dec. 1994, 5, and subsequent issues.

107. Interview with Franz, 10 Nov. 1992. On the bottom of the minutes to the 3 June 1987 Washington Office Coordinating Council meeting, one participant had written "Is MCC a group that uses right-wing dollars to promote left-wing causes?" For a discussion of a similar issue in the Presbyterian Church (PCUSA), see Anne Motley Hallum, "Presbyterians as Political Amateurs," in *Religion in American Politics,* ed. Charles W. Dunn (Washington: Congressional Quarterly Press, 1989), 63–73.

108. This is even slightly higher than the 68 percent who said they are satisfied with the overall program and emphases of MCC. Also, it should be noted that in a similar 1972 survey, only 55 percent of those responding said they favored the work of the Washington office (the Ottawa office was not founded until three years later). This is an increase of 17 percent, a rather dramatic jump in seventeen years. Kauffman and Driedger, *Mennonite Mosaic,* 177.

109. Mike Klassen, *The Mennonite,* 13 Oct. 1992, 435. But see also J. Daryl Byler, "A Vote for More Government," *Washington Memo* 27 (2) (Mar.–Apr. 1995): 2.

110. Driedger, *Mennonite Identity,* 16.

111. Hertzke, *Representing God,* 203, claims that "for some of the liberal denominations, such as the United Church of Christ or the Mennonite Central Committee, political activity is indeed reasonably well integrated into church life." As I've been saying, Mennonites' political activity is not "reasonably well integrated into church life," although in recent decades there have been movements in that direction. On 107, Hertzke also suggests that "for these small [peace] churches, we would not expect to find the same degree of tension between lobby policy and members' opinions as might exist elsewhere." This may be true in comparison with some denominational lobbying organizations and their constituent bodies, but a relatively high degree of tension remains even for some *peace* Protestants.

112. Results of the 1972 survey can be found in Kauffman and Harder, *Anabaptists.*

113. James Davison Hunter, *American Evangelicalism* (New Brunswick: Rutgers Univ. Press, 1983), 115.

114. It is striking that although the most conservative Mennonite groups claim to be apolitical, for many years one of their primary print vehicles, *Guidelines for Today,* contained more political articles than any other Mennonite publication. During the late 1980s, the publication included six to eight pages of social and political news briefs, generally on moral issues such as alcohol use, abortion, and the entertainment industry. The editor wrote a regular section on "Church and State," and another commentator, James R. Hess, frequently wrote on political issues in his column, "In My Opinion." In Jan. 1990, after the death of editor Sanford G. Shetler, the periodical was merged with another conservative publication, *The Sword and the Trumpet.* See J. R. Burkholder, "Apolitical Nonresistance," in Burkholder and Nelson Gingerich, *Mennonite Peace Theology,* 30–34. Burkholder says the basic logic of *Guidelines* might be stated as "pray, pay and obey," except when obedience would clearly violate God's commandments.

115. In Franz's files are many letters written in response to conservative critics James Hess, George R. Brunk II, Sanford Shetler, and others. On several occasions, Franz also met with some of these critics to discuss their differences.

116. Occasionally the office hears from one of these constituents. One postcard states: "I am sad to see you still advocating our writing Reagan/lobbying the government. Do you really think 1) that we have time to lobby for nuclear freezes, etc., given that it is 4 minutes to midnight? 2) that there really is democracy in the U.S., given the power of the Corps. i.e.: GE, Lockheed, Rockwell, etc.? 3) that the nuclear system is under government control or has it become controlled by its own momentum/technique?? I look forward to the day when I hear MCC call us to active resistance to nuclear madness, i.e., war tax resistance, Plowshares style witnesses, etc., where Xns are called to assume personal responsibility for this insanity and are not allowed to pass the buck to alleged government disarmament processes which if anything have legitimized an increased arms race over the years!" (Robert V. Peters to Franz, 30 Nov. 1981). Available in MCC Washington files.

117. Ebersole, *Church Lobbying in the Nation's Capital* (New York: Macmillan, 1951), 179.

118. King, "A Report," 29.

119. Lehman to Franz, 11 Mar. 1969. Available in AMC IX-6-3, file "DF 1969."

120. The statement was made by Paul G. Landis, then secretary of Lancaster Conference. Participants at the Smoketown conference were from the Mennonite Church, General Conference Mennonite Church, Conservative Conference of the Mennonite Church, and the Beachy Amish. For a report, see Dave Graybill, "Make Salvation Central, Ad-Hoc Group Tells Church," *Gospel Herald,* 24 July 1979, 586.

121. See, e.g., Wuthnow, *The Restructuring,* especially chap. 7. In *The Good Society,* 189, Bellah and his associates write: "If they are to be engaged with their own public without becoming driven as interest groups, the para-church advocacy groups must listen more closely to their local members and the people with whom they converse culturally beyond the pews. They need to talk with them more deeply and persuasively about the meaning of faith lived out in a good society." On this general point, see also the early work by Jeffrey Hadden, *The Gathering Storm in the Churches* (Garden City: Doubleday, 1969).

122. Interview with McGovern, 23 Feb. 1993.

123. Interview with Rendon, 24 Feb. 1993.

124. Interview with Martin, 2 Dec. 1992.

125. Interview with Goering, 8 Nov. 1992. In his 1963 report to the executive committee of MCC Peace Section, John Unruh said he hoped a witness to government "might reflect our concern for other persons and groups by urging that they receive the just treatment they are guaranteed in theory but often denied in practice." Unruh said concerns for others were partly a response to Mennonites' guilt feelings about witnessing to government only about their own needs and interests. Two decades later Phil Baker-Shenk, a public-service attorney in Washington, stated that "[s]elf-interested pleadings (as in exemption from conscription) rather than love of neighbor characterized our relations with government in the past. . . . We are now maturing into a love for neighbor." Cited in Sue C. Steiner, "Mennonites and Politics," *Christian Century,* 8 May 1985, 463.

126. It should be noted that Old Colony Mennonites are outside of MCC's constituent bodies.

127. "Stranded Mennonite Immigrants at Seminole, Texas, and Boley, Oklahoma: A Report for the Congressional Efforts to Resolve the Problem," submitted by MCC, 6 June 1979. Available in MCC Washington file "Archival: Old Colony Mennonites' Immigration to Texas."

128. The comment was cited in Rick Casey's sharply critical "Casey's Column . . . Choosing Your Aliens," *National Catholic Reporter,* 4 Nov. 1977, 3.

129. See, e.g., Karl S. Shelly, "Health Care Questions and Answers," *Washington Memo* 26 (3) (May–June 1994): 4. An analysis of Mennonite agencies' conflicting responses to health care reform would make a provocative study of its own.

130. See "Guidelines for the Washington Office of MCC U.S. Peace Section," Exhibit 9 at the MCC U.S. Executive Committee Meeting, 15–16 Dec. 1982, available in MCC Washington files.

131. Interview with Greg Goering, 1 Sept. 1992.

132. Interview with Peachey, 9 Nov. 1992.

133. Interview with Tate, 24 Feb. 1993.

134. Hofrenning, *In Washington,* 126–27.

135. Hertzke, *Representing God,* 70–79. On 73, Hertzke describes religious persons' difficulty with strategic thinking and compromise as a "unique psychological impediment to mastering the details of the legislative process."

136. Hertzke acknowledges, 79, that Hyman Bookbinder of the American Jewish Committee did function as the "quintessential Capitol insider."

137. The percentage is from the staff's 1989 "Self-Study." My observation would be that far less than 10 percent of staffers' time is spent in conversation with or in writing letters to legislators or legislative aides.

138. Franz had only one appointment in the White House during the Reagan-Bush years, and that was 31 Aug. 1992, just two months before the election that President Bush lost. Bush had called together a dozen representatives from disaster relief organizations to discuss clean-up efforts after Hurricane Andrew. MCC's Akron headquarters asked Franz to represent Mennonite Disaster Service, one of MCC's programs, at the meeting. The UCC's Jay Lintner provided a short history of mainline religious advocates' relationship with the White House. He said during

the Eisenhower and Kennedy eras, the mainline churches had a lot of clout with the president. "When the agenda shifted from Civil Rights to Vietnam, Johnson got a little miffed at the churches," observes Lintner. "And Nixon was paranoid. Needless to say, that was when the total shutdown occurred. He just said, 'No more church people in here.' And he didn't talk to anyone except for Billy Graham, practically. Then Ford didn't really change that. When Carter came, it was incredible. He opened up the White House—it wasn't just meetings with him. We'd take a delegation of urban mission people into the White House, and we'd meet a delegation of rural mission people coming out. We were in there regularly, not just to meet with Carter personally, but he'd turn over the whole first floor of the White House to receptions. . . . Carter's basic thing was that he didn't trust the establishment, and the churches were out of the establishment. . . . Reagan never invited the mainline churches in except basically the southern evangelicals. . . . And I think the only time I got in the Reagan White House was to meet with Vice President Bush, who convened a group to talk about foreign aid." Interview with Lintner, 4 Sept. 1992.

139. Mennonite theologian Norman Kraus made this observation following my presentation on this point at the twenty-fifth anniversary celebration of MCC Washington.

140. Interview with Tiller, 6 Nov. 1992.

141. Interview with Lintner, 4 Sept. 1992.

142. Interview with Franz, 10 Nov. 1992.

143. Interview with Jacob Ahearn, 26 Feb. 1993. "Inside the Beltway" is a reference to Interstate 95, which makes a broad loop around the District of Columbia.

144. Interview with Schmidt, 1 Sept. 1992. Schmidt is among those who was both impressed with and bothered by Franz's quiet style. Mennonite ethicist John Richard Burkholder suggests that while Franz was not "corrupted" by being in Washington, he believes directors of MCC's Washington office should stay only five-year terms so they do not "get stuck in that Washington orbit." "It's the same thing we say about Congress," explains Burkholder. "I think it would be healthy both ways—to have people with the Washington experience out there pastoring or in colleges or whatever in the church" (Interview with Burkholder, 1 Oct. 1992).

145. Interview with Gingrich, 9 Nov. 1992.

146. Interview with Schrag Lauver, 24 Feb. 1993. Schrag Lauver is a Mennonite who has worked in Washington for many years.

147. An overview of the Anabaptist principle and practice can be found in Robert Friedmann, "Gelassenheit," in H. S. Bender et al., eds., *Mennonite Encyclopedia II* (Scottdale, Pa.: Mennonite Publishing House, 1956), 448–49. See also Schlabach's extensive work with Mennonites' "humility theology" in *Peace, Faith*. Some Mennonite groups have emphasized humility more than others. Some Mennonite and non-Mennonite critics would say this humility is not necessarily a good thing, since being humble has often taken precedence over demanding justice.

148. Interview with Trenkle, 26 Feb. 1993.

149. Interview with Rendon, 24 Feb. 1993.

150. Interview with Jim McGovern, 23 Feb. 1993.

151. Interview with Tate, 24 Feb. 1993. Hertzke notes that few issues have the moral clarity of the Civil Rights Act, which the churches helped pass in 1964,

but he says mainline lobbies have a tendency to treat complex policy issues with a similar moral urgency and clarity. "Whether the issue is labor law, environment, day care, immigration, military doctrine, or trade with Mexico, the church leaders are there, arguing that the 'churches' stand for this or that," he says. See "An Assessment," 51.

152. Interview with Tate, 24 Feb. 1993.

153. Ibid. Tate claims that deciding to vote for the use of force was a traumatic decision for him and Rep. Leach. "For me, having volunteered to go to Vietnam for a year and having gotten out after a year, I tried to use that experience to learn how I might help that kind of thing from happening again. And of course here it was, and I couldn't find a way out of it."

154. Among the church leaders besides Goering and Franz were Vern Preheim, general secretary of the General Conference Mennonite Church; Arthur Jost and Vernon Wiebe, Mennonite Brethren representatives; Owen Burkholder, Mennonite Church representative; and James Lapp, executive secretary of the Mennonite Church. The delegation marked the fourth time in MCC Washington's history that representatives officially designated by denominations went to Washington. The other inter-Mennonite delegations to government officials that MCC Washington coordinated were in 1972 related to the Vietnam War; in 1982 regarding military conscription laws; and in 1983 to discuss Central American issues.

155. Interview with Goering, 8 Nov. 1992.

156. Interview with Schrag Lauver, 24 Feb. 1993.

5. REPORTING FROM THE FIELD

1. In one recent year the total service workers, local volunteers, salaried employees, and other MCC staffers totaled 919, 539 of whom were in the United States and Canada and 380 of whom were overseas. About a third of those persons with North American assignments have administrative roles in Akron, Winnipeg, or one of the regional offices. The remainder are doing other forms of hands-on service. Of the overseas workers, 112 were in Africa, 78 in Asia, 28 in Europe, 131 in Latin America, and 31 in the Middle East.

2. MCC, "Faith, Power."

3. Franz, "Origins," 2.

4. Ibid.

5. Friesen to Kassebaum, 9 Oct. 1992. Available in MCC Washington files.

6. Although not as relevant for the work of MCC Washington, it should be noted that some MCC workers have contact with national government officials or American embassy employees in countries where they serve.

7. Franz, Betsy Beyler, and Earl Martin to MCC Country Representatives and MCC Area Secretaries, 10 May 1984.

8. Franz to Titus and Linda Peachey, 31 July 1990.

9. The MCC worker was Blake Byler Ortman, who had served many years in El Salvador.

10. The mediation efforts led to a kidnapping threat on Lederach's spouse and four-year-old daughter. The Lederachs were living in Costa Rica at the time.

11. Information gleaned from a schedule of appointments for Lederach, Shogreen, and Sider, 1 Dec. 1987, and a follow-up letter, dated 3 Dec. 1987, from Franz to Sider. Both documents are available in MCC Washington files. In the letter, Franz adds, "Perhaps it was only coincidental and unrelated, but for the first time to my knowledge (on the afternoon of MCC delegation's arrival), a voice from an incoming phone call said, 'We are watching you'—and hung up."

12. Franz to Urbane Peachey, LeRoy Friesen, and William Snyder, "Follow-Up of LeRoy Friesen's Washington Appointments," 16 Aug. 1976. Available in MCC Washington files.

13. See Franz to John Stoner, Urbane Peachey, and John Lapp, 4 May 1977. Available in MCC Washington files.

14. Franz, "Mennonites Carry Torch for Vietnam in Washington," 19 Dec. 1975. MCC news release available in MCC Washington files.

15. Cited in Hertzke, *Representing God,* 78.

16. AFSC, founded in 1917 to send conscientious objectors to aid civilian victims during World War I, has its headquarters in Philadelphia, Pa. Its structure and history have many similarities with MCC, although it is considerably smaller, especially in terms of overseas workers. AFSC carries on programs of service, development, justice, and peace in twenty-two countries and forty-three program sites in the United States.

17. Among the others are the Washington Office on Development Policy of Church World Service and Lutheran World Relief.

18. Matlack, "American Friends Service Committee Program Description," May 1992. Available from the AFSC Washington office.

19. MCC has deliberately avoided scheduling press conferences for its returning service workers. Often MCC Washington staffers send press releases about the visits to Mennonite and Brethren in Christ publications, but they do not make similar contacts with the secular press. MCC U.S. board member Susan Goering expressed frustration about this practice. In the case of the kidnapping threats on Lederach's family, she had wondered why the office had not informed the mass media. Franz told her he had spoken with MCC Executive Secretary John Lapp and he had said, "We're not going to go to the press. We're going to try to deal with this in a private way."

20. Interview with Walter Owensby, 9 Nov. 1992.

21. Interview with Trenkle, 26 Feb. 1993.

22. Interview with Rendon, 24 Feb. 1993.

23. Interview with Murray, 23 Feb. 1993. At the time of the interview, Somalia was regularly covered in the media because of the United States–United Nations intervention there. Bosnia's "ethnic cleansing" also appeared regularly on the nation's front pages.

24. J. R. Burkholder, "Pacifist Ethics and Pacifist Politics," in Cromartie, *Peace Betrayed,* 198.

25. Ibid., 205. See also Wilbert Shenk, "Missions, Service and the Globalization of North American Mennonites," *Mennonite Quarterly Review* 70 (1) (Jan. 1996).

26. One of the organizational oddities of MCC Washington's international dimension is the fact that it comes under the auspices of MCC U.S., by virtue of its being a U.S.-based office. In its initial years the Washington office was directly under

MCC's Peace Section, but later the Peace Section was divided into a U.S. branch and an international branch. MCC Washington then came under the MCC U.S. Peace Section. With the dissolution of the Peace Section in 1992, the office was placed in a Peace and Justice Ministries cluster directly under MCC U.S. rather than MCC International.

27. Interview with McGovern, 23 Feb. 1993.

28. King, "A Report."

29. Franz, 1969 "Report," 2.

30. Franz, "Biblical/Theological Perspectives on Church and Government," *Washington Memo* 21 (1) (Jan.–Feb. 1989): 3.

31. Praxis's new primacy in theology, Chopp writes, is derived from three sources: "First of all, an orientation in much theology to structural and cultural crises such as poverty, the Holocaust, sexism, racism, and psychic destructiveness. Secondly, [it] arises from the influence of various contemporary theories that stress the importance of praxis in terms of the social situatedness of reason, the cultural-structural formation of anthropology and history, and historical aims of freedom. Thirdly, praxis is important due to renewed attention in Christian theology to faith as not only in existential or inward experience, but as the embodied activity of Christian faith and its communal character in transforming situations and experiences of suffering into those of freedom." See Chopp's "Praxis," in *The New Dictionary of Catholic Spirituality,* ed. Michael Downey (Collegeville: Liturgical, 1993), 756. See also, e.g., Gustavo Gutiérrez, *A Theology of Liberation* (Maryknoll, N.Y.: Orbis, 1973).

32. MCC Washington's epistemological basis, then, may loosely parallel that of various contemporary theologians: feminists, who begin with women's experience of injustice; and certain Latin Americans, who focus on the poor and oppressed in their countries.

33. Franz observes that, in retrospect, in his MCC work he "probably would have been better off to identify my agenda with domestic issues," adding that he shifted to Latin American and Mideast concerns because of the organization's concerns for international affairs. Had Franz chosen a domestic rather than international focus, one can expect that the office dynamics and MCC Washington's role in the capital may have shifted dramatically. Interview with Franz, 29 June 1992.

34. Goering to Pat Fons, 2 Oct. 1991. Available in MCC Washington files.

35. Interview with Goering, 1 Sept. 1992. Franz agrees that both the MCC Washington office and political leaders in Washington take *domestic* experience for granted. Franz mentioned the odd imbalance of giving someone working in Africa, or even an African national, more credibility than someone who grew up in the inner-city U.S. Interview with Franz, 25 Feb. 1993.

36. Mennonites were first in the Middle East in 1896, when some Mennonites reached out to the Armenians during a time of national disaster. An excellent source on MCC and other Mennonite mission and service efforts in the Middle East is LeRoy Friesen, *Mennonite Witness in the Middle East: A Missiological Introduction* (Elkhart, Ind.: Mennonite Board of Missions, 1992).

37. Interview with Whitlatch, 10 Nov. 1992.

38. C-MEP, "Background Paper on the Gulf Crisis," 7 Sept. 1990. Available in MCC Washington files. While Franz (and others who edited the statement) did not quote Scripture, they made essentially the same argument as what follows in the MCC statement.

39. MCC, "MCC Statement on the Use of Food as a Weapon," 6 Sept. 1990. Available in MCC Washington files.

40. Information gleaned from MCC, *MCC Workbook 1991.* Available from MCC Akron.

41. Franz, "Lifting Embargo on Food and Medicines for Suffering Children of Iraq," 5 July 1991. Available in MCC Washington files. This was MCC Washington's only *Hotline* related to Iraq during or after the Persian Gulf War.

42. Olfert to Peter J. Davies, 25 Nov. 1992. Available in MCC Washington files.

43. See AFSC, "A Statement by the American Friends Service Committee on the Situation in Somalia," 8 Dec. 1992. Available from AFSC.

44. Mary Yoder Holsopple, Elroy Holsopple, and Cindy Mullett, "Readers Say," *Gospel Herald,* 2 Mar. 1993, 5. Some other observers did, of course, disagree with the MCC workers' assessments.

45. Franz, "Origins," 2. The first two of the following stories were gleaned, in parts verbatim, from Franz's description.

46. This case is one of the best examples of how direct experiential testimony, combined with a single letter from a Mennonite constituent, can have tremendous impact on public policy. Franz mentions this incident in "The Washington Office: Reflections After Ten Years," *Washington Memo* 10 (4) (July–Aug. 1978): 2. Franz says the Hieberts were half of "the total American presence (other than three embassy personnel)" in Laos, and "their voice at the State Department was pivotal in obtaining U.S. release of 10,000 tons of grain so urgently needed in that famine area."

47. A 27 Aug. 1978 article by Richard Dudman, chief Washington correspondent for the *St. Louis Post Dispatch,* verified that the quiet intercession of the Hieberts resulted in the Laotians' release of the bodies of the airmen.

48. Richard A. Kauffman, David E. Hostetler, and Lois Barrett, "The Patty Erb Story—One Year Later," *Gospel Herald,* 27 Sept. 1977, 726–27. Two other sources on this story are David Shelly, "Two Tell of Torture in South America," *Mennonite Weekly Review,* 18 Aug. 1977, 6; and Kreider and Waltner Goossen, *Hungry, Thirsty,* 325–27. All of these sources were used in this summary.

49. *Congressional Record,* 15 June 1977.

50. In "The Washington Office," Franz also mentions that a letter from Mennonite missionary LaVerne Rutschmann about the torture of innocents in Latin America was quoted in a floor speech by his senator. The senator's legislation terminated a Washington-area military-police academy where officials from Third World regimes were being trained.

51. Former Eastern Mennonite Board of Missions and Charities missionary Don Jacobs asked Franz to schedule the Washington appointments for Kivengere. This story is told, in part, in Franz, "Ugandan Bishop Testifies in Washington," MCC Washington news release, Oct. 1977. Available in MCC Washington files.

52. Cited in Franz, "A Ugandan Bishop Came to Washington," an unpublished summary of Kivengere's visits written in 1988. Available in MCC Washington files. Other parts of this account are from Franz's summary.

53. Unfortunately, the speech was never given, adds the legislative aide. "By looking at the public record one can't fully see all that's going on," she says. Interview with Temple Brown, 26 Feb. 1993.

54. Ibid.
55. Interview with Franz, 10 Nov. 1992.
56. Interview with Martin, 2 Dec. 1992.
57. Interview with Franz, 10 Nov. 1992.
58. Interview with Gingrich, 9 Nov. 1992.
59. Interview with Capps, 25 Feb. 1993.
60. Interview with Whitlatch, 10 Nov. 1992.
61. Interview with Friesen, 26 Feb. 1993.
62. Interview with Franz, 10 Nov. 1992. Similar assessments of MCC's experience-based credibility were made in Canada and at the United Nations in New York. See, e.g., Rempel, "Work by the Church," 8. William Janzen, director of MCCC's Ottawa office, claims, "More than once when I've called people in the External Affairs Department, they've said, 'You say you're with the Mennonites? Well, I know your people from Bangladesh, or Jordan, or Tanzania, or wherever.' It really establishes credibility. It doesn't mean what one says about policy is meaningful, but at least you get a chance to say it." From my transcription of Janzen's 13 Feb. 1992 presentation at American Mennonite Biblical Seminaries. See also Janzen, "I thought the Mennonites might be able to help Canadian society on the question of caring for children" (*Peace Office Newletter* 23 [5] [Sept.–Oct. 1993]: 8).
63. Interview with Gingrich, 9 Nov. 1992.
64. Interview with Peachey, 9 Nov. 1992.
65. Interview with McCormick, 26 Feb. 1993.
66. Interview with Murray, 23 Feb. 1993. Franz contends that MCC's Middle East workers have been told repeatedly that theirs was the first voice to be heard reflecting the plight of the Palestinians. Two MCC *Peace Office Newsletters* illuminate Mennonite Central Committee's views of "Seeking Peace in Palestine" and "Anti-Semitism." See the Jan.–Feb. 1993 and Mar.–Apr. 1993 newsletters, which are fully devoted to these topics.
67. Interview with Jacob Ahearn, 26 Feb. 1993.
68. Interview with Volk, 9 Nov. 1992.
69. Interview with Goering, 8 Nov. 1992.
70. Interview with Matlack, 26 Feb. 1993.
71. Interview with Owensby, 9 Nov. 1992. Owensby adds: "But when that religious voice that is underscored by MCC's on-the-ground experience comes up against the lobbying interests of the arms firms, or VAPAC, or whomever, that may have more leverage than the churches do. Then despite the moral arguments, those may tend to get discounted in favor of other political considerations."
72. Interview with Ahearn, 26 Feb. 1993.
73. Interview with McCormick, 26 Feb. 1993.
74. Interview with Ahearn, 26 Feb. 1993.
75. Interview with Sprunger, 25 Feb. 1993.
76. Interview with Ahearn, 26 Feb. 1993.
77. Interview with McCormick, 26 Feb. 1993.
78. Interview with Murray, 23 Feb. 1993.
79. Interview with Semmel, 25 Feb. 1993.
80. Interview with McCormick, 26 Feb. 1993.
81. Interview with Rendon, 24 Feb. 1993.

82. Interview with McGovern, 23 Feb. 1993.

83. Interview with Sprunger, 25 Feb. 1993.

84. The term is from McGovern, who remarks, "I know it sounds kind of matter of fact, but there are a lot of people up here who come off like lunatics, I mean well-intentioned lunatics, but this is a very conservative atmosphere here on Capitol Hill, and everyone hugs the center and they don't want to be associated with people who are far off to the right or to the left. They want to be credible. And I think that the MCC here is able to operate in that credible margin" (Interview with McGovern, 23 Feb. 1993).

85. Interview with Semmel, 25 Feb. 1993.

86. MCC, "Faith, Power."

87. This is not to suggest that MCC or any other organization's experience is somehow "pure" or free of ideological tainting. MCC workers function with an often unarticulated ideological sieve that helps them sort through their personal experiences. Interpretation of events is based both on the experience itself and reflection on them. Evidence that particular commitments and prior experiences affect how events are interpreted by MCC workers is their response to the possibility of United States and United Nations military intervention in Somalia in 1992. Many other relief agencies with long-term involvements in Somalia supported the military assistance, but volunteers with MCC and the AFSC did not.

88. Interview with Lintner, 4 Sept. 1992.

89. Interview with Gingrich, 9 Nov. 1992.

90. Mark Neufeld, "Critical Theory and Christian Service: Knowledge and Action in Situations of Social Conflict," *Conrad Grebel Review* 6 (3) (Fall 1988): 249–61.

91. See Habermas, *Knowledge and Human Interests* (London: Heinemann, 1972). The description here is based largely on Neufeld's account.

92. Neufeld, "Critical Theory," 258.

93. See Appendix 1 for the full text of MCC's guiding principles.

94. Noted in Ray Brubacher, "Responses," *Conrad Grebel Review* 7 (1) (Winter 1984): 63–65. See also Ted Grimsrud and Helmut Harder's responses in the same issue, 65–69, as well as the critique of Neufeld in Suderman, "Liberation Pacifism."

95. See, e.g., Habermas, *Toward a Rational Society: Student Protest, Science and Politics* (Boston: Beacon, 1970).

96. Habermas, "On Systematically Distorted Communication," *Inquiry* 13 (1970): 205–18; and "Towards a Theory of Communicative Competence," *Inquiry* 13 (1970): 360–75.

97. Habermas, *The Structural Transformation.* Habermas does not make this link clear, nor does he indicate whether or not this "ideal speech situation" has been a historical reality or whether it is simply an "ideal" for which we should strive. On this, see, e.g., Wuthnow et al., *Cultural Analysis,* 227.

98. Wuthnow et al., *Cultural Analysis.* But see also the critique of the *singularity* of Habermas's public *sphere* in Nancy Fraser's "Rethinking the Public Sphere: A Contribution to the Critique of Actually Existing Democracy," *Social Texts* 25–26 (1990): 56–80.

99. See, e.g., Habermas, "Conservatism and Capitalist Crisis," *New Left Review* 115 (May–June 1979): 73–84; and "New Social Movements," *Telos* 49 (Fall 1981): 33–37.

100. The language is again from Fraser's "Rethinking," 66.

101. Interview with Gingrich, 9 Nov. 1992.

102. Interview with McGovern, 23 Feb. 1993.

103. Franz, "Review of MCC Peace Section Washington Office," 23 Mar. 1976, 3. Available in MCC Washington files.

6. SPEAKING MULTIPLE LANGUAGES

1. Franz, "The Washington Office: Reflections," 3.

2. Brueggemann, "The Legitimacy of a Sectarian Hermeneutic: 2 Kings 18–19," in *Education for Citizenship and Discipleship,* ed. Mary C. Boys (New York: Pilgrim, 1989), 13. Brueggemann's use of the term "illegitimate" is based on the theoretical work of Habermas. See, e.g., Habermas's *Legitimation Crisis* (Boston: Beacon, 1975). In a concise summary on 10–11, Brueggemann says: "Habermas characterizes the crisis of legitimacy as the separation of instrumental functions of administration from expressive symbols that evoke assent. By instrumental functions he means the autonomous, secularized, scientific modes of managing people, managing the means of production, and managing the supportive ideology. The crisis is that such administrative claims rest, he suggests, on appeals to power, deception, and pragmatism, because they are largely cut off from the symbols that genuinely authorize. And so one must cover over the loss of energizing symbols by more consumer goods, by diversionary activity, or by fabrication of false symbols. Such a way is illegitimate because it does not touch the actual life of people. While the deception may prevail, it cannot be compelling at bottom and therefore is illegitimate."

3. Harrington Watt, "United States," 265.

4. Brueggemann, "The Legitimacy," 9.

5. Ibid., 6–7.

6. Bellah et al., *The Good Society,* 193.

7. Interview with Goering, 1 Sept. 1992.

8. From my transcription of a 4 Sept. 1992 MCC Washington staff meeting at which Franz, Goering, Schmidt, and Gingrich discussed Brueggemann's "The Legitimacy."

9. Ibid.

10. Ibid.

11. Ibid.

12. This collective voice is *still* distinguishable from Washington's right-leaning religious lobbies, who usually are not part of the Methodist Building chorus.

13. Interview with Gingrich, 30 June 1992.

14. From 4 Sept. 1992 staff meeting.

15. Ibid.

16. Brueggemann, "The Legitimacy," 13.

17. Franz, "Self-Study," 6.

18. From 4 Sept. 1992 staff meeting.

19. These principles were derived from a draft of Friesen's paper, "An Anabaptist Understanding of the Church and Its Approach to Public Policy," and from Franz, "Summary Report," 3. On rights language, see, e.g., Donald E. Miller, "A Biblical Approach to Human Rights," in *Peace, Politics, and the People of God,* ed. Paul Peachey (Philadelphia: Fortress, 1986), 163–65.

20. These quotes and passages are gleaned from handwritten notes for a variety of seminars. The biblical passages generally are cited directly from Franz's notes. Available in MCC Washington files.

21. Franz, "Biblical/Theological Perspectives on Church and Government," *Washington Memo* 21 (1) (Jan.–Feb. 1989): 4.

22. All from Franz, "A New Historical Moment: Biblical/Theological Perspectives," *Washington Memo* 24 (1) (Jan.–Feb. 1992): 1–2.

23. Franz, "New Occasions Teach New Duties," *Washington Memo* 24 (2) (Mar.–Apr. 1992): 1.

24. Franz, "The Rich Man and Lazarus: A Reality in Haiti," *Washington Memo* 24 (4) (July–Aug. 1992): 1.

25. Beyler, "Federal Priorities for the 80's: Racking the Poor to Pay the Pentagon," *Washington Memo* 13 (2) (Mar.–Apr. 1981): 1.

26. Franz, "The Law of Unintended Consequences," *Washington Memo* 23 (3) (May–June 1991): 1.

27. Franz, "Violence Escalates in the Middle East: Peace Initiative Pending," *Washington Memo* 17 (4) (July–Aug. 1985): 1–3.

28. Franz, "Bridging the Gap," *Washington Memo* 2 (6) (Nov.–Dec. 1970): 7.

29. Interview with Goering, 1 Sept. 1992.

30. Interview with Friesen, 26 Feb. 1993.

31. Franz, "On Speaking," 1.

32. From 4 Sept. 1992 staff meeting.

33. Franz, "Middle Axioms: An Appropriate Mode of Thinking and Speaking to Public Policy Decision-Makers by People with an Absolute Ethic?" This undated nine-page paper presumably was prepared for a conference in 1970. See also a response by Paul Peachey entitled "The Mennonite Central Committee in Washington: Notes Toward the 'Middle Axioms' of Political Witness," paper dated January 1970. Both papers are available in MCC Washington files.

34. Cited in Paul Ramsey, *Basic Christian Ethics* (New York: Charles Scribner's Sons, 1953), 349.

35. John H. Yoder, *The Christian Witness to the State* (Newton, Kans.: Faith and Life Press, 1964), 33.

36. Ibid., 38–39. Yoder, whose thought Franz followed closely, attempts to differentiate this perspective from that of the classical Roman Catholic and Lutheran views, as well as those of Calvinist theocracy, liberal pacifism, Reinhold Niebuhr, various sectarians, and even traditional Amish-Mennonites. For a critique of Yoder's use of "middle axioms," see Koontz's "Mennonites and the State," in *Essays on Peace Theology and Witness,* ed. Willard M. Swartley (Elkhart, Ind.: Institute of Mennonite Studies, 1988), 49–50.

37. Franz, "Middle Axioms," addendum 2.

38. Franz, "The Relationship," 2.

39. Greg Goering, "Learning to Speak Second Languages," unpublished paper dated 5 May 1991. Available from the author.

40. Interview with Martin, 2 Dec. 1992.

41. Goering to Specter, 27 Sept. 1989. Emphasis mine.

42. MCC's Overseas Peace Office also has wrestled at length with these dilemmas. One helpful resource on understanding these debates within the larger MCC context is the May–June 1993 *Peace Office Newsletter,* which focuses on "Moral Dilemmas: Sanctions and Peacekeeping Forces."

43. Much of this description is from Franz's interpretation in a 24 Aug. 1992 letter to Anne Meyer Byler. See also four articles in the May–June 1993 *Peace Office Newsletter* 23 (3) (May–June 1993): Janzen, "U.N. Military Enforcement Action: Should Mennonites Condemn It?" 8–9; Joanne Epp, "Canada and Peacekeeping: An Overview," 10; Franz, "United Nations Peacekeeping," 11; and John Rempel, "The Mission of the Church and Modern Humanitarian Institutions: The Case of the U.N.," 12.

44. Cited in Franz, "The Growth of Terrorism in the Middle East: Some Causes and Some Remedies," *Washington Memo* 16 (2) (Mar.–Apr. 1984): 1.

45. Ibid., 3.

46. Carl R. Denman to Franz, 14 Apr. 1984.

47. Yoder, *The Christian Witness,* 36.

48. Franz, "Peacekeeping Role of U.N. Imperiled?" *Washington Memo* 24 (2) (Mar.–Apr. 1992): 7. On this difficult issue, see also Ernie Regehr's response to Charlton's "Pursuing Justice."

49. Judy Zimmerman Herr, "MCC and Sanctions," a working paper for discussion by the MCC Overseas Department, 5 Aug. 1992. Most of the information in these paragraphs is gleaned from the paper. See also her "Sanctions and Pacifists," *Peace Office Newsletter* 23 (3) (May–June 1993): 4–5.

50. "This was a new step for MCC, which moved in the direction of deliberate civil disobedience in defying sanctions, rather than following past precedent of sending supplies through some other legal route," says Zimmerman Herr, "MCC and Sanctions," 8. The U.S. government did provide MCC with a license in time, so the organization was able to legally send its supplies.

51. Cited in ibid., 1. The letter, from D. R. Yoder of Atlanta, was published in the 18 July 1991 issue of *Mennonite Weekly Review.*

52. Ibid., 11. She also refers to Mennonite ethicist Duane K. Friesen's distinctions between "violence" and "coercion." "Coercion, he suggests, is the ability to force compliance with a rule, while violence is that which violates or harms a person or persons. Coercion may not be violent if it does not injure persons and if it provides the possibility for wholeness and reconciliation. It then is performing an ordering function." See Friesen's *Christian Peacemaking,* 150–54. Some ethicists—Mennonites and others—see this distinction between coercion and violence as problematic.

53. Zimmerman Herr, "MCC and Sanctions," 16.

54. *Washington Memo* 1 (1) (Jan. 1969): 2–3.

55. Beyler, "Federal Priorities," 2, 6.

56. Bowman to *Washington Memo,* 17 June 1978.

57. Gingrich, "Major Global Changes: A Time for Real Disarmament," *Washington Memo* 23 (6) (Nov.–Dec. 1991): 3.

58. "An MCC U.S. Call to Reduce the Military Budget," *Washington Memo* 24 (1) (Jan.–Feb. 1992): 4.

59. This may sound like Ronald Reagan's "peace through strength," but it was suggested to me by two Mennonite graduate students working in the area of international politics. See also Koontz's "Mennonites and the State," 43–44. In private correspondence, Koontz said his words should not be used to imply that he has supported increased U.S. defense budgets. "I have always felt, even on 'realist' grounds, that they could be cut substantially," he writes.

60. Interview with Gingrich, 9 Nov. 1992.

61. Interview with Peachey, 9 Nov. 1992.

62. Interview with Franz, 10 Nov. 1992.

63. The fact that I ask these questions ought not imply that I believe Reagan was right.

64. Reichley, *Religion,* 354–55.

65. Harrington Watt, "United States," 264.

66. Brueggemann, "The Legitimacy," 12.

67. Ibid., 27.

68. Cited in Bellah et al., *The Good Society,* 194. Bellah's pseudonym for the church advocate is Mel Reese.

69. Brueggemann, "The Legitimacy," 28–29.

70. D. Friesen, *Mennonite Witness,* 17.

7. ENGAGING WISELY AND INNOCENTLY?

1. Meredith B. McGuire, *Religion: The Social Context* (Belmont, Calif.: Wadsworth, 1987), 18.

2. Weber, *The Protestant Ethic,* 182.

3. Interview with Franz, 10 Nov. 1992.

4. Interview with Gingrich, 9 Nov. 1992.

5. Interview with Goering, 1 Sept. 1992.

6. Interview with Franz, 10 Nov. 1992.

7. Schweizer, *The Good News,* 240.

8. Friesen, "Review," 344.

9. Fraser is responding to Habermas's work on the public sphere, critiquing its claim to be "the public arena in the singular." Fraser agrees that something like Habermas's public sphere is needed, but she challenges the assumption that "a multiplicity of competing publics" is a "step away from, rather than toward, greater democracy"; she also challenges the idea that public discourse "should be restricted to deliberation about the common good," making the appearance of "private interests" and "private issues" undesirable. Fraser argues that contestation among a plurality of competing publics better promotes the ideal of participatory parity than does a single, comprehensive, overarching public. Fraser, "Rethinking," 62–63, 66.

10. The more complete term Fraser uses for such groups is "subaltern counterpublics," which describes various "discursive arenas where members of subordinated social groups invent and circulate counterdiscourses." The counterpublics have a dual character: they function, on the one hand, "as spaces of withdrawal and regroupment; on the other hand, they also function as bases and training grounds for agitational activities directed toward wider publics" (ibid., 67–68).

11. Koontz, "Mennonites and the State," 46–50. Gerald W. Schlabach argues that "Mennonites ought to rework what is left of their theology of two kingdoms before it and they are left hopelessly fragmented" in "Beyond Two-/ vs. One-Kingdom Theology: Abrahamic Community as a Mennonite Paradigm for Christian Engagement in Society," *Conrad Grebel Review* 11 (3) (Fall 1993): 187–209. See also Duane Friesen's "Response to Schlabach," *Conrad Grebel Review* 12 (1) (Winter 1994): 87–89, along with Schlabach and Friesen's ongoing responses in Conrad Grebel Review 13 (2) (Spring 1995): 189–96.

12. Koontz, "Mennonites and the State," 54.

13. Friesen, *Christian Peacemaking,* 107–8. For a careful critique of Friesen and John H. Yoder by a political scientist, see Neufeld, "Responding to Realism," 43–62.

14. Friesen, *Christian Peacemaking,* 19. See also Friesen's "Peacemaking as an Ethical Category: The Convergence of Pacifism and Just War," in *Ethics in the Nuclear Age: Strategy, Religious Studies, and the Churches,* ed. Todd Whitmore (Dallas: Southern Methodist Univ. Press, 1989), 161–80.

15. Interview with Franz, 10 Nov. 1992.

16. Much of what has been done in this regard by Mennonites in recent years has to do with providing typologies of pacifism. These typologies include elements of church-state models implicit within each type. See, e.g., Burkholder and Nelson Gingerich, *Mennonite Peace Theology;* Yoder, *Nevertheless;* and Tom Yoder Neufeld, "Varieties."

17. In his critique of a paper I presented at the 1993 annual meetings of the Society for the Scientific Study of Religion, Mark Chaves helped me more clearly articulate this point. See personal correspondence from Chaves, 15 Nov. 1993. In a refinement of DiMaggio and Powell's new institutionalism, Chaves speaks about a "subset of an organizational population resisting the external institutional pressures and thereby maintaining a certain amount of diversity within the organizational population." While most institutionalization literature focuses on establishing the pervasive power of institutional pressures, Chaves notes the limits of those pressures. "When one subunit of an organization is subordinate to another subunit, that subordination may serve to block institutionalization," he writes. "Political dynamics internal to organizations enhance or suppress institutionalization and, consequently, contribute to the overall degree of diversity or homogeneity within an organizational population." See "Intraorganizational Power and Internal Secularization in Protestant Denominations," *American Journal of Sociology* 99 (1) (July 1993): 42–43.

18. More work needs to be done on how the MCC Washington case might challenge Chaves's notions of secularization and his use of Weber's various forms of authority—traditional, charismatic, and bureaucratic. In the MCC Washington example, we do not see bureaucratic authority inexorably overwhelming traditional and charismatic forms of authority. Nor is either organizational field—that of MCC or that of Washington's religious lobbies—controlled solely by one of Weber's ideal types of authority. It is not a case of "nuts and bolts rationality" on Capitol Hill versus "ultimate values" in Akron. In both locations, one finds a dense, complex mixture of various kinds of authority.

19. Interview with Lapp, 22 July 1993.

20. For an argument *for* a Mennonite "public church," see, e.g., Scott Holland, "God in Public: A Modest Proposal for a Quest for a Contemporary North American Anabaptist Paradigm," *Conrad Grebel Review* 4 (1) (Winter 1986): 43–55. See also John Redekop's critique in *Conrad Grebel Review* 4 (2) (Spring 1986): 156–58.

21. Hertzke, "An Assessment," 73. Hertzke goes on to cite Alexis de Tocqueville, the nineteenth-century French observer of American life. De Tocqueville argued that religion in America "is most powerful in its indirect, cultural influence, educating people in their obligations to the community and directing their attention away from self-interest, materialism, and hedonism inherent in a society that celebrates individual freedom." See de Tocqueville's *Democracy in America* (New York: Knopf, 1945 [1835]).

22. Hauerwas, *A Community of Character: Toward a Constructive Christian Social Ethic* (Notre Dame: Univ. of Notre Dame, 1981), 6.

23. Hauerwas and Willimon, *Resident Aliens* (Nashville: Abingdon, 1989), 38.

24. Ibid., 48.

25. Wayne North, "A Final Look at the '80s," *Gospel Herald,* 22 May 1990, 356–57. On his copy of North's article in his MCC Washington office files, Delton Franz had written across the bottom: "This article leads me to want to keep working at interpreting why we are in Washington as Mennonites."

26. Miller, "Why I Sat," 1–3.

27. These denominations will need to judge whether the charge is relevant to them. On the critique of the mainline denominations, see also Hertzke's "An Assessment."

28. Interview with Peachey, 22 July 1993.

29. On this point I am in general agreement with Duane Friesen when he writes: "That is our task as a peace church—to be faithful as a church to the vision we have been given, to *be* the church, but from that base to seek the shalom of the city where we dwell *by engaging our culture* in [a] variety of ways. . . . [This] model overcomes a false dichotomy often phrased in Mennonite peace theology as whether we should first be the church *or* whether we should express our peace witness through the institutions of society. Our peace witness is *both/and.* Yes, we should be the church, but being the church is integrally connected with our witness and action in the world; through example, the institutions we create, the ethos we help create, our vocations in which we work, and how as citizens we help shape public policy." See his "Review," 348–49.

30. Stanley Hauerwas, "Will the Real Sectarian Stand Up?" *Theology Today* 44 (1) (Apr. 1987): 91. However, Hauerwas remains, at best, cautious and concerned about political involvements. Responding to a paper I presented at a June 1994 "Whither the Anabaptist Vision?" conference in Elizabethtown, Pa., Hauerwas wrote: "I have a quite critical attitude toward the Methodist lobbying effort in Washington. They think they're there to influence government. My own view is that they should think of themselves as spies who reside in Washington to report back to the troops what the sons of bitches are planning to do to us. The whole image of influencing government seems to me to be quite corrupting. . . . I think nothing is more corrupting than the notion of citizens participating in a democracy because that gives you the idea that somehow we are the government. Mennonites should know better" (Personal correspondence from Hauerwas, 5 July 1994).

31. Interview with McGovern, 23 Feb. 1993.

BIBLIOGRAPHY

BOOKS AND PUBLISHED ARTICLES

Adams, James L. *The Growing Church Lobby in Washington.* Grand Rapids: Eerdmans, 1970.

Albright, W. F., and C. S. Mann. *Matthew.* Garden City: Doubleday, 1971.

Allen, Joseph L. *Love and Conflict: A Covenantal Model of Christian Ethics.* Nashville: Abingdon, 1984.

————. *War: A Primer for Christians.* Nashville: Abingdon, 1991.

Ammerman, Nancy T. *Baptist Battles: Social Change and Religious Conflict in the Southern Baptist Convention.* New Brunswick: Rutgers Univ. Press, 1990.

————. "Denominations: Who and What Are We Studying?" In *Reimagining Denominationalism,* edited by Russell Richey and R. Bruce Mullin, 111–33. New York: Oxford Univ. Press, 1994.

Amstutz, James F. S. "Dialogue with Washington: Mennonites and the Test of Faith." *Mennonite Life* 47 (1) (Mar. 1992): 27–34.

Arnett, Ronald C. "Conflict Viewed from the Peace Tradition." *Brethren Life and Thought* 23 (Spring 1978): 93–103.

Bainbridge, William, and Rodney Stark. "Sectarian Tension." *Review of Religious Research* 22 (2) (Dec. 1980): 105–24.

Bainton, Roland H. *Christian Attitudes Toward War and Peace: A Historical Survey and Critical Re-Evaluation.* New York: Abingdon, 1960.

Barlett, Donald, and James Steele. *America: What Went Wrong?* Kansas City: Andrews and McMell, 1992.

Bauer, Raymond A., Ithiel de Sola Pool, and Lewis Anthony Dexter. *American Business and Public Policy.* New York: Atherton, 1963.

Bauman, Clarence. "The Theology of the Two Kingdoms: A Comparison of Luther and the Anabaptists." *Mennonite Quarterly Review* 38 (7) (Jan. 1964): 37–49.

Bauman, Harvey W. "Pray—Vote: Which?" *Gospel Herald,* 31 Oct. 1950, 1071.

Beckford, James. "Religious Organizations." In *The Sacred in a Secular Age,* edited by Phillip E. Hammond, 125–38. Berkeley: Univ. of California Press, 1985.

Beechy, Atlee. "First They Make Enemies." *Peace Office Newsletter* 21 (2) (Mar.–Apr. 1991): 1–3.

Bellah, Robert N. "Civil Religion in America." In *Beyond Belief: Essays on Religion in a Post-Traditional World,* 168–89. New York: Harper and Row, 1970.

Bellah, Robert N., and Richard Madsen, William M. Sullivan, Ann Swidler, and Steven M. Tipton. *The Good Society.* New York: Knopf, 1991.

———. *Habits of the Heart: Individualism and Commitment in American Life.* New York: Harper and Row, 1985.

Bender, Harold S. "The Anabaptist Vision." *Mennonite Quarterly Review* 18 (2) (Apr. 1944): 67–88. Also in *Church History* 13 (Mar. 1944): 3–24.

———. "Church and State in Mennonite History." *Mennonite Quarterly Review* 13 (2) (Apr. 1939): 83–103.

———. "Mennonite Central Committee." In *Mennonite Encyclopedia III,* edited by Harold S. Bender et al., 605–9. Scottdale, Pa.: Mennonite Publishing House, 1957.

———. "Mennonite Peace Action Throughout the World." In *Proceedings of the Fourth Mennonite World Conference, 3–10 August 1948,* 262–69. Akron: Mennonite Central Committee, 1950.

———. "Outside Influences on Mennonite Thought." *Mennonite Life* 10 (1) (Jan. 1955): 45–48.

Bender, Ross T., and Alan P. F. Sell. *Baptism, Peace and the State in the Reformed and Mennonite Traditions.* Waterloo, Ontario: Wilfrid Laurier Univ. Press, 1991.

Bender, Urie A. *Soldiers of Compassion.* Scottdale, Pa.: Herald, 1969.

Bennis, Phyllis, and Michel Moushabeck, eds. *Beyond the Storm: A Gulf Crisis Reader.* Brooklyn, N.Y.: Olive Branch, 1991.

Benson, Peter, and Dorothy Williams. *Religion on Capitol Hill: Myths and Realities.* San Francisco: Harper and Row, 1982.

Berger, Peter L., and Richard John Neuhaus. *Movement and Revolution.* Garden City: Doubleday, 1970.

Berry, Jeffrey M. *Lobbying for the People: The Political Behavior of Public Interest Groups.* Princeton: Princeton Univ. Press, 1977.

Beschel, Robert P., Jr., and Peter D. Feaver. "The Churches and the War." *The National Interest* 23 (Spring 1991): 69–75.

Beyler, Betsy. "Federal Priorities for the 80's: Racking the Poor to Pay the Pentagon." *Washington Memo* 13 (2) (Mar.–Apr. 1981): 1–2, 6.

Bibby, Reginald W. *Fragmented Gods: The Poverty and Potential of Religion in Canada.* Toronto: Irwin, 1987.

Billingsley, Lloyd. *From Mainline to Sideline: the Social Witness of the National Council of Churches.* Washington: Ethics and Public Policy Center, 1990.

Boli-Bennett, John. "The Ideology of Expanding State Authority in National Constitutions, 1870–1970." In *National Development and the World System,* edited by John W. Meyer and Michael T. Hannan, 228–38. Chicago: Univ. of Chicago Press, 1979.

Brock, Peter. *Pacifism in the United States: From the Colonial Era to the First World War.* Princeton: Princeton Univ. Press, 1968.

—————. *Twentieth-Century Pacifism: New Perspectives in Political Science.* New York: D. Van Nostrand, 1970.

Brooks Thistlethwaite, Susan, ed. *A Just Peace Church.* New York: United Church, 1986.

Brubacher, Ray, Helmut Harder, and Ted Grimsrud. "Responses." *Conrad Grebel Review* 7 (1) (Winter 1984): 63–69.

Brueggemann, Walter. "The Legitimacy of a Sectarian Hermeneutic: 2 Kings 18–19." In *Education for Citizenship and Discipleship,* edited by Mary C. Boys, 3–34. New York: Pilgrim, 1989.

—————. "The Transformative Potential of a Public Metaphor." In *Interpretation and Obedience: From Faithful Reading to Faithful Living,* 70–99. Minneapolis: Fortress, 1991.

Burkholder, J. Lawrence. "Concern Pamphlets Movement." In *Mennonite Encyclopedia V,* edited by Cornelius J. Dyck and Dennis D. Martin, 177–80. Scottdale, Pa.: Herald, 1990.

—————. "The Dark Side of Responsible Love." *Gospel Herald,* 16 Mar. 1993, 6–7.

—————. "How Do We Do Peace Theology?" In *Essays on Peace Theology and Witness,* edited by Willard M. Swartley, 12–34. Elkhart, Ind.: Institute of Mennonite Studies, 1988.

—————. "Justice." In *Mennonite Encyclopedia V,* edited by Cornelius J. Dyck and Dennis D. Martin, 471–73. Scottdale, Pa.: Herald, 1990.

—————. "Mennonites on the Way to Peace." *Gospel Herald,* 19 Feb. 1991, 1–4, 8.

—————. "Nonresistance, Nonviolent Resistance, and Power." In *Kingdom, Cross and Community,* edited by John Richard Burkholder and Calvin Redekop, 131–37. Scottdale, Pa.: Herald, 1976.

—————. *The Problem of Social Responsibility from the Perspective of the Mennonite Church.* Elkhart, Ind.: Institute of Mennonite Studies, 1989 [1958].

—————. "The Peace Churches as Communities of Discernment." *Christian Century,* 4 Sept. 1963, 1072–75.

—————. "Some Background—Mostly Autobiographical." In *Sectarian Realism: A Conversation with J. Lawrence Burkholder,* edited by Scott Holland and Rodney J. Sawatsky. Waterloo: Conrad Grebel, 1993.

—————. "What Shall We Then Say to the State?" *Gospel Herald,* 31 Dec. 1991, 5–7.

Burkholder, John Richard. "Apolitical Nonresistance." In *Mennonite Peace Theology: A Panorama of Types,* edited by John Richard Burkholder and Barbara Nelson Gingerich, 30–34. Akron: Mennonite Central Committee Peace Office, Jan. 1991.

—————. "Can We Make Sense of Mennonite Peace Theology?" In *Mennonite Peace Theology: A Panorama of Types,* edited by John Richard Burkholder and Barbara Nelson Gingerich, 5–9. Akron: Mennonite Central Committee Peace Office, Jan. 1991.

—————. *Continuity and Change: A Search for a Mennonite Social Ethic.* Akron: Mennonite Central Committee Peace Section, 1977.

—————. "Historic Nonresistance." In *Mennonite Peace Theology: A Panorama of Types,* edited by John Richard Burkholder and Barbara Nelson Gingerich, 10–14. Akron: Mennonite Central Committee Peace Office, Jan. 1991.

271

————. "Mennonite Peace Theology: Reconnaissance and Exploration." *Conrad Grebel Review* 10 (3) (Fall 1992): 259–76.

————. *Mennonites in Ecumenical Dialogue on Peace and Justice.* Akron, Pa.: Mennonite Central Committee, Occasional Paper No. 7, Aug. 1988.

————. "Nonresistance." In *Mennonite Encyclopedia V.* Ed. Cornelius J. Dyck and Dennis D. Martin, 637–38. Scottdale, Pa.: Herald, 1990.

————. "Pacifist Ethics and Pacifist Politics." In *Peace Betrayed? Essays on Pacifism and Politics,* edited by Michael Cromartie, 193–206. Washington, D.C.: Ethics and Public Policy Center, 1990.

————. "Peace." In *Mennonite Encyclopedia V.* Ed. Cornelius J. Dyck and Dennis D. Martin, 681–85. Scottdale, Pa.: Herald, 1990.

————. "A Perspective on Mennonite Ethics." In *Kingdom, Cross and Community,* edited by John Richard Burkholder and Calvin Redekop, 151–66. Scottdale, Pa.: Herald, 1976.

————. "Sociopolitical Activism." In *Mennonite Encyclopedia V.* Ed. Cornelius J. Dyck and Dennis D. Martin, 837–38. Scottdale, Pa.: Herald, 1990.

Burkholder, John Richard, and Barbara Nelson Gingerich, eds. *Mennonite Peace Theology: A Panorama of Types.* Akron, Pa.: Mennonite Central Committee Peace Office, Jan. 1991.

Burkholder, John Richard, and Ted Koontz. "When Armed Force Is Used to Make Relief Work Possible." *Gospel Herald,* 12 Jan. 1993, 6–7.

Burkholder, John Richard, and Calvin Redekop, eds. *Kingdom, Cross, and Community.* Scottdale, Pa.: Herald, 1976.

Byler, J. Daryl. "Do Mennonites Want to Send a Message to Washington?" *Gospel Herald,* 20 Dec. 1994, 5.

————. "A Vote for More Government." *Washington Memo* 27 (2) (Mar.–Apr. 1995): 2.

Cagan, Leslie. "Reflections of a National Organizer." In *Collateral Damage: The New World Order at Home and Abroad,* edited by Cynthia Peters, 373–85. Boston: South End, 1992.

Carlson Brown, Joanne, and Carole R. Bohn, eds. *Christianity, Patriarchy and Abuse: A Feminist Critique.* New York: Pilgrim, 1989.

Carter, Stephen L. *The Culture of Disbelief: How American Law and Politics Trivialize Religious Devotion.* New York: Basic Books, 1993.

Casey, Rick. "Casey's Column . . . Choosing Your Aliens." *National Catholic Reporter,* 4 Nov. 1977, 3.

Chambers, John Whiteclay, II, ed. *The Eagle and the Dove: The American Peace Movement and United States Foreign Policy, 1900–1922,* 2d ed. Syracuse: Syracuse Univ. Press, 1991.

Chapman, Audrey R. *Faith, Power, and Politics: Political Ministry in the Mainline Churches.* New York: Pilgrim, 1991.

Charlton, Mark W. "Pursuing Human Justice in a Society of States: The Ethical Dilemmas of Armed Humanitarian Intervention." *Conrad Grebel Review* 12 (1) (Winter 1994): 1–20.

————. "Trends in Political Participation Among Brethren in Christ Ministers: 1975–1980." *Brethren in Christ History and Life* 4 (2) (1981): 142–62.

Chaves, Mark. "Denominations as Dual Structures: An Organizational Analysis." *Sociology of Religion* 54 (2) (Summer 1993): 147–69.

———. "Intraorganizational Power and Internal Secularization in Protestant Denominations." *American Journal of Sociology* 99 (1) (July 1993): 1–48.

Cherry, Conrad, and Rowland A. Sherrill, eds. *Religion, the Independent Sector, and American Culture.* Atlanta: Scholars, 1992.

Childress, James F. "Contemporary Pacifism: Its Major Types and Possible Contributions to Discourse about War." In *The American Search for Peace: Moral Reasoning, Religious Hope, and National Security,* edited by George Weigel and John P. Langan, S.J., 109–31. Washington: Georgetown Univ. Press, 1991.

———. *Moral Responsibility in Conflicts: Essays on Nonviolence, War, and Conscience.* Baton Rouge: Louisiana State Univ. Press, 1982.

Chopp, Rebecca S. *The Power to Speak: Feminism, Language, God.* New York: Crossroad, 1989.

———. "Praxis." In *The New Dictionary of Catholic Spirituality,* edited by Michael Downey, 756–64. Collegeville: Liturgical, 1993.

"Christian Witness Growing in Ottawa." *Mennonite Brethren Herald,* 27 Apr. 1979, 2–5.

Claassen Franz, Marian. "Pastors, Prophets, and Politicians." *Mennonite Life* 37 (1) (Mar. 1982): 24–29.

Clasen, Claus-Peter. *Anabaptism: A Social History, 1525–1618.* Ithaca: Cornell Univ. Press, 1972.

Coggins, Jim, ed. "Family Violence." *Mennonite Brethren Herald,* 20 Jan. 1989, 1–9, 17.

Cohen, Richard E. "Getting Religion." *National Journal,* 14 Sept. 1985, 2080–84.

Cohn, Bob, and Eleanor Clift. "Shaking up the Snake Pit." *Newsweek,* 11 July 1994, 16.

Craig, Robert H. *Religion and Radical Politics: An Alternative Christian Tradition in the United States.* Philadelphia: Temple Univ. Press, 1992.

Cromartie, Michael, ed. *Peace Betrayed? Essays on Pacifism and Politics.* New York: Univ. Press of America, 1990.

Derksen Hiebert, Chris. "Response" *Conrad Grebel Review* 13 (1) (Winter 1995): 102–6.

de Tocqueville, Alexis. *Democracy in America.* New York: Knopf, 1945 [1835].

Detweiler, Richard C. *Mennonite Statements on Peace 1915–1966.* Scottdale, Pa.: Herald, 1968.

DiMaggio, Paul, and Walter W. Powell. "The Iron Cage Revisited: Institutional Isomorphism and Collective Rationality in Organizational Fields." In *The New Institutionalism in Organizational Analysis,* edited by Paul J. DiMaggio and Walter W. Powell, 63–82. Chicago: Univ. of Chicago Press, 1991.

Dintamin, Stephen F. "The Spiritual Poverty of the Anabaptist Vision." *Conrad Grebel Review* 10 (2) (Spring 1992): 205–8.

"Disarming America—A Real Cause for Alarm." *Guidelines for Today* (May–June 1969): 2.

Douglas, Mary, and Steven M. Tipton, eds. *Religion in America: Spiritual Life in a Secular Age.* Boston: Beacon, 1982.

Drescher, John M., ed. "Vietnam Issue." *Gospel Herald,* 25 Jan. 1966, 65–96.

Driedger, Leo. "The Anabaptist Identification Ladder: Plain Urbane Continuity in Diversity." *Mennonite Quarterly Review* 51 (4) (Oct. 1977): 278–91.

———. "The Christian Involvement in Politics and Government." *The Canadian Mennonite,* 26 Oct. 1962, 5, 7.

———. *The Ethnic Factor: Identity in Diversity.* Toronto: McGraw-Hill Reyerson, 1989.

———. "Identity and Assimilation." In *Anabaptist-Mennonite Identities in Ferment,* edited by Leo Driedger and Leland Harder, 159–81. Elkhart, Ind.: Institute of Mennonite Studies, 1990.

———. *Mennonite Identity in Conflict.* Lewiston, N.Y.: Edwin Mellen, 1988.

———. "The Peace Panorama: Struggle for the Mennonite Soul." *Conrad Grebel Review* 10 (3) (Fall 1992): 289–308.

———. "Some Guides to Consider in Political Involvement." *The Canadian Mennonite,* 2 Nov. 1962, 5, 7.

———, ed. *The Canadian Ethnic Mosaic—A Quest for Identity.* Toronto: McClelland and Stewart, 1978.

Driedger, Leo, and Leland Harder, eds. *Anabaptist-Mennonite Identities in Ferment.* Elkhart, Ind.: Institute of Mennonite Studies, 1990.

Driedger, Leo, and J. Howard Kauffman. *The Mennonite Mosaic: Identity and Modernization.* Scottdale: Herald, 1991.

———. "An Urbanization of Mennonites: Canadian and American Comparisons." *Mennonite Quarterly Review* 66 (3) (July 1982): 269–90.

Driedger, Leo, and Donald B. Kraybill. *Mennonite Peacemaking: From Quietism to Activism.* Scottdale, Pa.: Herald, 1994.

Driedger, Leo, and Calvin Redekop. "Sociology of Mennonites: State of the Arts and Science." *Journal of Mennonite Studies* 1 (1983): 33–63.

Duek, Abe. "Church and State: Developments Among Mennonite Brethren in Canada Since World War II." *Direction* 10 (3) (July 1981): 30–47.

Duek, John. "Forsake a 400-year-old Tradition: Mennonites Enter Politics by the Dozen." *Mennonite Reporter,* 12 Jan. 1976, 10–11.

Dunn, Charles W., ed. *Religion in American Politics.* Washington: Congressional Quarterly Press, 1989.

Durnbaugh, Donald F., ed. *On Earth Peace: Discussions on War/Peace Issues Between Friends, Mennonites, Brethren and European Churches, 1935–1975.* Elgin: Brethren, 1978.

Dyck, Cornelius J., ed. *From the Files of MCC.* Scottdale, Pa.: Herald, 1980.

———. *Introduction to Mennonite History.* Scottdale, Pa.: Herald, 1993.

———. *Responding to Worldwide Needs.* Scottdale, Pa.: Herald, 1980.

———. *Something Meaningful for God.* Scottdale, Pa.: Herald, 1981.

———. *Witness and Service in North America.* Scottdale, Pa.: Herald, 1980.

Dyck, Peter. "A Theology of Service." *Mennonite Quarterly Review* 44 (3) (July 1970): 262–80.

Ebersole, Luke Eugene. *Church Lobbying in the Nation's Capitol.* New York: Macmillan, 1951.

Ediger, Elmer. "A Christian's Political Responsibility." *Mennonite Life* 9 (3) (July 1956): 143–55.

Elbaum, Max. "The Storm at Home: The U.S. Anti-War Movement." In *Beyond the Storm: A Gulf Crisis Reader,* edited by Phyllis Bennis and Michel Moushabeck, 142–59. New York: Olive Branch, 1991.

Elmer, Michael. "Bolivian Regime Moves Against the Church." *Christian Century* 87 (27) (8 July 1970): 851–52.

Elshtain, Jean Bethke. *But Was It Just? Reflections on the Morality of the Persian Gulf War.* New York: Doubleday, 1992.

Epp, Frank H. *Mennonite Peoplehood: A Plea for New Initiatives.* Waterloo: Conrad Grebel, 1977.

———. *Partners in Service: The Story of Mennonite Central Committee Canada.* Winnipeg: Mennonite Central Committee, 1983.

———. "Reflections on an Evolving Christian Vocation." *Mennonite Reporter* 10 (9) (29 April 1980): 9.

———. *A Strategy for Peace: Reflections of A Christian Pacifist.* Grand Rapids: Eerdmans, 1973.

———. *Visions: Speeches and Articles by Frank H. Epp.* Winnipeg: MCC Canada, 1991.

Epp, Joanne. "Canada and Peacekeeping: An Overview." *Peace Office Newsletter* 23 (3) (May–June 1993): 10.

Epp Weaver, Alain. "Options in Postmodern Mennonite Theology." *Conrad Grebel Review* 11 (1) (Winter 1993): 63–76.

Fenn, Richard K. *Liturgies and Trials: The Secularization of Religious Language.* New York: Pilgrim, 1982.

Finke, Roger, and Rodney Stark. *The Churching of America, 1776–1990: Winners and Losers in Our Religious Economy.* New Brunswick: Rutgers Univ. Press, 1992.

Fitzgerald, Gerry. "Religious Groups Orchestrate Opposition to 'Contra' Aid." *Washington Post,* 23 Apr. 1985.

Forell, George, ed. *Christian Social Teachings: A Reader in Christian Social Ethics from the Bible to the Present.* Garden City: Anchor, 1966.

Fowler, Robert Booth. *Religion and Politics in America.* Metuchen, N.J.: Scarecrow, 1985.

———. *Unconventional Partners: Religion and Liberal Culture in the United States.* Grand Rapids: Eerdmans, 1989.

Franz, Delton. "Advocacy: A Biblical Calling." *Washington Memo* 25 (5) (Sept.–Oct. 1993): 1.

———. "Beginnings: Peace Section Washington Office." *Peace Office Newsletter* 22 (5) (Sept.–Oct. 1992): 8.

———. "Biblical/Theological Perspectives on Church and Government." *Washington Memo* 21 (1) (Jan.–Feb. 1989): 3–4.

———. "Bridging the Gap." *Washington Memo* 2 (6) (Nov.–Dec. 1970): 7.

———. "Connecting." *Washington Memo* 23 (4) (July–Aug. 1991): 1–2.

———. "The Growth of Terrorism in the Middle East: Some Causes and Some Remedies." *Washington Memo* 16 (2) (Mar.–Apr. 1984): 1–3.

———. "How We Do Our Work: The Mennonite Voice to Government: Then and Now." *Washington Memo* 21 (1) (Jan.–Feb. 1989): 1–2.

———. "Human Need and Military Demands." *Washington Memo* 1 (1) (Jan. 1969): 2–3.

———. "Lobbying." In *Mennonite Encyclopedia V,* edited by Cornelius J. Dyck and Dennis D. Martin, 528. Scottdale, Pa.: Herald, 1990.

———. "The Law of Unintended Consequences." *Washington Memo* 23 (3) (May–June 1991): 1.

———. "Motives and Modes for the Christian's Interaction with Government." *Washington Memo* 18 (5) (Sept.–Oct. 1986): 1–2.

———. "Nazism Revisited: The Horror of Ethnic Cleansing." *Washington Memo* 25 (2) (Mar.–Apr. 1993): 1.

————. "New Occasions Teach New Duties." *Washington Memo* 24 (2) (Mar.–Apr. 1992): 1.

————. "A New Historical Moment: Biblical/Theological Perspectives." *Washington Memo* 24 (1) (Jan.–Feb. 1992): 1–2.

————. "On Speaking to Government." *Washington Memo* 16 (3) (May–June 1984): 1–2.

————. "Peacekeeping Role of U.N. Imperiled?" *Washington Memo* 24 (2) (Mar.–Apr. 1992): 7.

————. "The Relationship of the Church to the State: Diverse Perspectives within the MCC Family." *Washington Memo* 19 (6) (Nov.–Dec. 1987): 1–2.

————. "The Rich Man and Lazarus: A Reality in Haiti." *Washington Memo* 24 (4) (July–Aug. 1992): 1.

————. "The Spirituality of Advocacy: To Do Justice: Reflections After 20 Years." *Washington Memo* 20 (6) (Nov.–Dec. 1988): 1–2.

————. "United Nations Peacekeeping." *Peace Office Newsletter* 23 (3) (May–June 1993): 11.

————. "Violence Escalates in the Middle East: Peace Initiative Pending." *Washington Memo* 17 (4) (July–Aug. 1985): 1–3.

————. "The Washington Office: Reflections After Ten Years." *Washington Memo* 10 (4) (July–Aug. 1978): 1–2.

Franz, Delton, as interviewed by Robert Kreider. "Planting a Church in a Changing City." *Mennonite Life* (Mar. 1988): 23–27.

Franz, Delton, Carl Kreider, and Andrew and Viola Shelley. *Let My People Choose.* Scottdale, Pa.: Herald, 1969.

Fraser, Nancy. "Rethinking the Public Sphere: A Contribution to the Critique of Actually Existing Democracy." *Social Texts* 25–26 (1990): 56–80.

Fretz, Herbert. "Germantown Anti-Slavery Protest." *Mennonite Life* 13 (4) (Oct. 1958): 183–86.

Fretz, J. Winfield. "Should Mennonites Participate in Politics?" *Mennonite Life* 11 (3) (July 1956): 139–40.

————. *The Waterloo Mennonites: A Community in Paradox.* Waterloo: Wilfrid Laurier Univ. Press, 1989.

Frey, Marv, and Ed Epp. "Are We Being Swayed by a 'CNN Theology' of Peace?" *Mennonite Reporter,* 8 Feb. 1993, 7.

Friedmann, Robert. "Gelassenheit." In *Mennonite Encyclopedia II,* edited by Harold S. Bender et al., 448–49. Scottdale, Pa.: Mennonite Publishing House, 1956.

Friesen, Bert. *Where We Stand: An Index of Peace and Social Concern Statements by the Mennonites and Brethren in Christ in Canada (1787–1982).* Winnipeg: Mennonite Central Committee, 1986.

Friesen, Duane K. *Christian Peacemaking and International Conflict: A Realist Pacifist Perspective.* Scottdale, Pa.: Herald, 1986.

————. "A Critical Analysis of Narrative Ethics." In *The Church as Theological Community: Essays in Honour of David Schroeder,* edited by Harry Huebner, 223–46. Winnipeg: CMBC Publications, 1990.

————. *Mennonite Witness on Peace and Social Concerns, 1900–1980.* Akron, Pa.: Mennonite Central Committee, 1982.

————. "Mennonites and Social Justice: Problems and Prospects." *Mennonite Life* 37 (1) (Mar. 1982): 18–23.

————. "Peacemaking as an Ethical Category: The Convergence of Pacifism and Just War." In *Ethics in the Nuclear Age: Strategy, Religious Studies, and the Churches,* edited by Todd Whitmore, 161–80. Dallas: Southern Methodist Univ. Press, 1989.

————. "Response to Gerald W. Schlabach's 'Beyond Two-/ vs. One-Kingdom Theology: Abrahamic Community as a Mennonite Paradigm for Christian Engagement in Society.'" *Conrad Grebel Review* 12 (1) (Winter 1994): 87–95.

————. "Response to Gerald Schlabach's Response to Duane Friesen's Response to 'Beyond Two-/ vs. One-Kingdom Theology.'" *Conrad Grebel Review* 13 (2) (Spring 1995): 193–96.

————. "Review of *Mennonite Peace Theology: A Panorama of Types.*" *Conrad Grebel Review* 10 (3) (Fall 1992): 341–49.

Friesen, Ken Martens, et al. "Celebrating 25 Years in Washington." *Washington Memo* 25 (5) (Sept.–Oct. 1993): 3–6.

Friesen, Lauren. "Culturally Engaged Pacifism." In *Mennonite Peace Theology: A Panorama of Types,* edited by John Richard Burkholder and Barbara Nelson Gingerich, 15–25. Akron: Mennonite Central Committee Peace Office, Jan. 1991.

Friesen, LeRoy. *Mennonite Witness in the Middle East: A Missiological Introduction.* Elkhart, Ind.: Mennonite Board of Missions, 1992.

Funk Wiebe, Katie. *Day of Disaster.* Scottdale, Pa.: Herald, 1976.

Gaeddart, Albert. "Christian Love in Action: An Essential Aspect of Nonresistance." *Proceedings of the Fourth Mennonite World Conference, 3–10 August 1948,* 257–62. Akron: Mennonite Central Committee, 1950.

Geddert, Ron, ed. "The Church and Sexual Abuse," *Mennonite Brethren Herald,* 7 Dec. 1990, 1–9.

Geyer, Alan F., and Barbara G. Green. *Lines in the Sand: Justice and the Gulf War.* Louisville: Westminster/John Knox, 1992.

Gingerich, Melvin. *The Mennonites in Iowa.* Iowa City: State Historical Society of Iowa, 1939.

————. *Service for Peace: A History of Mennonite Civilian Public Service.* Akron, Pa.: Mennonite Central Committee, 1949.

Gingrich, Keith. "Major Global Changes: A Time for Real Disarmament." *Washington Memo* 23 (6) (Nov.–Dec. 1991): 3.

Goering, Greg W. "Prophetic Witness to the Nations: The Church's Witness to Government." *Washington Memo* 24 (3) (May–June 1992): 1, 12.

Goetz Lichdi, Dieter. *Mennonite World Handbook.* Carol Stream, Ill.: Mennonite World Conference, 1990.

Good, Merle. "Why I Haven't Voted." *Gospel Herald,* 11 Oct. 1988, 698–99.

Graber Miller, Keith. "Bumping into the State: Developing a Washington Presence." *Mennonite Quarterly Review* 70 (1) (Jan. 1996): 81–106.

————. "Mennonite Lobbyists in Washington: Wise as Serpents, Innocent as Doves?" *The Annual of the Society of Christian Ethics* (Nov. 1995): 177–99.

————. "Whirling Toward Similitude? Mennonite Lobbyists in the U.S. Capital." *Conrad Grebel Review* 12 (3) (Fall 1994): 283–97.

Graybill, Dave. "Make Salvation Central, Ad-Hoc Group Tells Church." *Gospel Herald,* 24 July 1979, 586.

Greenawalt, Kent. *Religious Conviction and Political Choice.* New York: Oxford Univ. Press, 1988.

Guth, J., T. G. Jelen, L. A. Kellstedt, C. E. Smidt, and K. D. Wald. "The Politics of Religion in America." *American Politics Quarterly* 16 (3) (July 1988): 357–97.

Gutiérrez, Gustavo. *A Theology of Liberation.* Maryknoll, N.Y.: Orbis, 1973.

Gwyn, Douglas, George Hunsinger, Eugene F. Roop, and John H. Yoder. *A Declaration on Peace: In God's People the World's Renewal Has Begun.* Scottdale, Pa.: Herald, 1991.

Habermas, Jürgen. "Civil Disobedience: Litmus Test for the Democratic Constitutional State." *Berkeley Journal of Sociology* 30 (1985): 96–116.

———. *Communication and the Evolution of Society.* Boston: Beacon, 1979.

———. "Conservatism and Capitalist Crisis." *New Left Review* 115 (May–June 1979): 73–84.

———. *Knowledge and Human Interests.* London: Heinemann, 1972.

———. *Legitimation Crisis.* Trans. T. McCarthy. Boston: Beacon, 1975.

———. "New Social Movements." *Telos* 49 (Fall 1981): 33–37.

———. "On Systematically Distorted Communication." *Inquiry* 13 (1970): 205–18.

———. *The Structural Transformation of the Public Sphere: An Inquiry into a Category of Bourgeois 1.* Trans. Thomas Burger. Cambridge: MIT Press, 1989 [1962].

———. *The Theory of Communicative Action,* Vols. 1 and 2. Trans. T. McCarthy. Boston: Beacon, 1984, 1987.

———. *Toward a Rational Society: Student Protest, Science and Politics.* Boston: Beacon, 1970.

———. "Towards a Theory of Communicative Competence." *Inquiry* 13 (1970): 360–75.

Hackman, Walton. "The Peace Section's Washington Office." *Washington Memo* 1 (1) (Jan. 1969): 1.

Hadden, Jeffrey K. *The Gathering Storm in the Churches.* Garden City: Doubleday, 1969.

Hamm, Peter M. *Continuity and Change Among Canadian Mennonite Brethren.* Waterloo: Wilfrid Laurier Univ. Press, 1987.

Harding, Vincent. "The Peace Witness and Modern Revolutionary Movements." In *The Witness of the Holy Spirit,* edited by Cornelius J. Dyck. Elkhart, Ind.: Mennonite World Conference, n.d., ca. 1967.

Harrington Watt, David. "United States: Cultural Challenges to the Voluntary Sector." In *Between States and Markets: The Voluntary Sector in Comparative Perspective,* edited by Robert Wuthnow, 243–87. Princeton: Princeton Univ. Press, 1991.

Hartzler, J. S., and Daniel Kauffman. *Mennonite Church History.* Scottdale, Pa.: Mennonite Book and Tract Society, 1905.

Hauerwas, Stanley. *Against the Nations: War and Survival in a Liberal Society.* San Francisco: Harper and Row, 1985.

———. *Christian Existence Today: Essays on Church, World and Living in Between.* Durham: Labyrinth, 1988.

———. *A Community of Character.* Notre Dame: Univ. of Notre Dame Press, 1981.

———. "Pacifism: A Form of Politics." In *Peace Betrayed? Essays on Pacifism and Politics,* edited by Michael Cromartie, 133–41. Washington: Ethics and Public Policy Center, 1990.

———. *The Peaceable Kingdom.* Notre Dame: Univ. of Notre Dame Press, 1983.

———. "Will the Real Sectarian Stand Up?" *Theology Today* 44 (1) (Apr. 1987): 87–94.

Hauerwas, Stanley, and William H. Willimon. *Resident Aliens: Life in the Christian Colony.* Nashville: Abingdon, 1989.

Hawkley, Louise, and James C. Juhnke, eds. *Nonviolent America: History through the Eyes of Peace.* North Newton, Kans.: Bethel College, 1993.

Hawley, Amos. "Human Ecology." In *International Encyclopedia of the Social Sciences,* edited by David L. Sills, 328–37. New York: Macmillan, 1968.

Hehir, J. Bryan. "The Catholic Bishops and the Nuclear Debate: A Case Study of the Independent Sector." In *Religion, the Independent Sector, and American Culture,* edited by Conrad Cherry and Rowland A. Sherrill, 97–112. Atlanta: Scholars, 1992.

Hero, Alfred O., Jr. *American Religious Groups View Foreign Policy: Trends in Rank-and-File Opinion, 1937–1969.* Durham: Duke Univ. Press, 1973.

Hershberger, Guy F. "Historical Background to the Formation of the Mennonite Central Committee." *Mennonite Quarterly Review* 44 (2) (July 1970): 213–44.

———. *The Mennonite Church in the Second World War.* Scottdale, Pa.: Mennonite Publishing House, 1951.

———. "A Mennonite Office in Washington?" *Gospel Herald,* 27 Feb. 1968, 186.

———. *Mennonites and Their Heritage, Number V: Christian Relationships to the State and Community.* Akron, Pa.: Mennonite Central Committee, 1942.

———. *Non-resistance and the State—The Pennsylvania Experiment in Politics, 1682–1756.* Scottdale, Pa.: Mennonite Publishing House, 1936.

———. *War, Peace and Nonresistance.* Scottdale, Pa.: Herald, 1944. Revised in 1953 and 1969.

———. "Washington Visitation on Vietnam." *Gospel Herald,* 15 June 1965, 520.

———. *The Way of the Cross in Human Relations.* Scottdale, Pa.: Herald, 1958.

———, ed. *The Recovery of the Anabaptist Vision.* Scottdale, Pa.: Herald, 1957.

Hertzke, Allen D. "An Assessment of the Mainline Churches Since 1945." In *The Role of Religion in the Making of Public Policy,* edited by James E. Wood Jr. and Derek Davis, 43–79. Waco: J. M. Dawson Institute of Church-State Relations, 1991.

———. *Representing God in Washington: The Role of Religious Lobbies in the American Polity.* Knoxville: Univ. of Tennessee Press, 1988.

———. "The Role of Religious Lobbies." In *Religion in American Politics,* edited by Charles W. Dunn, 123–36. Washington: Congressional Quarterly Press, 1989.

Hess, James R. "In My Opinion: AIMM ('Accuracy in Mennonite Media') vs. Deceptions—Lies—Disinformation." *Guidelines for Today* (May–June 1987): 7, 11.

Hiebert, P. C., and Orie O. Miller. *Feeding the Hungry: Russia Famine, 1919–1925.* Scottdale, Pa.: Mennonite Central Committee, 1929.

Hildebrand, Mary Anne. "Domestic Violence: A Challenge to Mennonite Faith and Peace Theology." *Conrad Grebel Review* 10 (1) (Winter 1992): 73–80.

Hillerbrand, Hans J. "The Anabaptist View of the State." *Mennonite Quarterly Review* 32 (2) (Apr. 1958): 83–110.

Hobbes, Thomas. *Leviathan,* edited by Michael Oakeshott. New York: Collier Books, 1962 [1651].

Hofrenning, Daniel J. B. *In Washington But Not of It: The Prophetic Politics of Religious Lobbyists.* Philadelphia: Temple Univ. Press, 1995.

Holderread Heggen, Carolyn. *Sexual Abuse in Christian Homes and Churches.* Scottdale, Pa.: Herald, 1993.

279

Holland, Joe, and Peter Henriot, S.J. *Social Analysis: Linking Faith and Justice.* Washington: Center of Concern, 1980.

Holland, Scott J. "God in Public: A Modest Proposal for a Quest for a Contemporary North American Anabaptist Paradigm." *Conrad Grebel Review* 4 (1) (Winter 1986): 43–55.

———. "The Problems and Prospects of a 'Sectarian Ethic': A Critique of the Hauerwas Reading of the Jesus Story." *Conrad Grebel Review* 10 (2) (Spring 1992): 157–68.

Hollenbach, David, S.J. "The Role of the Churches in the American Search for Peace." In *The American Search for Peace: Moral Reasoning, Religious Hope, and National Security,* edited by George Weigel and John P. Langan, S.J., 237–66. Washington: Georgetown Univ. Press, 1991.

Horsch, James E. *Mennonite Yearbook 1995.* Scottdale, Pa.: Mennonite Publishing House, 1995.

Horst, Irvin. *Handbook of Information on the Mennonite Central Committee.* Akron, Pa.: Mennonite Central Committee, 1950.

———. *A Ministry of Goodwill: A Short Account of Mennonite Relief, 1939–1949.* Akron, Pa.: Mennonite Central Committee, 1950.

Hrebenar, Ronald J., and Ruth K. Scott. *Interest Group Politics in America,* 2d ed. Englewood Cliffs: Prentice Hall, 1990.

Huebner, Harry. "Christian Pacifism and the Character of God." In *The Church as Theological Community: Essays in Honour of David Schroeder,* edited by Harry Huebner, 247–72. Winnipeg: CMBC Publications, 1990.

———. "Mennonites in Dialogue with Governments." *Peace Office Newsletter* 23 (5) (Sept.–Oct. 1993): 1–3.

Hunsinger, George, ed. *Karl Barth and Radical Politics.* Philadelphia: Westminster, 1976.

Hunter, James Davison. *American Evangelicalism: Conservative Religion and the Quandary of Modernity.* New Brunswick: Rutgers Univ. Press, 1982.

———. *Culture Wars: The Struggle to Define America.* New York: Basic, 1991.

———. "The Evangelical Worldview Since 1890." In *Piety and Politics: Evangelicals and Fundamentalists Confront the World,* edited by Richard John Neuhaus and Michael Cromartie, 19–53. Washington: Ethics and Public Policy Center, 1987.

———. *Evangelicalism: The Coming Generation.* Chicago: Chicago Univ. Press, 1987.

Janzen Longacre, Doris. *More-with-Less Cookbook.* Scottdale, Pa.: Herald, 1976.

Janzen, Rod A. *Terry Miller: The Pacifist Politician, from Hutterite Colony to State Capitol.* Freeman, S.D.: Pine Hill Press, 1986.

Janzen, William. "I thought the Mennonites might be able to help Canadian society on the question of caring for children." *Peace Office Newsletter* 23 (5) (Sept.–Oct. 1993): 8.

———. *Mennonite Submissions to the Canadian Government: A Collection of Documents Prepared by the Ottawa Office of Mennonite Central Committee Canada, 1975–1990.* Ottawa: MCC Canada, 1990.

———. "Politics—Is It for Mennonites?" *With* (October 1976): 6–9.

———. "Sharing Our Perspectives and Pressing Them." *Mennonite Brethren Herald,* 6 Nov. 1981, 20–21.

———. "U.N. Military Enforcement Action: Should Mennonites Condemn It?" *Peace Office Newsletter* 23 (3) (May–June 1993): 8–9.

Johnson, Benton. "Church and Sect Revisited." *Journal for the Scientific Study of Religion* 10 (2) (1971): 124–37.

Johnson, James Turner. *Ideology, Reason and the Limitation of War: Religious and Secular Concepts, 1200–1740.* Princeton: Princeton Univ. Press, 1975.

———. *Just War Tradition and the Restraint of War: A Moral and Historical Inquiry.* Princeton: Princeton Univ. Press, 1981.

Johnson, James Turner, and George Weigel. *Just War and the Gulf War.* Washington: Ethics and Public Policy Center, 1991.

Jonsen, Albert R. "Responsibility." In *The Westminster Dictionary of Christian Ethics,* edited by James F. Childress and John Macquarrie, 545–49. Philadelphia: Westminster, 1986.

Juhnke, James C. "Mennonite History and Self Understanding: North American Mennonitism as a Bipolar Mosaic." In *Mennonite Identity: Historical and Contemporary Perspectives,* edited by Calvin Redekop and Samuel Steiner, 83–99. Lanham: Univ. Press of America, 1988.

———. "A Mennonite Runs for Congress." *Mennonite Life* 26 (1) (Jan. 1971): 8–11.

———. "Our Almost Unused Political Power." *Gospel Herald,* 9 Jan. 1968, 38–39.

———. *A People of Two Kingdoms: The Political Acculturation of the Kansas Mennonites.* Newton, Kans.: Faith and Life Press, 1975.

———. "Political Attitudes." In *Mennonite Encyclopedia V,* edited by Cornelius J. Dyck and Dennis D. Martin, 710–11. Scottdale, Pa.: Herald, 1990.

———. *Vision, Doctrine, War: Mennonite Identity and Organization in America, 1890–1930.* Scottdale, Pa.: Herald, 1989.

Kamens, David H., and Tormod K. Lunde. "Institutional Theory and the Expansion of Central State Organizations, 1960–1980." In *Institutional Patterns and Organizations: Culture and Environment,* edited by Lynne G. Zucker, 169–95. Cambridge: Ballinger, 1988.

Kauffman, J. Howard. "Boundary Maintenance and Cultural Assimilation of Contemporary Mennonites." *Mennonite Quarterly Review* 51 (3) (July 1977): 227–40.

———. "Dilemmas of Christian Pacifism Within a Historic Peace Church." *Sociological Analysis* 49 (4) (Winter 1989): 368–85.

Kauffman, J. Howard, and Leo Driedger. *The Mennonite Mosaic: Identity and Modernization.* Scottdale, Pa.: Herald, 1991.

Kauffman, J. Howard, and Leland Harder. *Anabaptism Four Centuries Later: A Profile of Five Mennonite and Brethren in Christ Denominations.* Scottdale: Herald, 1991.

Kauffman, Richard A. "Innocence Lost?" *Gospel Herald,* 6 Mar. 1984, 16.

Kauffman, Richard A., David E. Hostetler, and Lois Barrett. "The Patty Erb Story—One Year Later." *Gospel Herald,* 27 Sept. 1977, 726–27.

Keener, Carl S. "Some Reflections on Mennonites and Postmodern Thought." *Conrad Grebel Review* 11 (1) (Winter 1993): 47–61.

Kehler, Larry. "The Many Activities of the Mennonite Central Committee." *Mennonite Quarterly Review* 44 (3) (July 1970): 298–315.

———. "The State Needs the Christian Witness." *The Mennonite,* 10 Jan. 1967, 22–24.

Keim, Albert N. *The CPS Story: An Illustrated History of Civilian Public Service.* Intercourse, Pa.: Good Books, 1990.

———. "Service or Resistance? The Mennonite Response to Conscription in World War II." *Mennonite Quarterly Review* 52 (2) (Apr. 1978): 141–55.

Keim, Albert N., and Grant M. Stoltzfus. *The Politics of Conscience: The Historic Peace Churches and America at War, 1917–1955.* Scottdale, Pa.: Herald, 1988.

Kelley, Dean M. *Why Conservative Churches Are Growing.* New York: Harper and Row, 1972.

Keohane, Robert O. "International Institutions: Two Research Programs." *International Studies Quarterly* 32 (4) (Dec. 1988): 379–96.

Kephart, William M. *Extraordinary Groups: The Sociology of Unconventional Lifestyles.* New York: St. Martin's, 1976.

Kimball, Charles A. *Religion, Politics and Oil: The Volatile Mix in the Middle East.* Nashville: Abingdon, 1992.

Kissinger, Henry A. *Nuclear Weapons and Foreign Policy.* New York: Harper and Row, 1957.

Klaassen, Walter. *Anabaptism: Neither Catholic nor Protestant.* Waterloo: Conrad, 1973.

———. "The Christian and the State." *The Mennonite,* 9 July 1974, 428–29.

———. "'Of Divine and Human Justice': The Early Swiss Brethren and Government." *Conrad Grebel Review* 10 (2) (Spring 1992): 169–85.

———. "The Quest for Anabaptist Identity." In *Anabaptist-Mennonite Identities in Ferment,* edited by Leo Driedger and Leland Harder, 13–26. Elkhart, Ind.: Institute of Mennonite Studies, 1990.

———, ed. *Anabaptism in Outline: Selected Primary Sources.* Scottdale, Pa.: Herald, 1981.

Klassen, Mike. "Why U.S. Mennonites Talk Democrat But Vote Republican." *The Mennonite,* 13 Oct. 1992, 435–37.

Koontz, Ted. "Christian Ethics and Political Ethics: An Irreducible Conflict?" In *Prophetic Vision Applied to One's Academic Discipline,* edited by John Rempel and Robert Charles, 11–25. Elkhart, Ind.: Mennonite Board of Missions, 1979.

———. "Church-State Relations." In *Mennonite Encyclopedia V,* edited by Cornelius J. Dyck and Dennis D. Martin, 159–62. Scottdale: Herald, 1990.

———. "Hard Choices: Abortion and War." *The Mennonite,* 28 Feb. 1978, 132–34.

———. "Mennonites and 'Postmodernity.'" *Mennonite Quarterly Review* 63 (4) (Oct. 1989): 401–27.

———. "Mennonites and the State: Preliminary Reflections." In *Essays on Peace Theology and Witness,* edited by Willard M. Swartley, 35–60. Elkhart, Ind.: Institute of Mennonite Studies, 1988.

———. "Reflections on American Mennonites and Politics." *The Window* 10 (1) (Oct. 1982): 1–2.

———. "Theology, Ethics, and the 'Facts.'" *The Mennonite,* 22 Dec. 1981, 744.

———. "The Theology of MCC: A Christian Resource for Extending God's Blessing." *Mennonite Quarterly Review* 70 (1) (Jan. 1996).

Krahn, Cornelius, J. Winfield Fretz, and Robert Kreider. "Altruism in Mennonite Life." In *Forms and Techniques of Altruistic and Spiritual Growth,* edited by Pitirim Sorokin, 309–28. Boston: Beacon, 1954.

Krasner, Stephen D., ed. *International Regimes.* Ithaca: Cornell Univ. Press, 1983.

Kraus, C. Norman. *Christians and the State.* Scottdale, Pa.: Mennonite Publishing House, 1956.

Kraybill, Donald B., ed. *The Amish and the State.* Baltimore: Johns Hopkins Univ. Press, 1993.

Kraybill, Donald B. "From Enclave to Engagement: MCC and the Transformation of Mennonite Identity." *Mennonite Quarterly Review* 70 (1) (Jan. 1996): 23–58.

———. "Modernity and Identity: The Transformation of Mennonite Ethnicity." In *Mennonite Identity: Historical and Contemporary Perspectives,* edited by Calvin Redekop and Samuel Steiner, 153–72. Lanham: Univ. Press of America, 1988.

———. "Modernity and Modernization." In *Anabaptist-Mennonite Identities in Ferment,* edited by Leo Driedger and Leland Harder, 91–109. Elkhart: Institute of Mennonite Studies, 1990.

———. *Our Star-Spangled Faith.* Scottdale, Pa.: Herald, 1976.

Kreider, Robert. "The Anabaptists and the State." In *The Recovery of the Anabaptist Vision,* edited by Guy F. Hershberger, 180–93. Scottdale, Pa.: Herald, 1957.

———. "The Impact of MCC Service on American Mennonites." *Mennonite Quarterly Review* 44 (3) (July 1970): 245–61.

Kreider, Robert, and Rachel Waltner Goossen. *Hungry, Thirsty, Stranger: The Mennonite Central Committee Experience.* Scottdale, Pa.: Herald, 1988.

Lapp, John A. "The Christian and Politics: How Do We Participate: Hold Office, Vote, or Primarily Pray?" *The Christian Leader,* 26 Oct. 1967, 6–7.

———. "Civil Religion Is But Old Establishment Writ Large." In *Kingdom, Cross and Community,* edited by John Richard Burkholder and Calvin Redekop, 196–207. Scottdale, Pa.: Herald, 1976.

———. "If I Were Writing the History of MCC Peace Testimony." *Peace Office Newsletter* 22 (5) (Sept.–Oct. 1992): 2–3.

———. "The Peace Mission of the Mennonite Central Committee." *Mennonite Quarterly Review* 44 (3) (July 1970): 281–97.

———. "Review of *The Struggle for America's Soul.*" *Conrad Grebel Review* 8 (2) (Spring 1990): 232–35.

———, ed. *Peacemakers in a Broken World.* Scottdale, Pa.: Herald, 1969.

Lawton, Kim. A. "Lobbying for God." *Christianity Today,* 16 July 1990, 32–34.

Leamon, David. "Politicized Service and Teamwork Tensions: MCC in Vietnam, 1966–1969." *Mennonite Quarterly Review* 70 (1) (Jan. 1996).

Lehman, M. C. *The History and Principles of Mennonite Relief Work: An Introduction.* Akron, Pa.: Mennonite Central Committee, 1945.

Lehman Schlozman, Kay, and John T. Tierney. *Organized Interests and American Democracy.* New York: Harper and Row, 1986.

Levitt, Theodore. *The Third Sector: New Tactics for a Responsible Society.* New York: AMACOM, 1973.

Lewy, Guenter. *Peace and Revolution: The Moral Crisis of American Pacifism.* Grand Rapids: Eerdmans, 1988.

Liechty, Daniel. "Witness to the State Is a Part of Faith Itself." *Gospel Herald,* 22 Sept. 1993, 6–8.

Lind, Millard. *Monotheism, Power, Justice.* Elkhart, Ind.: Institute of Mennonite Studies, 1990.

Lindbeck, George. "The Sectarian Future of the Church." In *The God Experience,* edited by Joseph P. Whalen, 226–43. Paramus: Newman, 1971.

Lintner, Jay. *Just Peace Theology and the Gulf War.* Washington: United Church of Christ Office for Church in Society, Feb. 1991.

Littell, Franklin H. "The Inadequacy of Modern Pacifism." *Christianity and Society* 11 (2) (Spring 1946): 18–23.

————. "The New Shape of the Church-State Issue." *Mennonite Quarterly Review* 40 (3) (July 1966): 179–89.

Loewen, Esko. "Church and State." *Mennonite Life* 11 (3) (July 1956): 141–42.

Loewen, Harry. "The Anabaptist View of the World: The Beginning of a Mennonite Continuum?" In *Mennonite Images: Historical, Cultural, and Literary Essays Dealing with Mennonite Issues,* edited by Harry Loewen, 85–95. Winnipeg: Hyperion, 1980.

————. "Church and State in the Anabaptist-Mennonite Tradition: Christ *Versus* Caesar." In *Baptism, Peace and the State in the Reformed and Mennonite Traditions,* edited by Ross T. Bender and Alan P. F. Sells, 145–65. Waterloo: Wilfrid Laurier Univ. Press, 1991.

————, ed. *Mennonite Images: Historical, Cultural and Literary Essays Dealing with Mennonite Issues.* Winnipeg: Hyperion, 1980.

Loewen, Howard John. "A Response to John Richard Burkholder: Mennonite Peace Theology: Continuing the Reconnaissance and Exploration." *Conrad Grebel Review* 10 (3) (Fall 1992): 277–87.

Loewen Reimer, Margaret. "MCC Board Discusses Somalia, Approves New Peace Statement." *Gospel Herald,* 16 Mar. 1993, 11.

MacGregor, G. H. C. *The New Testament Basis of Pacifism and the Relevance of an Impossible Ideal: An Answer to the Views of Reinhold Niebuhr.* Nyack: Fellowship, 1954.

————. *The Relevance of the Impossible.* London, 1941.

MacMaster, Richard K. *Land, Piety, Peoplehood: The Establishment of Mennonite Communities in America, 1683–1790.* Scottdale, Pa.: Herald, 1985.

MacMaster, Richard K., Samuel L. Horst, and Robert F. Ulle. *Conscience in Crisis: Mennonites and Other Peace Churches in America, 1739–1789: Interpretation and Documents.* Scottdale, Pa.: Institute of Mennonite Studies, 1979.

Martin, David. *Pacifism: An Historical and Sociological Study.* New York: Schocken, 1966.

Martin, Harold S. "Humanistic Tendencies in the Peace Churches." *Brethren Revival Fellowship Witness* 14 (5) (1979): 1–8.

Martin, Luke, James Metzler, Everett Metzler, and Donald Sensenig. "A Missionary Concern." *The Mennonite* (25 Jan. 1966): 63.

Marty, Martin E. "Church, State, and Religious Freedom." In *Religion and the Public Good: A Bicentennial Forum,* edited by John F. Wilson, 81–99. Macon, Ga.: Mercer Univ. Press, 1988.

————. "On 'Being Prophetic.'" *Christian Century* (14 May 1980): 559.

————. *The Public Church: Mainline—Evangelical—Catholic.* New York: Crossroad, 1981.

"MCC Presents Vietnam Letter." *Gospel Herald,* 21 Nov. 1967, 1069–70.

"An MCC U.S. Call to Reduce the Military Budget." *Washington Memo* 24 (1) (Jan.–Feb. 1992): 4.

McCann, Dennis P. "Liberation Theology." In *The Westminster Dictionary of Christian Ethics,* edited by James F. Childress and John Macquarrie, 349–50. Philadelphia: Westminster, 1986.

McCann, Dennis P., and Charles R. Strain. *Polity and Praxis: A Program for American Practical Theology.* Minneapolis: Winston, 1985.

McDowell, Stephen D. "Mennonites, The Canadian State, and Globalization in International Political Economy." *Conrad Grebel Review* 12 (1) (Winter 1994): 21–42.

McGuire, Meredith B. *Religion: The Social Context.* Belmont, Calif.: Wadsworth, 1987.

Mead, Sidney E. *The Lively Experiment: The Shaping of Christianity in America.* New York: Harper and Row, 1963.

———. *The Nation with the Soul of a Church.* New York: Harper and Row, 1975.

Mendel Schmidt, Doris, ed. *Handbook of Information, General Conference Mennonite Church.* Newton, Kans.: General Conference Mennonite Church, 1992.

Mennonite Central Committee. *Mennonites and Their Heritage: A Series of Six Studies Designed for Use in Civilian Public Service Camps.* Akron, Pa.: Mennonite Central Committee, 1942.

———. *A New Look at the Church and State Issue.* Akron, Pa.: MCC, Mar. 1966.

———. *Twenty-Five Years, The Story of MCC, 1920–1945.* Akron, Pa.: Mennonite Central Committee, 1946.

Mennonite Church. *Mennonite Confession of Faith.* Scottdale, Pa.: Herald, 1963.

"The Mennonite Church's Political Stance of the Past Two Decades." *Guidelines for Today* (Mar.–Apr. 1989): 22–23.

Mennonite Church and General Conference Mennonite Church. *Justice and the Christian Witness.* Scottdale, Pa.: Mennonite Publishing House, 1982.

Mennonite General Conference. *Peace and the Christian Witness.* Scottdale, Pa.: Herald, 1951.

Mennonite World Conference. "Mennonite and Brethren in Christ World Directory 1994." *Courier* 9 (1) (First Quarter 1994): 9–15.

Menos, Dennis. *Arms Over Diplomacy: Reflections on the Persian Gulf War.* Westport, Conn.: Praeger, 1992.

Metzler, James. *From Saigon to Shalom.* Scottdale, Pa.: Herald, 1985.

Meyer, John W., and Brian Rowan. "Institutionalized Organizations: Formal Structure as Myth and Ceremony." In *The New Institutionalism in Organizational Analysis,* edited by Walter W. Powell and Paul J. DiMaggio, 41–62. Chicago: Univ. of Chicago Press, 1991.

Miguez Bonino, Jose. *Doing Theology in a Revolutionary Situation.* Philadelphia: Fortress, 1975.

Milbrath, Lester W. *The Washington Lobbyists.* Westport, Conn.: Greenwood, 1963.

Miller, Donald E. "A Biblical Approach to Human Rights." In *Peace, Politics, and the People of God,* edited by Paul Peachey, 163–75. Philadelphia: Fortress, 1986.

Miller, John W. "Schleitheim Pacifism and Modernity: Notes toward the Construction of a Contemporary Mennonite Pacifist Apologetic." *Conrad Grebel Review* 3 (2) (Spring 1985): 155–63.

Miller, Joseph S., ed. "Mennonite Experience Between the Wars." *Mennonite Quarterly Review* 60 (1) (Jan. 1986): 5–103.

Miller, Larry. "Global Mennonite Faith Profile: Past, Present, Future." *Mennonite Weekly Review,* 9 Sept. 1993, 1–2.

Miller, Levi. "Daniel Musser and Leo Tolstoy." *Mennonite Historical Bulletin* 54 (2) (Apr. 1993): 1–7.

———. "Why I Sat Out the Gulf War." *Gospel Herald,* 5 May 1992, 1–3.

Miller, Richard B. *Interpretations of Conflict: Ethics, Pacifism, and the Just-War Tradition.* Chicago: Univ. of Chicago Press, 1991.

Moller Okin, Susan. *Justice, Gender, and the Family.* New York: Basic, 1989.

Morgenthau, Hans J. *In Defense of the National Interest.* New York: Knopf, 1951.

Motley Hallum, Anne. "Presbyterians as Political Amateurs." In *Religion in American Politics,* edited by Charles W. Dunn, 63–73. Washington: Congressional Quarterly Press, 1989.

Mouw, Richard J. *Political Evangelism.* Grand Rapids: Eerdmans, 1973.

———. *Politics and the Biblical Drama.* Grand Rapids: Eerdmans, 1976.

Musser, Daniel M. *Non-Resistance Reasserted: or the Kingdom of Christ and the Kingdom of this World Separated.* Lancaster: Elias Barr and Co., 1864.

Muste, A. J. *Pacifism and Perfectionism.* New York, ca. 1951.

National Conference of Catholic Bishops. *The Challenge of Peace: God's Promise and Our Response.* Washington: U.S. Catholic Conference, 1983.

National Council of Churches. *Pressing for Peace: The Churches Act in the Gulf Crisis.* New York: National Council of Churches Middle East Office, 1991.

Nelson Gingerich, Barbara. "Radical Pacifism." In *Mennonite Peace Theology: A Panorama of Types,* edited by John Richard Burkholder and Barbara Nelson Gingerich, 42–51. Akron: Mennonite Central Committee Peace Office, Jan. 1991.

Nelson-Pallmeyer, Jack. *Brave New World Order: Must We Pledge Allegiance?* Maryknoll, N.Y.: Orbis, 1992.

Neufeld, Elmer. "Christian Responsibility in the Political Situation." *Mennonite Quarterly Review* 32 (2) (Apr. 1958): 141–62.

Neufeld, Mark. "Critical Theory and Christian Service: Knowledge and Action in Situations of Social Conflict." *Conrad Grebel Review* 6 (3) (Fall 1988): 249–61.

———. "Responding to Realism: Assessing Anabaptist Alternatives." *Conrad Grebel Review* 12 (1) (Winter 1994): 43–62.

Neufeld, Vernon H., ed. *If We Can Love: The Mennonite Mental Health Story.* Newton, Kans.: Faith and Life, 1983.

Neuhaus, Richard John. *The Naked Public Square: Religion and Democracy in America.* Grand Rapids: Eerdmans, 1984.

Neuhaus, Richard John, and Michael Cromartie. *Piety and Politics: Evangelicals and Fundamentalists Confront the World.* Washington: Ethics and Public Policy Center, 1987.

News Services. "Hope Turns to Hostility in Somalia." *Atlanta Constitution,* 15 Dec. 1992, 1.

Niebuhr, H. Richard. *Christ and Culture.* New York: Harper and Row, 1951.

———. *The Social Sources of Denominationalism.* Gloucester: Peter Smith, 1984.

Niebuhr, Reinhold. *Christian Realism and Political Problems.* New York: Scribner's, 1953.

———. *Christianity and Power Politics.* New York: Charles Scribner's Sons, 1969 [1940].

———. *An Interpretation of Christian Ethics.* New York: Harper and Brothers, 1934.

———. "Liberalism: Illusions and Realities." *New Republic* 133 (4 July 1955): 11–12.

———. *Love and Justice: Selections from the Shorter Writings of Reinhold Niebuhr,* edited by D. B. Robertson. Philadelphia: Westminster, 1957.

———. *Moral Man and Immoral Society: A Study in Ethics and Politics.* New York: Charles Scribner's Sons, 1932.

———. "Why the Christian Church Is Not Pacifist." In *The Essential Reinhold Niebuhr: Selected Essays and Addresses,* edited by Robert McAfee Brown, 102–19. New Haven: Yale Univ. Press, 1986 [1939].

———. *Reinhold Niebuhr on Politics: His Political Philosophy and Its Application to Our Age as Expressed in His Writings.* Edited by Harry R. Davis and Robert C. Good. New York: Charles Scribner's Sons, 1960.

Nisly, Hope. "Witness to the Way of Peace: The Vietnam War and the Evolving Mennonite View of Their Relationship to the State." *The Maryland Historian* 20 (1) (1989): 7–23.

Noll, Mark A. *One Nation Under God? Christian Faith and Political Action in America.* San Francisco: Harper and Row, 1988.

———, ed. *Religion and American Politics: From the Colonial Period to the 1980s.* New York: Oxford Univ. Press, 1990.

Nolt, Steve. "The CPS Frozen Fund: The Beginning of Peace-Time Interaction Between Historic Peace Churches and the United States Government." *Mennonite Quarterly Review* 67 (2) (Apr. 1993): 201–24.

North, Wayne. "A Final Look at the '80s." *Gospel Herald,* 22 May 1990, 356–57.

Olshan, Marc. "The National Amish Steering Committee." In *The Amish and the State,* edited by Donald B. Kraybill, 67–84. Baltimore: Johns Hopkins Univ. Press, 1993.

Osgood, Robert. *Limited War: The Challenge to American Strategy.* Chicago: Univ. of Chicago Press, 1957.

Oyer, John S. *Anabaptists, the Law and the State.* Washington: Marpeck Academy, 1985.

———, ed. "Anabaptist Dialogue with Liberation Theology." *Mennonite Quarterly Review* 63 (2) (Apr. 1989): 150–209.

Payne, Keith B., and Karl P. Payne. *A Just Defense: The Use of Force, Nuclear Weapons and Our Conscience.* Portland: Multnomah, 1987.

"Peace Churches Polarized by Peace Witness." *The Mennonite,* 16 Feb. 1971, 102–3.

"Peace Section Opens Washington Office." *Gospel Herald,* 13 Aug. 1968, 733.

Peachey, J. Lorne. "Feeding the Hungry with Messy Theology." *Gospel Herald,* 12 Jan. 1993, 16.

———. "If I Were a Voting Mennonite." *Gospel Herald,* 27 Oct. 1992, 16.

Peachey, Paul. *Biblical Realism Confronts the Nation.* Fellowship Publications, 1963.

———. "The 'Free Church': A Time Whose Idea Has Not Come." In *Anabaptism Revisited,* edited by Walter Klaassen, 173–88. Scottdale, Pa.: Herald, 1992.

———. "Identity Crisis Among American Mennonites." *Mennonite Quarterly Review* 42 (3) (July 1968): 243–59.

———. "The Peace Churches as Ecumenical Witness." In *Kingdom, Cross and Community,* edited by John Richard Burkholder and Calvin Redekop, 247–58. Scottdale, Pa.: Herald, 1976.

———, ed. *Peace, Politics, and the People of God.* Philadelphia: Fortress, 1986.

Peachey, Titus, and Linda Gehman Peachey. *Seeking Peace.* Intercourse, Pa.: Good Books, 1991.

Peachey, Urbane, ed. *Mennonite Statements on Peace and Social Concerns.* Akron: MCC U.S. Peace Section, 1980.

———. *The Role of the Church in Society: An International Perspective.* Carol Stream, Ill.: International Mennonite Peace Committee, Mennonite World Conference, 1988.

Peachey, Urbane, et al. "Anabaptism, Oppression and Liberation in Central America." *Mennonite Quarterly Review* 58, Supplement (Aug. 1984): 232–43.

Perry, Michael J. *Love and Power: The Role of Religion and Morality in American Politics.* New York: Oxford Univ. Press, 1991.

———. *Morality, Politics, and Law.* New York: Oxford Univ. Press, 1988.

Peters, Cynthia, ed. *Collateral Damage: The New World Order at Home and Abroad.* Boston: South End, 1992.

Pitkin, Hanna Fenichel. *The Concept of Representation.* Berkeley: Univ. of California Press, 1967.

———. *Representation.* New York: Atherton, 1969.

Powell, Walter W., and Paul J. DiMaggio, eds. *The New Institutionalism in Organizational Analysis.* Chicago: Univ. of Chicago Press, 1991.

Preheim, Rich. "MCC Official Attends Mideast Peace Ceremony." *Mennonite Weekly Review,* 16 Sept. 1993, 1.

———. "Mennonite Candidates Feel Called to Political Action." *Mennonite Weekly Review,* 22 Oct. 1992, 1–2.

———. "Mennonite Politicians May Face Challenges When They Take Beliefs Into Politics." *Mennonite Weekly Review,* 29 Oct. 1992, 1–2.

Price, Tom. "Conservative Mennonites, Amish Raise Voices in Political Arenas" and "Old Order Amish Flex Political Muscle." *Gospel Herald,* 29 Mar. 1994, 10–11.

———. "Pacifist Heritage Forgotten in Some Denominations" and "A Warning to Mennonites?" *Mennonite Reporter* 22 (1) (2 Nov. 1992): 9.

Radford Ruether, Rosemary. *Sexism and God-Talk: Toward a Feminist Theology: With a New Introduction.* Boston, Beacon, 1993.

Ramsey, Paul. *Basic Christian Ethics.* New York: Charles Scribner's Sons, 1953.

———. *Speak Up for Just War or Pacifism: A Critique of the United Methodist Bishops' Pastoral Letter "In Defense of Creation."* University Park: Pennsylvania State Univ. Press, 1988.

———. *Who Speaks for the Church?* New York: Abingdon, 1967.

Ratzlaff, Don. "Ultimate Church Committee Knows Message." *Mennonite Weekly Review,* 9 Feb. 1989, 1.

Rawls, John. "Justice as Fairness: Political Not Metaphysical." *Philosophy and Public Affairs* 14 (3) (Summer 1985): 223–51.

———. "Kantian Constructivism in Moral Theory: Rational and Full Autonomy." *Journal of Philosophy* 77 (9) (Sept. 1980): 515–72.

———. *A Theory of Justice.* Cambridge: Harvard Univ. Press, 1971.

Redekop, Calvin. "The Mennonite Central Committee Story: A Review Essay." *Mennonite Quarterly Review* 67 (1) (Jan. 1993): 84–103.

———. "The Mennonite Identity Crisis." *Journal of Mennonite Studies* 2 (1984): 87–103.

———. *Mennonite Society.* Baltimore: Johns Hopkins Univ. Press, 1989.

———. "The Organizational Children of MCC." *Mennonite Historical Bulletin* 56 (1) (Jan. 1995): 1–8.

———. "A New Look at Sect Development." *Journal for the Scientific Study of Religion* 13 (1974): 345–52.

———. "Religion and Society; a State Within a Church." *Mennonite Quarterly Review* 47 (4) (Oct. 1973): 339–57.

———. "Sectarianism and Cultural Mandate." In *Mennonite Encyclopedia V,* edited by Cornelius J. Dyck and Dennis D. Martin, 806–7. Scottdale, Pa.: Herald, 1990.

———. "Sectarianism and the Sect Cycle." In *Anabaptist-Mennonite Identities in Ferment,* edited by Leo Driedger and Leland Harder, 59–83. Elkhart, Ind.: Institute of Mennonite Studies, 1990.

———. "The Sociology of Mennonite Identity: A Second Opinion." In *Mennonite Identity: Historical and Contemporary Perspectives,* edited by Calvin Redekop and Samuel J. Steiner, 173–92. Lanham: Univ. Press of America, 1988.

Redekop, Calvin, and Samuel Steiner, eds. *Mennonite Identity: Historical and Contemporary Perspectives.* Lanham, Md.: Univ. Press of America, 1988.

Redekop, John H. "Canadian and U.S. Election Campaigns Change Roles." *The Mennonite,* 17 Oct. 1972, 601–2.

———. "Canadian Pacifism." In *Mennonite Peace Theology: A Panorama of Types,* edited by John Richard Burkholder and Barbara Nelson Gingerich, 60–68. Akron: Mennonite Central Committee Peace Office, Jan. 1991.

———. "Church and State: the Boundaries Blur." *Peace Office Newsletter* (Sept.–Oct. 1993): 10–12.

———. "Church and State in Canada." In *The Believers' Church in Canada,* edited by Jarold K. Zeman and Walter Klaassen, 191–205. Brandford: Baptist Federation of Canada and MCC Canada, 1979.

———. "Evangelical Christianity and Political Ideology." *Christian Living* (May 1970): 26–27.

———. "Involvement in the Political Order." *The Christian Leader,* 27 Sept. 1977, 10–14.

———. *Making Political Decisions: A Christian Perspective.* Scottdale, Pa.: Herald, 1972.

———. "Mennonite Politicians." *Mennonite Brethren Herald,* 23 Dec. 1988, 8.

———. "Mennonites and Politics in Canada and the United States." *Journal of Mennonite Studies* 1 (1983): 79–105.

———. "A Perspective on Anabaptist Pacifism in Canada." In *Mennonite Peace Theology: A Panorama of Types,* edited by John Richard Burkholder and Barbara Nelson Gingerich, 60–68. Akron: Mennonite Central Committee Peace Office, Jan. 1991.

———. "Politics." In *Mennonite Encyclopedia V,* edited by Cornelius J. Dyck and Dennis D. Martin, 711–14. Scottdale, Pa.: Herald, 1990.

———. "A Re-Assessment of Some Traditional Anabaptist Church-State Perspectives." In *Essays on Peace Theology and Witness,* edited by Willard M. Swartley, 61–72. Elkhart, Ind.: Institute of Mennonite Studies, 1988.

———. "The State and the Free Church." In *Kingdom, Cross and Community,* edited by John Richard Burkholder and Calvin Redekop, 179–95. Scottdale, Pa.: Herald, 1976.

Regehr, Ernie. "Response to Mark W. Charlton's 'Pursuing Human Justice in a Society of States: The Ethical Dilemmas of Armed Humanitarian Intervention.'" *Conrad Grebel Review* 12 (2) (Spring 1994): 217–21.

———. "Two Formative Influences on the Post–World War II North American Mennonite Church." *Peace Office Newsletter* 21 (6) (Nov.–Dec. 1991): 7.

Regehr, Ernie, and Simon Rosenblum. *The Road To Peace.* Toronto: James Lorimer, 1988.

Regehr, John. "Jesus and the State." *Direction* 5 (3) (July 1976): 30–33.

Reichley, A. James. *Religion in American Public Life.* Washington: Brookings Institution, 1985.

Reimer, A. James. "Toward a Christian Theology from a Diversity of Mennonite Perspectives." *Conrad Grebel Review* 6 (2) (Spring 1988): 147–59.

Rempel, John. "The Mission of the Church and Modern Humanitarian Institutions: The Case of the U.N." *Peace Office Newsletter* 23 (3) (May–June 1993): 12.

————. "Spirituality and Peacemaking among Mennonites: An Overview." *Peace Office Newsletter* 23 (4) (July–Aug. 1993): 1–2.

————. "Work by the Church Does Make a Difference." *Gospel Herald,* 10 Nov. 1992, 8.

Rempel, John, et al. "Mennonites Working with the United Nations." *Peace Office Newsletter* 25 (1) (Jan.–Mar. 1995): 1–12.

Richard, Phil. "Native American Leaders Oppose Legalizing Peyote." *Mennonite Weekly Review,* 24 June 1993, 3.

Richey, Russell. "Institutional Forms of Religion." In *Encyclopedia of the American Religious Experience,* edited by Charles H. Lippy and Peter W. Williams, 31–50. New York: Scribner's, 1988.

Richey, Russell, and R. Bruce Mullin, eds., *Reimagining Denominationalism.* New York: Oxford Univ. Press, 1994.

Roof, Wade Clark, and William McKinney. *American Mainline Religion: Its Changing Shape and Future.* New Brunswick: Rutgers Univ. Press, 1987.

Rorty, Richard. "The Priority of Democracy Over Philosophy." In *The Virginia Statute for Religious Freedom,* edited by Merrill D. Peterson and Richard Vaughan, 257–82. New York: Cambridge Univ. Press, 1988.

Rousseau, Jean-Jacques. *The Social Contract,* trans. by G. D. H. Cole. London: J. M. Dent and Sons, 1973 [1762].

Rubinson, Richard. "Dependence, Government Revenue, and Economic Growth, 1955–1970." In *National Development and the World System,* edited by John W. Meyer and M. T. Hannan, 207–222. Chicago: Univ. of Chicago Press, 1979.

Sandel, Michael J. *Liberalism and the Limits of Justice.* New York: Cambridge Univ. Press, 1981.

————. "The Procedural Republic and the Unencumbered Self." *Political Theory* 12 (1) (Feb. 1984): 81–96.

Sartre, Jean-Paul. *Dirty Hands.* In *No Exit and Three Other Plays,* 131–248. New York: Vintage, 1955.

Sawatsky, Rodney J. *Authority and Identity: The Dynamics of the General Conference Mennonite Church.* North Newton, Kans.: Bethel College, 1987.

————. "Beyond the Social History of the Mennonites: A Response to James C. Juhnke." In *Mennonite Identity: Historical and Contemporary Perspectives,* edited by Calvin Redekop and Samuel Steiner, 101–8. Lanham, Md.: Univ. Press of America, 1988.

————. "Defining 'Mennonite' Diversity and Unity." *Mennonite Quarterly Review* 57 (3) (July 1983): 282–92.

————. "The One and the Many: The Recovery of Mennonite Pluralism." In *Anabaptism Revisited,* edited by Walter Klaassen, 141–54. Scottdale, Pa.: Herald, 1992.

————. "Pacifism and Mennonite Identity." In *Call to Faithfulness: Essays in Canadian Mennonite Studies,* edited by Henry Poettcker and Rudy A. Regehr, 189–96. Winnipeg: Canadian Mennonite Bible College, 1972.

————, ed. "A Concern Retrospective." *Conrad Grebel Review* 8 (2) (Spring 1990): 107–204.

Schipani, Daniel S., ed. *Freedom and Discipleship: Liberation Theology in an Anabaptist Perspective.* Maryknoll, N.Y.: Orbis, 1989.

Schlabach, Gerald W. "Beyond Two-/ vs. One-Kingdom Theology: Abrahamic Covenant as a Mennonite Paradigm for Christian Engagement in Society." *Conrad Grebel Review* 11 (3) (Fall 1993): 187–209.

———. "Response to Duane Friesen's Response to 'Beyond Two-/ vs. One-Kingdom Theology.'" *Conrad Grebel Review* 13 (2) (Spring 1995): 189–92.

Schlabach, Theron F. *Gospel Versus Gospel: Mission and the Mennonite Church, 1863–1944.* Scottdale, Pa.: Herald, 1980.

———. "Mennonites, Revivalism, Modernity—1683–1850." *Church History* 48 (1979): 398–415.

———. *Peace, Faith, Nation: Mennonites and Amish in Nineteenth-Century America.* Scottdale, Pa.: Herald, 1988.

———. "Politics and Peoplehood." *Goshen College Bulletin* 65 (4) (July 1980): 6–7.

Schrock-Shenk, David. "25 Years of Washington Witness." *Mennonite Weekly Review,* 12 Aug. 1993, 3.

Schroeder, David. "Nationalism and Internationalism: Ground Rules for a Discussion." *The Mennonite,* 9 July 1974, 426–27.

———. "Will Mennonites Still Stand for Peace in 2001?" *Mennonite Reporter,* 2 Nov. 1992, 8.

Schweizer, Eduard. *The Good News According to Matthew.* Trans. David E. Green. Atlanta: John Knox, 1975.

Scriven, Charles. *The Transformation of Culture: Christian Social Ethics After H. Richard Niebuhr.* Scottdale, Pa.: Herald, 1988.

Sensenig, Pearl. "Military Role in Relief an Issue: Somali Situation Prompts Forum on Humanitarian Aid." *Mennonite Weekly Review,* 31 Dec. 1992, 1–2.

Shelley, Maynard, ed. "A Manual for Action and Witness." *The Mennonite,* 25 Jan. 1966, 49–72.

Shelly, David. "Two Tell of Torture in South America." *Mennonite Weekly Review,* 18 Aug. 1977, 6.

Shelly, Karl S. "Health Care Questions and Answers." *Washington Memo* 26 (3) (May–June 1994): 4.

Shelly, Patricia. "Winona Lake Memories." *Peace Office Newsletter* 21 (6) (Nov.–Dec. 1991): 1–2.

Shenk, Steve. "MCC Washington Office Affirmed at 20th Anniversary Consultation." *Gospel Herald,* 31 Jan. 1989, 76–77.

Shenk, Wilbert. "Missions, Service and the Globalization of North American Mennonites." *Mennonite Quarterly Review* 70 (1) (Jan. 1996): 7–22.

Shetler, Sanford J. "Is the Mennonite Central Committee Peace Section Becoming Political?" *Guidelines for Today* (Sept.–Oct. 1974): 15, 20.

Sider, Ronald. "An Evangelical Theology of Liberation." In *Piety and Politics: Evangelicals and Fundamentalists Confront the World,* edited by Richard John Neuhaus and Michael Cromartie, 143–60. Washington: Ethics and Public Policy Center, 1987.

Sider, Ronald, et al. "Are We Willing to Die for Peace?" *Gospel Herald,* 25 Dec. 1984, 898–903.

Skillen, James W. *The Scattered Voice: Christians at Odds in the Public Square.* Grand Rapids: Zondervan, 1990.

Skillen, James W., and Rockne M. McCarthy, eds. *Political Order and the Plural Structure of Society.* Atlanta: Scholars, 1991.

Smith, Hedrick. *The Power Game: How Washington Works.* New York: Ballantine Books, 1989.

Snyder, C. Arnold. *The Life and Thought of Michael Sattler.* Scottdale, Pa.: Herald, 1984.

———. "Reflections on Mennonite Uses of Anabaptist History." In *Mennonite Peace Theology: A Panorama of Types,* edited by John Richard Burkholder and Barbara Nelson Gingerich, 84–86. Akron: Mennonite Central Committee Peace Office, Jan. 1991.

———. "The Relevance of Anabaptist Nonviolence for Nicaragua Today." *Conrad Grebel Review* 2 (2) (Spring 1984): 123–37.

———, ed. "In a Mennonite Voice: Women Doing Theology." *Conrad Grebel Review* 10 (1) (Winter 1992): 1–85.

Stackhouse, Max. "Religion, Society and the Independent Sector: Key Elements of a General Theory." In *Religion, the Independent Sector, and American Culture,* edited by Conrad Cherry and Rowland A. Sherrill, 11–30. Atlanta: Scholars, 1992.

Stark, Rodney, and William Sims Bainbridge. *The Future of Religion.* Berkeley: Univ. of California Press, 1985.

Stassen, Glen. *Just Peacemaking: Transforming Initiatives for Justice and Peace.* Louisville: Westminster/John Knox, 1992.

Stauffer Hostetler, Beulah. *American Mennonites and Protestant Movements: A Community Paradigm.* Scottdale, Pa.: Herald, 1987.

———. "Nonresistance and Social Responsibility: Mennonites and Mainline Peace Emphasis, ca. 1950 to 1985." *Mennonite Quarterly Review* 64 (1) (Jan. 1990): 49–73.

Stayer, James M. *Anabaptists and the Sword.* Lawrence, Kans.: Coronado Press, 1972.

———. "The Easy Demise of a Normative Vision of Anabaptism." In *Mennonite Identity: Historical and Contemporary Perspectives,* edited by Calvin Redekop and Samuel Steiner, 109–16. Lanham, Md.: Univ. Press of America, 1988.

Stayer, James M., Klaus Depperman and Werner Packull. "From Monogenesis to Polygenesis: The Historical Discussion of Anabaptist Origins." *Mennonite Quarterly Review* 49 (2) (Apr. 1975): 83–121.

Steiner, Sam. "Politics—Is It for Mennonites?" *With* (Oct. 1976): 9–12.

Steiner, Sue C. "Mennonites and Politics." *Christian Century* (May 1985): 463–64.

Steinfels, Peter. "Reshaping Pacifism to Fight Anguish in a Reshaped World." *New York Times,* 21 Dec. 1992, 1–2.

Stoner, John K., and Robert S. Kreider. "Patriotism." In *Mennonite Encyclopedia V,* edited by Cornelius J. Dyck and Dennis D. Martin, 679–80. Scottdale, Pa.: Herald, 1990.

Stout, Jeffrey. *Ethics After Babel: The Languages of Morals and Their Discontents.* Boston: Beacon, 1988.

Strege, Merle D. "The Demise (?) of a Peace Church: The Church of God (Anderson), Pacifism and Civil Religion." *Mennonite Quarterly Review* 65 (2) (Apr. 1991): 128–40.

Stuckey, Harley. "Should Mennonites Participate in Government?" *Mennonite Life* 14 (1) (Jan. 1959): 12, 34–38.

Suderman, Robert J. "Liberation Pacifism." In *Mennonite Peace Theology: A Panorama of Types,* edited by John Richard Burkholder and Barbara Nelson Gingerich, 69–77. Akron: Mennonite Central Committee Peace Office, Jan. 1991.

Swalm, E. J., comp. *Nonresistance Under Test: A Compilation of Experiences of Conscientious Objectors as Encountered in Two World Wars.* Nappanee, Ind.: E. V. Publishing House, 1949.

Swartley, Willard, ed. *Essays on Peace Theology and Witness.* Elkhart, Ind.: Institute of Mennonite Studies, 1988.

Swartley, Willard, and Cornelius J. Dyck, eds. *Annotated Bibliography of Mennonite Writings on War and Peace.* Scottdale, Pa.: Herald, 1987.

Swartzendruber, Fred. "A Mennonite Lobby in Washington?" *Forum* (Dec. 1978): 1–3.

Swidler, Ann. "Culture in Action: Symbols and Strategies." *American Sociological Review* 51 (Apr. 1986): 273–86.

Tinder, Glenn. *The Political Meaning of Christianity: An Interpretation.* Baton Rouge: Louisiana State Univ., 1989.

———. "Republic and Liberal State." *Emory Law Journal* 39 (1) (Winter 1990– Fall 1990): 191–202.

Toews, Paul. "The Concern Movement: Its Origins and Early History." *Conrad Grebel Review* 8 (2) (Spring 1990): 109–26.

———. "The Impact of Alternative Service on the American Mennonite World: A Critical Evaluation." *Mennonite Quarterly Review* 66 (4) (Oct. 1992): 615–27.

———. "The Long Weekend or the Short Week: Mennonite Peace Theology." *Mennonite Quarterly Review* 60 (1) (Jan. 1986): 38–57.

———. *Mennonites in America, 1930–1970: Modernity and the Persistence of Religious Community.* Scottdale, Pa.: Herald, 1996.

———. "Mennonites in American Society: Modernity and the Persistence of Religious Community." *Mennonite Quarterly Review* 63 (3) (July 1989): 227–46.

Tolstoy, Leo. *The Kingdom of God Is Within You.* Trans. Constance Garnett. Lincoln: Univ. of Nebraska Press, 1984 [1893].

———. *The Kingdom of God and Peace Essays.* Trans. Aylmer Maude. London: Oxford Univ. Press, 1974.

Troeltsch, Ernst. *The Social Teachings of the Christian Churches,* Vols. 1 and 2. New York: Harper and Row, 1960 [1911].

United Methodist Council of Bishops. *In Defense of Creation: The Nuclear Crisis and a Just Peace.* Nashville: Graded, 1986.

Unrau, Ed. "MB Debate on 'Peace' Sets Worrisome Tone." *Mennonite Mirror* 20 (5) (Jan. 1991): 30.

———. "A Fascination with Politics that Led to the Premier's Office." *Mennonite Mirror* (Jan. 1982): 17.

Unruh, John D. "How Does the Church Relate to the State?" *The Canadian Mennonite,* 22 Sept. 1964, 1–2.

———. *In the Name of Christ: A History of Mennonite Central Committee.* Scottdale, Pa.: Herald, 1952.

Unruh, Richard S. "Classical Patterns of Church-State Relations." *Direction* (July 1976): 22–26.

U.S. News and World Report. *Triumph Without Victory: The Unreported History of the Persian Gulf War.* New York: Random House, 1992.

Vaux, Kenneth L. *Ethics and the Gulf War: Religion, Rhetoric, and Righteousness.* Boulder: Westview, 1992.

Wald, K. D. *Religion and Politics in the United States.* New York: St. Martin's, 1987.

Walzer, Michael. *Just and Unjust Wars: A Moral Argument with Historical Illustrations.* New York: Basic, 1977.

———. "Political Action: The Problem of Dirty Hands." In *War and Moral Responsibility,* edited by Marshall Cohen, Thomas Nagel, Thomas Scanlon, and Richard B. Brandt, 62–82. Princeton: Princeton Univ. Press, 1974.

———. *Spheres of Justice: A Defense of Pluralism and Equality.* New York: Basic, 1983.

Warner, Michael. *Changing Witness: Catholic Bishops and Public Policy, 1917–1994.* Washington: Ethics and Public Policy Center, 1995.

Warner, R. Steven. *New Wine in Old Wineskins.* Berkeley: Univ. of California Press, 1987.

Watson, Russell, et al. "It's Our Fight Now." *Newsweek,* 14 Dec. 1992, 31–35.

Weathering the Storm: Christian Pacifist Responses to War. Scottdale, Pa.: Herald, 1992.

Weaver, J. Denny. "Mennonites: Theology, Peace, and Identity." *Conrad Grebel Review* 6 (2) (Spring 1988): 119–45.

———. "We Must Continue to Reject Just War Thinking." *Gospel Herald,* 27 Apr. 1993, 6–8.

———. "Where Mennonites Are Headed in the 1980s." *Christianity Today* 27 (9) (20 May 1983): 74.

Weber, Max. *From Max Weber: Essays in Sociology.* Trans. and ed. H. H. Gerth and C. Wright Mills. New York: Oxford Univ. Press, 1946.

———. *The Protestant Ethic and the Spirit of Capitalism.* Trans. Talcott Parsons. New York: Charles Scribner's Sons, 1958.

———. *The Sociology of Religion.* Trans. Ephraim Fischoff. Boston: Beacon, 1963 [1922].

Weber, Theodore R. "Christian Realism, Power, and Peace." In *Theology, Politics, and Peace,* edited by Theodore H. Runyon. Maryknoll, N.Y.: Orbis, 1989.

———. "Political Authority and Obedience." *Worldview* 17 (5) (May 1974): 27–34.

Weigel, George, and John P. Langan, S.J., eds. *The American Search for Peace: Moral Reasoning, Religious Hope, and National Security.* Washington: Georgetown Univ. Press, 1991.

Wenger, J. C., ed. *The Complete Writings of Menno Simons.* Scottdale, Pa.: Herald, 1956.

Will, Emily. "Twenty Years Experience Brings New Views of Hunger." *Gospel Herald,* 1 June 1993, 6–7.

Wilson, Bryan, ed. *Patterns of Sectarianism: Organisation and Ideology in Social and Religious Movements.* London: Heinemann, 1967.

Wink, Walter. *Engaging the Powers: Discernment and Resistance in a World of Domination.* Minneapolis: Fortress, 1992.

Witham, Larry. "Mennonites Witness Here." *Washington Times Magazine,* 25 May 1983.

Wogaman, J. Philip. *Christian Perspectives on Politics.* Philadelphia: Fortress, 1988.

Wood, James E., Jr., and Derek Davis, eds. *The Role of Religion in the Making of Public Policy.* Waco: J. M. Dawson Institute of Church-State Studies, 1991.

Wuthnow, Robert. *The Restructuring of American Religion: Society and Faith Since World War II.* Princeton: Princeton Univ. Press, 1988.

———. "Sources of Doctrinal Unity and Diversity." In *Views from the Pews,* edited by Roger A. Johnson, 33–56. Philadelphia: Fortress, 1983.

———. *The Struggle for America's Soul: Evangelicals, Liberals, and Secularism.* Grand Rapids: Eerdmans, 1989.

———. "The Voluntary Sector: Legacy of the Past, Hope for the Future?" In *Between States and Markets: The Voluntary Sector in Comparative Perspective,* edited by Robert Wuthnow, 3–27. Princeton: Princeton Univ. Press, 1988.

————, ed. *Between States and Markets: The Voluntary Sector in Comparative Perspective*. Princeton: Princeton Univ. Press, 1991.

Wuthnow, Robert, James Davison Hunter, Albert Bergesen, and Edith Kurzweil. *Cultural Analysis: The Work of Peter L. Berger, Mary Douglas, Michel Foucault and Jürgen Habermas*. London: Routledge and Kegan Paul, 1984.

Yoder, Edward. "The Obligation of the Christian to the State and Community—'Render Unto Caesar.'" *Mennonite Quarterly Review* 13 (2) (Apr. 1939): 104–22.

Yoder, Elizabeth G. *Peace Theology and Violence Against Women*. Elkhart, Ind.: Institute of Mennonite Studies, 1992.

Yoder, John H. "The Anabaptist Dissent." *Concern* 1 (1954): 45–68.

————. *Christian Attitudes to War, Peace, and Revolution: A Companion to Bainton*. Elkhart, Ind.: Co-Op Bookstore, 1983.

————. *The Christian Witness to the State*. Newton, Kans.: Faith and Life, 1964.

————. "The Historic Peace Churches; Heirs to the Radical Reformation." In *Peace, War and God's Justice*, edited by Thomas D. Parker and Brian J. Fraser, 105–22. Toronto: United Church, 1989.

————. "Just War Tradition: Is It Credible?" *Christian Century*, 13 Mar. 1991, 295–98.

————. "Mennonite Political Conservatism: Paradox or Contradiction." In *Mennonite Images: Historical, Cultural and Literary Essays Dealing with Mennonite Issues*, edited by Harry Loewen, 7–16. Winnipeg: Hyperion, 1980.

————. *Nevertheless: The Varieties of Religious Pacifism*. Scottdale, Pa.: Herald, 1971. Revised in 1992 and retitled *Nevertheless: The Varieties and Shortcomings of Religious Pacifism*.

————. *The Politics of Jesus*. Grand Rapids: Eerdmans, 1972. Revised and expanded in 1994.

————. *The Priestly Kingdom: Social Ethics as Gospel*. Notre Dame: Univ. of Notre Dame Press, 1984.

————. "The Prophetic Dissent of the Anabaptist." In *The Recovery of the Anabaptist Vision*, edited by Guy F. Hershberger, 93–104. Scottdale, Pa.: Herald, 1957.

————. "Questions on the Christian Witness to the State." *Gospel Herald*, Apr. to Aug. 1963, Series.

————. "Reinhold Niebuhr and Christian Pacifism." *Mennonite Quarterly Review* 29 (2) (Apr. 1955): 101–17.

————. "Review of Gordon Kaufman's *The Context of Decision*." *Mennonite Quarterly Review* 37 (2) (Apr. 1963): 133–38.

————. "Sacrament as Social Process: Christ the Transformer of Culture." *Theology Today* 48 (3) (Apr. 1991): 33–44.

————. *When War is Unjust: Being Honest in Just War Thinking*. Minneapolis: Augsburg, 1984.

————. "Why Speak to Government?" *Gospel Herald*, 25 Jan. 1966, 73–74.

Yoder, John H., ed. and trans. *The Legacy of Michael Sattler*. Scottdale, Pa.: Herald, 1973.

Yoder, Michael L. "Findings from the 1982 Mennonite Census." *Mennonite Quarterly Review* 69 (4) (Oct. 1985): 307–49.

Yoder Neufeld, Tom. "Varieties of Contemporary Mennonite Peace Witness: From Passivism to Pacifism, From Nonresistance to Resistance." *Conrad Grebel Review* 10 (3) (Fall 1992): 243–57.

Young, Oran R. "International Regimes: Toward a New Theory of Institutions." *World Politics* 39 (1) (Oct. 1986): 104–22.

Zerwick, Max, and Mary Grosvenor. *A Grammatical Analysis of the Greek New Testament.* Rome: Biblical Institute, 1981.

Zimmerman Herr, Judy. "Sanctions and Pacifists." *Peace Office Newsletter* 23 (3) (May–June 1993): 4–5.

Zucker, Lynne G. "Institutional Theories of Organizations." *Annual Review of Sociology* 13 (1987): 443–64.

———. "Organizations as Institutions." In *Research in the Sociology of Organizations,* edited by S. B. Bacharach, 1–42. Greenwich, Conn.: JAI Press, 1983.

———. "The Role of Institutionalization in Cultural Persistence." In *The New Institutionalism in Organizational Analysis,* edited by Walter W. Powell and Paul J. DiMaggio, 83–107. Chicago: Univ. of Chicago Press, 1991.

DISSERTATIONS, THESES, AND UNPUBLISHED MATERIAL

Beitler, Alan J. "The Impact of Social Context on Theological Belief and Political Involvement: The Life Stories of Three Mennonite Men." M.A.P.S. thesis, Associated Mennonite Biblical Seminaries (hereafter AMBS), 1985. Available in AMBS Library.

Bowie Wiesel, Barbara. "From Separation to Evangelicalism: A Case Study of Social and Cultural Change among the Franconia Conference Mennonites, 1945–1970." Ph.D. diss., University of Pennsylvania, 1974.

Braun, Will. "Political Theology and the Anabaptist-Mennonite Tradition of Faith." Term paper, Toronto School of Theology, 1983.

Burkholder, John Richard. "Continuity and Change: An Analysis of Mennonite Experience in the Political Order." Paper presented at Conversations on Faith II, Laurelville, Pa., 7–9 Mar. 1985. Available in Mennonite Historical Library, Goshen, Ind. (hereafter MHL).

———. "Forms of Christian Witness to the State: A Mennonite Perspective." Paper prepared for Goshen College convocation, 12 Mar. 1976. Available in MHL.

———. "Radical Pacifism Challenges the Mennonite Church." Paper prepared for meeting of the Mennonite Theological Study Group, Jan. 1960. Available in MHL.

———. "Talking Back to Caesar: The Christian Witness to the State." Paper prepared for the C. Henry Smith Lecture, Bluffton College, 26 Mar. 1985. Available in MHL.

Bush, Perry J. "Drawing the Line: American Mennonites, the State and Social Change, 1935–1973." Ph.D. diss., Carnegie Mellon University, 1990.

Charles, J. Robert. "Mennonite International Peacemaking During and After the Cold War: A Review of Contexts and Options." Paper prepared for the "Consultation on Mennonite Peacemaking After the Cold War," Mennonite Central Committee, Akron, Pa., 4–5 Nov. 1993. Available from the author.

Churches for Middle East Peace. "Background Paper on the Gulf Crisis." 7 Sept. 1990. Available in MCC Washington files.

Dula, Peter. "Pacifism After Babel: Does It Stretch, or Will It Break?" M.A.T.S. thesis at Associated Mennonite Biblical Seminary, 1995. Available in AMBS library.

Enns, Monique. "A History of the MCC Ottawa Office as Drawn from MCC Files." Paper for a course on Mennonite studies, 7 Apr. 1986. Available in MCCC Ottawa files.

Epp, Ed. "Military Intervention in Somalia: A Case Study." Jan. 1993. Available in MCC Washington files.

Epp, Esther Ruth. "The Origins of Mennonite Central Committee Canada." M.A. thesis, University of Manitoba, 1980.

Epp, Frank H. "Relationships Between American and Canadian Mennonites in the Context of MCC." Paper prepared for the MCC annual meeting, 21–27 June 1977. Available in AMBS Library.

Epp, Frank H., and Marlene G. Epp. "The Progressions of the Mennonite Central Committee Peace Section," 1985. Available in MCC Akron files.

Franz, Delton. "The Christian and Government, Part I." Available in Archives of the Mennonite Church, Goshen, Ind. (hereafter AMC) IX-6-3, file "DF 1969."

———. "Mennonites Carry Torch for Vietnam in Washington." News release dated 19 Dec. 1975. Available in MCC Washington files.

———. "Middle Axioms: An Appropriate Mode of Thinking and Speaking to Public Policy Decision-Makers by People with an Absolute Ethic?" Undated [1970?] paper. Available in MCC Washington files.

Franz, Delton, et al. "A Comprehensive Constituency Advocacy Proposal." Attachment to a 29 May 1990 memo to Linda Gehman Peachey and Titus Peachey. Available in MCC Washington files.

———. "The MCC Peace Section Washington Office: A Review." Attachment II to the MCC Peace Section minutes, 29–31 Mar. 1973. Available in AMC.

———. "Origins of the Washington Office." 1981. Available in MCC Washington files.

———. "Self-Study." Paper on the MCC Washington office prepared for the 12–14 Jan. 1989 "20th Anniversary Consultation on the Washington Office." Available in MCC Washington files.

———. "Washington Office Coordinating Council." 8 Jan. 1977. Available in MCC Washington files.

Friesen, Duane K. "An Anabaptist Understanding of the Church and Its Approach to Public Policy." Paper presented at the 12–14 Jan. 1989 "20th Anniversary Consultation on the Washington Office." Available in MCC Washington files.

Goering, Greg W. "Learning to Speak Second Languages." 5 May 1991. Available from the author.

———. "The Prophetic Role to the Nations and the Church's Witness to Government." 29 Jan. 1992. Great Plains Seminary. Available from the author.

Goosen, Rick. "A New Vision or a Shattering Vision? Canadian Mennonites and Political Participation." Fourth-year paper in history, Simon Fraser University, 1982.

Harder, Leland. "The Quest for Equilibrium in an Established Sect: A Study of Social Change in the General Conference Church." Ph.D. diss., Northwestern University, 1962.

Hershberger, Betty Ann. "A Pacifist Approach to Civil Government: A Comparison of the Participant Quaker and Non-Participant Mennonite View." B.A. thesis, Swarthmore College, 1980.

Hershberger, Guy F. "The Committee on Peace and Social Concerns, Dissent: Past and Present." Confidential paper dated Nov. 1966. Available in AMC.

———. "Questions Raised Concerning the Work of the Committee on Peace and Social Concerns." 1967. Available in MHL.

Horsch, John. "The Difference Between Our Peace Program and the Program of Other Peace Movements." In "Mennonite Conference on War and Peace," 16–20. Mimeographed copy of the conference papers. 15–17 Feb. 1935, Goshen College. Available in MHL.

Horst, Irvin B. "Some Principles and Limitations Guiding the Christian Witness to the State." Report of Group C. Papers of Peace Problems Committee, Laurelville Conference, 21–22 Sept. 1956.

Huebner, Harry. "Biblical/Theological Implications for the Washington Office." Paper prepared for 12–14 January 1989 "20th Anniversary Consultation on the Washington Office." Available in MCC Washington files.

Janzen, William. "How Should MCCC Address Questions of National Defence?" Paper presented in Winnipeg, Manitoba, 17 Sept. 1988.

———. "The Limits of Liberty in Canada: The Experience of Mennonites, Hutterites and Doukhobors." Ph.D. diss., Carleton University, 1980.

———. "Mennonites in Canada: Their Relations with and Effect on the Larger Society." Paper prepared for inter-church conference on Christianity and Canadian Culture, Toronto, 20–22 Oct. 1988. Available in AMBS Library.

———. "Militarism and the Response of Canadian Mennonites from the 1940s to the 1980s." Discussion paper presented to MCCC, 12 Sept. 1966.

———. "A Perspective for Approaching Government." Written 10 May 1985 following an oral presentation in Mar. 1985 to MCCC Executive Committee.

———. "Supporting Constitutional Reform: A Mennonite Central Committee Canada Discussion Paper." 18 Jan. 1992. Available in AMBS Library.

Janzen, William, and Freda Enns. "Canadian Mennonites in Politics." Paper written for 1990 Mennonite World Conference. Available in AMBS Library.

Jeavons, Thom. "When the Bottom Line is Faithfulness: An Examination of the Place, Functions and Management of Christian Service Organizations." Ph.D. diss., Union Institute, 1992.

Keeney, William C. "The Establishment of the Washington, D.C., and Ottawa Offices" (First Draft). 1977. Available in MCC Washington files.

———. "Report and Recommendation Concerning a Washington Office." Exhibit 1, to MCC Peace Section Executive Committee Meeting, Chicago, 18 Jan. 1968. Available in AMC, "Peace Section Minutes and Reports," IX-7-8, Box 3.

King, Dwight Y. "A Report, Including Recommendations, to the MCC Peace Section on an Investigation of the Washington Scene in Order to Illumine Further Consideration of a Mennonite Office in the Nation's Capital," 1 Sept. 1966. Available in MCC Washington files.

Klassen, J. M. "Statement Regarding an MCC (Canada) Office in Ottawa." Paper presented at the 1974 annual meeting of MCCC. Available in MCCC Ottawa files.

Koontz, Ted. "Peace Section Experience Regarding Coalition and Lobby Efforts." MCC U.S. Ministries meeting, 15–16 Mar. 1976. Available in MCC Washington files.

Lapp, John A. "The Church and the Political Process." Paper presented at the Canadian Inter-Mennonite Consultation, Kitchener, Ontario, 8–10 Jan. 1975. Available in MHL.

———. "Missions, Missionaries and the Political Process." In "Missionary Retreat 1976," a collection of papers from the June 1976 General Conference Mennonite Church Committee on Overseas Ministries Retreat. Available in MHL.

Leaman, Hershey. "MCC Thoughts on Food and Hunger." Paper presented at MCC's 1993 annual meeting, Niagara-on-the-Lake, Ontario. Available in MCC Akron files.

Mennonite Central Committee. "Consultation: Mennonite Peacemaking After the Cold War," report of the 4–5 Nov. 1993 consulation in Akron, Pa. Available in MCC Akron files.

———. "Faith, Power and Politics: Questions and Answers." Brochure published by MCC's Akron office, 1992.

Mennonite Central Committee Peace Section. "A Message to Mennonite and Brethren in Christ Church Leaders and Peace Committees." 19 Jan. 1967. Available in AMC IX-7-8, Box 3, "Peace Section Minutes and Reports."

Metzler, Edgar. "Mennonite Witness to the State: Attitudes and Actions, World War I–1956." Paper presented at the Laurelville Conference on Nonresistance and Political Responsibility, Peace Problems Committee, 1956. Available in MHL.

———. "Why Another Look at Church-State Relations?" Report to MCC, undated. Available in MHL.

Mihevc, Joe. "The Politicization of the Canadian Mennonite Peace Witness in the Twentieth Century." Ph.D. diss., St. Michael's College, University of Toronto, 1988.

Miller, Joseph S. "A Mennonite Witness in Washington, D.C." Typewritten article and interview with Delton Franz. Available in MCC Washington files.

Miller, Louis Lawrence. "The Rise and Growth of New Social Interests Among the Mennonites." B.Div. thesis, Chicago Theological Seminary, June 1919.

Nisly, Hope Renae. "Witness to a Way of Peace: Renewal and Revision in Mennonite Peace Theology, 1950–1971." M.A./M.L.S. thesis, University of Maryland, 1992.

Nisly, Weldon. "Change Project: MCC Peace Section Washington Office." Paper at Associated Mennonite Biblical Seminaries. 1 June 1976. Available from the author.

Oral History Institute. "Mennonite Response to the Persian Gulf War." Oral interviews and newspaper clippings, 1991. Available in Bethel (Kans.) College Library.

Peachey, Paul. "The Mennonite Central Committee in Washington: Notes Toward the 'Middle Axiom' of Political Witness." Jan. 1970. Available in MCC Washington files.

Redekop, Calvin. "The Sectarian Black and White World." Ph.D. diss., University of Chicago, 1959.

Redekop, John H. "Evaluation of MCC (Canada) Ottawa Office." 21 Nov. 1978. Available in AMC.

Royer, Don. "The Acculturation Process and the Peace Doctrine of the Church of the Brethren." Ph.D. diss., University of Chicago, 1955.

Sawatsky, Rodney J. "History and Ideology: American Mennonite Identity Definition Through History." Ph.D. diss., Princeton University, 1977.

———. "The Influence of Fundamentalism on Mennonite Nonresistance, 1908–1944." M.A. thesis, University of Minnesota, 1973.

Stutzman, Ervin R. "From Nonresistance to Peace and Justice: Mennonite Peace Rhetoric, 1951–1991." Ph.D. diss., Temple University, 1993.

"Summary Report of the 20th Anniversary Consultation on the MCC Washington Office." 12–14 Jan. 1989. Available in MCC Washington files.

United Methodist General Board of Church and Society. "The United Methodist Building." Undated.

Unruh, John D., Jr. "Report to the Peace Section Executive Committee on the Washington Witness to Government." 6 Sept. 1963. Available in AMC IX-7-8, file 3/1.

Walters, L. "Five Classic Just War Theories." Ph.D. diss., Yale University, 1971.

Yeatts, John R., and Ronald J. Burwell. "The Brethren in Christ and Public Policy." Paper presented at the annual meeting of the Society for the Scientific Study of Religion, 1990.

Yoder, John H. "Richard Niebuhr—Christ and Culture: An Analysis and Critique." Paper written for Student Services Summer Seminar, Aug. 1964. Available in AMBS Library.

Zimmerman Herr, Judy. "MCC and Sanctions." Working paper prepared for MCC's Overseas Department, 5 Aug. 1992. Available in MCC Akron files.

INDEX

Emmanuel Mennonite Church, 217n, 233n
enemies, 177
Energy and Ecology Task Force, 98
England, 31, 158
Enns, Freda, 219n
Enns, Monique, 219n
environment, 35, 38, 97, 100, 114, 119,
 125, 158, 165, 176, 192, 208, 257n
Episcopal Church, 51
Epp, Ed, 243n, 244n
Epp, Esther Ruth, 217n
Epp, Frank H., 83, 215n, 217n, 226n,
 231n, 246n
Epp, Joanne, 265n
Epp, Marlene, 226n
Erb, Patricia, 146–47
Ergada, 144
Esther, 168
ethics, 64, 164, 173–76, 194–96, 199, 214n;
 see also social ethics
Ethiopia, 143, 243n
evangelical, 60, 71
Evangelical Mennonite Church, 217n, 233n
evils, 175, 191, 194
excommunication, 219n
experience: as a basis for lobbying, 3, 8,
 76–77, 115, 118, 122, 124–60, 185,
 187, 202–3, 260n; of MCC Washington
 workers, 133–38, 188

Faith and Life Press, 97
faithfulness, 49, 84–90, 121–22, 145, 159,
 170, 193
Feaver, Peter D., 54, 234n, 235n
Federal Council of Churches, 237n
Fellowship of Evangelical Bible Churches,
 217n
Fellowship of Reconciliation (FOR), 72,
 75, 140–41
Festival Quarterly, 97
Fine, James, 142
fish, 35
Foley, Tom, 128
Ford, Gerald, 256n
foreign aid, 67, 88, 150
Foreign Policy and Military Spending Task
 Force, 67, 88, 92, 165
Forell, George W., 26, 222n
France, 31, 36, 158, 227n

Franz, Delton, 23, 34–35, 47–50, 64–65,
 70–71, 80, 87, 94, 97, 99, 101, 113,
 115, 118–22, 125, 127–30, 132, 134–
 36, 139, 141–42, 146–51, 153, 155,
 159, 161–62, 164, 166, 168–69, 171–
 72, 174–78, 180–81, 183, 185, 189–91,
 194–95, 202, 228n, 229n, 232n, 233n,
 239n, 240n, 241n, 245n, 248n, 249n,
 250n, 251n, 252n, 253n, 254n, 255n,
 256n, 257n, 258n, 259n, 260n, 261n,
 263n, 264n, 265n, 266n, 267n, 268n
Franz, Marian Claassen. *See* Claassen Franz,
 Marian
Fraser, Nancy, 193, 262n, 266n
freedom, 57, 268n
French, Paul C., 91
French Revolution, 100
Frey, Marv, 243n, 244n
Friends Committee on National Legislation, 42, 46, 63–64, 66, 74, 78, 81,
 131, 152, 230n, 232n, 235n
Friends, Society of. *See* Quakers
Friends War Problems Committee, 91
Friesen, Duane K., 109, 167–68, 186–87,
 192, 194–96, 221n, 224n, 235n, 238n,
 252n, 263n, 266n, 267n, 268n
Friesen, Ken Martens, 47, 126, 136, 151,
 173–74, 229n, 257n, 261n, 264n
Friesen, LeRoy, 128, 141, 258n, 259n
fundamentalism, 101, 111, 242n
Funk Wiebe, Katie, 224n

Gandhi, Mahatma, 59, 238n
Geddert, Ron, 236n
Gelassenheit, 119, 256n
General Conference Mennonite Church
 (GCMC), 11, 13–15, 29–30, 43–44,
 47, 105, 110, 121, 212, 213n, 217n,
 232n, 237n, 240n, 253n, 254n, 257n
German Baptists, 62
Germany, 14, 31, 36, 158, 169, 177, 227n
Geyer, Alan F., 242n
Gingerich, Martin, 154
Gingerich, Melvin, 225n, 248n
Gingrich, Keith, 70, 86–87, 119, 136,
 150–51, 155–56, 159, 165, 181–82,
 190–91, 229n, 240n, 241n, 247n, 256n,
 261n, 262n, 263n, 265n, 266n
Glickman, Dan, 128

313